The Changing Academy – The Changing Academic Profession in International Comparative Perspective 17

Scope of the series

The landscape of higher education has in recent years undergone significant change. This has been particular the case for research training, academic life, employment, working conditions and entrepreneurial activities of universities around the globe. The academy is expected to be more professional in teaching, more productive in research and more entrepreneurial in everything. Some of the changes involved have raised questions about the attractiveness of an academic career for today's graduates. At the same time, knowledge has come to be identified as the most vital resource of contemporary societies.

The Changing Academy series examines the nature and extent of the changes experienced by the academic profession. It aims to address these changes from an international comparative perspective, focusing at both the higher education system level as well as the STEM fields of science, technology, engineering and mathematics in particular. It explores both the reasons for and the consequences of these changes.

The series considers the implications of the changes for the attractiveness of the academic profession as a career and for the ability of the academic community to contribute to the further development of knowledge societies and the attainment of national goals. It provides analyses on these matters drawing initially on available data-sets and qualitative research studies with special emphasis on the international studies of the Changing Academic Profession and the national surveys in STEM fields. Among the themes featured will be:

- Relevance of the academy's work
- Enrolment, graduation and the institutional setting of STEM
- Research, development and technology policies with regards to STEM
- Internationalization of the academy governance and management
- The new generation in the academic profession – the doctoral graduates

More information about this series at http://www.springer.com/series/8668

Heather Eggins
Editor

The Changing Role of Women in Higher Education

Academic and Leadership Issues

 Springer

Editor
Heather Eggins
University of Sussex
Brighton, UK

The Changing Academy – The Changing Academic Profession in International
Comparative Perspective
ISBN 978-3-319-42434-7   ISBN 978-3-319-42436-1   (eBook)
DOI 10.1007/978-3-319-42436-1

Library of Congress Control Number: 2016953104

Printed on acid-free paper

This Springer imprint is published by Springer Nature
The registered company is Springer International Publishing AG Switzerland

FOR ROSANNE AND ALEX

NEXT GENERATIONS

AND BRENDA, HILARY, MARGARET AND RAE

COLLEGE FRIENDS

Foreword

At the end of the twentieth century, it seemed inevitable that the advances made by women in higher education would continue. Yet 15 years into the twenty-first century, it's clear that there is still some way to go before women achieve anything approaching real equality in academic and leadership roles.

In this comprehensive survey of women in higher education across the world, Heather Eggins draws together evidence from a variety of countries with varying records on women's equality. A wide range of contributors argue that patriarchy is still strongly felt in the academe, that women are becoming better educated but that is not reflected in salary scales, that legislation is not necessarily the answer to achieving equality in higher education and that the most discriminated against are women of colour.

The book looks at detailed case studies from many different countries, including the UK, the USA, Greece, Netherlands, Brazil, Malaysia, South Africa and Ghana. The different chapters are written by established leaders in their field, with insights drawn from a wide range of disciplines. It's perhaps not surprising to learn of the importance of female role models, with Dilma Rousseff presidency in Brazil prompting 80 % of Brazilian graduates to say they are planning to seek top jobs, compared to 53 % in the USA.

The conclusions to be drawn from this wide-ranging look at the situation of women in higher education are to some extent encouraging: there is evidence of growing international support for gender equality, and new perspectives are opening up for the enhanced social engagement of graduate women, in cooperation with supportive male counterparts.

As the twenty-first century unfolds, the debate on women in higher education will inevitably become more important as the knowledge economy grows. This book is an essential reading for those wishing to understand the gains made so far and the challenges for the future.

Cambridge, UK   Jackie Ashley
November 2015

Acknowledgements

The editor would like to thank the many colleagues, friends and relatives who have taken part in discussions relating to this volume and in particular those at the Centre for Higher Education and Equity Research, University of Sussex, and fellow members of the Consortium of Higher Education Researchers. Valuable support with the texts has been given by Jack Simmons, Rosanne Hargreaves and colleagues at Staffordshire University.

This volume should also acknowledge the inspiration of the editor's suffragist grandmother, Isabel Wilson Parker, who imbued in the editor a recognition of the equality of women and of the importance of education.

Contents

Author Biographies

Bahiyah Dato' Hj. Abdul Hamid (PhD) is an associate professor at the School of Language Studies and Linguistics, Faculty of Social Sciences and Humanities, Universiti Kebangsaan Malaysia (UKM). She is currently the deputy director of the Tun Fatimah Hashim Women's Leadership Centre, UKM. Her research interest focuses on language and gender, identity construction, code alternation and code choice and discourse and semiotics analysis. Bahiyah has headed an international research study funded by Qatar Foundation on linguistic sexism and gender role stereotyping and has headed numerous research projects nationally and at university level. She has worked extensively with government agencies and NGOs at national level and has worked with regional universities and women's associations such as those in the Philippines, Thailand, Vietnam and Indonesia on activities related to gender and women's issues. She was the vice president of SAMA-Southeast Asian Association for Gender Studies (Malaysia branch) and is a life member of the Malaysian Social Science Association (PSSM).

Jackie Ashley has stalked the corridors of power in Westminster for over 30 years, working as a prominent political journalist and broadcaster, sitting on influential commissions and chairing conferences. Jackie Ashley is a columnist for *The Guardian* and has previously been a presenter of BBC Radio 4's 'The Week in Westminster', political editor of the *New Statesman* and political correspondent for ITN. Since her husband, the broadcaster Andrew Marr, suffered a serious stroke in 2013, Jackie has been campaigning for more rehabilitation provision for stroke survivors and for better rights for carers, including carer's leave. Jackie, a graduate of St Anne's College, Oxford, was appointed president of Lucy Cavendish College, Cambridge, in September 2015. Lucy Cavendish is the only women's college in Europe exclusively for students aged 21 or over and a unique part of the University of Cambridge.

Madeline Berma is currently an associate professor at the Faculty of Economics and Management, Universiti Kebangsaan Malaysia (UKM). She is the director of the Tun Fatimah Hashim Women's Leadership Centre, UKM. Madeline has done extensive research and published on economic development, focusing on rural development, women in development, poverty and the indigenous communities. She also worked extensively with government agencies and NGOs, particularly on economic empowerment programs. Currently, she is heading an action research to evaluate the effectiveness of Malaysia's Ministry of Women, Community and Family Development's economic empowerment programmes. Madeline was a member of the Malaysian Government's delegation to the United Nations Commission on the Status of Women (CSW) in year 2015 and 2016. Madeline was appointed by the prime minister of Malaysia to be a member of four national consultative committees: the National Unity and Consultative Committee, Women's Advisory and Consultative Council, National Consultative Committee on Political Funding, and Committee to Promote Inter-religious Harmony and Understanding.

Bojana Culum works as assistant professor at the University of Rijeka's Faculty of Humanities and Social Sciences, Department of Education, Croatia. Her research focuses on university third and civic mission, university-community engagement and changes in academic profession with particular interest for early career (female) researchers' socialisation into academia. She was a Fulbright Visiting Scholar at Portland State University, USA, during the academic year 2015/2016.

Miriam E. David is professor emerita of sociology of education at University College London's Institute of Education. She has a worldwide reputation for her research on education, family, feminism, gender and policy. She has published widely and most recently a personal memoir *Reclaiming Feminism: Challenging Everyday Misogyny* (Bristol, Policy Press, 2016) and *A Feminist Manifesto for Education* (Cambridge: Polity Press, 2016). Her study *Feminism, Gender and Universities: politics, passion and pedagogies* (Farnham: Ashgate 2014) is based upon interviews with over 100 international academic feminists and activists. Together with colleagues in the USA, she is editing the *Sage Encyclopaedia of Higher Education* to be published in 2018.

Heather Eggins is visiting professor at Sussex University, visiting professor at Staffordshire University and fellow commoner at Lucy Cavendish College, University of Cambridge. Her areas of higher education research include gender issues, access and equity, quality assurance and enhancement, policy and strategy and globalisation. She was a Fulbright New Century Scholar in 2005–2006 and has served as director of the Society for Research into Higher Education. She has considerable editorial experience, and her books include, as editor and contributor, *Access and Equity: Comparative Perspectives* Rotterdam, Sense Publishers, 2010; *Drivers and Barriers to Achieving Quality in Higher Education* Rotterdam, Sense Publishers, 2014; and *The Changing Roles of Women in Higher Education* Rotterdam, Springer, 2016.

Carol Frances served 7 years as chief economist of the American Council on Education (ACE). ACE is based in Washington DC and represents the interests of the higher education community. While at ACE, she conducted two studies funded by the Ford Foundation on women and minorities in higher education administration. She is a member of the International Association for Feminist Economics. She is currently developing information on the participation of women in the STEM fields of science, technology, engineering and mathematics.

Gaële Goastellec is a sociologist and assistant professor (MER) at the University of Lausanne, Switzerland. She leads comparative research on higher education systems and social inequalities. She has been a Lavoisier fellow (2004–2005) and a Fulbright New Century Scholar fellow (2005–2006). Amongst her latest books are (with G. Felouzis) (Eds), 2014, *Les inégalités scolaires en Suisse. Ecole, société et politiques éducatives*. Genève, Peter Lang; with T. Fumasoli and B. Kehm (Eds), 2014, *Academic careers in Europe: trends, challenges, perspectives*. Springer; and with F. Picard (Eds), 2014, *Higher Education and the fabric of societies. Different scales of analysis*, Sense Publishers.

Fei Guo is a postdoctoral research fellow at the Institute of Education in Tsinghua University in China. She holds an MA and a PhD in Economics and Education from Teachers College, Columbia University. She received a BA in International Economics from Shanghai Jiaotong University in China. Fei Guo conducts research to explore factors influencing college students' academic achievement, cognitive and non-cognitive development and labour market performance. Her research interests include student development and learning outcomes in higher education, economic returns to higher education and educational equality and equity in China.

Mary Henkel now retired, was until recently professor and then professor associate of the Department of Politics and History, Brunel University, UK. She has researched and published extensively on higher education, science and evaluation policies. Her primary focus during the last 20 years has been on the implications of such policies for academic work and identities. Her main publication in this field is *Academic Identities and Policy Change in Higher Education* (Jessica Kingsley Publishers, 2000).

Bengü Hosch-Dayican holds a PhD in Political Science from the University of Twente. She is a postdoctoral researcher for Professor of Higher Education at the Center for Higher Education (zhb) at TU Dortmund University. Her research interests include the processes and influences of higher education governance and policies, particularly on the nature of academic work as well as on the gender differences in academic career advancement. Her work has been published in *Acta Politica, Journal of Workplace Rights and Social Science Computer Review*.

Belinda Lee Huang is principal of Celadon Leadership Development, which offers customised leadership programmes based on her research on faculty of colour, pathways to senior leadership for women of colour and postdoctoral scholars. Recently, Doctor Huang served as the executive director of the National Postdoctoral Association, managing operations, developing and promoting national policies and programming that benefited the postdoctoral community and the scientific research community. She has taught Asian American Studies at UC Berkeley, University of Pennsylvania and CSU, East Bay, and was an affiliate faculty for the Educational Leadership program at Loyola University. Previously, as associate director for student affairs, she led an undergraduate student affairs programme developing leaders at the Wharton School, University of Pennsylvania. As an organisational leadership consultant, she developed a leadership development programme for Asian American Pacific Islander college women and presented it at 15 liberal arts and research institutions. Her publications include the American Council on Education monograph *Raising Voices, Lifting Leaders: Asian Pacific Islander American Leaders in Higher Education* (2013) and the *National Postdoctoral Association Institutional Policy Report 2014: Supporting and developing postdoctoral scholars*. Doctor Huang holds a PhD in Higher Education Administration, Education Policy from the University of Maryland.

Mary-Louise Kearney (New Zealand/France) held director posts at UNESCO in Higher Education and in External Relations, including management of the *UNESCO Forum on Higher Education, Research and Knowledge*.

After establishing Kearney Consulting, she collaborated with the OECD on projects related to higher education, R&D and innovation and has been a senior research fellow of Oxford University. She is vice president of the Society for Research into Higher Education (SRHE), special issues coeditor for the *SRHE* journal, *Studies in Higher Education,* and a board member of the *European Journal of Higher Education* (EJHE). A member of the Oxford Education Society and the Auckland University Society, she is also associated with international NGOs and fora which promote issues related to women graduates and has authored numerous publications on Higher Education, including gender issues.

Carole Leathwood is an emeritus professor at the Institute for Policy Studies in Education (IPSE), London Metropolitan University. With a disciplinary background in sociology and women's studies, Carole specialises in research related to inequalities in higher and post-compulsory education. Research interests include gender, academic subjectivities and the affective in HE, developments in higher education and research policy and issues in widening participation. Recent publications include *Research policy and academic performativity: Contestation, compliance and complicity, Studies in Higher Education* (with B. Read, 2013, *Studies in Higher Education*: 38:8, 1162–1174.); *Re/presenting Intellectual Subjectivity: Gender and Visual Imagery in the Field of Higher Education* (2013, *Gender and Education* 25, 2, 133–154); and a co-authored book (with B. Read) *Gender and the Changing Face* *of Higher Education: A feminised future?* (2009, SRHE/OUP). Carole is a fellow of the Society for Research into Higher Education (SRHE), a consulting editor for *Women's Studies international Forum*, an associate editor for *Gender, Work and Organisation* and a member of the editorial board of the *Journal of Education Policy*.

Liudvika Leišytė is professor of Higher Education at the Center for Higher Education (zhb) at TU Dortmund in Germany. Her major research interests lie in the nexus between organisational change and academic work, including impact of governance shifts and evaluation practices on teaching-research nexus, professional autonomy, academic entrepreneurship and academic identities. Gender in academic profession is a cross-cutting theme in her work. Professor Leišytė has published three books, numerous chapters and articles in higher education and science policy as well as public management journals. She is the co-convener of *Higher Education Section* (22) at the European Association of Educational Research.

Elisabeth Lillie is emeritus professor of Language Learning and Teaching at the University of Ulster. One strand of her research focuses on diverse aspects of teaching and learning in higher education. Her other main area of work is the literature and thought of nineteenth-century France, in particular the author Ernest Renan. She has a range of publications reflecting these various interests.

Yeukai A. Mlambo, M.A. is a doctoral candidate in the Higher, Adult and Lifelong Education programme at Michigan State University. Her research interests include issues related to the recruitment, retention and the persistence of women in the academy with a focus on science, technology, engineering and mathematics (STEM) fields. Broadly, her interests include issues of diversity and gender mainstreaming in higher education, higher education in Africa, comparative and international higher education and the experiences of international students in higher education institutions. Her current research explores the career choice processes of Black African women engineers in South Africa with the aim of understanding the post-apartheid underrepresentation of this population in engineering academe.

Louise Morley FAcSS is a professor of Education and Director of the Centre for Higher Education and Equity Research (CHEER) (http://www.sussex.ac.uk/education/cheer/) at the University of Sussex, UK. Louise has an international profile in the field of the sociology of gender in higher education and has made keynote conference presentations on five continents.

She has recently completed research on women and leadership in higher education in South Asia for the British Council and is now working on a Horizon 2020 Marie Skłodowska-Curie-funded project *Higher Education Internationalisation and Mobility: Inclusions, Equalities and Innovations (HEIM)* (www.sussex.ac.uk/education/cheer/heim). She has undertaken research for the Leadership Foundation for Higher Education on women and leadership, for the ESRC/DFID on Widening Participation in Higher Education in Ghana and Tanzania (www.sussex.ac.uk/

education/cheer/wphegt), for the ESRC on knowledge exchange, for the HEFCE on graduate employability and for the Carnegie Corporation of New York and the Department for International Development on Gender Equity in Commonwealth Universities.

Louise is on the editorial board of *Studies in Higher Education, Teaching in Higher Education* and *Higher Education Research and Development*. She was previously a member of the editorial board of *Gender and Education*. Louise is a fellow of the Academy of Social Sciences, a fellow of the Society for Research into Higher Education and a guest professor at the University of Gothenburg, Sweden (2016–17); was a senior research fellow at the Centre for Gender Excellence, University of Örebro, Sweden (2011); and the 2013–2014 inaugural chair of the Women's Leadership Centre, Universiti Kebangsaan, Malaysia. Louise has published widely in the field of higher education studies. See Sussex Research Online – http://sro.sussex.ac.uk/view/creators/461.html.

Marília Moschkovich is a Brazilian sociologist. Her MA in Education was obtained in 2013 at the State University of Campinas (UNICAMP), Brazil, with the dissertation 'Glass ceiling or firewalls? : A study on gender in the academic carrer and the brazilian case of UNICAMP'. She is now a PhD candidate in the area of Sociology of Education/Sociology of Knowledge at the Education School of UNICAMP, with a research that investigates the reception of the concept of gender in Latin America. She is also a writer and author of a sociology textbook used in high school education. Her main research interests are gender inequalities, gender studies, higher education, academic careers, sociology of intellectuals and academics, sociology of education, sociology of knowledge and sociology of gender.

Terhi Nokkala is a senior researcher at the Finnish Institute for Educational Research, University of Jyväskylä, Finland. Her research focuses on the interplay between policy, technological developments, organisational parameters and individual experiences in higher education, with specific interest in academic work and careers, internationalisation, research collaboration and university autonomy. She is coeditor of *Journal of the European Higher Education Area*.

Tatiana Fumasoli is a senior lecturer and researcher at the Department of Education, University of Oslo, Norway. Her research focuses on institutional change in the academic field and on the multilevel dynamics in the so-called 'knowledge society'. She is coeditor of *Higher Education Quarterly*.

Reitumetse Obakeng Mabokela is the vice provost for International Affairs and Global Strategy and professor of Higher Education at the University of Illinois at Urbana-Champaign. Her research examines experiences of marginalised populations and aims to inform policies that affect these groups within institutions of higher education. Professor Mabokela employs interdisciplinary approaches, drawing largely on theoretical approaches from Comparative and International Education, Policy Studies and Sociology to study higher education issues in developing and transitional societies. She is the author, co-author, editor or coeditor of seven books and has published extensively on these issues in a variety of academic journals.

Antigoni Papadimitriou is an assistant professor, School of Education, at The Johns Hopkins University, Baltimore, MD, USA. She also teaches as adjunct Institutional Research at Baruch College/CUNY. Additionally, she is a visiting professor at Solvay School of Economics and Open University HCMC in Vietnam where she teaches Performance Evaluation. She received her PhD from the University of Twente, School of Management and Governance, Center for Higher Education Policy Studies (CHEPS) in the Netherlands. She holds a Master of Science in Higher Education Administration from Baruch College, School of Public Affairs, City University of New York, and a Baccalaureate in Business Economics, from Aristotle University, Thessaloniki, Greece. She was a postdoctoral fellow in the Department of Educational Research at the University of Oslo, Norway. Doctor Papadimitriou specialises in quality management, organisational leadership, strategic planning and organisational change. She is a specialist in mixed methods research with an international reputation for her work on quality in higher education. She is a member of Comparative and International Education Society (CIES) Higher Education Sig (HESIG) Awards Committee, executive board member for the EAIR (European Higher Education Society) and treasurer of the Mixed Methods International Research Association (MMIRA).

Massimiliano Vaira is associate professor of Economic Sociology at the Department of Political and Social Sciences of Pavia University (Italy), where he teaches Organisation and Governance of Education Systems, Sociology of Organisation and Sociological Theory. He is also member of the Interdepartmental Centre of Studies and Researches of Higher Education Systems (CIRSIS) at the same institution and of the Consortium of Higher Education Researchers (CHER). His main research interests are policy, reform and organisational change of higher education, comparative analysis of higher education systems, academic work and career, evaluation of higher education and university-economy relationships. Amongst his most recent publications are *Questioning Excellence in Higher Education. Policies, Experiences and Challenges in National and Comparative Perspective* (coedited with M. Rostan), Rotterdam, Sense Publisher, 2011; *The Permanent Liminality. Transition and Liminal Change in the Italian University. A Theoretical Framework and Early Evidences*, in Branković J., M. Klemenčič, P. Lažetić, P., P. Zgaga (eds.) *Global Challenges, Local Responses in Higher Education*, Rotterdam Sense Publisher, 2014; and *Between Tradition and Transition: The Academic Career in Italy*, in V. Meira Soares, U. Teichler, M. de Lourdes Machado-Taylor (eds.) *Challenges and Options: The Academic Profession in Europe*, Dordrecht, Springer (forthcoming).

Zhou Zhong is associate professor of the Institute of Education, Tsinghua University. Zhou graduated from Peking University (BA) and the University of Oxford (MSc and DPhil). Her research interest is in comparative, international and interdisciplinary studies of higher education, with special reference to the impact of internationalisation and globalisation. Her recent studies have involved a gendered perspective in access to education, faculty development, global mobility, international collaboration and e-learning. She has a special interest in integrating the teaching, research and practice of innovation in education.

Introduction

Women in Higher Education: Charting the Trajectory

Charting the Trajectory

This volume has been written in response to the continuing concern that despite the efforts that have been made by governments and institutions to bring about equality for women in the workplace, there remain some areas of that labour market that have not responded to those pressures. One such area is higher education and particularly so in terms of leadership positions in academia.

The present book is essentially an update of an earlier volume published by the editor, *Women as Leaders and Managers in Higher Education*, Open University Press 1997. That book, when set alongside this volume, underlines the major changes in the attitude to women in senior positions in academia. The earlier volume discusses 'the relative invisibility of women as major leaders within their own campuses and communities'. No longer, in 2016, are those leaders invisible: those of ability are becoming accepted for the skills they offer, no longer as tokens in an all-male community. This volume charts a shift in cultural attitudes, which, while still needing to develop further, is certainly noticeable.

The earlier volume examined the initiatives recently established to advance and support the development of women in higher education, because support had been sadly lacking. The Report of a Commission on Women in Higher Education, established by the American Council on Education, had presented a bleak picture. At the time of the first Report, 1973, there were just 148 women heads of US higher education institutions, out of a total of 2500. As a result, the National Network for Women Leaders in Higher Education was established to support the recognition and promotion of women. Slowly, very slowly, the effects of such initiatives, echoed in many Western countries and now in Eastern countries, as evidenced in this volume, are effecting change. It takes a generation, but it has, and is, happening.

Much of the research findings on women, as discussed by Robin Middlehurst in the earlier volume (pp. 3–16), hold true and are more widely understood. The Ohio and Michigan Leadership Studies to which she refers still carry weight: the four dimensions of support behaviour, thus enhancing a sense of worth; interaction-facilitation, exemplified by mutually satisfying relationships; commitment to achieving particular goals; and work facilitation, by enabling planning, organisation and coordination. Each of these dimensions remains true in 2016 and is touched on in a number of chapters in this new volume. Networking, for instance, viewed as a somewhat novel approach in the late 1990s, is now mainstream and used by women very effectively (cf. Chap. 14).

There are differences in the academy of 1997 and 2016: aspects which were viewed as additional extras in higher education society have now become embedded. The first is the curriculum area of gender studies. With the growing awareness of the need to understand and appreciate the role of women came the growth of gender studies and related areas such as equity studies and access studies. Considerable research funding was made available, and the pool of knowledge in these areas was enhanced by high-quality scholarship. Today the research funds have shrunk considerably in this field, though there is still excellent work done, as exemplified in this volume, but the priority has moved elsewhere. However, the cultural shift is by no means complete, and the dearth of funding for those of high calibre with expertise in these areas is to be regretted.

Another area which has undergone mutation is that of equal opportunities. In the late 1990s, equal opportunities was an add-on in higher education institutions, with a separate group of staff, often viewed as managers more than academics, who were expected to carry out the mission of fostering equal opportunities to career advancement for all staff. Often there was an equal opportunities officer in each faculty. With the coming of Equality Acts enacted by many Western governments, this area is no longer an add-on, but has been subsumed into the structure of the higher education institutions, thus marking a significant cultural shift.

Unlike the first volume, this book examines the issue in a global context, and that in itself indicates the new importance of the world view and the awareness of the global village all academics are intensely aware of. The first volume offered a range of transatlantic initiatives and with that an essentially Western perception of policy relating to gender equality. In this new volume, it is clear that the issues considered are shared at some level by every nation and that Eastern nations are also now in the forefront of change.

Part One sets the scene in global terms, with studies from a world policymaker's view to those from two great powers, the USA and China, and a study from Africa. Kearney (Chap. 1) presents a world view which provides the policy setting for the book, examining the ability of women to respond to the demands and pressures of the technological age. Frances (Chap. 2) makes a statistical assessment of the US scene, and Zhong and Guo (Chap. 3) offer a detailed study of educational opportunities and employment prospects for women in China. It is instructive that in 2016 Chinese research carries a weight that would not have been discerned in the 1990s.

Africa, the BRIC countries and the Far East all contribute to this volume, unlike its predecessor: their research findings echo those of the European authors.

Part Two takes the theme of adjusting to change, with a mix of policy approaches and sociological research studies. The country study of the Netherlands and the comparative study on Italy and Switzerland trace detailed findings on aspects of academic women's careers, while the Greek study shows how higher education academics in that country are adjusting to the exigencies of the Greek political situation. The study of Malaysia offers a government-backed research initiative which is aimed at improving the lot of academic women in that country. And the US piece on the position of women of colour in higher education indicates the challenges that they face and overcome in achieving career advancement.

Part Three offers the findings from a range of specific groups in academia, all of whom are seeking gender equality. David considers the topic from a UK point of view, as does Leathwood who examines academic researchers; Henkel asks whether academic career progression in the UK and Germany is a matter of time; Lillie reports on those who teach languages in Europe. The book concludes with two contrasting studies which emphasise the range of situations of women in academia who are affected by the issues and challenges of gender equality. One study is European and offers new findings on early career women in academia; the other is a study of women professors, but in a BRIC country. Thus, the global nature of the changing academic profession for women is underlined.

Indeed, the global economy is such that all nations are interconnected, whether they like it or not. Change is inevitable. Any major fall in the Chinese stock market reverberates around the world, and although individual countries may attempt to insulate themselves against the global pressures, in the end, they fail to do so. Despite highly diverse global populations, certain trends are echoed in country after country, as can be seen in the studies in this volume (e.g. Morley, Goastellec and Veira).

The knowledge economy brings opportunities for women and particularly for graduate women who have developed the skills to contribute to national wealth. Women worldwide seek education and crowd into the universities: in the last 30 years, they have aspired to learn and have taken opportunities to better themselves. The recent UNESCO global gender parity index for female/male enrolments in higher education stands at 1.08, indicating that more women than men choose to study. Morley (2013) points out that the number of women participating in higher education has increased by 600% in the last 40 years.

Major changes have taken place in the shape of society, and it is these cultural shifts, notably in Western and OECD countries, that have presaged the changes in women's roles. No longer is the man expected to be the major breadwinner for the family, and no longer is the woman expected to be confined to the home. Flexibility has become a keyword. Women now commonly work for much of their lives, and men commonly contribute time and effort to child-rearing. The shift to teamwork, approaching tasks together, is a far cry from the separation of domains seen in earlier Western societies. Economic necessity still drives, but responses are much more flexible in terms of gender roles.

Demographics remain a major factor; Western Europe has been affected for many years by declining birth rates. Germany has been noticeably affected. A study by the German auditing firm BDO with the Hamburg Institute of International Economics pointed out in May 2015 that Germany's birth rate had slumped to the lowest in the world, with 8.2 children born per 1000 inhabitants in the past 5 years, a lower figure than Japan. In Europe, Portugal and Italy came second and third with an average of 9.0 and 9.3 children, respectively. France and the UK both had 12.7 children per 1000 inhabitants. The shrinking of population impacts powerfully on the labour market, and shortages of skills appear which cannot easily be remedied. The German study notes that the percentage of people of working age in Germany will drop from 61 to 54 % by 2030, leading to likely higher wage costs. Arno Probst, a BDO board member, warned that without strong labour markets, Germany could not maintain its economic edge. The report argued that one of the ways to enable Germany to hold its economic position was to expand the number of women in the workforce. In the past, there have been some examples, such as the period following the Second World War, when the paucity of qualified men for university positions enabled more women to be appointed. Demand outstripped supply of those from the traditional mould. Mabokela (Chap. 4) points out that there are similar effects in South Africa where the shift in political power opened up greater opportunities for educated black women to teach in the universities. Hence, in certain times, demographics act in women's favour.

However, it is cultural shift that can be seen as arguably the most important factor in enabling the role of women to change in the academy. It is slow, and it can take generations. The speed at which countries move is very variable, as evidenced by New Zealand giving the vote to women in 1893 and Saudi Arabia in 2015. Slow cultural shifts can be traced in all countries and all professions, particularly in the most conservative of professions. In the UK, it was only in 2015 that women bishops were appointed to the Anglican Church, and although there has been a steady smattering of women vice-chancellors in British universities, what is curious is that the percentage holding these posts has barely shifted over time. The numbers range between 15 % and 21 % over the last decade. The shift in numbers is very slight. Those posts are still fought for, hard, and many factors come into play. The part played by search agencies themselves, in view of the fact that they prepare the long list of candidates from which the university chooses its shortlist, needs researching. Even so, the present likelihood of many more than 20 % of women becoming vice-chancellors in the UK does not appear high.

A number of authors in this volume examine the situation for women's academic career advancement in their own countries. Moschkovich presents a detailed discussion of the institutional mechanisms and cultural norms that contribute to the existing gender inequalities in Brazil; Huang offers an insight into the situation of women of colour in US higher education; and Leisyte and Hosch-Dayican consider the balance of teaching and research in the Netherlands, which has the effect of cutting down on opportunities to reach top career levels. Leathwood examines the situation of those working solely in research. Henkel's study of gender equality in the UK and Germany traces the contrasts and commonalities of academic working lives.

Papadimitriou's research documents the effect of the financial collapse of Greece on women academics in its higher education system, and Morley, Berma and Hamid present a major study in Malaysia, which considered a wide range of issues relating to the position of women in higher education.

Some changes in society, which affect both women and men, have been important in enabling women to reposition themselves in society and in the academy. The power of globalisation in the twenty-first century, combined with the growing importance of the knowledge economy, has brought new pressures to bear on the cultures of all countries. Digital communication enables the immediacy of news worldwide. The media can fuel aspiration and facilitate achievement of educational goals.

The expansion of opportunity to study, linked with rising demand worldwide from those who wish to study, is a factor in pushing undergraduate figures for women into the majority in very many countries (Kearney). The study by Zhong and Guo in this volume traces the rapid growth in educational opportunities in China and points out that not only are women students now a majority in higher education but they also perform better both in learning approaches and outcomes.

The actions of the government in facilitating cultural change in the role of women in society are explored in a number of ways in this volume. A decade ago, China took the decision to expand its higher education system hugely, and this has offered new opportunities of access (Zhong and Guo). New universities were built; an elite group of research universities was established; and higher education opportunities were made available to those who were geographically isolated in the West. The demand for access has become a worldwide phenomenon, with new institutions and new methods of delivery being seen in almost every country.

European legislation is and has been a major factor in the modernisation of Europe's higher education systems and can be arguably seen as bringing about critical cultural change. David's chapter traces the effect in the UK of The Robbins Report (1963) which brought about the founding of new universities, expanded the university system and ushered in a new system of grants for study, which offered women from all backgrounds, however poor, the chance to enter university. The effect was to free up individual and social mobility in an unprecedented manner and, arguably, reinvigorate the innovative abilities of the country as a whole. The effects are still being seen today.

The Bologna Process, established in 1999 by the ministers of education in 29 European countries, ensures compatibility in the standards and quality of higher education in Europe. The European Higher Education Area has been created which has considered a range of topics including, in November 2010, The Social Dimension of Higher Education: Building Excellence and Equality. Lillie argues that although European measures promote equality of opportunity and legislation supports women in their careers and can play a positive role in fostering egalitarian workplaces, those women teaching languages in higher education still encounter a range of problems that need to be addressed.

Within the different European countries, considerable legislation on equality issues has been enacted. Henkel's chapter refers to the national agendas in the UK and Germany which have ushered in equal opportunities policies and gender main-streaming. Government support for childbearing, childcare and family responsibili-ties has affected women's perceptions of career possibilities and opened up opportunities for advancement. Both Lillie's and Nokkala, Culum and Fumasoli's research reported in this volume examine these aspects. The latter study specifically examines the situation of those academics still at an early career stage.

Equality legislation has been enacted in the majority of EU countries; in Norway a 2008 law laid down that at least 40 % of males and 40 % of females should be appointed to public boards. This has been very successful, and the movement to raise the numbers of women on public boards in other European countries has gath-ered momentum. Encouragement, though, rather than legislation, is a slower way of proceeding; in the UK, for instance, only 12 % of chairs of higher education govern-ing bodies are women (2013 figure), a far cry from 40. However, the climate is changing, and the general acceptance of women as capable leaders and managers is now widespread. The transfertilisation of the corporate world, the public world and the academic world, backed by government policy, is a major factor in OECD coun-tries in enabling women to be recognised and valued for their potential contribution to society.

Affirmative action has been important in the USA, and predated much of the European legislation. Title IX of the Education Amendments of 1972 is a compre-hensive federal law that prohibits discrimination on the basis of sex in any federally funded education programme or activity. This applies to all traditional educational institutions such as colleges, universities and elementary and secondary schools and also, from 2000, all education programme providers and recipients funded by other federal agencies.

Following on from equality legislation, leadership programmes for women have been developed in many OECD countries in recent years, and these can attract pub-lic funding: the Association of Commonwealth Universities (ACU) offers a gender programme as does the Office of Women in Higher Education in the USA. The Equality Challenge Unit (UK) has been established to further and support equality and diversity for staff and students. It is a registered charity, funded by the UK higher education funding bodies and representative organisations. Among other projects, it is currently involved in a multi-country European project to address the issue of promoting gender equality in research institutions and the integration of the gender dimension in research contexts. The research is part of the European Union's Seventh Framework Programme, and the partners involved include France, Spain, Norway, Switzerland, Ireland, Belgium, Cyprus, Slovenia, Canada and the USA. The presence and roles of women in research are examined by Leathwood in this volume.

At an institutional level, change is being achieved, though from a low base in many cases. Science and technology has had markedly low numbers. The Norwegian University of Science and Technology increased the number of its women profes-sors from 9 to 14 % in 5 years, a 55 % increase; the Excellentia programme of the Austrian Council for Research and Technology Development enabled a rise to 20 % of women professors from 13 % 6 years earlier (2005–2011). Thus, the figures for women professors are improving, though slowly, as is evidenced in a number of chapters in this volume.

Change interventions to support women's advancement are widespread and at a range of levels. By putting equality legislation on the statutory book, governments signal their support for equality and encourage action to be taken to implement it. Morley, Derma and Hamid's chapter is an example of research and recommendations on the issue, backed by government support.

Local communities can support women in achieving their goals with childcare facilities and group support, using a range of communication techniques including Facebook, messaging and Skype. Institutions can put in place gender equality policies, processes and practices expressed in audits and reviews, in flexible working patterns and university frameworks that support women's career development and leadership. Actions need to be underpinned by a commitment to natural justice and a commitment that universities should reflect and represent their societies as well as a commitment to developing fully the human resource potential of their staff.

Supportive, positive mentoring can be offered to the individual, with opportunities to prepare for advancement and to develop networks to which she can contribute and draw support from. Self-esteem and the knowledge that she is equal and has every right to assert herself can enable the individual to develop her full potential.

Cultural shifts in the attitude of society, for whatever plethora of reasons, appear to be the key to major change, and Hofstede's work on values dimensions in national cultures provides some insight into the behaviours, intentions and attitudes of society. What is interesting is that the calls in the media for full equality of women and men are becoming more frequent. The acknowledged leaders are the Nordic countries, Sweden, Norway, Denmark and Finland, whose gender equality policies have achieved real change, and are arguably leaders in other areas – health outcomes, educational outcomes and social welfare programmes. But the enlightened attitudes of the Nordic countries are now echoed elsewhere. Lucy Clark, writing in *The Guardian* (15.1.16) from an Australian point of view, calls for parity: 'What we must have, first and foremost, is a culture of parity – equal numbers of women and men in positions of power and leadership'.

Women are equal, and this volume, while examining the current position for women in higher education, also presages the shift in societal acceptance of the opening up of the range and seniority in position that women can now aspire to, not only throughout professions, such as medicine, the law and the church, but also in higher education. I conclude with a positive and cheering example: whereas the women chairs of governing councils of English universities remain in 2016 at 14%, by August of 2016, Scotland will have just over 50% who are women. Equality can be reached; society's acceptance of and respect for women's abilities are integral to the overall development of universities in terms of both equality and quality.

University of Sussex, Brighton   Heather Eggins
United Kingdom

References

Clark, L. (2016). *And now Jamie Clements*: *Equal numbers is the only way to create a culture of respect* www.theguardian.com/commentisfree/2016/Jan/15. Hamburg Institute of International Economics and BDO.

Equality challenge unit equality in higher education: *Statistical report 2014*, London: ECU.

Hofstede, G., Hofstede, G. J., Minkov, M. (2010). *Cultures and organisations*; *Software of the mind*, 3rd edn. New York: McGraw-Hill.

Morley, L. (2013). *Women and higher education leadership*: *Absences and aspirations*, London: The Leadership Foundation.

UNESCO Institute of Statistics. (2010). *Global education digest: Comparing education statistics across the world* (*a special focus on gender*), Paris: UNESCO.

Part I
Setting the Scene

Chapter 1
Whither Women Graduates in the Knowledge Economy?

Observations on the Advancement of Women in Politics, Higher Education and Business

Mary-Louise Kearney

Introduction: Situating the Issue

The overall objective of this chapter is to present thoughts and evidence regarding the issue of graduate women in the global economy where their academic credentials constitute a starting point for their personal and professional pathways.

This relates to their progress towards attaining tertiary education qualifications and their status quo in terms of current enrolment numbers and presence in higher education decision-making. However, their roles in the particular decision-making processes of politics and of business will also be examined. Today, these two critical areas, together with the academy, may be considered as the "golden triangle" for socio-economic development. The issue of leadership is quite different from the feminization of many professions (such as medicine and law) and from the fact that talented women without academic credentials may do well in politics and business, though these tend to be a minority. Even Mhairi Black (the Scottish National Party MP elected to the British Parliament in May 2015 and, at age 20, the youngest member of the House of Commons) campaigned for office while still an undergraduate and finished her degree in Politics at Glasgow University after election (*The Financial Times: 1 August 2015*). Leadership in these three areas is a crucial part of social decision-making. Given their importance, there are often calls for targets and quotas to remove barriers and to ensure a higher female presence. These are still necessary while imbalances continue. For example, 45 % of the new pan-African Parliament is expected to be female and many will be university-educated, according to Olesegun Obasanjo, president of Nigeria from 1999 to 2007. In contrast, women made up only 15 % of delegates to the 2014 Davos World Economic Forum

M.-L. Kearney (✉)
SRHE Journal Studies in Higher Education, Oxford University, Oxford, UK
e-mail: kearneyml@gmail.com

© Springer International Publishing Switzerland 2017   3
H. Eggins (ed.), *The Changing Role of Women in Higher Education*,
The Changing Academy – The Changing Academic Profession in International
Comparative Perspective 17, DOI 10.1007/978-3-319-42436-1_1

(*Source:* The Economist 2014) and despite the growing numbers of female graduates in business-related studies, only 4.6 % of CEOs leading the celebrated Fortune 500 companies are women. In a 2013 Harvard Business School survey of New Zealand company boards members where only 7.5 % are female, 88 % of these women had advanced degrees compared with 45 % of their male counterparts (*Source*: The New Zealand Herald 2014). Clearly much progress is yet to be made; yet the steadily rising number of women graduates should mean that they would be increasingly prominent in these fields in the future.

For this reason, it is important to consider the wider context of the world, today and beyond. At the present time, the global economy is knowledge-based where, in principle, highly qualified people stand in good stead. But powerful forces can impact negatively on this context. Lisa Kahn, a Yale University economist, has investigated how periods of recession affect graduate employment (particularly for those with credentials which are not in high demand by the labour market), debt levels and delayed entry into adult life (The New York Times 2014). Moreover, this situation will evolve further in the years ahead as established socio-economic paradigms undergo major changes leading to a new world order dominated by new nations with growing resources and dynamic young and mobile populations. Ghana, Nigeria, South Africa, Brazil, Mexico, Algeria, Egypt and Indonesia are just a few salient examples and contrast with embattled industrialized economies with ageing populations such as Canada, Germany, the United Kingdom and Denmark. (*Source*: http://world.bymap.org/Young Populations). This situation triggers a range of important questions, which affect the particular fortunes of women graduates, whatever their cultural or socio-economic background may be. A few important questions are listed below:

- What are the major international advocacy strategies used to promote and monitor the access of women to higher education, as well as to politics and the economy, and do they lead to effective policies in this regard?
- What are the returns for women holding tertiary education qualifications and do these hold good in today's labour market?
- Who are the current international role models for women and how do these interface with personal and local narratives, experiences and challenges?
- What might be the next objectives for qualified women, as the present social and economic contexts will continue to evolve?
- Is gender research keeping adequate track of the evolving situation of women in the Knowledge Economy?

While this chapter will examine these particular areas, others will analyse in depth the important issue of women in the academy itself and offer convincing evidence concerning current trends and desirable future directions to correct imbalances. The status quo of women as leaders in the academy is now a specific – and critical – matter since the entire question of academic careers has shifted significantly in recent years. Governments are now dealing with the reality of massified – or even universal – higher (and, more broadly, tertiary) education where 60 % or more of the national 18–25 year age cohort have access to this level of study and where the demand for lifelong learning has accelerated sharply to meet the changing needs of the labour market. Women often dominate both the initial enrolment figures and the overall demand for further education and training. Consequently, highly qualified women enter – and often constitute the majority in – certain areas of the skilled workforce. This trend, along with other future realities such as increased demand from female adults for flexible learning opportunities, was predicted as long ago as 1998 by the OECD's seminal report entitled *Redefining Tertiary Education* (OECD 1998). From one viewpoint, it might be said that the educational objective advocated by the women's movement during the latter decades of the twentieth century, has been attained – namely that women can access postsecondary study and then reap the benefits of their credentials in their professional lives. However, the story has moved on rapidly from there and it is important to analyse the current factors in play to ensure that progress continues in this new and more complex landscape.

Because development is not a linear process, the issue of women in higher education is obviously part of an evolving process. Since 2008, the fragile recovery from the post-crisis labour market has created grave problems affecting the stability of the labour market. Graduates, while much better equipped than the poorly qualified, are certainly not immune to this situation and must consider more frequent job changes and greater mobility of employment as part of their career plans. Concurrently, the academic profession is encountering a period of change. Tenure is under serious scrutiny and is an area where women are already in the minority, e.g. 64% men and 36% women in the USA according to a study by Catherine Hill, Research Director of the American Association of University Women (Hill 2004). As well, levels of student debt are reaching alarming proportions and there is growing evidence that institutional interest (notably for universities seeking world-class status) has moved to attracting dynamic and productive research faculty and graduate students (Meek and Jacob 2012). This change process is accompanied by ever growing CIT (communication and information technology) potential, the applications of which have far reaching implications for academic teaching and research. In this regard, none other than Rafael Riefe, resident of MIT and an electronics engineer, has expressed the opinion that "*Universities in their present form are obsolete*" meaning that their teaching and research functions can be delivered in new and more effective ways; hence the rise of the MOOCs to provide open and IT-delivered educational programmes. Certainly, change is on the agenda. The inevitability of this evolution has led the OECD to propose the Modern Academy based on new approaches to *governance and management, funding, quality, equity, innovation, labour market links, and internationalization* which are the key components of higher education systems today (OECD 2008). Hence, a wider contextual analysis is necessary to ascertain how the reality of enhanced access for women to higher education is playing out, where the next challenges – both social and economic – for this group will lie and which policies will address the new issues with optimal effects.

As these questions are studied, a general overview of women in higher education – whether as students, academics or graduates – should be kept in mind. The following figure proposes the major factors affecting the fortunes of this group at the various stages of their studies; careers and personal lifestyles and these will recur throughout the issues discussed in this chapter. It can be argued the personal or professional path for any women may well be traced by her attitude and performance in relation to these key areas and their interaction.

This resonates closely with the 2015 OECD Report, *The ABC of Gender Equality in Education: Aptitude, Behaviour and Confidence*, designed to offer evidence-based policy guidance to governments. This examines the new gender gap between male and female achievement at school level and its probable later negative effects, which prevent the optimal development of citizen potential. In this regard, concern is also increasing about lower male achievement in education and in the workforce. Of course, numerous academics have written books to explain either the progress of women or their lack of advancement. One example, *Wonder Woman: Sex, Power and the Quest for Perfection by* Debora L. Spar, president of Barnard College, in New York, is noteworthy because it acknowledges that success or failure will inevitably result from a mix of factors, rather than one single element. Some emanate from the woman herself, others will originate in her context (such as institutional and cultural impediments or the influence of interlocutors notably family, teachers and peers). What then becomes paramount is how each woman navigates her particular course. These individual paths will gradually merge into the collective journey.

Achievements to Date: The Impact of International Advocacy

Due to advocacy, enormous progress towards gender equality was made during the twentieth century, which helped change the life of women in relation to political empowerment, access to education and presence in the middle and upper echelons of the workforce. Each of these advances has been a process in itself with its own time-line and landmarks in terms of achieving objectives, including the elaboration of necessary policies required. This achievement should never be underestimated. However, it is important to understand how the three areas – political, educational and economic – interconnect to ensure the continued progress of women, who constitute 51 % of humanity, towards real and universal equality.

For instance, in the case of women's suffrage, more than an entire century separates New Zealand where women won the right to vote in 1893 from Saudi Arabia where women's suffrage was finally achieved in 2015. In education, progress was more rapid. The post-World War II Baby Boomer generation enjoyed much wider access to study at all levels and particularly to university qualifications. As a result, higher education enrolments for men and women in high-income economies became massified by the late 1980s. In other socio-economic contexts, the pace has varied. While certain merging economies have made huge strides in this area, some low-income countries still lag far behind. An example is Afghanistan, which now spends only 0.5 % of GNP on higher education and where the Gross Enrolment Rate in this sector is only 5 %. With Chad and Eritrea, this is the lowest in the world (Atarupane 2013). In 2015, recently, the first female Minister of Higher Education (Farida Momand, a medical doctor) was appointed and must address this problem urgently. In general, women everywhere now understand much better what they have to gain from education and intend to seek opportunities for this. In the field of employment, the wave of graduates since the 1970s has assured a steady stream of skilled human capital – including much larger numbers of qualified women – into the workforce. This process was notable up to the 2008 crash, which shook the foundations of the labour market and continues to exert profound influence on the future of stable employment and, consequently, on social development itself. Already, it is now common practice for women to share (or to assure alone) the breadwinning role in households at all economic levels (except for the mega-wealthy who, as the American author F. Scott Fitzgerald observed in his famous novel, *The Great Gatsby*, are different from ordinary people – perhaps because money often marries money to ensure powerful alliances based on wealth).

These areas of politics, academia and business have specific significance for women graduates.

For instance, highly educated women are more likely to enter the political arena with, as previously mentioned, African parliaments leading the charge in this regard. According to the Inter-Parliamentary Union, some 20 % of all national parliamentarians were women in Sub-Saharan Africa in 2013 with Rwanda reporting an impressive 64 % (*Source:* The Economist 9 November 2013). Despite this success, data collected by New World Wealth states that only 22 % of women worldwide are deputies and 16 out of 34 OECD countries (including the USA and the United Kingdom) are failing to meet the 30 % benchmark of women representatives in lower houses and in ministerial positions (*Source: Time Magazine, 27 July 2015*). In terms of study choices, women now dominate certain disciplines (such as law, education and medicine) but still remain in the minority in the hard sciences and engineering. Concerning feminine leadership in the workplace, progress remains too slow and the Glass Ceiling prevails, notably in the business sector and in higher education management. Clearly, a new era – and a new campaign – must begin in this respect. These few examples, along with many others, merit their own analyses to help chart the progress of women graduates towards social and economic equality and the factors – whether old or new – impeding this. This is positive news for academic research, both for Gender Studies and for other disciplines because there is a rich store of new and critically relevant material to explore. Recent examples include collaborative neuroscience research at the American Universities of Duke and Southern California which suggest women perform well as decision-makers in high stress situations (*Source: Women, Men and Stress Tests,* International New York Times, 18 October 2014), and sociology research from Oslo University, Norway, challenging the thesis that men and women have different management styles (*Source: Sex in the Boardroom, The Economist, 6 June 2015*).

However, on the personal level, it is important that each woman student or graduate should view her own path in terms of the dimensions described in Fig. 1.1. Each will need self-confidence, application and support to take advantages of the

| 1. Self-perception/Aspirations | 2. Application/Perseverance |
| 3. Personal/Career Opportunities | 4. Support/Mentoring |

Fig. 1.1 Women with advanced educational credentials. Legend (*1*) These qualities designate the awareness of women regarding their own abilities and their own self-belief and confidence to articulate aspirations and to pursue these throughout life. (*2*) Application and perseverance are the usual prerequisites for success, whether personal or professional. (*3*) Opportunities usually arise for each and every person in their personal and work situations and should be seized. However, sometimes people must create these for themselves. Timing is a critical associated factor in this regard. (*4*) Each personal and professional journey offers encounters with persons who can help build self-confidence and offer useful advice for strategic choices. Such support systems are invaluable and need to be nurtured. Conversely, discouraging forces (e.g. institutional impediments) or persons need to be identified and countered (Source: The Author)

opportunities and avenues of support that usually materialize at some point in time. These will stand women in good stead in the present global context, which is characterized by social complexity and volatility, uneven political leadership, elusive sustainable growth and the emergence of a new economic world order. This approaching reality was reflected in the title of the 2013 Human Development Report, *The Rise of the South: Human Progress in a Diverse World.*

The existence of gender advocacy strategies at international level has a crucial objective, namely to help promote the formulation of better policies at national level – both in the gender domain and in related areas such as labour and social affairs. Overall, the fact that women are half of humanity – and often of the work force too – has finally hit home. The major components of advocacy action are women in the political arena, in higher/tertiary education and in the labour force. These domains are closely linked, as well-qualified women are more likely to rise to elevated roles of power in each. Though women are still in the minority regarding the level of top leadership, those who have succeeded have a responsibility to encourage others to follow in their footsteps so as to share decision-making. Strategies used by international and non-governmental organizations (such as UN agencies, IGOs, development banks and NGOs) now provide a wide-ranging and solid body of evidence both to record progress towards equality and to highlight underperformance when results leave room for improvement. In recent years, this proliferation of data collection on gender issues has become an invaluable tool for policy-makers seeking to bring about change, both in national legislation and in institutional management.

The annual Human Development Report (HDR), published by the United Nations Development Programme (UNDP) provides an ongoing statistical record on the progress of women, which is considered a critical benchmark for social progress. In this report, countries are ranked by level of development (from very high and high to medium and low) and the results posted for the status of women oblige governments to examine their own position in relation to other neighbours and to similar economies worldwide. A glance at the 2011 HDR, entitled *Sustainability and Equity: a Better Future for All*, shows the status of women in relation to politics, advanced educational qualifications and the economy. Sometimes, the correlation expected amongst the three areas does not occur which recalls the differences in politico- socio-economic contexts (Fig. 1.2).

These data emanate from the Gender Inequality Index (GII) of the UNDP's Human Development Report (HDR), which aims to stimulate urgently needed policy change in areas where women make a particularly vital contribution to national development. In this regard, their access to education, notably tertiary and higher education and training, economic participation and parliamentary presence are deemed critical. The specific importance of this data for socio-economic decision-making was first recognized 20 years ago by the GEM (Gender Empowerment Measure) which preceded the GII itself. Since then, research indicators and results have become more comprehensive as more needs to be known about the exact factors which help (or hinder) women's advancement in these areas. In contrast, the HDR's Gender Development Index (GDI) monitors the parity of male/female levels in health, education and economic empowerment to indicate overall national equality of citizenry. Assessing high, middle and low-income countries shows that certain countries may have strong overall human development ranking but average to poor results related to gender policies.

Thus, a sample of the countries – with varying levels of development – shows that their GII ranking may be higher, similar or lower than their GDI ranking. Hence, they are already renovating policies to promote women's advancement, or they are maintaining equal efforts for improvement or they should do more – and sometimes much more – in this domain (Fig. 1.3).

Position in the HDR Index	Country	Country Parliamentary Presence	Women 25 and older with Tertiary Education	Labour Force
1	Norway	39.6	99.3	63
3	Canada	24.9	92.3	62.7
12	Japan	13.6	80	47.9
30	UAE	22.5	76.9	41.9
39	Poland	17.9	79.7	46.2
44	Chile	13.9	67.3	41.8
61	Malaysia	14	66	44.4
84	Brazil	9.6	48.8	60.1
101	China	21.3	54.8	67.4
118	Botswana	7.9	73.6	72.3
123	South Africa	42.7	66.3	47
134	India	10.7	26.6	32.8
143	Kenya	9.8	20.1	76.4
154	Yemen	0.7	7.6	19.9
172	Afghanistan	27.6	5.8	33.1
183	Chad	14.3	0.9	62.7
187	Congo	9.4	10.7	56.5

Fig. 1.2 Female representation % in key sectors (Source: Human Development Report, UNDP 2011)

Fig. 1.3 Country position
in the HDI index in 2014
(Source: Human
Development Report,
UNDP 2014)

1. Norway	GII 9	GDI 5
2. Australia	GII 19	GDI 40
5. USA	GII 47	GDI 7
6. Germany	GII 3	GDI 61
8. Canada	GII 23	GDI 24
17. Japan	GII 25	GDI 79
19. Israel	GII 17	GDI 29
26. Italy	GII 8	GDI 61
33. Estonia	GII 8.5	GDI 29
34. Saudi Arabia	GII 56	GDI 112
41. Chile	GII 68	GDI 61
43. Hungary	GII 45	GDI 4
57. Russian Federation	GII 52	GDI 61
62. Malaysia	GII 39	GDI 91
70. Kazakhstan	GII 11.8	GDI 59
71. Mexico	GII 73	GDI 85
100. Tonga	GII 90	GDI 54
109. Botswana	GII 100	GDI 58
113. Bolivia	GII 97	GDI 93
125. Guatemala	GII 112	GDI 104
146. Pakistan	GII 127	GDI 145
147. Kenya	GII122	GDI 107
151. Rwanda	GII 79	GDI 80
154. Yemen	GII 152	GDI 146
187. Niger	GII 149	GDI 147

Particularly interesting statistics are found in the tertiary education domain where female representation varies considerably. In the case of Low Development Countries, the poor figures were explained by the precedence given to achieving the Millennium Development Goals (MDGs). This includes reaching their educational targets such as illiteracy eradication and access to basic education and constitutes the priority action for certain UN agencies notably UNESCO and UNICEF. In certain Medium Development Countries, female enrolments in tertiary education are also too low. In both cases, governments should foresee much higher investment in this area for women since demand from this group of the population will rise steadily (Fig. 1.4).

Still within the IGO space, the OECD (Organization for Economic Cooperation and Development) has worked on the elaboration of a Gender Initiative over recent years. This has involved all areas of the organization (inter alia, social policy, education, finance and enterprise, public governance, science, technology and innovation, statistics and development cooperation), thus demonstrating that gender equality pertains to numerous areas of expertise and should be a common priority. The comprehensive evidence collected is documented in OECD repositories such as the Social Institutions and Gender Index and the Gender, Institutions and Development Data Base. These are intended to inform and shape the work of national and institutional policy-makers.

The OECD strategy is designed to contribute to the ongoing and global campaign for gender equality. In particular, the integral economic aspects are emphasized, again recognizing that women constitute half of the world's population and often the majority of national workforces. In this respect, providing equal educational opportunities at all levels is the foundation and the steady rise in the numbers of women with tertiary level qualifications constitutes a significant advantage for national economic growth in the global knowledge economy (Figs. 1.5 and 1.6).

Given these gains, the next logical objective must be to increase the participation of qualified women in the workforce and notably in leadership and management roles. This duly reflects the new major thrust for gender advocacy and activism. For example, only 15 % of the delegates at the 2014 World Economic Forum were women (*Source:* The Economist 25 January 2014). This has not changed significantly in recent years, causing protests such as that in 2013 from a Ukrainian feminist group entitled Femen. The barriers to power remain numerous and strong

Position	Country	HRD Rating Sample	Position	Country	HRD Rating Sample
4	USA	85.9	96	Algeria	30.6
10	Sweden	71.5	113	Egypt	28.5
37	Qatar	10.2	155	Senegal	8.0
45	Argentina	69.4	156	Nigeria	10.1
56	Saudi Arabia	32.8	180	Sierra Leone	2.0
71	Lebanon	52.5			

Fig. 1.4 Tertiary education: gross enrolment rates 2001–2010 in % (Source: Human Development Report, UNDP 2011)

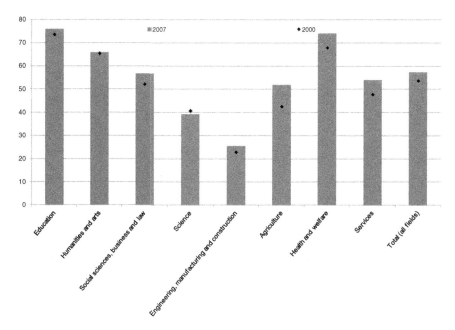

Fig. 1.5 Percentage of degrees awarded to women by subject 2000 and 2007. OECD average[1] OECD average does not include Greece or Luxembourg due to data constraints (Source: The OECD Innovation Strategy, Paris 2011)

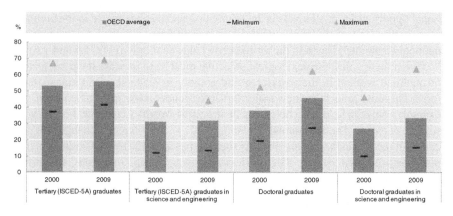

Fig. 1.6 Women graduates in the OECD area, 2000 and 2009. As a percentage of all graduates at the corresponding level (Source: The OECD STI Scoreboard, Paris 2011)

resistance to shared decision-making in political and socio-economic domains is a regrettable reality. While the progress of women in education is irrefutable, it must also be acknowledged that they are still excluded in certain instances from the natural benefits of this status such as equal pay scales and higher living standards.

Against this background, the OECD has built its strategy around three areas namely *education, employment and entrepreneurship*, since these are key pathways to better economic opportunities. Four pillars underpin the Gender Initiative: data on barriers to equality; indicators to measure progress; evidence about female entrepreneurship; and good practice to inform policy-makers. A Final Report on findings to date was published in 2012 and included issues such as the economic case for gender equality, retaining girls in school, the study choices made by women, achieving gender balance on company boards, shared support between women and men to handle work and domestic responsibilities, characteristics of women entrepreneurs and facilitating their access to credit. The latest addition to this body of evidence designed to inform national policy-makers is the aforementioned publication, *The ABC of Gender Equality: Achievement, Behaviour and Confidence*, produced within the framework of the PISA (Programme for International Student Assessment) series.

A further significant international force to help monitor gender issues is constituted by the non-governmental sector. These organizations assure the civil society perspective in this domain and can facilitate debate on fractious problems from a very early stage.

Regarding women in political leadership, the current female representation in world governments can be monitored thanks to the data collected by the Inter Parliamentary Union (IPU) and similar bodies at regional levels. The importance of this function was evidenced in January 2013 when it was announced that women would participate in Saudi Arabia's Shura Council with 20 % of seats. While this body is advisory and 50 % representation was sought, at least this decision starts to move the political agenda a little way forward for women in this country where they cannot drive. Although tertiary education is not a pre-requisite for holding political office, women graduates do form the majority of female parliamentarians and this trend is expected to continue in the future. At 31 October 2012, the IPU posted the following figures (Fig. 1.7).

In addition, 20 countries (out of 206 sovereign states) were led by women in 2012, while 17 countries (of varying socio-economic scales) have had more than

Parliamentarians in the world: 45.068

Women parliamentarians as part of this group: 9.339 (*e.g.* some 20/30%)

Regional Averages of Representation (*e.g.* single/lower house figures)

Nordic countries: 42%
Americas: 23.8%
Europe/OSCE * + Nordic countries: 23.6%
Europe /OSCE * - Nordic countries: 21.9%
Sub-Saharan Africa: 20.8%
Asia: 18.5%
Arab States: 14.9%
Pacific Region: 12.7%

*OSCE: Organization for Security and Co-operation in Europe
(Source: IPU, 2012)*

Fig. 1.7 Parliamentary data

one female leader: e.g. Switzerland has had five female presidents and Sao Tome and Principe has been led by two female prime ministers.

Advocacy remains crucial to ensure that feminine political leadership will increase in the future. In this regard, initiatives such as the Council of Women Leaders are essential. Established in 1996 by Vigidis Finnbogadottir, (then President of Iceland), with support from the Woodrow Wilson Centre, this networks past and present female political leaders to support the enhanced presence of women in political decision-making.

In contrast, charting the progress of women as leaders of Tertiary Education institutions is a notoriously difficult domain. Sadly the reported numbers continue to be too low and this fact is rendered more damning due to the fact that women constitute more than 50 % of all graduates in many high-income countries. According to the international journal, Scientometrics, there are some 17,000 tertiary education institutions (TEIs) in the world, of which some 9000 are universities. Of this latter group, approximately 50 would be considered as the top research universities (Super RUs) as recognized by the various Ranking Tables (*inter alia*, Shanghai Jiao Tong, THE, QS, European Union) and with a significant number located in the USA and the United Kingdom.

It is true that some of these elite institutions have had women presidents or vice-chancellors. Examples are Drew Gilpin Faust at Harvard, Susan Hockfield at MIT, Condoleezza Rice as Provost of Stanford, Alison Fettes Richard at Cambridge (who also chairs the Cambridge Network for academia and business), Brenda Gourlay at the Open University and Louise Richardson at St Andrews and now at Oxford University. Also, a significant number of women accede to VC and deputy VC and in certain contexts (e.g. Australia, New Zealand, Canada); this balance is now considered virtually obligatory. However, this situation might be regarded as another manifestation of the Glass Ceiling syndrome. Female leaders are more likely to be found further down the institutional rankings and in other types of TEIs such as university or community colleges (e.g. some 26% in the USA as of 2013). This further confirms that the top echelon of the academy remains amongst the areas of power dominated by men.

This issue is of major concern for women who have actually led these institutions. Action in this area is necessarily limited but an interesting example is the World Women University Presidents Forum, which has assembled some 600 women university and TEI leaders from 60 countries worldwide during its annual forum, which commenced in 2006. At the 2012 gathering in Zimbabwe, this group called for quotas to arrive at a more creditable representation of women leaders and insisted on the need for support from male counterparts in this struggle. Moreover, this sort of action is supported by major NGOs, notably the International Federation of University Women (IFUW) which has affiliates and members in over 100 countries worldwide. IFUW pioneered the right of women to pursue advanced studies as a human right based on gender equality. As that objective has been met, IFUW and similar bodies have shifted the focus of their advocacy and initiatives to bringing about the empowerment of women in leadership roles. This starts with tertiary and higher education institutions themselves but extends to political and socio-economic spheres where the solid contribution of qualified women to debate and action should be recognized. This networking amongst NGOs for the same purposes provides a valuable background support system as the women's movement evolves towards new goals.

Last but certainly not least in a globalized economy, women in business leadership have emerged as an area, which is frequently cited and considered increasingly important. This is logical given that women are very present in the commercial workforce both in high-income and emerging economies but predominantly in lower and mid-level jobs. As is well known, they are the majority of workers in the informal economy in developing countries. Moreover, women are especially active in small and medium size enterprises (SMEs), which account for some 70 % of all national business activity worldwide. When they create and run such businesses, they frequently have great success as demonstrated by the thriving textile industry in Benin. Because of their natural business acumen, women have been able to benefit from the positive impact of micro-credit schemes such as those offered by the Grameen Bank and similar sources. However, conditions vary widely worldwide. According to a study by Dell Research, women entrepreneurs fare best in the USA but continue to struggle elsewhere including in Russia and Pakistan (*Source: Time Magazine 22 June 2014*).

However, for this enquiry, our main interest is the advancement of highly qualified women in the private sector that has long been seen as very exclusionary for women. Nowhere is this greater than at the top echelons of the business world in fields such as banking, finance and manufacturing. Even for those with the requisite qualifications, cracking the glass ceiling into top management remains the toughest challenge. The very low figures speak for themselves. Due to its rarity, any new appointment of a woman to a Fortune 500 company is hailed in the media. For example, CNN's leading women programme interviewed Lynn J. Goode who has led Duke Energy since 2013. When the New York Times profiled Zhou Qunfei, CEO of Lens Technology, she was described as China's wealthiest entrepreneur (*Source: NYT, 1 August 2015*). In the OECD, the average for women with seats on company boards is one in five members, while in the USA, women account for only some 30 % of MBA students. But, this situation is slowly changing thanks to major advocacy efforts and increased numbers of women who undertake business studies and then work in the commercial field, whether in companies or as owners of small and medium-sized firms. Moreover, the important body of self-help literature, often written for women by qualified women to offer advice on professional advancement, have had an undeniable impact. When Lois Frankel, a psychotherapist and corporate coach, wrote *Nice Girls Don't Get the Corner Office* in 2004, she emphasized the importance of women's ability, behaviour and confidence – exactly the same elements cited by the OECD in its latest gender achievement report in 2015.

Starting with the UN's Global Compact, the concept of business as serving society has helped generate considerable philanthropy along with support for the idea of gender equality in commercial activity. This resonates with NGOs such as the World

Business Council for Sustainable Development (WBCSD), the Davos Economic Forum, the International Chamber of Commerce (ICC), and the International Federation of Business and Professional Women (IFBPW).

In fact, the private sector is doing a great deal to improve the status of women in business (and in other fields such as science) through its practices of sponsoring and branding. Examples are numerous: Goldman Sachs supports a programme to increase the numbers of African women with commercial qualifications; the appointment and stories of high-achievers in business and other domains are show-cased in a previously mentioned CNN programme entitled "Leading Women" which is sponsored by Omega; and L'Oreal, in collaboration with UNESCO, funds a large-scale award scheme to recognize women in science. Other initiatives link business with academia. One example is the partnership between Price Waterhouse Cooper and Bentley University in Boston, USA to support the latter's Centre for Women and Business; another such programme is run by the Forte Foundation, (a non-profit consortium of leading international business schools e.g. INSEAD/France, Wharton/USA, and the London Business School and major companies and banks e.g. AT and T, IBM, Barclays Bank, Ernst and Young, Bank of America Merrill Lynch, Deloittes and Deutsche Bank) to launch women into successful careers through business studies (often taken in addition to qualifications earned in other fields), grants, internship opportunities and networking.

The recognition of women's capacities both by the business sector and by academia (e.g. leading schools such as Harvard and Wharton are actually targeting parity in enrolments) is an encouraging sign. This is further supported by certain national and regional legislation (e.g. Norway and the European Community) to ensure quotas for women on company boards. Very importantly, it is clearly understood that women need not only the academic credentials but also other attributes such as self-confidence and networking skills.

Furthermore, the growing presence of more women as top business leaders in emerging economies is very significant as they are highly visible and influential role models for girls and female students in their specific societies. While in the past, access to such posts was often the precinct of the politically connected and mega-wealthy elites, this has changed as countries democratize and diversify their economies. China's has the world's highest number of self-made billionaires and women are figuring more often in this elite. As well, women who have earned international qualifications in business-related fields and gained experience abroad, often return home to attractive posts and can expect to rise more quickly in the ranks. In this regard, invaluable assistance can come from the national and local chapters of NGOs, both those that promote women in professional areas (e.g. Zonta) and also those that promote business cooperation such as Rotary and Lions' Clubs. These help to build contacts both amongst women themselves and with their male colleagues. Thus, as female enrolments in tertiary education become more prolific, it is obvious that women will be seeking to identify mentoring support and networks to help launch their careers and advise on important choices as they progress. As this change takes place, the influence of role models remains especially important.

Returns on Higher Education Qualifications

According to the OECD, investing in higher – or tertiary, which is the broader term preferred by this organization-education, is an investment which helps build sustainable economies. This investment is both national and personal and leads not only to better skilled work forces but also to more aware citizens who are more likely to make more prudent informed political and social choices.

A sample of benefits as listed in the annual OECD publication *Education at a Glance* is as follows:

- *Solid termination rates in tertiary education assure better skilled national workforces (Indicator A3)*
- *In OECD countries (where reliable statistics exist), the net public return from investment in tertiary education is more than US 5 K per student (Indicator A6)*
- *The role of skilled human capital in the knowledge economy justifies further investment (Indicator A9)*
- *Educational attainment links to long-term social outcomes, e.g. better health, political understanding, citizenship (Indicator A11).*

(Source: OECD 2012a, b)

Major progress in female enrolment at this level of study has been the most noteworthy aspect of this sector over the past two decades. This holds true both for the age cohorts (25–34 and 55–64) used to measure enrolments and for the net entry rates for tertiary education. In OECD countries, the results have been quite spectacular with women overtaking men in the composition of the student body. According to the OECD report entitled *Tertiary Education in the Knowledge Society*, the gap between female and male entry to tertiary-type **A** education had become sizeable by 2005:

- Iceland: females 96 % cf males 53 %
- Hungary: females 78 % cf males 57 %
- New Zealand: females 93 % cf males 64 %
- Norway: females 89 % cf males 63 %.

(Source: OECD 2008) (Fig. 1.8).

Naturally, this attainment success then translates into higher job expectations as women seek to use their credentials for attractive careers. Not surprisingly, this has led to new problems in terms of male attainment and social attitudes to better-qualified girls and women. Certain problems persist notably in technology and the hard sciences where female enrolments are less than 30 % and less than 40 % respectively in OECD countries. In contrast, women students are in the majority (more than 60 %) in the life sciences. Thus, in terms of the earlier objective of the women's movement to increase female enrolment in higher education, there is no doubt that this has been reached.

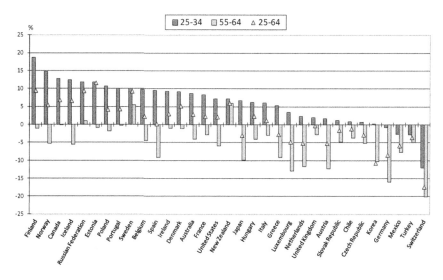

Fig. 1.8 Difference between the percentage of females and the percentage of males who have attained at least tertiary education, by age group, 2005. Countries are ranked in descending order of the difference between the percentage of females and the percentage of males, in the age group 25–34, who have attained at least tertiary education. Note: Years of reference are 2004 for Chile and 2003 for the Russian Federation (Source: Tertiary Education in the Knowledge Society, OECD, 2008)

Despite their educational achievements, their new status as the majority of university graduates poses new challenges for women. This affects where women work and their salary levels compared to men. Important gender differences still persist in labour force participation, hours spent in paid and unpaid work and in employment conditions and earnings. This is true not just in high-income countries (where women are playing an increasing role in the workforce and as consumers) but also more widely in the major emerging economies which now engage in regular dialogue with the OECD in relation to global economic development. The following graph illustrates some interesting current trends (Fig. 1.9).

In fact, the employment gender gap is smaller in China and the Russian Federation than in OECD countries. In India, where many women work in the informal sector, the gap has not narrowed over the last 30 years. However, middle-income countries need to re-orient their labour policies so that these benefit from better design, development and technology diffusion and can thus employ appropriately skilled women. At the present time, the OECD Development Assistance Centre reports that some 20 % of all aid funding is earmarked for women (e.g. some US$ 4.6 billion out of US$ 20 billion) but most of this goes to the rural sector. For women to be economically empowered, investment is needed in sectors in which women can work if they are appropriately skilled (such as environment, health, energy, transport, education and information, as well as in small and medium-sized enterprises). In contrast, most of their female counterparts in OECD countries tend to be seeking to use their qualifications in order to climb the career ladder and, for the most ambitious, break

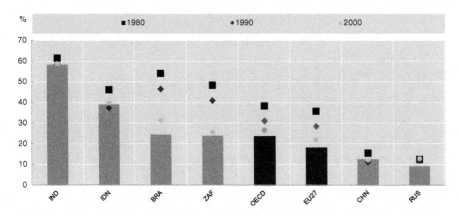

Fig. 1.9 Gender Gap in employment 1980–2009. Difference in male-female labour force partici-pation rates as a share of male labour participation rate (Source: The OECD STI Scoreboard, OECD 2011a, b and ILO Data Base, Geneva 2011)

the glass ceiling so as to accede to the highest decision-making levels of public and private sector employment.

Last but not least, the reality of earning credentials to access the global work force is fast gaining ground in all economic contexts. This is a direct consequence of the ongoing unemployment crisis and concerns men and women alike. In January 2015, the ILO reported unemployment to be running at 201 million worldwide with 25 % of this in OECD economies. Despite improved job creation in the Japanese and American economies, the problems of Greece in 2015 have impacted on Europe. Elsewhere, results are uneven and thus overall recovery from the 2008 crisis remains fragile. The ILO estimates 280 million new jobs are needed by 2019 to return to the pre-2008 levels of global employment (*Source*: ILO 2015). Youth and women remain especially vulnerable. Two telling examples come from Spain and China. In the former context, a report from the Davos Economic Forum highlighted young graduates seeking opportunities abroad in Europe or further afield (e.g. Germany and Brazil for engineers) to escape the dismal youth employment statistics of +50 % of 18–26 year olds. In China, an analysis of short-term business degrees (e.g. 1 year MBAs in finance, administration and human resources) shows that young women under the age of 30 dominate the enrolment figures and they are taking these quali-fications in order to seek work outside their own country whether elsewhere in Asia or further afield (*Source: CNBC Straight Talk, 25 January 2013*). This trend is expected to become more frequent until national employment figures become more robust which may not happen quickly. To combat this crisis, young people (includ-ing young women) will take charge of their own futures by acquiring portable quali-fications, including indispensable foreign language capacity. Thus, it can be expected that this trend will become increasingly common as the twenty-first cen-tury progresses.

As far as earnings are concerned, substantial salary differentials exist between men and women with tertiary level educational attainment. By way of example,

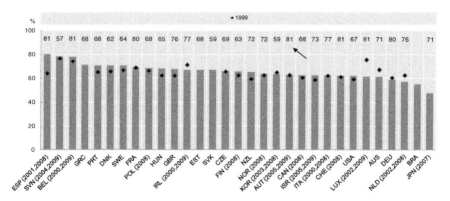

Fig. 1.10 Earning differentials at the tertiary level education attainment 1999 and 2009. Average annual earnings of women as a percentage of men's earnings (Source: The OECD STI Scoreboard, Paris 2011)

even in the OECD countries, women with tertiary education can expect to earn about 70 % of men's salaries on average (Fig. 1.10).

Sometimes, the gap in salary is due to difference of occupation or to the amount of time spent in the labour force. For example, women might prefer to opt for part-time work when raising families and if social assistance policies permit this choice. However, the main problem lies elsewhere. When women are well qualified but less well remunerated, they may decide to work in other countries (thus provoking a sort of academic brain drain) – or even not work at all if they have sufficient income from other sources. This might then become detrimental to the supply of labour and to the utilization of skills produced by their educational system, thus creating new problems for the retention of skilled workers in national labour markets. Last but not least, the moral argument for equal salaries merits the strongest support from governments and employers. In this regard, statistics must not be taken at face value. By way of example, the September 2014 Quarterly Employment Survey from Statistics New Zealand records that women hold 50.1 % of jobs and earn 87.1 % of male pay across the labour market. In some areas (forestry, mining, construction), pay is fully equal. Yet, in other domains where women constitute the large majority of workers, their pay gap is significant: 86 % in education/training, 68.7 % in health/social assistance, 62.9 % in finance/insurance (*Source*: NZ Statistics 2014). Given the present unjustified imbalances, this is clearly another battle for women to wage and win in both high-income and emerging economies.

Role Models and Personal Narratives: Charting the Progress of Women Graduates

Making sound observations on the clear advancement of graduate women requires not only statistical data but also examination of the "soft issues" where personal experience and self-awareness can offer useful lessons. These two areas provide evidence-based research but from differing perspectives. In this vein, both the household names with stellar careers and the growing mass of women managing successful personal and professional lives may serve as relevant role models to the coming generation of female graduates. It is important that academic gender research tracks this socio-economic progress.

On the global scene, a rapid survey of internationally recognized women leaders in a variety of fields attests to the fact that women graduates can succeed alongside their male counterparts.

Women run – or have run – countries (inter alia, Argentina, Australia, Brazil, Germany, Iceland, India, Ireland, Israel, Jamaica, Liberia, Lithuania, Kyrgyzstan, New Zealand, Poland, the Republic of Korea, the Philippines, Thailand) and female royals are held in high esteem for their exemplary statecraft (the Queens of England, Denmark and – until abdication – The Netherlands), hold high office in governments (e.g. the post of American Secretary of State) and sit on the Supreme Courts of many nations. The Church of England and certain other confessions now appoint female prelates. Women manage UN and other international organizations (e.g. IMF, UNDP, UNESCO, UN Women) and well-known universities (e.g. Oxford and Manchester, United Kingdom, Princeton, USA, Vaal University of Technology, South Africa and 9 of Australia's 39 universities). Increasingly, women are rising to the top of the business world (e.g. IBM, Yahoo, Facebook, PepsiCo, General Motors Latin America, Petrobas in Brazil, Sabanci Holdings in Turkey) and hold major posts in the media (e.g. CNN, the New York Times, the Huffington Post, Time Magazine, Newsweek). Even in traditionally male domains of work where women are few, success stories of women are evident. Examples abound: in 2014, Janet Yellen, a respected economist with an impressive four-decade academic career, was appointed to head the US Federal Reserve. Anne Lauvergeon (a physicist by training with experience in banking) has run Areva France's nuclear energy corporation; Austria's Helga Nowotny chairs the European Research Council; Zaha Hadidis an award-winning Iraqi-born architect; Chanda Kochharis CEO of ICICI, which is India's second-largest bank, while the Union Bank of Nigeria is headed by OlunfunkeIyabo Osibodu. Li Xiaolin heads the China Power International Development dealing with energy-generating companies and Chua Sock Koong is CEO of Singapore Telecommunications. Clara Furse, a Canadian, managed the London Stock Exchange from 2001 to 2009 and was its first female CEO. Nobel Prizes have been won by Elinor Ostrom in Economics and Kenya's Wangari Maathai in the Environment. Cherie Blair is a leading British court lawyer and judge and Sian Elias is New Zealand's Chief Justice. Stella Rimington was Director-General of MI5, the British espionage office and Australia's Sharan Burrowis

Secretary-General of the International Trade Union Confederation (ITUC). Other noteworthy areas are the military where 20 % of the American army are female (and as of 2013, able to access some major combat roles), and space exploration where, to date, 56 women astronauts have pursued careers in this field.

How have these women arrived at success? Each would have her own narrative where the four critical components – aspiration, application, opportunities, mentor and family support – would find their particular place. Two examples show the range of influences: Elisabeth Badinter, a former French Minister for Women and chair of Publicis, the advertising giant, attributes her confidence to her father's encouragement from her earliest years; in contrast, Mary Cranston, the first female chair of a global 100 law firm, Pillsbury Winthrop Shaw Pittman LLP in the USA, believes that successful women learn how to overcome gender stereotyping and refuse to be undermined by bias. The positive aspect of this situation is that such women become household names and inspire – albeit from afar – many younger women who now understand that many pathways are possible for them.

In contrast, personal narratives offer a significant complement to the visibility of international figures. Notwithstanding the success of the latter, it is most often dialogue with local individuals at various stages of their lives and careers which reveals much more concretely how the four components come into play and are addressed by each woman. Moreover, confidence and self-belief are critical qualities, which permit women to seek – rather than to avoid – major challenges that can prove turning points in their careers. Acquiring and feeling comfortable with such attributes and attitudes are discussed in detail by Sheryl Sanford, CEO of Facebook, in her 2013 book, *Lean In. Women, Work and the Will to Lead*, which urges women to overcome reticence and fears so as to better assert themselves in their workplace. Ms Sanford's ideas provoked a healthy and much needed debate with both supportive and dissenting voices. But, more importantly, it demonstrated that women of her generation have innovative approaches to their career paths and a strategy to achieve their goals.

As part of the research undertaken for this chapter, informal interviews were held with some 30 women graduates of all ages and at various stages of their careers. Conversations also took place with men whose support for the advancement of women graduates were known to be varied. The viewpoints expressed indicate that, like the development process itself, the journey towards gender equality is ongoing and the lessons learnt should be heeded.

Interview Results

The World Turns

Older women (notably over 45) who enjoyed moderate success in their careers at the middle management level felt that their own journey had been difficult in contrast to the wider support available for younger female graduates today. Thus, they saw themselves as trail blazers to some extent.

Social Mores Evolve

This group also considered that more women of their generation had elected to choose between career and marriage since social attitudes were less tolerant and support systems were much less developed than today.

Some Things Never Change

Younger women were aware both of the barriers still prevalent in male–dominated professions and noted that women still tend to avoid engaging in these areas due to the difficulties involved.

Today Women Have Choices

It was agreed that internships and similar work experiences have become essential to prepare young graduates for the reality of the workplace. In particular, these allow women to directly observe the effort required to pursue certain careers and to rise to the upper echelons of the workforce in general. Furthermore, based on their observations, some younger women, though well qualified academically, had already decided to seek a less stressful work and life balance.

Be Prepared: Like the Scouts

As well, young women felt that they must equip themselves as well as possible for upper echelon jobs often require both a variety of both academic credentials and other skills to perform well. These, for example, negotiation ability, political acumen, business sense, multilingual capacities, staff management, take considerable time to acquire. Perhaps men do not think preparation in these fields to be vital but women believe that they will be disadvantaged if they are not very well prepared for career steps which may interest them.

Some Areas Must Modernize

There was general agreement that, since two-income families are often the norm in high-income economies, the workplace must become more flexible to accommodate the domestic and professional demands faced by working women. Government and company policies are changing but still have significant progress to make in this regard.

Carpe Diem: And Make Sure That You Can Accept the Challenges

Opportunities for career advancement do indeed arise but there will surely be a cost. Often, this is higher than anticipated. In reality, the ability to respond to these openings depends greatly on accommodation and support within the couple and the family unit.

Nothing Is Perfect

Some younger women were surprised by the changing attitudes of family members (notably spouses or parents) at varying points in time as these were seen to exert pressure to advance specific agendas. For example, support was forthcoming for tertiary study per se but tended to be less evident when professional and domestic responsibilities had to be balanced. Maternity invariably affects career progress to some degree and for women who wished to continue along a chosen career path (rather than adapt to a more flexible rhythm during childrearing years) reported unexpected opposition to this option. This still seemed to indicate that women, rather than men, are expected to adapt to domestic responsibilities.

Learn to Listen to the Right People

There was universal agreement that mentoring is the most essential source of support for career advancement, regardless of gender. When women heed advice, they help develop the other types of intelligences (emotional, political, business) needed for professional activity. Sometimes, these are innate but in most instances, they must be acquired. As societies (and labour markets) grow increasingly diverse, academic intelligence is a base but qualifications will require complementary talents.

No Gain Without Pain

Amongst younger men, there was general acceptance that qualified women would work both as part of the couple's financial planning and also to pursue personal career fulfilment. However, it was admitted that more successful careers by women could cause tensions within personal relationships.

Pro-women Men

A special variety of male vital in professional life – notably those who were known for their support of women colleagues attributed this to their personal sense of justice, recognition for the principle of gender equality and their belief that talented people – male or female – should have equal opportunities as their skills are needed in professional life.

Hopeless Cases to Avoid

A number of young men admitted that they would not be comfortable with a female partner who possessed better academic credentials and earning potential. Hence, certain attitudes have yet to evolve significantly and this sort of person might be best avoided by women graduates wishing to fulfil rewarding careers because strife lies ahead.

Balancing life and career priorities has become a central challenge for the average woman who works in a post of responsibility and is a basic financial contributor to her household. This must be addressed adequately and concerns graduates and non-graduates alike.

According to research carried out by the USA Association which monitors women studying or holding MBAs, a set of golden rules is recommended:

- Identify a sound mentor (a family member or colleague) and consult with this person often.
- Recognize that life/work balance is a crucial challenge and comes with a price tag but this situation can be handled with solid personal support.
- Get help with the domestic duties of your life and personal commitments.
- Seize professional opportunities when they arise (even if they may appear unorthodox), and learn to be sensitive to good (or bad) timing.
- Do not wait to be discovered if interesting career openings are on the horizon.
- Network with peers and related persons who can advise and assist.
- Learn to negotiate notably in the area of salary (e.g. recent Cornell Business School research has shown that, when seeking higher pay, 57 % of men but only 7 % of women do this.)
- Stay flexible in one's planning as life and career paths change frequently.
- These points concern the personal lives and careers of men and women alike.

Reviewing both these points and the experiences of global and local role models, there is a remarkable correlation with the four components proposed earlier for women with academic credentials.

Levels of self-belief, confidence, aspiration and ambition (which may be described as a more articulated form of aspiration) are very personal traits and will differ in each individual. Some people will have unrealistic visions of their capacities while others seriously underestimate their talents. Self-belief and confidence, tempered with realism, are crucial for achieving one's desired goals. Otherwise, academic credentials should be relegated to the category of "nice to have".

There is no substitute for hard work. Exceptionally privileged people will always exist but the rank and file must apply themselves to work and persevere through difficulties, which are sure to occur. If a woman prefers not to commit to this level of professional application, this is her choice. Then, she should expect the challenges to be handled on the home front. Her career progress will usually reflect the decision taken and domestic management strategies put in place to support this.

Women are – or can become – well informed and they are now aware that certain countries (e.g. the Nordic states) and companies (e.g. Google) have attracted attention for their family-friendly policies and workplaces. This proves that positive action can be taken when there is common sense and good will because this makes sense for the national good and for commercial benefit.

Opportunities are sometimes hard to foresee, especially in today's volatile and mobile labour market. Predictable career paths will continue to occur but for a very small minority. Often openings are unexpected and their potential cannot be immediately perceived. Daring to break one's local mould to start realizing one's potential is a very important – and perhaps neglected – concept and more research is needed on women from all socio-economic groups who do this. Thus, recognition that risk-taking is part of any successful career is vital.

In each of these instances, mentor support is an essential factor. Hopefully, this can come from family (parents, siblings or relatives). However, in many cases, women meet more experienced colleagues who are better placed to recognize talent and propose indispensable advice. The importance of mentoring in building self-belief is growing and now involves official support schemes ranging across social strata and the barriers inherent in these. One example is the elite Paris Business school, ESSEC, whose students tutor socially disadvantaged young people with good academic potential so they can aim for better career credentials. However, conversely, this area also concerns the non-support that women can encounter. While it might be thought that this is a thing of the past and that normal gender balance has corrected such situations, considerable evidence can be cited to show that this is unfortunately not the case. Career rivalry in couples, parent and child pressures, colleague competition and outright cultural hostility are common realities and their occurrences indicate that conflicts and barriers must be resolved and surmounted. Again, objective mentor opinion can give much needed perspective to such stressful situations. Exceptional role models play a particular role in demonstrating that even the most entrenched opposition can be overcome. Many of today's autobiographies and biographies of such women have an impact far beyond their intended reach. All areas of the media can – and must – fulfil its social responsibility by documenting the paths of successful women who can inspire their peers and the coming generation. In this vein, outstanding cases are Aung San Suu Kyi, the long-term activist for democracy in Myanmar and now leader of the parliamentary opposition party who could lead the government after the 2015 elections, and Malala Yousafzai, the young Pakistani girl who won the 2014 Nobel Peace Prize after suffering brutal assault in 2012 for seeking to advance her education. Their examples can teach the world a great deal – including a reminder to women who already enjoy equality that nothing should be taken for granted.

Conclusion: The Journey Continues

This overview of the status quo for women graduates in three specific domains has endeavoured to show that gender equality is far from being an end in itself, especially in the current era. It is now urgent that qualified women can make their optimal contribution to the critical decision-making processes of national and international development. To this end, there must be gender parity in the areas of parliamentary representation (given the number of women citizens) and in the leadership of the tertiary and higher education sector (given their numbers as academics and students) and in the world of business (given their numbers in the workforce). Because this parity has yet to be achieved, the UNDP's Gender Inequality Index (GII) will continue to play a necessary role in charting how countries are advancing towards this goal in order to ensure that socio-economic decision-making will truly become an equally shared process.

A final comment might be useful with regard to the likely challenges for women graduates in the future.

Firstly, as the twenty-first century progresses, the tertiary/higher education sector will continue to change and probably in quite radically directions. Thus, a credential earned at this level will be a useful base that will permit women to plan their careers and its interface with their personal life.

Secondly, other professional skills (such as social capital and emotional intelligence) will be not just necessary but equally important for career success. So, training and mentoring in this area will be increasingly vital to obtain.

Thirdly, as the global knowledge economy evolves, professional mobility will increase obliging graduates to mix in a more varied cultural environment where different social attitudes will become apparent. By way of example, a December 2012 report on the impact of Dilma Rousseff's presidency on women's political and professional aspirations revealed that 80 % of Brazilian women plan to seek top jobs and 59 % consider themselves very ambitious as opposed to 53 % and 36 % of Americans in these areas (Source: The Dilma Effect 2012.

Fourthly, it is good news that international support for gender equality is growing overall. Also, it is significant that opprobrium is more often expressed when female citizens are not accorded respect and security – as evidenced by the national and worldwide outrage in December 2012 at the tragic death of a paramedical student who was gang raped in India. According to a BBC report in 2012, this is perhaps the worst country in the world for women in terms of social behaviour and attitudes. All women – educated or not – will benefit from heavy pressure on governments to create more security for this group and to punish criminal action. In these cases, highly educated women are obligated to use their articulate voices to criticize and censure such action.

Lastly, gender research should certainly continue and has fertile areas for investigation, ranging from the greater gender equality in the academy to the increased role and influence of highly educated women in the political and economic sectors where feminine attitudes to power and negotiation are known to be more conciliatory and so more productive. It is important to document that new per-spectives are opening for the enhanced social engagement of graduate women in full cooperation with their supportive male counterparts. This last imperative has inspired the new 2014 United Nations campaign entitled *He For She* which encourages efforts to achieve full equality as a joint and beneficial endeavour (*Source:* www.HeForShe.org). Unless the psychology of this approach prevails, newly emerging problems such as rising male dropout rates in education and the vulnerability of male workers in a volatile employment situation will become chronic. The collaboration which is essential to find solutions will be difficult to achieve and will require a broad and multi-disciplinary approach to social con-text. Indeed, there are recent suggestions that society should be free of gender issues. This could be ideal if equality is assured but disastrous if the equality debate ceases because the benefits of a fully equal citizenry will never be achieved.

Thus, as the world of the twenty-first century unfolds, the debate on women in higher education moves ahead in a socio-economic context where knowledge is the driving force. The journey towards equality continues and is increasingly complex. Women seek equality not domination. This brings new challenges for academic research, for government and for decision-makers in every domain where the role and contribution of women are essential for progress. There is no valid reason why this should be denied.

References

Altbach, P., & Jamil, S. (Eds.). (2011). *The road to academic excellence: The making of world class universities.* Washington, DC: The World Bank Group.

Altbach, P., et al. (2009). *Trends in global higher education: Tracking an academic revolution.* Paris: UNESCO.

Atarupane, Harsha (2013) *Higher education in Afghanistan: An emerging moonscape.* Working Paper, The World Bank, Washington, DC.

Badinter, E. (2012). The conflict: How modern motherhood undermines the status of women (Broche, Paris 2010, French version).

Banerjee, A., & Duflo, E. (2011). *Poor economics. A radical rethinking of the way to fight global poverty.* New York: Public Affairs.

Bjarnason, S., & Coldstream, P. (Eds.). (2003). *The idea of engagement: Universities in Society.* London: Association of Commonwealth Universities, ACU.

Caldwell, C. (2012) University looks like a bubble that is about to burst. Article in The Financial Times, 23–24 August.

Castells, M. (2009). *Communication power.* Oxford: Oxford University Press.

Collini, S. (2012). *What are universities for?* New York: Penguin.

Cranston, M. (2014). *Perception of bias obstacle to success.* Interview in The New Zealand Herald, 26 April 2014.

Eagly, A. H., & Carli, L. L. (2007). *Through the Labyrinth: The truth about how women become leaders.* New York: Harvard Business Review Press.

Frankel, L. (2004). *Nice girls don't get the corner office* (Reprint Editionth ed.). New York: Business Plus.

Gibbons, M., et al. (1994). *The new production of knowledge: The new dynamics of science and research in contemporary societies*. Thousand Oaks: Sage.

Gundara, J. (2007). *Some current intercultural issues in multicultural societies*. Commissioned paper for the UNESCO Forum on higher education, research and knowledge, UNESCO, Paris 2007.

HeForShe. United Nations initiative for gender equality launched in September 2014 (www. HeForShe.org)

Hill, C. (2004). *Tenure denied: Cases of sexual discrimination in academia*. Report of the American Association of Academic Women, Washington, DC. 2004

http://world.bymap/org/YoungPopulations

Hudson, W. J. (1993). *Intellectual capital*. New York: Wiley.

ILO. (2015). *World employment and social outlook. Trends 2015*. Geneva: ILO.

International Federation of University Women. (2007). *Civil society partnerships and development policies. Emerging trends*. Commissioned paper for the UNESCO Forum on Higher Education, Research and Knowledge, UNESCO, Paris 2007.

International Herald Tribune Magazine. (2010). *Female factor. Around the world in the 21st century: Where women are and where they want to go*. www.global.nytimes.com/femalefactor

Kanter, R. M. (1993). *Men and women of the corporation*. New York: Basic Books.

Kanter, R. M. (2004). *Confidence: How winning streaks and losing streaks begin and end*. New York: Crown Publishing.

Kearney, M.-L. (2000). Towards gender equity in higher education. A global appraisal of policy and process. In E. Rosarii Griffin (Ed.), *Chapter in education in transition*. Oxford: Oxford University Press.

Kearney, M.-L., & Ronning, A. (Eds.). (2001). *Women, power and the academy*. New York: Berghahn Books.

Kearney, M.-L., & Yelland, R. (2010). *Higher education in a world changed utterly: Doing more with Less*. Issues paper for the OECD/IMHE Conference, Paris.

Kellermann, B., & Rhode, D. L. (2007). *Women and leadership. The state of play and strategies for change*. New York: Jossey-Bass.

Lauvergeon, A. (2012). *La Femme Qui Resiste*. Paris: Plon.

Meek V. L., & Merle J. (2012). *Scientific mobility and international research networks: Trends and policy tools for promoting research excellence and capacity-building*. Paper at the International Seminar on Research Universities, Boston College/OECD/Programme IHERD, USA.

Meek, V. L., Ulrich, T., & Kearney, M.-L. (Eds.). (2009). *Higher education, research and innovation: Changing dynamics*. Germany: INCHER, University of Kasse.

OECD. (1998). *Redefining tertiary education*. Paris: OECD.

OECD. (2008). *Tertiary education for the knowledge society: Volumes 1 and 2*. Paris: OECD.

OECD. (2010). *The OECD innovation strategy. Getting a headstart on tomorrow*. Paris: OECD.

OECD. (2011 and 2012). *Education at a glance*. OECD, Paris.

OECD. (2011b). *OECD science, technology and industry scoreboard 2011. Innovation and growth in knowledge economies*. Paris: OECD.

OECD. (2011c). *OECD yearbook 2011: Better policies for better lives*. Paris: OECD.

OECD. (2012). *Closing the gender gap: Act now*. Final report on the gender initiative. OECD, Paris.

OECD. (2012b). *The OECD development strategy*. Paris: OECD.

OECD. (2015). *The ABC of gender equality in education: Aptitude, bahaviour and confidence* (Directorate for Education and Skills (Pisa Series)). Paris: OECD.

OECD/CERI. (2010). *Higher education to 2030: Scenarios*. Paris: OECD/CERI.

Paglia, C. (2013, Dec 30). *The year men became obsolete? Essay*, Time Magazine.

Ronning, A. H., & Kearney, M.-L. (Eds.). (1996). *Women and the University curriculum*. London: Jessica Kingsley.

Sanberg, S. (2013). Lean. In *Women, work and the will to lead*. UK, Virgin Books.

Scientometrics. *Triannual journal*, Springer, The Netherlands.

Shea, C. (2010). *The end of tenure?* http://www.nytimes.com/2010/09/05/books/review/Shea-t. html+

Shipman, C., & Kay, K. (2009). *Womeconomics*. New York: Harper Business.

Slaughter, A.- M. (2015). *Unfinished business: Women, men, work, family.* New York: Random House.

Spar, D. L. (2014). *Wonder woman: Sex, power and the quest for perfection.* New York: Picador.

Statistics NZ. (2014, Sep). *New Zealand quarterly employment survey.*

The Dilma Effect. (2012, December 3). *How Brazil's ground – Breaking President is inspiring other women to run.* Women in the world foundation. www.womenintheworld.org/ stories/ entry/the-dilma-effect

The Economist. (2013, Nov 9). *Women are winning, Africa's female politicians.*

The Economist. (2014, Jan 25). *The data of Davos. Women in business.*

The European Science Foundation, Higher Education and Social Change ESF, Brussels, 2009–2011.

The International New York Times. (2014, June 21). *Out of school and nowhere to go.*

The New Zealand Herald. (2014, Feb 20). *Degrees of difference on boards.*

The Royal Society. (2011). *Knowledge networks and nations: Global scientific collaboration in the 21st century.* London.

Time Magazine, Go Glocal. Time Magazine (Europe Edition) 20 August 2012.

UK Grad Programme Review. (2004). *What do PhDs do?* London: UK Grad Programme.

UN Global Compact. www.unglobalcompact.org

UNDP. (2011). *Sustainability and equity. A better future for all.* Human Development Report. UNDP, New York.

UNDP. (2013). *The rise of the South: Human progress in a diverse world.* Human Development Report. UNDP, New York.

UNDP. (2014). *Sustaining human progress: Deducing vulnerabilities and building resilience.* Human Development Report. UNDP, New York.

UNDP. (2015). *Rethinking work for human development.* Human Development Report UNDP, New York.

UNESCO. (1998). *Higher education in the twenty-first century: Vision and action.* Paris: UNESCO.

UNESCO. (2005). *Towards knowledge societies.* Paris: UNESCO.

UNESCO. (2008). *Trends in postgraduate education: UNESCO forum on higher education, research and knowledge.* Paris: UNESCO.

UNESCO. (2009a). *Innovation for development. The forum on higher education: Research and knowledge.* Paris: UNESCO.

UNESCO. (2009). Ed. Heather E. *Sharing research agendas on knowledge systems.* UNESCO Forum on Higher Education, Research and Knowledge Occasional Paper No 16. UNESCO, Paris.

UNESCO/International Social Science Council. (2010). *The world social science report.* Paris: UNESCO Publishing.

FT Weekend Magazine, Women of 2011. Special Issue 2011, The Financial Times, London.

World Bank. (2010). *The MDGs after the crisis. The World Bank global monitoring report.* Washington, DC: World Bank.

World Bank. (2013). *World development report.* Washington, DC: World Bank.

Chapter 2
Women in American Higher Education: A Descriptive Profile

Carol Frances

Women Faculty Gains

Women have made extremely impressive gains moving in huge numbers into the faculty ranks of American colleges and universities. The number of women working as faculty almost trebled in the short span of just 24 years from 1987 to 2011. The U.S. Department of Education reported that there were 264,000 women employed as faculty in American degree-granting institutions in 1987. By 2011 the number had increased by an astounding 471,000 – that is, almost trebling the number of women faculty in American higher education.

From 1987 to 2011 the total number of faculty employed in American colleges and universities almost doubled, increasing from about 790,000 to almost 1.5 million. The share of women of the total number of American faculty, including both women and men, increased from one-third of the total of just under 800,000 in 1987 to almost of half of the 1.5 million total in 2011. Trends in employment of faculty women and men over this period are shown on Chart 2.1.

We might well believe that we could celebrate without reserve this triumphant increase in the number of American women faculty. But hold on. These advances in employment of women as faculty members have not been accompanied with commensurate gains in their salaries as compared with the salaries of faculty men. Indeed, the gap between the salaries of women and men professors has widened since the 1970s. Measured in constant 2012–2013 U.S. dollars, the gap on average between the salaries of women and men professors in the mid-1970s was $10,822. The gap in constant dollars had increased by 2012–2013 to $16,915. Women professors' salaries as a percent of men professors' actually slipped from 88.7 % to 85.1 %. This erosion in their relative salaries occurred over the 37 years because the salaries

C. Frances (✉)
Carol Frances + Associates, 27711 Vista del Valle, Hemet, CA 92544-8394, USA
e-mail: carolfrances100@gmail.com

© Springer International Publishing Switzerland 2017
H. Eggins (ed.), *The Changing Role of Women in Higher Education*,
The Changing Academy – The Changing Academic Profession in International
Comparative Perspective 17, DOI 10.1007/978-3-319-42436-1_2

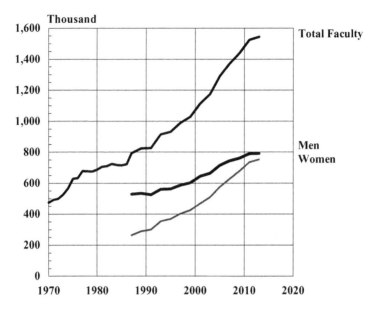

Chart 2.1 Trends in the number of instructional faculty in American colleges and universities by gender 1979–1987 (Source: U.S. Department of Education, National Center for Education Statistics, *Digest of Education Statistics*: 2014, Table 315.10)

of the men professors were higher than the salaries of the women in the beginning and their salaries grew over the years at a slightly faster rate than the salaries of the women professors.

The gap is salaries between women and men faculty grows as faculty ascend in rank, from instructor to assistant professor, then to associate professor, and finally to full professor. This chapter will document the trends in women's participation in American higher education, with emphasis on women faculty – and then put these trends into a broader context, including in particular comparisons of the women's experiences in academia with those of men.

Higher Education as an Industry

To put this discussion into a broader economic context, we can compare higher education with other "industries." Close to 4.0 million people were employed by American higher education institutions in 2015. This is considerably more than the 2.4 million employed in the auto industry.

From 1991 to 2011, the last year for which we have consistent data by gender, higher education added 1.3 million more employees, in effect doubling total employment in just 20 years. Of the 1.3 million increase in total employment over these 20 years, 60 % were women and only 40 % were men.

Thus, by 2011, the most recent years for which we have employment data by gender, more than half of the total number of all employees in American colleges and universities were women. Trends in total higher education employment are documented in Chart 2.2. In 2011, 2.1 million women were employed in higher education as compared with 1.8 million men. Yes, 300,000 more women were employed in American higher education than men and presumably the difference has widened in the years since then.

Comparative Trends in Higher Education Employment, by Type of Job and by Gender

While the primary focus of this chapter is on women faculty, we should understand that faculty is only one of five major categories used to describe people employed in colleges and universities. First, the jobs are divided into two groups, professional and nonprofessional.

There are major differences in the percentage of these jobs held by women. As shown in Chart 2.3, a smaller percentage of women hold professional jobs and a larger percentage hold nonprofessional jobs than do men employed in American colleges and universities.

Next, the professional group of employees is divided into four subcategories: (A) Executive, administrative, and managerial, (B) Faculty, (C) Other professionals, and (D) Graduate assistants. Trends in the employment of women and men in the four professional academic job categories are shown on Chart 2.4. The difference in the distribution of professional jobs by type and by gender is large in the faculty domain. Only 35 %, or just over one-third, of the women employed in higher education work

Chart 2.2 Trends in the total number of employees in degree-granting American colleges and universities by gender, 1991–2013 (Source: U.S. Department of Education, National Center for Education Statistics, *Digest of Education Statistics*: 2013, Table 314.20)

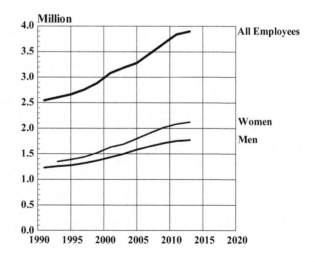

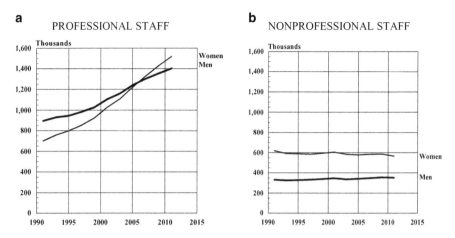

Chart 2.3 Trends in the number of staff employed in American colleges and universities by gender from 1991–2011 is shown on Chart 2.3. (Source: U.S. Department of Education, National Center for Education Statistics, *Digest of Education Statistics*: 2013, Table 314.20)

as faculty members as compared with 45 % of the men. The difference by gender is also large among "other professionals", with many more women than men employed in this group.

Comparative Trends in the Employment of Faculty Women and Men

There have been phenomenal increases in the number of faculty employed in American higher education institutions over the 20 years from 1991 to 2011. Total faculty employment soared from 826,000 in 1991 to 1.5 million in 2011. This is a huge increase of 697,000, or 84 %, in the total number of faculty employed.

According to the numbers published by the U.S., Department of Education in the 2013 Digest of Education Statistics, over these 20 years, 68 % of the increase in the number of faculty employed was accounted for by women. The number of women faculty increased by an astounding 144 %, almost three times the rate of increase in the number of men faculty which increased by only 50 %, though starting from a larger base. This means that the number of women faculty employed by American higher education institutions much more than doubled in just the 20 years from 1991 to 2011. Over these 20 years the number of women faculty employed increased by 434,000, from 300,000 in 1991 to 734,000 in 2011.

Thus, by 2011 the share of the full-time faculty who are women still differs enormously by rank, as shown in Chart 2.5. Only 29 % of the full-time professors are women, while 71 % are men. Women account for larger percentages of the faculty only at the lower ranks.

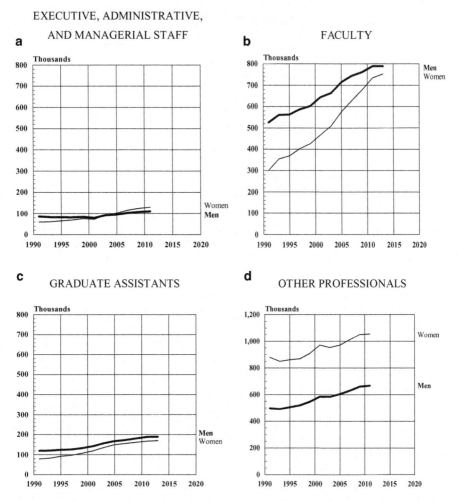

Chart 2.4 Trends in the number of employees in American colleges and universities by type of job by gender 1991–2013 (Source: U.S. Department of Education, National Center for Education Statistics, *Digest of Education Statistics*: 2013 and 2014, Table 314.20)

Trends in Faculty Employment by Full-Time and Part-Time Status and by Gender

The most recent data available about the patterns of full-time and part-time faculty employment by gender is for 2003. We do know that part-time faculty has increased to become close to half of all faculty employment, but we do not know the gender distribution of the current faculty full-time and part-time employment.

We can calculate the percentage distribution of women and men faculty between full-time and part-time employment for 2003. At that time, of the women faculty

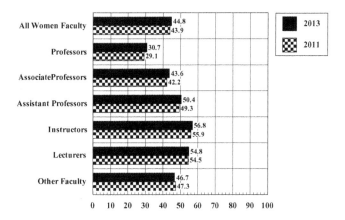

Chart 2.5 Percent of full-time faculty in American higher education who are women by faculty rank 2011 and 2013 (Source: U.S. Department of Education, National Center for Education Statistics, *Digest of Education Statistics*: 2014, Table 315.20)

employed by American colleges and universities, about half were employed full-time and half part-time. The division for men faculty was 60 % full-time and 40 % part-time.

From 1992 to 2003 the largest component of growth by employment status was the employment of part-time women faculty. This sector of employment increased by over 50 % compared with an increase of 32 % of part-time men faculty.

Though we do not have data on the salaries of part-time faculty by gender we can say that the salaries of a very large share of all of the part-time faculty are extremely modest. Almost two-thirds of the part-time faculty earned a base salary at their home institutions of $10,000 or less in 2003 while 90 % of the part-time faculty earned $25,000 or less in that year. In addition, many of the part-time faculty do not earn benefits equivalent to the benefits earned by full-time faculty, and some may not earn any benefits. The compensation of the part-time faculty, including salaries and benefits is so disproportionately low as compared with the compensation of full-time faculty that there is increasingly strident activism calling for higher compensation and better working conditions. Since a higher proportion of women than men faculty is part-time, these less fortunate conditions impact a greater share of the women than men faculty.

A good part of the explanation for the meager salaries of the part-time faculty is that almost 90 % hold a rank of instructor, lecturer, other rank, or no rank. Only 10 % hold a rank of assistant professor, associate professor, or professor.

It may also be explained in part by the fact that institutions pay women less than they pay men so they save money employing women. The U.S. Department of Education reports that on average, faculty women employed full-time earn 21.5 % less than faculty men across all accredited institutions. Women were paid $69,000 in 2012–2013 as compared with men who were paid $84,000, a stunning difference of $15,000 a year.

This salary gap is generated by a combination of four separate phenomena. First, there is the differing distributions of women and men faculty by type of institution. A higher percentage of the women are employed at the less prestigious, lower paying institutions. Second, a larger percentage of the women are employed in the lower paid ranks of associate and assistant professor ranks while a larger percentage of men faculty are employed in the higher paid rank of professor. Third, at each of the three faculty ranks, women are paid less than men. And fourth, on average the women are probably younger than the men because a larger share of them have been hired more recently and have accumulated less seniority.

What is dismaying to the women in American higher education is that not only are women paid less at all three major faculty ranks but the salary gap has widened between women and men professors over the last two decades and it has not narrowed between the salaries of women and men associate and assistant professors. This salary situation persists in spite of the efforts of the feminists to teach women more effective skills when it comes time to negotiate their salaries.

Women have made impressive gains in the number employed as faculty in American colleges and universities. In a fairly short 20-year period from 1990 to 2010 women accounted for 60 % of the increase in the total number of faculty and only 40 % were men. Over this period women rose from about a third of the total number of faculty to almost half.

Distribution of Women and Men Faculty and Instructional Staff, by Type and Control of Institution

Usually analysts working with higher education institutions distinguish between public and private control, and five different types: (1) Research, (2) Doctoral, (3) Comprehensive – all 4-year institutions, (4) Liberal arts colleges which are almost all private 4-year colleges, and (5) 2-year colleges, the majority of which are public.

The patterns of employment of women and men faculty and instructional staff are very different between full-time and part-time status. At virtually all of the institutions, at both public and private institutions, and at all five types of institutions, far fewer women are employed full-time than men. Generally, fewer than 40 % of the full-time faculty and instructional staff are women and more than 60 % are men. Of those employed part-time just under 50 % are women and just over 50 % are men (Chart 2.6).

Women Faculty in the For-Profit Sector

A private for-profit college or university is private property from which the owner seeks to earn income. Inadequate response by the public sector institutions to the growing demand for college education has created space for the growth of the

FULL-TIME   PART-TIME

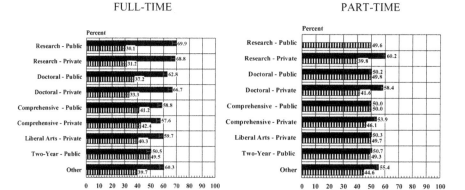

Chart 2.6 Percent distribution of faculty and instructional staff in postsecondary institutions by type and control, by gender, fall 2003 (Source: U.S. Department of Education, National Center for Education Statistics, *Digest of Education Statistics*: 2014, Table 315.50. Legend: *Solid Black Bars*=Men, Striped *Bars*=Women)

for-profit sector. The for-profit sector has expanded rapidly in the United States over the course of the most recent decades. Much of the growth in the private sector has been in the for-profit component, not the traditional non-profit sector. Actually, the private non-profit institutions are more similar to the public institutions than they are to the private for-profit institutions. The private for-profit institutions are sufficiently different from the private non-profit institutions that higher education should be characterized as having three sectors, not just the traditional two of public and private.

Women faculty have been a significant part of the growth of the for-profit sector. In 2013 there were close to 127,000 faculty employed in the for-profit colleges and universities. Of these, about 55 %, or 70,000 were women faculty. Actually, women faculty predominate in all of the four components of the for-profit sector, comprising 51.4 % of the 4-year for-profit full-time faculty and 54.4 % of the 4-year for-profit part-time faculty. Women account for an even slightly higher percentage of the 2-year for-profit faculty: 58.6 % of the full-time faculty in the 2-year for-profit sector and 60.9 % of the 2-year part-time faculty.

Women faculty in the for-profit sector may be working for lower salaries and fewer benefits, without the protection of tenure.

Faculty Salaries by Gender

While the increases in the numbers of women employed as faculty are very impressive, these employment gains are not accompanied by significant narrowing of the historic gap between the salaries of women and men faculty.

The gap in faculty salaries of all faculty by gender has not narrowed. Indeed, the salary gap has widened between women and men who are full professors. In constant 2012–2013 dollars, the gap between the salaries of women and men full professors has widened from just over $10,000 in 1986 to over $16,000 in 2012, as documented in Chart 2.7. Over a career these annual gaps in salary could amount to hundreds of thousands of dollars and significantly disadvantage women in the accumulation of essential social security benefits based on annual salary, as well as retirement benefits generally.

The lower salaries on average for the women faculty are accounted for in part by a different distribution of women and men faculty employed by types of institution, by faculty rank, by discipline, and by activity. A higher percentage of women are employed in less prestigious and lower paying institutions; a higher percentage of women are employed in lower faculty ranks; and a higher percentage of women are employed in lower paying disciplines. Finally, faculty employed by higher education institutions are considered to have one of three primary activities: instruction, research, and service. The patterns of primary activity differ by gender. Close to half of the faculty whose primary activity is instruction are women, and close to half of the faculty whose primary activity is service are women. There is a difference, however, among faculty whose primary activity is research. Close to 60 % of the faculty whose primary activity is research are men while only about 40 % are women, as shown on Chart 2.8. Faculty engaged in research generally earn more than faculty in instruction. As a consequence, the lower percentage of women in research could help to explain the lower salaries of women.

Women Faculty with Tenure

We begin with two questions: first, what is tenure? And second, does tenure impact faculty women the same as faculty men, or differently?

Historically, American higher education was characterized by the tenure system at most of the 4-year colleges and especially at the prestigious universities. The core principles combine academic freedom and tenure in the belief that freedom of teachers to teach and of students to learn requires protection from dismissal except for cause, such as moral turpitude. Since the promulgation of the original Statement of Principles of Academic Freedom and Tenure by the American Association of University Professors (AAUP) in 1915 it has evolved over decades in negotiation with the institutions with refinements incorporated in 1940. Institutions pressed to include financial exigency as a just cause for termination of faculty and the AAUP countered seeking to avoid manufactured crises insisting that the exigency be demonstrably real.

The public institutions have tended to maintain their tenure systems, while the private institutions have managed a substantial move away from tenure. Often tenure at the private institutions is replaced with term contracts. Tenure is virtually nonexistent in the for-profit institutions.

As the management of institutions focused increasingly on balancing budgets in the face of diminishing outside resources, the granting of tenure came to be seen as

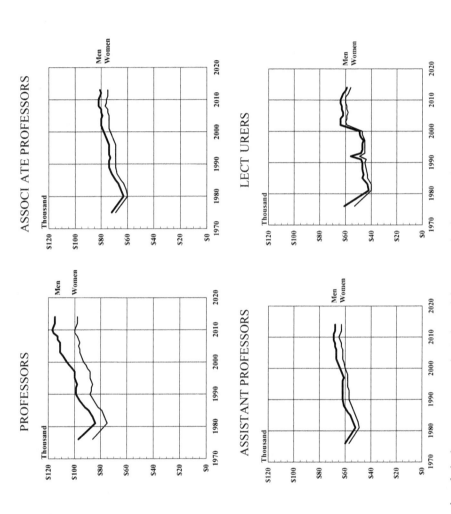

Chart 2.7 Gaps in faculty salaries between women and men by rank in constant 2013–2014 dollars 1974–1975 to 2013–2014 (Source: U.S. Department of Education, National Center for Education Statistics. *Digest of Education Statistics: 2014*, Table 316.10)

Chart 2.8 Faculty activity percent by gender 2003 (Source: U.S. Department of Education, National Center for Education Statistics, *Digest of Education Statistics*: 2013, Table 314.40)

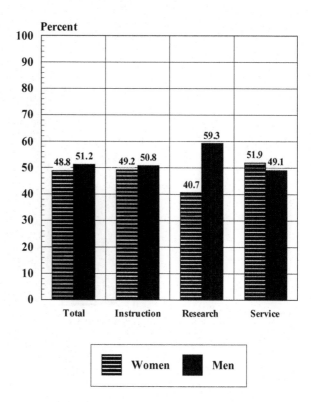

creating very large fixed costs limiting the ability of the institutions to respond to necessary change. Consequently, pressures mounted on many campuses to terminate tenure. What happened instead, however, was that rather than take on the faculty in a direct confrontation, the tenure system was simply eroded by offering employment to new faculty only on a non-tenure track basis. Further, many of the new hires were only in part-time positions.

Thus, many men were hired in the past while institutions were still embracing tenure. Women are now seeking employment as faculty in an era when opportunities for tenure-track positions are no longer being offered, or at least are offered much less often. Typically, as documented by one self-reflective study by the Harvard Faculty of Arts and Sciences (Harvard 2005), women are offered only a small fraction of the tenure-track positions that are offered to men.

While women generally have about the same percent with tenure as men within each faculty rank, a smaller percentage are employed in the faculty ranks with the highest percent with tenure. Chart 2.9 shows that 91.2 % of the men employed as professors as well as 90 % of the women employed as professors. The gap in the percent of women in all ranks with tenure is explained by the fact that many fewer women than men are employed as professors.

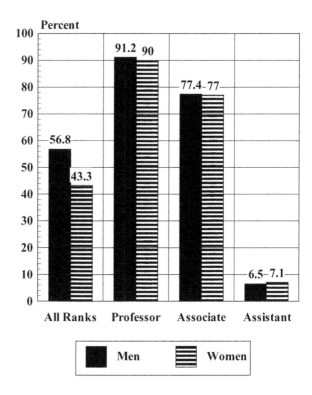

Chart 2.9 Percent of faculty with tenure at institutions with a tenure system by rank, by gender (Source: U.S. Department of Education, National Center for Education Statistics, Digest of Education Statistics: 2014, Table 316.80)

Women in the Higher Education Pipeline

Actually, for women the higher education pipeline begins in the elementary grades, encouraging girls to excel in school and take the classes, including math classes that are prerequisites for college, that will prepare them to apply. We will begin here with the next step, which is to enroll in college. Subsequent steps are to complete an undergraduate curriculum, and then enter graduate school. Women who are preparing to teach at the college level then go on for a master's degree and ultimately a doctorate. Once entering a career in academia, women could aspire to become department chairs, deans, provosts or vice presidents for academic affairs. At the pinnacle of a career in academia women could become college presidents and possibly members of the governing boards of trustees. This section of the chapter compares the participation of women with that of men at each major milestone along the pipeline.

Enrollment of Women Students in Colleges and Universities

While the focus of this chapter is primarily on faculty, it is important to take at least a brief glance at women students enrolled in colleges and universities. They account for more than half of the entrants into the pipeline that ultimately produces women eligible to become faculty members.

Chart 2.10 documents the trends in college enrollment of women and men from 1950 to 2012. Up until about 1980 men enrolled in college had always significantly outnumbered women. Beginning about 1980, however, women students began to outnumber men. Amazingly, there was very little increase in the college enrollment of men for a period of almost 25 years from the mid-1970s until the late 1990s. During this entire period, while the enrollment of men was almost flat, the number of women increased almost continually. Since 2000 the number of men enrolled in colleges has begun to increase again, but the gap previously created by the women continues to widen. By 2012 there were close to 2.8 million more women than men enrolled in American colleges and universities.

The trend in enrollment from 1950 until 2012 in American colleges and universities by gender is shown on Chart 2.10.

Women in the STEM Pipeline

In recent years in the United States there has been a particular focus on the STEM fields: science, technology, engineering, and mathematics. President Obama has declared that excellence in the STEM fields is essential to our national well-being and success in global economic competition. An immediate question is what is the role of women in these fields. We know that few of the faculty in these fields are women, but is the number of women in the pipeline increasing? One possible indicator is the number of BA degrees awarded to women in the STEM fields. It would be reasonable to take data on the number of degrees awarded to women in the physical sciences, information technology, engineering, and mathematics as proxies for the more broadly defined STEM fields.

The unfortunate answer is that in all four of these STEM fields the number of BA degrees awarded to women has either plateaued or actually declined. As the trend data in Chart 2.11 document, BA degrees awarded to women in science, engineering, and mathematics increased significantly in the 1970s and 1980s. They peaked more than 10 years ago around 2000 and have since plateaued or declined. In the field of information technology the percentage of BA degrees awarded to women peaked in the mid-1080s and since then has plummeted to less than half the peak percent.

Interestingly, in some of the STEM fields, particularly in information technology and engineering, a higher percentage of the MA and PhD degrees are awarded to

Chart 2.10 Trends in the enrollment of women and men in American colleges and universities, from 1947 to 2013, are shown on Chart 2.10 (Source: U.S. Department of Education, National Center for Education Statistics, *Digest of Education Statistics*: 2014, Table 303.10)

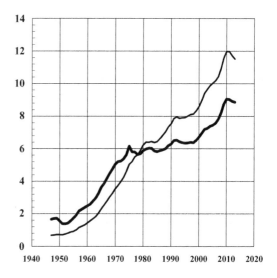

Chart 2.11 Trends in the percent of BA degrees in stem fields awarded to women 1950–2013 (Source: U.S. Department of Education, National Center for Education Statistics, *Digestof Education Statistics*: 2014, Table 325)

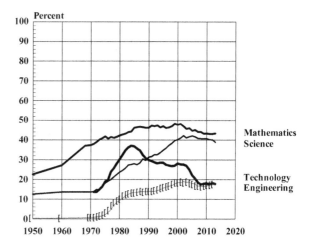

women than the percentage of BA degrees awarded to women. The detailed percentages are shown on the following Table 2.1.

Doctorate Degrees Awarded to Women

In judging the appropriateness of the share of faculty at American colleges and universities who are women it would be relevant to assess the number of women in the pool of people who might be considered for appointment as faculty. Most senior faculty in American institutions of higher education hold doctorate degrees.

Table 2.1 The percent of B.A., M.A., and Ph.D. degrees awarded to women in the stem fields

	B.A.			M.A.			Ph.D.		
			Percent			Percent			Percent
	Total	Women	Women	Total	Women	Women	Total	Women	Women
Science	28,050	10,907	38.9	7,011	2,636	37.6	5,514	1,868	33.9
Technology	50,962	9,088	17.8	22,777	6,239	27.4	1,826	353	19.3
Engineering	102,984	18,351	17.8	45,325	10,831	23.9	9,467	2,162	22.8
Mathematics	20,453	8,851	43.3	6,957	2,779	39.9	1,823	531	29.1

Source: U.S. Department of Education, National Center for Education Statistics, Digest of Education Statistics: 2014, Table 325

Chart 2.12 Doctorate degrees awarded by American colleges and universities by gender 1976–77 – 2012–13 (Source: U.S. Department of Education, National Center for Education Statistics, *Digest of Education Statistics*: 2014, Table 324.20)

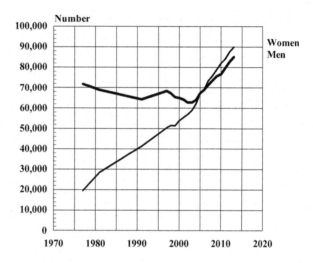

Consequently, it is relevant to develop information about the number of women earning doctorate degrees, as compared with the number of men.

In the mid-1970s, close to four times as many men as women earned doctorates in American colleges and universities. In academic year 1976–1977 men earned almost 72,000 doctorates while women earned only about 19,500. Then, the number of doctorates earned by men slipped to a low point of 63,000 in 2002, before climbing back up – but the number of doctorates earned by men in 2006–2007, was still fewer than the number earned by men 30 years earlier in 1976–1977. Meanwhile, the number of doctorates earned by women increased so rapidly and steadily, that by 2005 women earned as many doctorates as men, and by 2012–2013 women earned almost 5,000 more doctorates than men, 90,000 for women as compared with 85,000 for men. These trends by gender are shown in Chart 2.12

It is important to recognize, however, that the pattern of degrees earned by discipline by women is completely different from the pattern of degrees earned by men. Men dominate the fields of engineering as well as the fields of physical sciences, mathematics, and computer sciences. Men earned 77.5 % of the doctor's degrees in engineering in 2011–2012 as compared with only 22.3 earned by women. Likewise, men earned 71.4 % of the doctor's degrees in the combined fields of physical sciences, mathematics, and computer sciences compared with only 28.5 % earned by women.

On the other hand, women dominate the fields of life sciences, social sciences, and psychology, and especially education. Women earned 68.7 % of the doctorates in education in 2011–2012, as compared with only 31.3 % earned by men. The single field where women and men earn about the same share of the doctor's degrees is the humanities. Women earned 51.7 % while men earned a fairly close 48.3 %. The shares of doctorates earned by gender in selected disciplines is shown on Chart 2.13

Women College and University Presidents

Women have made great strides at the highest executive levels with increasing numbers being appointed college and university president, including at highly prestigious institutions. Hannah Grey notably moved from serving as Provost at Yale to become Acting President in 1977–1978 on the occasion of the unexpected resignation of Kingman Brewster, the President of Yale to become the American Ambassador to the Court of Saint James. Hannah Gray was then appointed to be President of the University of Chicago serving for 15 years from 1978 to 1993. She was the first women President of a major university in the history of the United States. Drew Gilpin Faust became the 28th, but first women, president of Harvard University in 2007 after creating and then being appointed the first Dean of the Radcliff Institute for Advanced Studies established after the merger of Radcliff with Harvard.

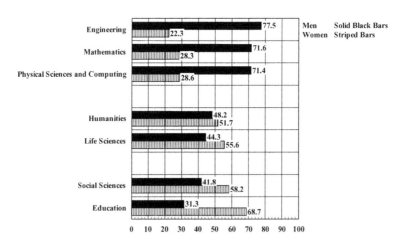

Chart 2.13 Percent of persons receiving doctoral degrees in selected disciplines by gender 2011–2012 (Source: U.S. Department of Education, National Center for Education Statistics, *Digest of Education Statistics*: 2014, Table 324.80)

Interestingly, President Faust was appointed after the resignation of President Laurence Summers in the wake of strong faculty criticism about remarks he had made respecting the capabilities of women. At a press conference on the Harvard campus after her appointment Drew Faust observed "I hope that my own appointment can be one symbol of an opening of opportunities that would have been inconceivable even a generation ago." She also added, "I'm not the woman president of Harvard, I'm the president of Harvard."

Since 1986 the American Council on Education has conducted surveys of the American College Presidents and in 2014 published the eighth edition of a comprehensive report. In 1986 women held 11 % of the presidents of American colleges and universities. Many were presidents of women's colleges and when these colleges became co-educational, were merged with other institutions, or were closed there were fewer opportunities for women to become college presidents. By 2014, however, women accounted for almost one-third of the college presidents, though a high proportion of them head smaller, less prestigious institutions.

The 2014 ACE study shows that in 2011 overall a higher percentage of public institutions (29.4 %) than private (21.9 %) are headed by women presidents. Generally speaking, the percentage of women presidents is lowest (between 5 % and 10 %) among the most prestigious universities, and increases (up to 30–40 %) for the 2-year associate institutions, as the prestige of the institutions diminishes.

Women on College and University Boards of Trustees

Considering women in positions of leadership in American higher education it is extremely important to examine the representation and role of women trustees on the governing boards of institutions. The increasing numbers of women serving as trustees has, according to surveys of the Association of Governing Boards of Colleges and Universities (AGB), shifted the priorities of the boards somewhat toward academic quality and the student experience with less emphasis on finances.

All of the public and private non-profit (also known as "independent") colleges and universities in the United States are governed by Boards of Trustees, while for-profit institutions are guided by their business owners. The public and private non-profit Boards set policy guidelines and generally select and evaluate the performance of the president. Members of a public institution board may be appointed by the state governor and reflect political preferences. Often members are reappointed for several terms. The private nonprofit boards may be self-renewing, with a board committee nominating new board members at the expiration of the term of a previous board member.

In the realm of public institutions, women made great strides in their share of membership on governing boards for three decades, almost trebling from 11 % in the late 1960s to 30 % the late 1990s. In the following decade after 2000, the share of women on public college and university governing boards actually dipped slightly and did not regain their 30 % share until 2010. According to AGB's most recent

Chart 2.14 Percent of American college and university governing board members who are women 1970–2015 (Source; Association of Governing Boards of Colleges and Universities, 2010; Updated in the September/October 2015 issue of Trusteeship, page 2)

report, by 2015 the share of women governing board members at public institutions had only reached 31.5 %, in effect making virtually no gains at all in the last 15 years, as shown on Chart 2.14.

In the realm of private non-profit institutions, women have made almost steady gains from 1969 when they accounted for a mere 11 % of governing board members to 2015 when women rose to 31.7 %. Currently the share of women governing board members is virtually the same in the public and private institutions, again as shown on Chart 2.14.

There are still very few women serving as members of the most powerful board committees which are finance and audit. And very few women are serving as chairmen of either public or private governing boards. The tendency of boards to reappoint serving members at the end of their initial terms makes it difficult for women to break through the "old boy" networks.

Close to half of the members of the governing boards of American colleges and universities come from business. The fact that women are still not well represented among the senior ranks of American business executives may help explain why they are not a higher percentage of college and university board members. Very few board members are faculty members, whether women or men faculty.

Factors Outside Academia Affecting Women in American Higher Education: Critical Factors That Helped Women Succeed in American Higher Education in the Past

Title IX

Title IX was written into the 1972 Amendments to the original Higher Education Act passed by the U.S. Congress in 1964. It prohibits sex discrimination in any educational program or activity receiving any type of federal financial aid. It covers all programs at an institution if any program receives the financial aid. And it covers all programs, not just athletic programs. It was signed into law by Richard Nixon in 1972 and survived decades of legislative, regulatory, and judicial attempts to eliminate its provisions or at least vitiate them.

When the U.S. Department of Education was created in 1980 during the administration of President Jimmy Carter, it was given jurisdiction over Title IX through the Office of Civil Rights. It helped create a climate in which academic women sought to clarify and enforce their rights. Enforcement of Title IX, or at least the threat of a legal case based on Title IX, continues until today to be an important force is helping women succeed in academic pursuits.

Affirmative Action

The first use of the term "affirmative action" was in an Executive Order issued in 1961 by President John Kennedy that required federal contractors to take "affirmative action" to hire employees without regard to race, creed, or national origin. Gender was not initially taken into consideration but in subsequent years the criteria were expanded to protect women. Affirmative action is based in policies, not legislation. It is the outgrowth of the civil rights movement and attempts to create equal opportunity, primarily in education and employment, for members of underrepresented minorities and, subsequently, for women. It has been highly controversial as critiques claimed it would lead to deterioration of quality. Proponents argue that idea is absolutely wrong. Affirmative action is about actively broadening the pool of qualified candidates, not about lowering standards.

Affirmative action programs for women in education include actively broadening the pool of talent from which candidates for employment are selected. It also extends to grants and graduate fellowship programs aimed at helping women students move into fields where their participation has been discouraged, such as engineering, math, and the physical sciences.

Faculty Unions

The National Education Association (NEA) and the American Federation of Teachers (AFT) are unions of American teachers both of which have divisions organizing higher education faculty, and the American Association of Professors (AAUP) operates as a union in some circumstances.

Faculty unions could possibly have had some impact on relative faculty salaries by gender. Though the gap in the salaries of men and women faculty in the associate and assistant faculty ranks has not narrowed, the fact that the gap is relatively small could possibly be explained by the fact that the higher the membership in faculty unions, the smaller the gap between the salaries of women and men faculty.

Important Trends That Will Affect Women in American Higher Education in the Future

Demographic Trends

Both faculty and administrators are aging. A large share are older men will be facing normal retirement in very few years This will lead to shortages of faculty and administrators which will create new opportunities for women who are prepared.

Economic Trends

On one hand, institutions facing economic and financial constraints are trying to balance their budgets by hiring women at lower salaries than they pay men. Women advocates of equal pay for equal work are trying to eliminate discrimination against women to end the differential pay, but progress in slow.

Overall Conclusions About the Participation Rate and the Changing Role of Women in American Higher Education

The participation rate of women in American higher education simply measures the numbers. The changing role is a different assessment which examines whether the actual functions women perform in higher education are evolving over time.

The conclusions about the participation of women in American higher education are drawn primarily from analysis of trend data published by the U. S. Department

of Education, National Center for Education Statistics, in recent editions of the
Digest of Education Statistics. These trend data clearly document two conclusions:

The first conclusion about the participation of women is clearly positive: There has
    been a phenomenal increase in the participation of women in American higher
    education over at least the last two decades, as students, faculty, and
    administrators.

The second conclusion about the participation of women is clearly negative: A
    higher percentage of women than men are employed at lower-paying colleges
    and universities; a higher percentage of women than men are employed in lower-
    paying jobs at the lower-paying institutions, and in each of these jobs women are
    paid less than men. Most discouraging is the fact that the salary gap is not nar-
    rowing between women and men faculty at any rank, and at the rank of professor
    the gap in salaries continues to widen. Over the course of a professional career
    of, say, 35 years this difference could reach to as much as half a million dollars
    or more.

With respect to the changing role of women in higher education, the conclusion
would be modest. The teaching disciplines continue to be gendered, with women
representing a much higher percentage of faculty in education and the social sciences and a much lower percentage in the sciences. Movement of women into the
STEM fields could be characterized as a changing role, but gains in the STEM fields
in the 1980s have slipped away in the following decades. A few women are moving
into executive positions and taking on broader decision-making roles than they had
as faculty. And women have to a modest degree changed the priorities of college
and university governing boards from finances to the quality of education and student experiences. But summarizing the results of the Association of Governing
Board's 2015 survey of trends in the number of women trustees, Susan Johnston
AGB's Executive Vice President titled her report as "A Disappointing Showing."

Broader Questions Raised by These Trends

Trends documented in this chapter raise broader questions: One important question
is how were the higher education institutions able to increase faculty employment
by an astounding 84 % over the two decades, from 1991 to 2011, a period generally
characterized by constrained resources, while student enrollment increased by only
46 %?

A corollary question is why have the majority of these new hires been women?
Why were 62 % of the additional faculty hires over these same 20 years accounted
for by women? American higher education institutions have been hiring more
women than men for decades. Perhaps men have more lucrative opportunities in
business than women do, so some men choose an alternative career to academia.

Another important question is what is the current and expected future impact on
higher education of the use of instructional and communications technology and the

widespread use of online teaching and learning. Further, might the impact be different for women and men? The expanded use of instructional technology and greater reliance on online teaching was expected to reduce the number of faculty needed to teach face-to-face classes, but it apparently has not, at least not yet. Is the IT being used more to enhance face-to-face classes and not to replace those classes and reduce the number of faculty needed?

These questions are generated by hard, verifiable trend data documenting differences between the outcomes for women and men in academia. The answers to these questions range far into the realm of speculation. Searching for the explanations for these differences stimulates critical questions about the continuing role of direct and indirect discrimination against women in American higher education. Work needs to be done to replace these questions with factual answers to use as the basis for an action agenda.

References

"Affirmative Action Overview". National Council of State Legislatures, Online at www.ncsl.org/research/education/affirmative-action/overview.aspx/. Accessed 27 May 2015.

John Harvard's Journal. (2005, January–February). Tenure and gender. Online at http://harvardmagazine.com/2005/01/tenure-and-gender.html. Accessed on 23 May 2015.

Sources of Data

American Association of University Professors, Commission on Women.

American Council on Education series: The American College President, 1986–2012.   On the Pathway to the Presidency, 2013.   Gender Equity in Higher Education, 2010.

Association of Governing Boards of Colleges and Universities, based on a 2010 study of women serving on governing boards of colleges and universities. A summary of the results of the most recent AGB survey of the members of college and university boards of trustees was published in the September/October 2015 issue of the Trusteeship magazine published by AGB.

U. S. Department of Education, National Center for Education Statistics, National Survey of Postsecondary Faculty (NSOPF-03).

U.S. Department of Education, Office of Educational Research and Improvement, National Center for Education Statistics, National Study of Postsecondary Faculty, "Gender and Racial/Ethnic Differences in Salary and Other Characteristics of Postsecondary Faculty: Fall 1998. Statistical Analysis Report, (NCES 2002–170), 99 pages.

U.S. Department of Education, National Center for Education Statistics, Digest of Education Statistics: 2014, Chapter 3, and earlier editions.

Chapter 3
Women in Chinese Higher Education: Educational Opportunities and Employability Challenges

Zhou Zhong and Fei Guo

Women hold up half of the sky.

—Mao Zedong (1968)

Setting the Scene: The Macro Context of Women's Education in China

The development of women's talents in higher education is both a cause and a product of China's modernization. The Women's movement which begun in the Western world in the late nineteenth century has also effected profound changes in Chinese society. As China struggled to transform from a traditional society into a modern nation, Chinese women have become deeply involved in both the initiation and the resultant changes arising from such transformations. Educational development has been a major driving force in the rise of China over the past century. The recent unprecedented progress in education can be seen as both a continuum of this century-long momentum and also a major factoring the economic growth in China's new era of Reform and Open Door since 1977. The changing role of women students and professionals in higher education needs to be first examined in the context of China's legal, political and educational systems that protect the basic and evolving rights and interests of women.

Z. Zhong (✉) • F. Guo
Institute of Education, Tsinghua University, Beijing, China
e-mail: zhongzhou@tsinghua.edu.cn; feiguo0121@mail.tsinghua.edu.cn

© Springer International Publishing Switzerland 2017   53
H. Eggins (ed.), *The Changing Role of Women in Higher Education*,
The Changing Academy – The Changing Academic Profession in International
Comparative Perspective 17, DOI 10.1007/978-3-319-42436-1_3

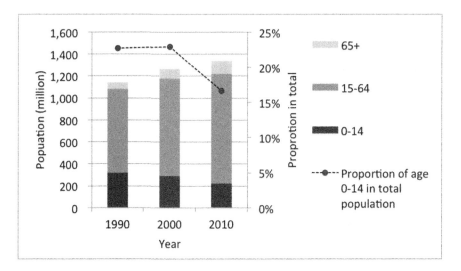

Fig. 3.1 Age structure in China in 1990, 2000 and 2010* (Source: NBS (2011). Note: the population statistical data of 1990, 2000 and 2010 came from the 4th, 5th and 6th national census of China)

Demographic Context

China, as the most populous country in the world, has undergone significant demographic change in the past three decades through the promotion of a birth-control policy since the late 1970s (Fig. 3.1). This policy has brought profound educational, economic and social changes to single-child families in the urban areas, gender imbalance with more men than women in the population, and an aging society during rapid economic and social progress. In particular, the size of the school-age population began to decline in 2006 and the college-age population consequently began to shrink accordingly from 2011. This fall is expected to last till 2028 (Yang 2011). From the positive point of view, the female child as the single child in urban areas or usually as one of no more than two children in rural areas has received better support in education, including better opportunities for higher education, a factor which has contributed to progress in gender equality against long-held gender discrimination in family, schools and society at large (Tian and Liu 2014).

Legal and Political Context

Rapid progress has been made in women's welfare in China over the past two decades. In terms of legal context, it was in 1949 upon the founding of the People's Republic of China that the women's equal status to men and their consequent rights were first set out in law through the Chinese Constitution. Underpinned by the Constitution, a system of support by law and regulation was gradually developed to ensure women's rights and entitlements. The principal law is the Law on the Protection of Rights and Interests of Women enacted in 1992, including political rights, rights and interests relating to culture and education, to work and social security, to property, to the individual person, to marriage and the family, and legal responsibility. Other major laws and regulations supporting women's rights in China include, but are not limited to, Marriage Law enacted in 1950, Inheritance Law in 1985, Compulsory Education Law in 1986, Labour Law in 1995, Labour Contract Law in 2007, Law on Maternal and Infant Health Care in 2005 and Special Rules on the Labour Protection of Female Employees in 2012.

In terms of the political context, the organisation of the Fourth United Nations World Conference on Women in Beijing in 1995 was a critical milestone in raising women's political and social status in China. It was on the occasion of this Conference that the Chinese government first established the principle of gender equality as one of China's basic national policies. Such a commitment not only reinstated the equal rights and opportunities for women and men, but also committed the Government to ensure equality in the resulting welfare distribution for both genders in the course of economic and social development. Consequently, the Chinese government has published a series of documents entitled Outline for the Development of Women in China since 1995. For example, the new 2011–2020 Outline identified 57 major goals and 88 policy measures in seven priority areas: women's health care and life quality, women's education rights, opportunity and attainment, economic resources and status, political participation and social affairs management, social protection and welfare, environmental decisions and their management, and legal guarantees. Detailed planning and implementation of the Outlines is supported by the central, regional and local governments at all levels with matching programmes.

The Attainment and Participation of Women in Chinese Higher Education

Over the past three decades the Chinese education has experienced increasing political commitment to, and funding resources for, increasing and widening access while enhancing quality. In the twenty-first century China has set itself the goal of transforming Chinese education, especially the higher education system, from a big system into a strong one that embraces both economic growth and social equity. As a result, education attainment and participation have achieved unprecedented improvement for both men and women. In contrast, graduate employment and especially women's graduate employment has experienced major challenges after the rapid expansion of higher education enrolment since 1999.

Women's Educational Attainment in China

During the period 1990–2010, while the adult male-female gap for educational attainment in general was widened from 0.86 years to 1.36 years for the 25+ age-group of the population the gender gap for those with higher educational attainment was reduced. Over the same period, China's average number of years of schooling of the 25+ age-group of the population grew by 2.7 years from 4.85 to 7.55 (Fig. 3.2). Nevertheless the female members of the same age-group still had a relatively lower level of educational attainment although that had risen from 4.42 average years of schooling to 6.87 years over the same period. People with lower or upper secondary education qualifications almost doubled while people with higher education qualifications grew over six fold (Fig. 3.3). China's improvement in educational attainment was driven by rapid expansion of enrolment at all levels, especially in the upper-secondary and higher education sectors (Fig. 3.4). As a result, the improved structure and performance of the Chinese education system has generated a growing capacity of human capital to drive China's economic growth.

According to the sixth national census of China, the total population of Mainland China in 2010 was 1,333 million; the population size of the 30–39 age cohort (born in 1971–1980) was 215.16 million, about twice of the 60–69 age cohort (born in 1940–1950) which was 99.78 million. The comparison of the educational attainment of the 2 age cohorts with three decades separation illustrates the rapid progress in education that China has achieved since the foundation of the new China in 1949. The development of women's educational attainment in China represented by the 2 age cohorts exhibited the following characteristics (Figs. 3.4 and 3.5, Table 3.1):

The size of female participation increased markedly and at a rate much faster than that of the male at all levels of education. It can be seen that, the higher the level of education, the greater the rate of increase was for both genders. The higher education sector registered the most dramatic increase in the rate of growth between the 2 age cohorts. The number of women with postgraduate attainment increased

Fig. 3.2 Educational attainment by average year of schooling in China in 1990, 2000 and 2010 (Source: National Bureau of Statistics of China (NBS) 2011)

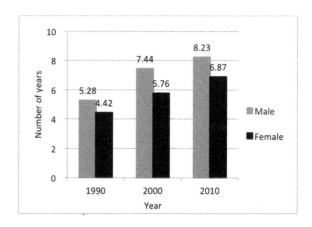

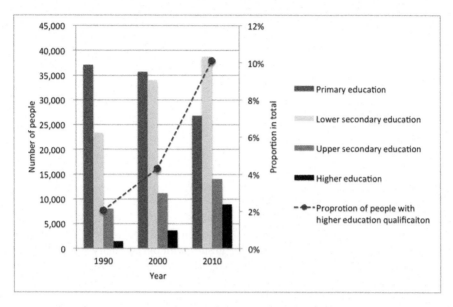

Fig. 3.3 Educational attainment by level of highest qualification per 100,000 inhabitants in China in 1990, 2000 and 2010 (Source: NBS 2011)

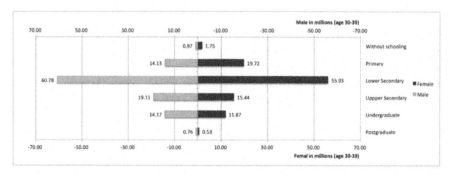

Fig. 3.4 Level of educational attainment by gender of age 30–39 in China in 2010 (Source: NBS 2011)

76.49 times from 6,992 to 534,807 as compared to the 28.98-times increase for men. The number of women with undergraduate attainment increased 11.38 times from 1.04 million to 11.87 million, as compared to the six-times increase for men. So the rate of growth in the size of population with higher education attainment was much faster for women than for men, with a factor of 2.64 times and 1.90 times respectively at postgraduate and undergraduate level.

The gender gap has been reduced significantly, despite there still being fewer women than men completing secondary and higher education in both age cohorts. The proportion of females in secondary and higher education increased from the

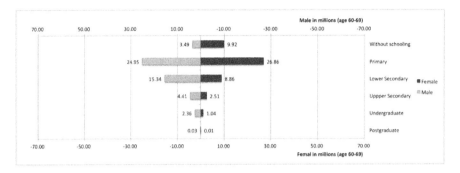

Fig. 3.5 Level of educational attainment by gender of age 60–69 in China in 2010 (Source: NBS 2011)

range of 41–49 % to the range 21–37 % between the 2 age cohorts, even though women were still over represented in the groups with only primary school level of education or without formal schooling. The male-female ratio was lowered from 3.73 to 1.31 at postsecondary level and from 2.26 to 1.19 at undergraduate level.

Women's Participation in Chinese Higher Education

The improvement in education attainment in China reflected the dramatic expansion in enrolment over the past two decades across all levels of education, with women's enrolment increasing more rapidly than that of men. The higher education enrolment soared with double-digit growth rate in 1999–2005 before stabilizing at a single-digit rate from 2006 onward, and the total enrolment reached 31 million in 2010. The gross enrolment rate rose from 3.4 % in 1990, 12.5 % in 2000, 25.9 % in 2010, and 34.5 % in 2013. The aim is to reach 40 % by 2020 (Fig. 3.6).

Rapid expansion has generated a more gender-balanced participation in the Chinese higher education in recent years. In this sector, the size of full-time women faculty, women faculty and staff and women students expanded respectively nearly 6 times, nearly 3 times and over 16 times between 1990 and 2013 (Figs. 3.7, 3.8, and 3.9). As a result, the proportion of professional women rose from about one third to close to one half in total and women students outgrew the men for the first time in recent years – firstly in the undergraduate associate-degree programmes in 2006, followed by the master's degree programmes in 2010, then in the bachelor degree programmes in 2011 (Fig. 3.8).

Despite women's increased participation in higher education, there were still marked gender achievement gaps in several areas. For example, in the PhD sector women students were still under-represented with 36.45 % of the total in 2012. Of course it was a result of both ability and personal choice. As another example, while there was a nearly fourfold increase in full-time women faculty from 0.18 million to 0.68 million in 2000–2013, and a higher proportion of women obtained professor-

Table 3.1 Level of educational attainment by gender of those aged 60–69 and those aged 30–39 in China in 2010

		Post-graduate education	Under-graduate education[a]	Upper secondary education	Lower secondary education	Primary education	No schooling
Age 30–39	Male	756,275	14,170,814	19,106,789	60,779,296	14,131,262	968,490
	Female	534,807	11,871,304	15,436,586	55,931,237	19,724,358	1,752,944
	Total	1,291,082	26,042,118	34,543,375	116,710,533	33,855,620	2,721,434
Age 60–69	Male	26,100	2,360,278	4,409,528	15,342,984	24,951,043	3,492,964
	Female	6,992	1,043,056	2,507,647	8,863,370	26,859,047	9,917,555
	Total	33,092	3,403,334	6,917,175	24,206,354	51,810,090	13,410,519
Growth rate: 60–69 group compared to 30–39	Male	28.98 %	6.0 %	4.33 %	3.96 %	0.57 %	0.28 %
	Female	76.49 %	11.38	6.16 %	6.31 %	0.73 %	0.18 %
	Total	39.01 %	7.65 %	4.99 %	4.82 %	0.65 %	0.2 %

Source: NBS (2011)

[a]Undergraduate degrees in China comprise both 4-year bachelor-degree programmes and 3-year associate-degree programmes

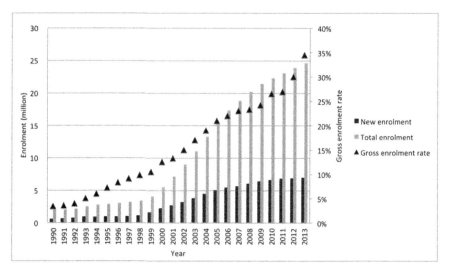

Fig. 3.6 Undergraduate enrolment in regular higher education in China, 1990–2013 (Source: Ministry of Education of China (MOE) 1991–2014)

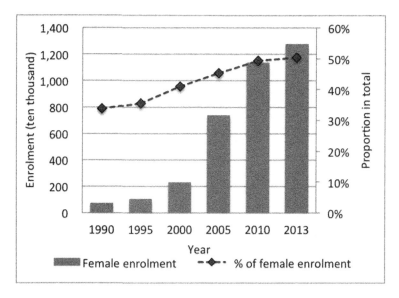

Fig. 3.7 Female undergraduate enrolment in regular higher education in China in selected years in 1990–2013 (Source: MOE (1991–2013); NBS (2015))

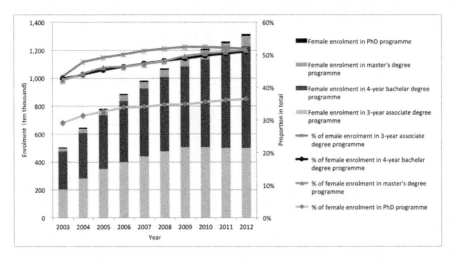

Fig. 3.8 Female enrolment in higher education in China in 2003–2012 (Source: MOE (2004–2013))

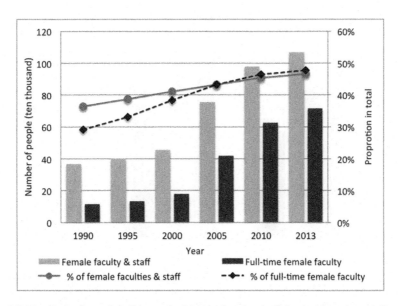

Fig. 3.9 Female faculty and staff in regular higher education in China in selected years (Source: MOE (1991–2013); NBS (2015))

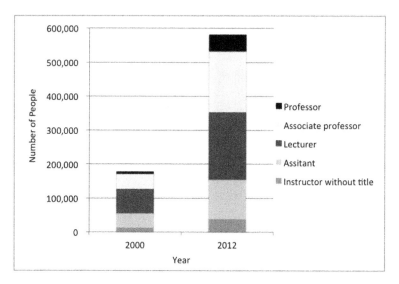

Fig. 3.10 The number of women faculty by academic title in 2000 and 2012 in regular higher education institutions in China (Source: MOE (2001, 2013))

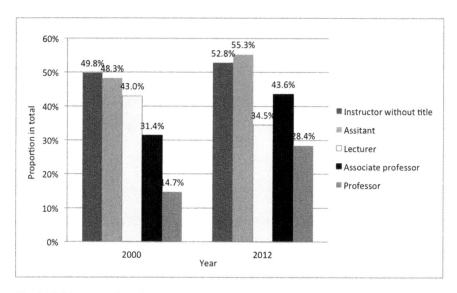

Fig. 3.11 The proportion of women faculty by professional title in 2000 and 2012 in regular higher education institutions in China (Source: MOE (2001, 2013))

ships (from 14.7 to 28.4 %) and associated professorships (from 31.4 to 43.6 %) there was a lower proportion of women who obtained lectureships (from 43.0 % to 34.5 %) (Figs. 3.10 and 3.11). Women were therefore still the minority in the medium to senior ranks of academic professionals, though they had now become the majority in the junior ranks of assistant and instructor without title. As a third example, the 39 leading universities in China had a total 42 female presidents, vice-presidents or leaders at similar levels, with at least one in each institution in 2014 (MOE 2014).

Employment Challenges of Women Graduates in Chinese Higher Education

A mass higher education system with increased access has also brought rising challenges in graduate employment, as Chinese higher education moved from an elite to a mass system when the gross higher education enrolment rate reached the threshold of 15 % in 2002 (Trow 1974). Then in 2009, the number of women graduates in higher education outgrew men for the first time and the proportion of women graduates in total continued to increase (CSICC and PKU 2011).

A Quantitative Analysis of Women Graduate Employment in China

Gender discrimination has long been a major challenge in women's employment, not only in higher education but also in the labour market in general, mainly because of China's long tradition of gender inequality (An 2001; Yang 2012). Challenges to women's graduate employment multiply as a result of the rapid expansion in higher education enrolment. Criticisms of graduate employment in general ensued as the number of higher education graduates expanded, with double-digit in the years 2002–2008 before becoming stable at single-digit growth from 2009 onwards. The number of graduates grew from 0.9 million in 1999 to 2.0 million in 2003 and 7.3 million in 2014. Concerns about employment centred on increased competition, the declining rate of employment on graduation, a declining starting salary for new graduates, qualification inflation, rising dissatisfaction with the quality of available employment, the mismatch in skills between education and the labour market, and the lack of research into graduate employment (Min et al. 2005; Xie et al. 2010).

According to the 1998 and 2003 national surveys of graduate employment, while significant gender differences existed in access to higher education and in the rate of employment in the first 6 months after graduation, there was little significant gender difference in student academic performance or employment quality (Wen 2005). In contrast, national surveys of graduate employment every 2 years in the period 2003–2013 consistently showed: (1) the quality of graduate employment had worsened since the first generation of graduates after the enrolment expansion entered the labour market in 2003; (2) the academic performance of women had improved as had their access to higher education; they had become more disadvantaged in terms of graduate employment compared to the period before the expansion of enrolment (Yue 2012; Cao and Yue 2011; Yue and Zhang 2014).

According to national surveys of graduate employment in 2007–2013, there were significant systematic disadvantages for women in terms of their first employment rate at 6 months after graduation, the level of starting salary, the level of satisfaction (reflecting the difference between the sense of satisfaction and the expectation concerning one's work). These disadvantages were not influenced by the manner in which the graduates were grouped, whether it was by qualification, by area of study or by type of institution (Ao and Ding 2011). For example, in 2007 and 2009 40.2 % and 38.6 % respectively of women graduates were still unemployed 6 months after graduation; for those did obtain employment only 45.4 and 48.2 % expressed satisfaction with their work, and their starting salaries were about US $224 and $323, or 90.1 % and 85.9 % of those of male graduates (Cao and Yue 2010).

A survey of 2009 national graduate employment (Yang 2012) and a regional survey of undergraduate graduate employment in 2004–2011 in Zhejiang province (a prosperous region in eastern coastal China) (Zhu et al. 2012) both confirmed a significant disadvantage for women in starting salary as well as in on-going salary. According to the 2009 national survey, female graduates in general earned 10 % less than their male counterpart in industry, and such a gender income difference could be wholly explained by the gender discrimination within each industry for the graduates with undergraduate degrees, but only partially explained for those with master's degrees, alongside the factor of individual difference.

The phenomena of "division of labour" and "mobility inertia" reflected structural problems in gender inequality in both educational access and graduate employment. On the "input" side, women were disadvantaged in terms of access to the strategically scarce resources of "key educational institutions" no matter where the female student's home location was, family socio-economic background, or type of qualification obtained except for the doctorate. Such key institutions are top-level universities and secondary schools that tend to cluster in major cities. For example, the proportion of women's access to the top 100 or so universities was 36.6 % in 2009, about 10 % lower than the average chance of women's access to higher education in general (Yue 2010).

On the "outcome" side, the area of work where women graduates tended to cluster was less dynamic and less mobile in terms of both quantity and quality of opportunities and choices of employment. For example in 2013, 75 % of women graduates sought employment in the service sector while nearly 50 % of men chose to work in the manufacturing sector, and more women graduates worked in the non-business sector while more men worked in the business sector (Yue 2014). The fact was that until 2012 the manufacturing sector had been the biggest sector in China's economy measured by the Gross Domestic Product (GDP), and the manufacturing and building industries generated 24.58 million new work places as compared to 5.63 million new work places in the non-business service sector in 2003–2012 (NBS 2013). In 2013 China's service sector outgrew the manufacturing sector as the largest sector measured by GDP. It is expected that the possible expansion of the service sector in terms of the generation of new employment might bring more new opportunities for graduates, especially for professional women (NBS 2014).

Moreover, female graduates exhibited "mobile inertia" as they were more reluctant than male graduates to relocate in terms of residence once they had accustomed themselves to one place. For example, the gender difference in mobility between regions was 19.5 and 23.77 % in terms of place of study and of employment respectively in 2009, and 11.7 % of employment in 2013 as men was 50.8 % and women was 39.1 % (Yue 2010, 2014).

Therefore even though women students may have achieved better academic performances during the process of their studies in higher education, they were still disadvantaged in mobility in both their access to, and exit from, higher education. Given both mobility and salary are indications of human capital, women graduate's employability, that is, the capability involving knowledge, skills and attitudes for gaining and maintaining employment (Hillage and Pollard 1998), was still not equal to that of men even when they received the same type of higher education. Gender inequality in graduate employment reflects not only a long-held wider social perception of gender roles and gender discrimination in the world of work, but also equality and efficiency issues in higher education in particular and in the education system at large. Recent studies argued that the educational attainment of the parents serves as a significant factor to predict the employment mobility and starting salary of the graduates (Du and Yue 2010; Yue 2014; Tian and Liu 2014). Therefore the improvement of women's educational attainment has positive inter-generation economic and social benefits.

A Qualitative Analysis of Women Graduate Employment in China

This section discusses the graduate profiles and employability issues of Chinese graduates viewed from both Chinese and European perspectives. The findings came from a recent China-EU China study conducted by the present authors with their European colleagues to examine the relevance and responsiveness of higher education systems in China and the EU in 2010–2011 (Ulicna and Zhou 2011) and its follow-up study (Zhong et al. 2014). The study conducted 162 interviews (82 in China and 80 in Europe) and all interviewees had direct experience with both Chinese and European higher education systems in terms of studying, teaching, research or programme design, or work experience involving Chinese and European graduates. About one third of all interviewees were women. All Chinese interviewees either studied or worked in leading universities in China. Most interviewees raised no issues of significant gender difference in terms of the profile and employability of Chinese graduates, but many Chinese women interviewees did discuss significant gender difference in mobility in relation to their decisions to study abroad and return home afterwards, and the opportunities and challenges faced by women graduates who returned to work in China.

The Main Characteristics in the Profile of Chinese Students and Graduates

The people interviewed for this study were asked to reflect on the similarities and differences they perceived in knowledge, skills and competences between students and graduates from Europe and China. The interviewees from China and Europe had very similar perspectives on these issues. In particular cases, of course, the distribution of knowledge, skills and competences differed radically from the generalised, somewhat stereotyped picture provided here, but few of the interviewees actually provided information that would contradict the general picture presented below.

With regards to knowledge within a given discipline, the Chinese education system from primary to tertiary level gives a strong emphasis on the acquisition of a solid foundation in quantitative skills and calculating solutions to complex problems. Mathematical competence is one of the key criteria in the highly selective routes of examination-based progression into higher levels of education. As a result, Chinese students and graduates tend to excel generally in theoretical knowledge in their discipline and have particularly strong foundations in quantitative and technical skills. They are proficient in mathematics-based solutions to problems. Shanghai's excellent performance in PISA in 2009 and 2012, especially in PISA mathematics, serve as an example in this regard.

With regards to the application of knowledge to practical situations and problem solving, the Chinese students and graduates were less flexible in moving from theory to practice. In general, students in China did not have sufficient opportunities during their studies to apply the theoretical knowledge they learned in the classroom to practice, though this was not the case as much in those disciplines where laboratory work is a standard requirement. Chinese students and graduates often excelled in solving problems with which they were more familiar. Since the Chinese education emphasises memorization, rote learning and problem solving exercises within a known framework, the Chinese students and graduates tend develop excellent skills and proficiency in solving theoretical and textbook problems when they have previously mastered the normative problem solving process for that area.

With regards to soft skills, the Chinese education system has a strong tradition of written culture, and until recently in the top schools and universities, the students did not have sufficient opportunities to develop their oral communication skills in terms of presentation, discussion or debate. Similarly, as they are mainly required to work individually, Chinese students have very few opportunities to develop their collaborative and teamwork skills. Moreover, Chinese students and graduates tend to work in a more clearly defined framework with clear tasks to carry out; they were less comfortable working autonomously and tend to have less developed management skills in planning, communication and interaction.

Labour Market Demand for Graduate Competences

All three types of employers i.e. those from the universities, Chinese domestic enterprises and international enterprises with Chinese branches, reported that the supply of competences such as working in teams, leadership, management skills, communication, problem solving or the ability to innovate usually fell below their expectations. In particular, the Chinese labour market was short of the following types of graduate competences.

Senior managers: The shortage of senior managers in China could be explained by the transformation of the Chinese labour market and the introduction of a meritocratic approach for promotion to management positions, rather than promotion based solely on seniority. Quite commonly, Chinese graduates with strong technical skills often did not have sufficient competence to manage colleagues effectively.

Researchers working in R&D centres: While the supply of people with excellent theoretical or technical knowledge in China was good, work in research and development centres of international enterprises, and increasingly so in more recent years in domestic enterprises, required more than the mastery of codified knowledge and routine process. It necessitates good communication with others involved in the innovation process, the capacity to think about an often vaguely-defined problem in an unconventional manner as well as the capacity to work autonomously and to cope with unpredictable situations.

Sales persons with a good understanding of the product or technicians with sales skills: Sales professions require strong negotiation, communication and interpersonal skills that people with more technical profiles and a good understanding of technical products seem to be lacking.

Employees with proficiency in foreign languages: Most interviewees mentioned that fluency in English and/or other foreign languages is at a good premium in the Chinese labour market. These skill shortages partly mirror the observations of the profile of both female and male graduates in China, and these shortages need to be put into the perspective that China's economy and consequently its occupational structures are undergoing dynamic transformations. This transformation comes with different competence requirements than those that were considered adequate in China's former centralised and planned economy.

Relevance and Responsiveness of Higher Education and Graduate Employability in China

The relevance of teaching content versus the relevance of learning process: The nature and quality of the learning process was identified as a major factor in improving the relevance of higher education in China. The holistic and stimulating learning process is as important in competence development as the learning of up-to-date content. To be relevant, students assimilate information in relation to other information and through a dynamic process of social interaction, rather than solely through the one-way professor-to-student transmission. This principle has been progressively embedded in higher education in China, and has become increasingly influential among leading Chinese universities, especially in the fields of engineering, medical studies and social sciences.

Actions to Improve Responsiveness

In China, institutional autonomy in teaching and learning varied by type of university and college. At the institutional level, top universities allow much greater freedom to their professors in groups or as individuals to make innovations to the content and method of their teaching, but for the majority of HEIs in China, standardised national or regional textbooks are still widely recommended for use everywhere from the institutional to the national levels. The positive aspect of this situation is that the central and regional governments have made a large investment in encouraging top-level scholars and experts to create state of the art textbooks in all major subjects and keep them updated to ensure their continued relevance to international standards. On the other hand, at the institutional or local level, the individual teacher's initiatives are not being encouraged sufficiently.

Moreover, an increasing number of Chinese HEIs have developed international collaborative programmes with foreign partners for mobility study, joint degrees, joint ventures and internship programmes. Such co-operation has also helped improve the responsiveness of higher education in China (Zhong 2010). Many of the Chinese and international employers interviewed pointed out the intensity of competition for experienced competent personnel in the labour market. Increasingly, many large-scale Chinese enterprises also provide scholarships, joint research projects or competitive extra-curricular entrepreneurial activities with universities. In addition, Chinese universities are increasingly shaping their practices to move up the ladder of international and national rankings (Zhong et al. 2014). While many international bench-markings are academic and research focused, China has also developed national rankings and annual reports with emphasis on employability issues to improve the employment prospects of the students.

At the system level, the MOE made graduate employment in terms of first employment rate a key benchmark in the 2004 *National Framework of Quality Assurance for Regular Higher Education Institution* (MOE 2004). It subsequently added the quality of graduate employment (the graduate's preparedness and career prospects for the work and the graduate's satisfaction with their employment) and the availability and quality of institutional career service into the graduate employment benchmark in the latest *2011 National Framework* (MOE 2011). The HEIs have put in place measures to ensure the responsiveness of their educational programme to labour market needs, and to collect and report employment opportunities for students after graduation as part of their internal and external quality assurance measures. Moreover, China has also established regional and national networks of university and college offices to offer employment guidance and career services.

These offices not only provide counselling to individual students but also function as liaison agents to communicate and collaborate with the employers and related government and non-government organisations.

China's latest policy for higher education structural rationalisation has a strong focus on the promotion of graduate employment. The goal is to convert over 600 out of 1,200 or so regional 4-year HEIs offering academic bachelor degrees into vocational colleges offering 3-year associate degrees and 5-year bachelor degrees (ChinaNews 2014). The reform is expected to meet local and institutional difficulty in implementation, because the HEIs in questions are mainly those which have been recently upgraded from college to university since the 1999 expansion of enrolment, and because, in general, Chinese society values academic study much more highly than vocational education and training regardless of its prospect of employability.

Competence-Based General Education

For China the task of operating the world's largest general education system across a land comparable in area to the whole of Europe is indeed challenging. Any reform of such a complex system has to be planned with a long-term perspective. China's latest curriculum reform of general education towards more competence-based and problem-based learning has been on-going at all levels of education including higher education since entering the twenty-first century. However, the extent to which general education contributed to the development of such desired innovative attributes such as creativity, communication, teamwork and management skills has frequently been questioned by the interviewees for this study.

The implementation of new national curriculum reform has met numerous difficulties, including inadequacies in teacher quality, resources, and reform of the paper-based national entrance examination to university which itself is not yet competence-based. In higher education in particular, as faculty employment and promotion are increasingly research-oriented and in the general context of the expansion of enrolment, criticism has surged concerning the relative neglect of teaching and learning support by the faculty and the university in general. Nevertheless, a national consensus has been reached that this curriculum reform, like Chinese education reforms in general, has to become an evolving process within the framework of a far-sighted master plan. According to the Chinese saying, it is a process that "has no ending but only a beginning."

An Ideal Graduate

The interviewees were also asked to describe an image of the ideal graduate from higher education. Such an profile turned out to be generally the same for all interviewees in China and Europe: (1) a strong knowledge base in one's academic and professional area; (2) a solid skill foundation, especially in terms of literacy, numeracy, and digital competence; (3) the capacity to apply the knowledge and skills to concrete situations and problems that arise in the work environment; (4) competence to work with others and to efficiently communicate ideas; (5) the ability to lead or follow the leadership of others according to the situation; (6) autonomy in making decisions in accordance with his/her responsibilities; (7) international experience, combined with the mastery of at least one foreign language; (8) the ability to recognise new opportunities and to develop new ranges of products or services; (9) the willingness to invest in himself/herself through further learning.

Given the above consensus on the image of the 'ideal graduate', it remains unclear whether employment structures and labour markets actually offer sufficient opportunities for people who possess these qualities to excel. As the number of graduates continues to grow and the higher education system has increasingly tiered and diversified in China, varied requirements and expectations have developed for different types of graduates. Nevertheless, the interviews showed that the personal attributes mentioned above were highly valued by employers in China, who often had difficulties in finding people who matched these characteristics. For both male and female graduates in China, those who fit the profile appear to be in an attractive position to take advantage of a broad range of opportunities.

Conclusion and Recommendations

The development of higher education for women has achieved remarkable progress over the past two decades in the context of rapid economic development, slowed population growth under the birth-control policy, explicit national development policy for women and more importantly the massive expansion of educational opportunities for all throughout the education system in China. In recent years there were already more women than men participating in all levels of higher education except at PhD level, and women are truly competitive in academic performance, especially in the leading universities. As more female students are provided with more and better opportunities in education, a main challenge remains for women as professionals to be offered more and better development opportunities outside education in society at large.

At the forefront, equal work for equal pay in general is still not a reality in China, whether for women with or without higher education qualifications. Moreover, women remain in the minority in senior academic and administrative group, and leadership is still more difficult for women professionals to achieve both within and beyond the higher education sector. Gender disparity in graduate employment is a complex result of the combined forces of individual ability and effort, organisational and industry policy, macro-economic, political and legal institutions as well as social and cultural norms.

For policy recommendations to improve gender equality in higher education and beyond, it is therefore imperative to raise political commitment to, and social awareness of, gender-smart policy underpinned by the principle of equal-but-different. Equality means equal rights for both genders, while difference highlights meeting women's special needs taking account of physical and mental characteristics and professional and occupational preferences. Gender-smart policy in education and beyond needs to be supported through cross-field policy integration and legal development to protect women's equal rights.

First of all, it is essential to integrate women's education policy written in the *Outline for the Development of Women in China* into the mainstream education policy represented by major documents such as the 5-year educational planning and the guidelines for mid- to long-term educational reform and development from national to local and institutional levels.

Accordingly, it is also important to strengthen the monitoring and evaluation of the gendered development in education and all other aspects of national life through statistical monitoring at all levels. For example, the national yearbook of education added several new gender related indicators from 2003 onwards, such as female enrolment by qualification and women professionals by academic status in both regular and adult higher education sectors, but most indicators still lack the gender perspective, such as enrolment by field of study or by type of institution. Neither aggregated nor gender-specific data on graduate employment are available in the educational statistical yearbook. Findings of large-scale national surveys of graduate employment are available in academic publications such as journal papers but usually they are not open and not easily accessible to the general public.

Secondly, the government at all levels should seriously consider establishing a more competitive labour market and one which also ensures equality and equity It must give targeted support to women and other conventionally disadvantaged groups, such as employability education and training as well as pre-service and in-service employment counselling services. Indeed, the issue of gender equality was mentioned once in the latest master reform document for China's reform promulgated in 2013—the *Decision of the Central Committee of the Communist Party of China on Some Major Issues Concerning Comprehensively Deepening the Reform.* With regards to promoting employment and the development of entrepreneurship through institutional innovation, the *Decision* reinstated the commitment to regulating employment policies and eliminating all institutional obstacles and social discriminations concerning urban-rural location, industry, social status and gender. The *Decision* gave special emphasis to promoting higher education graduate employment, particularly through expanding the capacity of public administration and social service to increase employment opportunities for graduates.

With special regard to higher education policy, it is most important to continue to implement gender-smart strategic goals and policy measures put forward by the 2010–2020 plan for the Development of Women in China: fully implementing the principle of gender equality in education; raising the educational attainment of the female labour force to 11.2 years of schooling; raising women's gross enrolment rate in upper secondary education to 90 %, with equal opportunity for women to have access to upper secondary education; raising women's gross enrolment rate in higher education to 40 %, with equal proportion of female and male students in HEIs; further promoting the adoption of women's studies courses in HEIs; full adoption of the principle and concept of gender equality in the curriculum and in teaching and learning processes at all levels and in all forms of education.

The academic roles and leadership roles of women in Chinese higher education are improving in the twenty-first century, as women students have become approximately equal in numbers to male ones, and women professionals have come to play an increasingly important role in Chinese higher education today in the context of expanded educational opportunities for all in China. There is still a long to go to improve gender equality in Chinese society but the higher education sector has already set a good example to drive this change. After all, women hold up half of the Chinese higher education now.

References

An Shufen. (2001). Anthology of the study on women in higher education towards the 21st century (ed., pp. 91–93). Beijing: Higher Education Press.

Ao Shan, & Ding Xiaohao. (2011). Employment characteristics study of college graduates based on gender differences. *Education & Economy, 2011*(2), 1–7.

Cao Xing, & Yue Changjun. (2010). Gender gap in Chinese college graduates' employment status. *Journal of Higher Education, 31*(1), 68–72.

Cao Xing, & Yue Changjun. (2011). Literature review of gender gap in Chinese college graduates' employment. *Education Research Monthly, 2011*(2), 10–14.

ChinaNews. (2014, February 26). State Council: Guiding the conversion of a number of regular undergraduate HEIs into applied technological HEIs. ChinaNews. http://www.chinanews.com/gn/2014/02-26/5887245.shtml

CSICC (China Student Information and Career Centre) & PKU (Peking University School of Education). (2011). China's national information of higher education graduate employment (2009–2010). Beijing: Peking University Press.

Hillage, J., & Pollard, E. (1998). Employability: Developing a framework for policy analysis, Department for Education and Employment (DfEE) of UK. Research Report no. RR85. London: DfEE. http://www.moe.edu.cn/publicfiles/business/htmlfiles/moe/s7168/201403/165457.html

Min Weifang, Ding Xiaohao, & Wen Dongmao. (2005). An empirical study of the employment of graduates in 2005. *Journal of Higher Education, 27*(1), 31–38.

MOE. (1991–2013), MOE (2004–2013), MOE (2001, 2013). Educational statistical yearbook of China 1990–2012. Beijing: People's Education Press.

MOE. (1991–2014). Statistical bulletins of China's national educational development, 1999–2014.

MOE. (2004). Temporary national framework of quality assurance for regular higher education institution, Department of Higher Education [2004] 21.

MOE. (2011). National framework of quality assurance for regular higher education institution, MOE Department of Higher Education [2004] 21 [2011] 2.

MOE. (2014). MOE: Each project 985 University has a women president, the speech of Vice Minister of MOE Li Weihong at the opening of the 6th World Women University Presidents Forum on 5 September 2014. http://news.sina.com.cn/c/2014-09-07/043930806030.shtml

NBS. (2011). *China statistical yearbook 2011*. Beijing: China Statistical Publisher.

NBS. (2013). *China statistical yearbook 2013*. Beijing: China Statistical Publisher.

NBS. (2014). A primary study of China's GDP in 2013, issued on 21 January 2014. http://www.stats.gov.cn

NBS. (2015). Report on the implementation of the outline for the development of Chinese women (2011–2020) in 2013, issued on 3 February 2015. http://www.stats.gov.cn/tjsj/zxfb/201501/t20150122_672472.html

Tian Feng, & Liu Yulong. (2014). The impact of higher education on the differentiation between the only child and non-only child. *Population & Economics, 206*, 51–61.

Trow, M. (1974). *The transition from elite to mass higher education.* Paris: OECD.

Ulicna, D. and Zhong Zhou. (2011). EU and China: Race for talent: Relevance and responsiveness of education and training: A joint study of the European Commission and the Ministry of Education, China, and jointly conducted by the GHK Consultancy and Tsinghua University.

Wen Dongmao. (2005). A comparative study on gender disparity in higher education opportunity, achievement and graduate employment in China. *Tsinghua Journal of Education, 26*(5), 16–21.

Xie Zuoxu, Wang Weihong, & Chen Xiaowei. (2010). A study of women's access to higher education in rural and urban China: An analysis across different types of higher education institutions. *Chinese Education and Society, 43*(4), 32–40.

Yang Dongping. (2011). Education blue book: China education development report 2011, Beijing: 21st century Education Research Institute.

Yang Po. (2012). Education, industry segregation and gender wage gap: Evidence from college graduate surveys in China. *Peking University Review, 10*(3), 95–114.

Yue Changjun. (2010). A comparative study of gender disparity in higher education and labour market. *Tsinghua Journal of Education, 31*(6), 75–81.

Yue Changjun. (2012). A comparative study of on graduate employment surveys, 2003–2011. *Peking University Education Review, 10*(1), 33–47.

Yue Changjun. (2014). Gender and inter-provincial migration from college graduates. *Education & Economy, 2014*(1), 31–39.

Yue Changjun, & Zhang Kai. (2014). Research on job-hunting result and starting salary of college graduates and its influential factors. *Educational Research, 2014*(11), 72–83.

Zhong Zhou., Ulicna, D., & Han Shuangmiao (2014). Relevance and responsiveness of higher education, China and the EU Compared, in the European Association for International Education (EAIE) (ends.) Handbook of Internationalisation of Higher Education, 19th Supplement (III-2014).

Zhong Zhou. (2010). Beijing banks on C9 to break into higher education's elite. In T. Martin (Ed.), *QS Worldclass 2010 showcase.* London: QS.

Zhu Ruhua, Zhen Yueqiao, & Yang Leijing. (2012). Gender gaps in college graduate employment quality: A case study of Zhejiang Province. Heilongjiang Education (Higher Education Research and Appraisal) 1008: 79–80.

Chapter 4
Women, Leadership, and Organizational Culture in Higher Education: Lessons Learned from South Africa and Ghana

Reitumetse Obakeng Mabokela and Yeukai A. Mlambo

Introduction

Globalization has played a significant role in redefining the role and identity of higher education institutions across the world, and universities in developing countries are no exception. Education policies in many developing countries have historically favored and funded the development of basic education; however there has been a gradual shift in national policies towards investing in the higher education sector. This chapter examines how the intersection of gender, socio-cultural factors, and organizational culture impacts professional experiences of women academics in Africa. Given the glaring absence of women in academic positions across many African universities, particularly at senior ranks, this chapter seeks to provide an understanding of challenges and opportunities that influence the upward mobility of women academics and academic leaders.

According to Amina Mama (2003), access to higher education remains inequitable and even with formal restrictions removed women's entry into higher education as both students, faculty and administrators remains uneven. Mama (2003) states that contrary to institutional claims of gender neutrality, the cultures of many African higher education institutions continue to be infused with sexual and gender dynamics that impact professional experiences, especially for women.

Mama (2003) attributes the underrepresentation of women to the masculine culture of the academy that dates back to the historical origins of universities across

R.O. Mabokela (✉)
University of Illinois at Urbana-Champaign, Champaign, IL, USA
e-mail: mabokela@illinois.edu

Y.A. Mlambo
Michigan State University, East Lansing, MI, USA
e-mail: mlamboye@msu.edu

© Springer International Publishing Switzerland 2017   75
H. Eggins (ed.), *The Changing Role of Women in Higher Education*,
The Changing Academy – The Changing Academic Profession in International
Comparative Perspective 17, DOI 10.1007/978-3-319-42436-1_4

the African continent, which were informally designated as male spaces and where women were absent for a long period of time. For example, Makerere University in Uganda established in 1922, and one of the oldest universities in sub-Sahara Africa, only admitted the first women in 1945. Similarly, the National University in Congo established in 1954 admitted the first female students in 1962 (Mama 2003). This chapter clearly conveys that while African universities have developed beyond the early colonial days, there are persistent patterns of marginalization of women academics and administrators. The legacy of exclusion continues to manifest in the under-representation and sometimes, stark absence of women in senior academic and leadership positions. The persistent lack of a critical mass of women as advanced doctoral students, researchers, and academic staff limits the pool of potential women academic leaders available. Even in academic disciplines where women are the majority such as Education and Social Work, male academics disproportionately occupy senior academic and administrative ranks.

Drawing from institutions of higher education in Ghana and South Africa in particular, this chapter provides an overview of the status and experiences of women in higher education leadership in these countries, focusing on senior administrative positions. The ensuing discussion highlights the status of women in higher education in a global context, to provide a framework for understanding where the experiences of academic leaders in Ghana and South Africa are situated. It is important to understand the experiences of African academic leaders within this broader global context.

Global Patterns of Gender Marginalization

An examination of literature on women in higher education suggests that the marginalization of women scholars and administrators, with varying degrees of success and disparities, is a global phenomenon. Dines (1993) indicates that, "the global picture is one of men outnumbering women at about five to one at middle management level and at about twenty or more to one at senior management level" (p. 11).

In country after country we find that women hold less than 50 % of academic and administrative posts in higher education institutions (Jarboe 2013; The White House Project 2009). They tend to be overrepresented in lower level academic and middle management positions and their participation relative to men decreases at successively higher levels (Madsen 2012). Representation varies between about 10 and 20 % at middle management level and from 0 to 10 % at senior management level. Representation in the committee system follows a similar pattern with women more likely to be members of departmental and faculty committees than on governing boards or councils. A consequence of this pattern of decreasing representation at successively higher level is that senior women frequently find themselves isolated in hierarchies, which are predominantly male (Dines 1993).

Brooks (1997) research on academic women in the United Kingdom and New Zealand reveals disturbing patters of exclusion for female students, faculty and administrators. Although patterns of representation of female students in the UK have shifted from complete exclusion at the turn of the twentieth century, to the point where they represented 50 % of the student population in the 1990s, female scholars and administrators continue to be marginalized (Jarboe 2013). That is, the increase in the student population has not translated into a significant change in the representation of female faculty and administrators, even in departments where female students have been heavily recruited. Brooks (1997) notes that in 1991, female faculty comprised 4.7 % of full professors, 10.3 % of senior lecturers and readers and 23.1 % of lecturers. Further, a disproportionately high percentage of women are employed as contract workers (non-tenure track) and occupy the lowest academic ranks; that is, lecturers, junior lecturers, or tutors (Brooks 1997). Similar patterns of inequity are prevalent in institutions of higher education in other countries including Canada (Acker and Feuerverger 1997), and the United States (Acker and Feuerverger 1997; Glazer-Raymo 2001); Martin 2000; (Martinez and Renn 2002; The White House Project 2009). While the socio-cultural conditions and political particularities in these countries differ significantly from each other, the conditions of female academics are remarkably similar.

Even with limited quantitative and qualitative data from official sources, it is safe for us to claim that the east and the west meet when it comes to the under-representation of women leaders in higher education. But local and cultural factors, along with the "glass ceiling" effect, impact more significantly on women scholars in developing countries, such as India, Malaysia, Indonesia, and Arab States (Chitnis 1993); Hammoud 1993; (Luke 2002; Omar 1993; Setiadarma 1993). These factors may include psychological, political, historical, religious, cultural, racial, social, and familial status of women in these countries, which exhibit both commonalities and distinctions compared with what their western counterparts experience.

In comparison with their western counterparts, academic women in developing countries suffer more in their professional progression from insufficient access to higher education. For example, in developed countries women comprise 52 % of tertiary students, while such access ranges from 33 % in China to 49 % in Latin America and the Caribbean (Singh 2002). India boasts one of the largest higher education systems in the world, with the number of women's colleges increasing substantially from 780 colleges in 1986–1987, 1,195 in 1996–1997 and 1,600 in 2002. Even so, women's enrolment only accounts for 40 % of the total enrolment (Cheney 2005) Furthermore, as noted by Chitnis (1993), the representation of Indian women scholars is extremely small and highly skewed in terms of disciplines and their geographically location. Similar patterns of marginalization of women scholars have been observed in South Africa, where race has also exacerbated their situation. In the USA, Blacks and women tend to be relegated to the lower ranks with a disproportionate number in service as opposed to academic and administrative positions. A study conducted by Mabokela (2000) demonstrates that in a 13-year period between 1983 and 1995, the proportion of women in senior administrative positions at one prestigious university increased very slightly from 14.55 % in 1983 to 15.35 %. At another university there was 1 woman administrator on the staff in 1983 compared to 57 male colleagues, 13 years later in 1995, there were 5 women and 92 male (Mabokela 2000) administrators.

It is even harder for women in some Asian countries to reach top management positions in higher education institutions due to the deeply ingrained feudal social and cultural prejudice against females. Some scholars advocate the use of similar approaches in Asian countries to those in the West: legislative and infrastructure support, financial and social measures to increase women's enrolment in postgraduate education, training programs and courses, establishment of networks, and mentoring (Chitnis 1993); Hammoud 1993; (Omar 1993; Setiadarma 1993; Singh 2002). However, Luke (1999) contends that the western emphasis on individualism and goal-directed self-promotion for women's career mobility may not necessarily apply in "Asian" cultural contexts.

When we examine Arab States as an example, where Islamic law governs the legal codes of personal status, even with advances in recent decades, the status of women in this region of the world is still inferior to that of men. Women accounted for only between 10 and 15 % of the total labor force, recorded as among the lowest in the world. Data from Arab states also showed that women are underrepresented in both academic and administrative posts at higher education institutions, particularly in top administrative positions. Hammoud (1993) reported that in the institutions of his study, women constituted 15.5 % of the total academic staff, 16.7 % of the total administrative directors, 16 % of the total chairpersons of academic departments, 5 % of the total numbers of Deans of Colleges, and top level positions (President and Vice-President as well as Board of Trustees members) are almost 100 % male. Of the factors impeding women's access to higher education management in Arab states, traditional attitudes and stereotypes in these areas are most noteworthy. Women are primarily deemed as wife and mother, physiologically and intellectually inferior to men, naturally emotional and lacking in self-discipline, and thus not fit for leadership and decision-making positions (Hamdan 2005; Hammoud 1993). The most irrevocable prejudice comes from women themselves as surveys in Arab states showed female respondents believed women should be confined to some traditional professions if they chose to work and they should discontinue work if it conflicted with family duties (as cited in Hammoud 1993).

As the preceding discussion indicates, there are common threads that transcend the professional experiences of women scholars and administrators regardless of their social, political, and cultural context. These trends present a disturbing global pattern of continuing disparities and institutionalized practices of inequity, which continue to place women scholars and administrators on the margins. Turning to Africa, the discussion that follows in this chapter focuses on the African continent as a whole and then uses Ghana and South Africa as case studies to help understand issues surrounding the leadership of women in higher education.

The Status of Women in Higher Education in the African Context

As mentioned previously, historically women were excluded from higher education both as students and staff (Mama 2003). Reliable continental statistics are hard to find but over the years research in different African countries has revealed some general figures that can provide insight into the status of women in higher education. In 1996 only 3 % of Africa's professoriate were women with only 25 % of women enrolled as students in institutions of higher learning (Mama 2003). Across different African countries women represent a significantly high number of support staff with miniscule numbers of academic staff. Table 4.1 shows how males dominate the higher education space as academic and research staff and this has implications for the gender composition of leadership tiers given that a larger male contingency already exists in the academy.

Although the gender composition varies across the continent, the consistent pattern is that few women are employed in senior administrative and leadership positions. In the rare cases where women in leadership are found, they occupy managerial positions that can be viewed as gendered and more suitable for women to lead such as departments related to student welfare and human resources (Mama 2003). A closer analysis of South Africa and Ghana reveals general trends on the continent to help facilitate a better understanding of the status of women in higher education.

Table 4.1 Percentage distribution of male to female academic and research staff in African countries

Country	% Male research and academic staff	% Female research and academic staff
Ethiopia	93.9 %	6.1 %
Uganda	80.3 %	19.7 %
Nigeria	87.6 %	12.4 %
Sierra Leone	87.1 %	12.9 %
Malawi	71 %	29 %
Mozambique	69 %	31 %
Namibia	56.9 %	43.1 %
South Africa	53.5 %	46.5 %
Zambia	75 %	25 %
Ghana	76 %	24 %

Sources: Adapted from Kotecha et al. (2012), Tettey (2010), and World Bank (2007)
Sierra Leone data from World Bank (2007)
Note: Some figures were calculated by the authors based on initial figures extracted from original sources

South Africa

As shown in Table 4.1, women in South Africa represent close to 47 % of research and academic staff in higher education (Kotecha et al. 2012). Although this number is relatively higher than other African countries what is not visible in these figures is that while more women are indeed present in academia, they are densely populated in lower ranks compared to their male counterparts (Corneilse 2009; Mabokela 2001). The lower the academic rank, the more women one encounters in higher education. Males occupy the majority of professoriate roles and women are mostly employed as junior lecturers or lecturers (see Table 4.2; Mabokela 2001; Maürtin-Cairncross 2009; Tettey 2010).

Occupying close to 60 % of lecturer, junior lecturer and below junior lecturer positions, women are burdened with large teaching responsibilities that limit time available for research (Mabokela 2001). Furthermore, the patriarchal culture of higher education institutions and "androcentric ideologies, particularly as applied to promotion, continue to inhibit women's advancement within institutions" (Maürtin-Cairncross 2009, para. 1). Other challenges women in higher education face such as the lack of support and mentorship (Mabokela 2001; Maürtin-Cairncross 2009) and not being taken seriously or considered to be incompetent for the job. All these barriers negatively impact the ability of women in institutions of higher education to climb the ladder resulting in a limited number of senior academic women from whom institutional leaders are usually selected.

Data on the number of women in senior leadership positions are dated and not easy to verify. As indicated in Table 4.3, data from Higher Education Resource Services (HERS) in 2007 indicates that men dominate senior leadership positions in pubic universities in South Africa (Maürtin-Cairncross 2009). Seven years later, few changes have taken place. A quick perusal of institutional websites in 2014 reveals similar gender disparities. Out of the 24 universities and universities of technology; including the 2 institutions opened in 2014, only 5 (about 20 %) have females as vice-chancellors and often these women are the first to hold such positions in the history of the institutions further confirming the long-standing legacy of patriarchy of South African higher education.

Race, Gender and Leadership in Post-Apartheid South Africa

Emerging from a legacy of apartheid where race and gender inequalities were the social norm, the status of women in education and higher education in South Africa cannot be separated from race relations. Early South African higher education policies recognized the underrepresentation of women and Black people (that is Africans, Coloreds and Indians) in senior academic and administrative positions (White Paper 1997: 2.94).

Table 4.2 Rank of academic staff by gender in 2005

Gender	Professor		Associate Professor		Director		Associate Director		Senior Lecturer		Lecturer		Junior Lecturer		Below Junior Lecturer	
	M	F	M	F	M	F	M	F	M	F	M	F	M	F	M	F
Number	1,630	370	997	424	75	14	169	65	2,451	1,597	3,018	3,139	289	373	29	37
%Female	19%		30%		16%		28%		39%		51%		56%		56%	

Sources: In Maürtin-Cairncross (2009) adapted from the South African Department of Education 2006 report

Table 4.3 Gender distribution of senior leadership positions in South African higher education, 2007

	Vice Chancellor		Deputy Vice Chancellor		Registrar		Executive Director		Deans	
Gender	M	F	M	F	M	F	M	F	M	F
Number	19	4	71	14	18	5	101	21	151	41
%Female	17%		16%		22%		17%		21%	

Source: HERS cited in Maürtin-Cairncross (2009)

In 1993, as South Africa was transitioning to a democracy, Black people represented only 36% of academic staff at historically Black universities (HBUs), 15% at historically English speaking White universities (HWUs) and only 5% at Afrikaans speaking institutions (Organization for Economic Cooperation and Organization for Economic Cooperation and Development 2008). By the year 2003, Black staff represented 70% and 20% of staff at HBUs and English speaking HWUs, respectively (Department of Education 2004). Although more Black people were employed in higher education, they continued to be clustered in institutions that had previously been designated for Black people under apartheid. Black people mostly occupy over 97% of service staff positions (e.g. cleaners, ground and maintenance positions) and only count for 45% of instructional staff in all public institutions (Department of Education 2010). Even though these figures are an improvement from previous years (e.g. 30% in 2001), few Black people are senior academics (i.e. associate or full-time professors) a useful credential to have when promotion to leadership positions is considered. In the year 2012, of the 193 African professors, African women accounted for only 34. Similarly, out of 94 colored professors, Colored women represented only 29 of full-time professors in the country (Price 2014). Such figures are alarming not only in terms of racial disparities but mostly in terms of gender disparities especially for Black women who are relegated to the periphery of higher education even more than African males.

Institutions such as the University of Cape Town argue that there is a limited pool of qualified Black candidates for professorship providing the following justifications: (1) it takes more than 20 years to be promoted to a professor after one obtains his or her PhD (approximately 5 years per stage from junior lecturer, lecturer, senior lecturer, associate professor to professor); (2) Very few Black people pursue academic careers, instead they opt for careers in the civil service and private sector (Price 2014). These factors, UCT argues, contribute to the absence of Black professors not only at UCT, but also across the country.

Although the UCT argument is one possible explanation for the absence of Black senior academics in South African institutions, other research provides counter explanations. For example, Mabokela (2000) examined faculty diversification programs at the University of Cape Town and Stellenbosch University (both historically White universities). From the findings it is evident that the status of Blacks and women has remained unchanged in 20 years at these two institutions as the employment and recruitment of Black academics remains poor (Mabokela 2000).

In 1994 Africans represented 4.01 % of permanent faculty members at UCT, Coloreds 2.14 % and Indians 1.60 % compared to Whites who accounted for 92.25 % of faculty members (Mabokela 2000). In the same year, women represented 22.72 % of faculty members and only 14.63 % (6 out of 41) of executive administrators (Mabokela 2000). Mabokela's study also found that despite the existence of an institutional Equal Opportunity Employment Policy there was no active attempt to find and employ qualified Black academics. The argument posited to support the persistent absence of Blacks in the academy was that they pursued career opportunities in professional sectors outside of higher education (Mabokela 2000). These two institutions are merely examples of the lack of effort among South African higher education institutions to change the gender dynamics within higher education spaces.

In a more recent news article almost 14 years after Mabokela's year 2000 article similar findings persist. In the article Professor Jonathan Jansen, the Rector of the University of the Free State articulates how the under-representation of women in professorships, departmental headships and senior management positions in higher education is usually explained away using excuses about the lack of qualified candidates or as previously mentioned, that women leave academia to pursue careers in government or corporate South Africa. Instead Jansen (2014) argues that the truth is "women are simply not a priority" (para. 5). Jansen argues that higher education leadership remains male-heavy and vice-chancellors, deans and heads of department rarely if at all, make a true effort to "find, nurture, retain and advance women in middle and senior management leadership in higher education" (para. 6). In addition, institutional sexism perpetuates a belief that men are better suited for leadership positions. By and large institutions do not accommodate women and there is no effort to cultivate the next generation of leaders. The argument runs that the failure to develop future women leaders from those entering or already in the pipeline is the reason there is a limited pool of women suitable for leadership positions.

According to Jansen (2014), higher education institutions and their leaders do not invest in the development of women and when they do, the development opportunities provided to the women are inadequate and insufficient. For example, "dropping women into week-long workshops, and then returning them to universities with little evidence of a sustained mentorship programme for promising leadership candidates" (para. 29) coupled with an institutional culture that is hostile to women's advancement results in most women withdrawing from the leadership race. In conclusion Jansen (2014) states that higher education leaders should stop making excuses to explain the underrepresentation of women in leadership. Instead, leaders should cultivate and expand the pool of women academics and administrators and then actually select these women for the various positions they have been nurtured for.

Although higher education leaders often use the absence of suitable women candidates for leadership positions in higher education as an excuse, as Jansen reveals; the statistics show that this excuse is indeed a reality. Without absolving institutions and their leadership of responsibility, we enter this conversation to reveal some of the reasons why so few women leadership candidates are available and how this impacts the underrepresentation of women in leadership in higher education in South Africa, Ghana and the rest of the African continent.

Ghana

While South Africa's emergence from apartheid is relatively recent and vestiges of segregation are still evident, Ghana represents a different history of colonization and race-relations, and a more mature democracy with less racial tensions. Given that the overwhelming majority of the population is Black African, demographic data are usually reported according to the differences in ethnic groups rather than race. Despite different historical paths in these two countries, there are very similar patterns of gender disparity. Women constitute the majority of the total population at 51.2% with men representing the remaining 48.8% (Ghana Statistical Services [GSS] 2013). Even though they represent the majority, women in Ghana exist in a social and cultural patriarchy where women are considered to be subordinate to men and this permeates academic institutions as well as other public spaces (Ohene 2010). For example, women represent only 15% of parliamentarians and less than 10% of directors in different ministries, political spaces with significant power to influence national level gender relations. In higher education, women represent only 24% of research and academic staff, less than half of women's representation in South Africa (Ohene 2010).

Women's underrepresentation in higher education impacts the number of women available for promotion to leadership positions. However, the number of women available is merely a product of other factors associated with the higher education institutional place, space and culture. First, Ohene (2010) suggests that historically universities in Ghana were established as places where men could be educated. Women were viewed as being academically and intellectually inferior thus they were excluded from academic work (Ohene 2010). The legacy of higher education as a male space is consistent with Mama's (2003) analysis of the history of academe on the African continent. Masculine organizational cultures are a barrier to women's participation in higher education institutions in other African countries (Mabokela and Magubane 2004). Second, the negative experiences of women who have managed to enter academic spaces serve as barriers to women's career advancement in the academy. Tsikata's (2007) study on the experiences of faculty members at the University of Ghana highlighted how women academics at the university struggled to navigate and advance their careers in the institution in which men occupy almost all senior positions. Tsikata's findings correspond with the notion of institutional sexism as articulated by Jansen (2014) such that men occupy leadership positions and the culture within higher education in Ghana continues to believe that leadership positions are fit for men and not for women.

Intersections of Race and Gender: Tokenism, Isolation, and the Pressure to Prove

The continuing impact of race noted in the South Africa and to a lesser in Ghana, is evident in other countries. A review of the literature revealed a number of common themes that have emerged, that continue to impact the professional journeys of African women academics and administrators, even those considered to be success-ful. Some examples can be found in the United States, a country that has a long history of legislative and other interventions to address disparities.

> Tokenism masks racism and sexism by admitting a small number of previously excluded individuals to an institution. At the same time a system of tokenism maintains barriers of entry to others. (Greene 1997, p. 89)

In the US, women of African descent in particular are under-represented in the faculty and administrative ranks. Even in academic disciplines such as education and the other social sciences, which have historically graduated a slightly higher proportion of under-represented minorities, Gregory (1995) notes that these schol-ars tend to be relegated to lower rank, non-tenure track positions in the 2-year col-lege sector. This is a trend that has also been observed in African universities.

It is disconcerting to note that after 50 years of affirmative action programs and other federally mandated measures to address historical racial and gender dispari-ties in the US, many African American women scholars continue to be the first, the only or one of very few in their respective academic departments. There are serious challenges that come with the position of being the first or the only, a phenomenon that has been observed among the few African women leaders in South Africa and Ghanaian universities. Kanter (1977) contends that women, whom she identifies as "tokens" in predominantly male organizations (or academic disciplines), are placed under constant psychological pressure, scrutiny from colleagues, and isolation because of their small representation. While African academic leaders do not char-acterize themselves as "tokens," they (we) acknowledge that their chronic under-representation places them in the spotlight, where it is impossible for these individuals to remain anonymous and have any privacy, when all of their profes-sional actions are public.

This professional isolation may manifest in terms of the value placed on the research and intellectual contributions that African scholars and leaders make to a given department, institution, or academic discipline. Potgieter and Moleko (2004) illuminate this professional isolation in their assertion that knowledge production within the academy is a "Eurocentric, masculinist process" (p. 86) that devalues intellectual contributions of African women. The fact that African scholars and administrators (as the only Black or one of very few) often do not have colleagues in their departments who share their research interests means that they have limited opportunities for collaboration in research projects and grant activities within their departments. This is particularly critical for new scholars who would not only ben-efit immensely from the intellectual exchange that emerges from collaborative work, but also from the opportunity to engage their senior colleagues who could potentially serve as mentors. Professional relationships that stem from these collaborative activities do not only provide networking opportunities, but may become especially critical in the tenure and review process where senior colleagues could serve as cultural translators, to assist new scholars to unravel the subtle nuances of their department. Therefore, by being isolated, African women scholars miss these critical opportunities. By being the only, or one of very few, African women academics rarely have opportunities for meaningful intellectual dialogue and exchanges that can contribute constructively to their research. While colleagues may view the research of some African academics as "interesting" or "different," this does not necessarily translate into active interest to understand or engage this work. Therefore, not only does marginalization continue but more critically, negative evaluations may result from colleagues who may not necessarily understand the scholarship of African academics.

This isolation can be further exacerbated by the tendency of colleagues from the dominant groups – be it race or gender – to view successful academic women and administrators "special" or "different," rather than intelligent individuals who can make significant contributions. Implicit in this statement is the flawed but deeply ingrained perception that African women academics and administrators are intellectually inferior (Woods 2001). Therefore, those who succeed are the anomaly. This unfounded perception absolves the institution from any responsibility it may have or role it may play in creating the institutional conditions that impede the professional accomplishments of African women faculty and administrators.

Potgieter and Moleko (2004) argue that another way in which tokenism manifests itself is by acknowledging the professional accomplishments of individual women, while maintaining the perception that the group is below standard. With statements such as *"You are so different; how have you managed to kick all the cultural socialization? ... I even at times forget that you are Black"* (p. 88), there is an implicit attitude that in order to be successful as academics Blacks have to be different from their peer group, and this difference means embracing more Eurocentric ways of knowing and doing. The preceding example highlights a phenomenon Kanter (1977) identifies as symbolic consequence, where members of a minority group experience pressure to become representatives of their race and gender in response to the stereotypical beliefs of their majority peers, and the subsequent treatment that follows from that stereotyped portrayal. Due to the visibility of underrepresented African women in the academy, majority faculty members may project their stereotypical views onto them and when they fail to respond in the expected way, they may be dismissed as untrue representatives of their race. Collins (2000) asserts that those African women who accept these stereotypical projections about the roles and contributions of Black scholars are "likely to be rewarded by their institutions, but often at significant personal costs; those challenging them run the risk of being ostracized." Therefore, there is an expectation that the Black faculty and administrators will adjust themselves to the organization (university), but with little acknowledgement that the presence of African academics and administrators will also impact the institution. As Maphai (1989), explains,

> Most (organizations) operate from the assumption that Blacks are defective. Often no question is raised regarding the institution. Black(s) are provided with a mentor(s) who will assist (them) to adjust to the company. There is no remedial course for the company to adjust to Blacks.

Emerging from the pervasive tendency to define the professional accomplishments of African academics in terms of the "blackness" rather than their disciplinary expertise, Black scholars are faced with the additional burden of having to prove their intellectual worth to their colleagues and in some cases, their students as well. Many African American academics experience the additional burden to establish themselves as *qualified* experts to overshadow their *token status* and the pervasive perception that they are *affirmative-action hires*. Because of the historical racial relationship between Black and Whites in South Africa (as well as in other countries (for example, United States), where race relations have been particularly turbulent, women are sometimes presented in the care-taker, mother role. Hooks (1999) contends that this care-taker role manifests in relationships and expectations that African American women have with colleagues and students on their university campuses. As she explains (p. 154),

> Racist and sexist assumptions that Black women are somehow innately more capable of caring for others continue to permeate cultural thinking about Black female roles. As a consequence, Black women in all walks of life, from corporate professionals and university professors to service workers, complain that colleagues, co-workers, and supervisors, etc, ask them to assume multi-purpose caretaker roles ... to be that all nurturing breast – to be the mammy.

The challenge is that the service responsibilities that come with this mothering role are often not acknowledged in the reward structures of the university. Therefore, these become extra responsibilities, in addition to their teaching, research, and service obligations. Adusah-Karikari (2008) states that these extra responsibilities that are often helping pastoral roles do not have benefits for women's advancement in the academy. Those African scholars who do not embrace this caretaker role, with selfless and self-sacrificing zeal are projected in negative ways, as if they are neglecting part of their responsibility. Adusah-Karikari (2008) highlights how in Africa "gender-based social roles irrelevant to the workplace are carried into the workplace" (p. 48). Universities in Ghana perpetuate the sexual division of labor such that men who are viewed as natural leaders serve in most senior positions and women occupy lower-paid and insecure jobs, ultimately confirming universities as patriarchal spaces (Adusah-Karikari 2008).

Retention is another manifestation of professional isolation that many African academics and administrators experience. As Cose (1993) and Maphai (1989) have observed, the acculturation of new employees into an organization seems to be a one-way process, where new employees are expected to adjust themselves to the norms and values of their organization. There is little acknowledgment that the new entrants may in turn impact the culture of the organization. There are various issues that may compromise the ability of an institution to retain its African academics and administrators.

The preceding discussion highlights some of the persistent challenges that continue to affect the professional lives of African women scholars and administrators. The discussion clearly demonstrates that while there are pockets of success for African academic leaders, there are continuing race and gender disparities. Critically, there are institutional barriers that fail to take full advantage of the expertise and contributions that African women academic leaders could make.

Future Considerations

The status of academic women in higher education in Africa and around the world has been documented time and again with very little action taken to redress the gender inequalities found in higher education leadership. Even though women are participating in higher education at increasing rates, especially at the undergraduate level, these trends in enrollment are not reflected in increased representation in senior academic or administrative positions. Emerging from the discussion in this chapter, we offer recommendations that institutions need to consider to address the underrepresentation of women in higher education leadership on the African continent.

First, higher education spaces and cultures need to be more receptive to professional contributions that women academics and administrators can make. The traditional notion of higher education and knowledge creation being a male domain needs to be discarded. While one recognizes that these gendered ideas stem from wider societal cultures and norms, institutions of higher learning have the responsibility to lead by example and not be satisfied with perpetuating gender and other inequalities (Adusah-Karikari 2008). Achieving the goals of gender equity will require fundamental organizational change in the culture and climate of universities. Verbeke, Volgering and Hessels (as cited in Allen 2003) define organizational climate as "the reflection of the way people perceive and come to describe the characteristics of their environment" and organizational culture as reflecting "the way things are done in an organization" (p. 63). Both climate and culture work together to guide the actors in an organization. Such a cultural and climatic change requires the input of all actors within the university space, from leadership to students and support/facilities staff. However, Jansen (2014) places onus on leadership in particular as being the main driving force in changing the role and status of women in higher education.

Second, as articulated by Jansen (2014), institutions need to not only cultivate talented women but also actively select these women for leadership positions when the openings are available. It is of no use to have these women prepared to take on certain roles if there is no show of good faith in their ability to do so. Women have a great deal to offer in the higher education environment and their contributions need to be recognized and supported. In order for the culture and climate of higher education to change leaders and all other actors in the organization need to be able to see how the presence of women in leadership positions is directly linked and beneficial to the goals of the institution (Katz and Miller 1996). Drafting these ideas and engaging in dialogue with all institutional stakeholders where a shared meaning and value of women is fostered, will yield positive results.

Finally, in addition to redefining higher education as a gender inclusive place, the spaces and practices of higher education need to be accommodate women's socio-cultural roles outside of the institution. The requirements to participate in research, teaching, and service coupled with the extra responsibilities outside of the work-place (e.g. childcare) serve as a barrier to promotion for significant numbers of women in higher education. Existing promotion structures favor men over women as often teaching and service are not awarded the same weight as research, thus disadvantaging women who are already responsible for the bulk of teaching in their lower faculty positions. In addition, as women are often wives and mothers, these responsibilities do not allow for them to be as engaged in their scholarship as their male counterparts (Rhoton 2011). Therefore, providing adequate financial, mentor-ship and other institutional support such as daycare facilities and breastfeeding rooms for new mothers (Jansen 2014) will allow women to compete with their male counterparts without being taken away from the workplace as much as they are cur-rently forced to.

Women are an important part of the development of any country and continent. With impending retirements of many senior and mostly male academics and admin-istrators expected within the next decade, as well as competition from other sectors for qualified candidates, universities do not have the luxury to marginalize women and exclude them from the pool of potential applicants for future academic posi-tions. African universities of the twenty-first century will only be globally competi-tive when they can harness and engage the talents and expertise of all their employees.

References

Acker, S., & Feuerverger, G. (1997). Enough in never enough: Women's work in Academe. In C. Marshall (Ed.), *Feminist critical policy analysis: A perspective from post-secondary educa-tion* (pp. 122–140). London: Falmer Press.

Adusah-Karikari, A. (2008). *Experiences of women in higher education: A study of women faculty and administrators in selected public universities in Ghana.* Doctoral dissertation. Athens: University of Ohio.

Allen, D. K. (2003). Organisational climate and strategic change in higher education: Organisational insecurity. *Higher Education, 46,* 61–92.

Association of American Colleges and universities (AACU). (2009). Global perspective. *On Campus With Women, 38*(1). Retrieved from: http://www.aacu.org/ocww/volume38_1/global.cfm

Brooks, A. (1997). *Academic women.* Bristol: Society for Research Into Higher Education and Open University Press.

Cheney, G. R. (2005). *India education report.* National Center on Education and the Economy. Retrieved from, http://www.ncee.org/wp-content/uploads/2013/10/India-Education-Report.pdf

Chitnis, S. (1993). The place of women in the management of higher education in India. In E. Dines (Ed.), *Women in higher education management* (pp. 81–103). Paris: United Nations Educational, Scientific and Cultural Organization (UNESCO)/Commonwealth Secretariat.

Collins, P. H. (2000). Towards an afrocentric feminist epistemology. In P. Kivisto (Ed.), *Social theory: Roots and branches* (pp. 329–339). Los Angeles: Roxbury Publishing.

Corneilse, C. (2009). *Living feminism in the academy: South African women tell their stories.* Doctoral dissertation. College Park: University of Maryland.

Cose, E. (1993). *The rage of a privileged class.* New York: Harper Perennial.

Department of Education. (2004). *Education statistics in South Africa at a glance in 2002.* Pretoria: Department of Education.

Department of Education. (2010). *Education Statistics in South Africa in 2008.* Pretoria: Department of Education.

Dines, E. (1993). Overview. In E. Dines (Ed.), *Women in higher education management* (pp. 11–29). Paris: United Nations Educational, Scientific and Cultural Organization (UNESCO)/Commonwealth Secretariat.

Ghana Statistical Services. (2013). *2010 Population and housing census: National analytical report.* Ghana: Ghana Statistical Services.

Glazer-Raymo, J. (2001). *Shattering the myths: Women in academe.* Baltimore: Johns Hopkins University Press.

Greene, L. S. (1997). Tokens, roles models and pedagogical politics: Lamentation of an African American Law professor. In A. K. Wing (Ed.), *Critical race feminism* (pp. 88–95). New York: New York University Press.

Gregory, S. (1995). *Black women in the academy: Their secrets to success and achievement.* New York: University Press of America.

Hamdan, A. (2005). Women and education in Saudi Arabia: Challenges and achievements. *International Education Journal, 6*(1), 42–64.

Hammoud, R. S. (1993). Bahrain: The role of women in higher education management. In E. Dines (Ed.), *Women in higher education management* (pp. 31–51). Paris: United Nations Educational, Scientific and Cultural Organization (UNESCO)/Commonwealth Secretariat.

Hooks, B. (1999). Theory as liberatory practice. *Yale Journal of Law and Feminism, 1,* 1–12.

Jansen, J. (2014, August 8). The academy must bridge the gender divide. *Mail & Guardian.* Retrieved: http://mg.co.za/article/2014-08-08-the-academy-must-bridge-the-gender-divide

Jarboe, N. (2013). *Women count: Leaders in higher education 2013.* UK, Women Count Org. Retrieved: http://www.kpmg.com/UK/en/IssuesAndInsights/ArticlesPublications/Documents/PDF/Market%20Sector/Education/women-count-leaders-higher-education-2013.pdf

Kanter, R. M. (1977). Some effects of proportions on group life: Skewed sex ratios and responses to token women. *American Journal of Sociology, 82*(5), 965–990.

Katz, J. H., & Miller, F. A. (1996). Coaching leaders through culture change. *Consulting Psychology Journal: Practice and Research, 48*(2), 104–114.

Kotecha, P., Wilson-Strydom, M., & Fongwa, S. N. (2012). *A profile of higher education in Southern Africa – Vol. 2 National Perspectives.* Southern African Regional Universities Association. Retrieved from, http://www.sarua.org/files/publications/SARUA%20leadership%20Dialogue%20Series/SARUA%20Profiles%20of%20HE%20Vol%202.pdf

Luke, C. (1999). *Women's career mobility in higher education: Case studies in Southeast Asia.* Association of Commonwealth Universities Bulleti of Current Documentation, 139.

Luke, C. (2002). *Globalization and women in Southeast Asian Higher Education Management.* Retrieved February 10, 2003 from http://www.tcrecord.org/Content.asp?ContentID=10843

Mabokela, R. O. (2000). 'We cannot find qualified Blacks': Faculty diversification programmes at South African universities. *Comparative Education, 36*(1), 95–112.

Mabokela, R. O. (2001). Hear our voices!: Women and the transformation of South African higher education. *The Journal of Negro Education, 70*(3), 204–218.

Mabokela, R. O., & Magubane, Z. (2004). *Hear our voices: Race, gender and the status of Black South African women in the academy.* Pretoria: Unisa Press.

Madsen, S. R. (2012). Women and leadership in higher education: Current realities, challenges and future directions. *Advances in Developing Human Resources, 14*(2), 131–139. doi:10.1177/1523422311436299.

Mama, A. (2003). Restore, reform but do not transform: The gender politics of higher education in Africa. *Journal of Higher Education in Africa, 1*(1), 101–125.

Maphai, V. T. (1989). Affirmative action in South Africa: A genuine option. *Social Dynamics, 15,* 1–24.

Martin, R. J. (2000). *Coming of age in academe: Rekindling women's hopes and reforming the academy.* New York: Routledge.

Martinez, A. A. M., & Renn, K. A. (2002). *Women in higher education: An encyclopedia.* Santa Barbara: ABC CLIO.

Maürtin-Cairncross, A. (2009). A still chilly climate: Experiences of women in leadership positions in South African higher education. Association of American Colleges and Universities: *On Campus with Women, 38*(1). Retrieved from, http://www.aacu.org/ocww/volume38_1/global.cfm

Morley, L. (2013). *Women and higher education leadership: Absences and aspirations. Stimulus paper.* London: Leadership Foundation for Higher Education. Retrieved from: http://www2.hull.ac.uk/pws4/pdf/LFHE_%20Morley_SP_v3.pdf.

Ohene, I. (2010). *Gender and leadership in higher educational institutional: Exploring perceptions and practices in University of cape Coast, Ghana.* Doctoral dissertation. UK: University of Sussex. Retrieved from: http://sro.sussex.ac.uk/6293/1/Ohene%2C_Isaac.pdf

Omar, A. H. (1993). Women managers in higher education in Malaysia. In E. Dines (Ed.), *Women in higher education management* (pp. 121–133). Paris: United Nations Educational, Scientific and Cultural Organization (UNESCO)/Commonwealth Secretariat.

Organization for Economic Cooperation and Development [OECD]. (2008). *Reviews of national policies for education.* South Africa: OECD.

Potgieter, C., & Moleko, A. S. (2004). Stand out, stand up, move out: Experiences of Black South African women at historically White universities. In R. O. Mabokela & Z. Magubane (Eds.), *Hear our voices! Race, gender and the status of Black South African women in the academy* (pp. 80–95). Pretoria: University of South Africa (UNISA) Press.

Price, M. (2014, July 14). *Staff transformation at UCT. University of Cape Town.* Retrieved from, http://www.uct.ac.za/dailynews/?id=8752

Rhoton, L. A. (2011). Distancing as a gendered barrier: Understanding women scientists' gender practices. *Gender & Society, 25*(6), 696–716.

Setiadarma, M. (1993). Indonesian women in higher education management. In E. Dines (Ed.), *Women in higher education management* (pp. 105–119). Paris: United Nations Educational, Scientific and Cultural Organization (UNESCO)/Commonwealth Secretariat.

Singh, J. K. S. (Ed.). (2002). *Women and management in higher education: A good practice handbook.* Paris: UNESCO.

Tettey, W. J. (2010). *Challenges of developing and retaining the next generation of academics: Deficits in academic staff capacity at African universities. Partnership for Higher Education in Africa.* Retrieved from, http://www.foundation-partnership.org/pubs/pdf/tettey_deficits.pdf

The White House Project. (2009). *The White House Project: Benchmarking women's leadership.* New York: The White House Project. Retrieved, http://www.in.gov/icw/files/benchmark_wom_leadership.pdf.

Tsikata, D. (2007). Gender, institutional cultures and the career trajectories of faculty of the University of Ghana. *Feminist Africa 8: Rethinking Universities, 1*(8), 26–41.

University World News. (2008). *South Africa: Where are the women?* http://www.universityworld-news.com/article.php?story=20080413130436148

White Paper 3: A Programme for the Transformation of higher Education (1997). Pretoria: Department of Education. Retrieved http://www.che.ac.za/sites/default/files/publications/White_Paper3.pdf

Woods, R. L. (2001). Invisible women: The experiences of Black female doctoral students at the University of Michigan. In R. O. Mabokela & A. L. Green (Eds.), *Sisters of the academy: Emergent black women scholars in higher education* (pp. 105–115). Sterling: Stylus Publishing.

World Bank. (2007). *Education in Sierra Leone: Present challenges, future opportunities.* Washington, DC: World Bank Publications.

Part II
Adjusting to Change

Chapter 5
Gender and Academic Work at a Dutch University

Liudvika Leišytė and Bengü Hosch-Dayican

Introduction

European higher education institutions have undergone significant transformation in the past two decades partly due to the New Public Management (NPM) inspired reforms and relatively strong convergence of European higher education systems due to inter-governmental agreements such as the Bologna process (Leisyte and Dee 2012). Universities have been shifting their structures and processes from being 'loosely coupled' to 'tightly coupled' organizations (De Boer et al. 2007). As part of this process a gradual shift away from the classical Humboldtian model of teaching and research unity within the professional role of an academic toward structurally differentiated academic roles has been observed (Leisyte and Dee 2012).

We argue that the increasing division of academic labor may lead either to the emergence of, or the intensification of, already existing inequalities. As research output is often valued more than teaching experience in recruitment and promotion procedures,[1] the disproportionate division between teaching and research roles in academia can produce a segregation of academic roles among marginalized groups, since work tasks with lower status in performance evaluations (teaching) is likely to be concentrated among such groups in an organization (Leisyte and Hosch-Dayican 2014). Consequently, marginalized groups will not have the capacity or opportunity to engage in high status activities (research) and therefore will encounter problems with career advancement. Gender inequality in academia, for example, is highly

---

[1] Success in research remains one of the most important criteria required for promotion to higher-ranked academic positions. A large number of research outputs and grants seems to conform better with contemporary notions of performance, while teaching has fewer measurable outputs (Blackmore and Sachs 2007).

L. Leišytė (✉) • B. Hosch-Dayican
Center for Higher Education (zhb), TU Dortmund University, Dortmund, Germany
e-mail: liudvika.leisyte@tu-dortmund.de; bengue.dayican@tu-dortmund.de

© Springer International Publishing Switzerland 2017   95
H. Eggins (ed.), *The Changing Role of Women in Higher Education*,
The Changing Academy – The Changing Academic Profession in International
Comparative Perspective 17, DOI 10.1007/978-3-319-42436-1_5

likely to be fuelled by this kind of development. Female academics already form a disadvantaged group since they are underrepresented in senior academic positions (see e.g. Eveline 2005; Grummell et al. 2009; Van den Brink 2010). As evidence from recent research suggests, female academics tend to be more involved in teaching than in research or leadership than their male counterparts (e.g. Berg et al. 2003; Barry et al. 2012). Thus, the shifting teaching-research nexus is more likely to introduce a constraint for their career progression for female than for male academics (Leisyte and Hosch-Dayican 2014).

The purpose of this study is to understand the change of academic roles for female academics and the implications of this change for their career opportunities. We focus on the Dutch academic system in general and on one university in particular. The Dutch higher education system is chosen as it is currently one of the poorest performers in Europe when it comes to the female academic representation in the professorial positions.[2]

In this chapter we therefore aim to answer the following research questions:

1. How have the changes in the NPM affected the division of academic labor in the Dutch higher education system?
2. What academic role differentiation can be found in the Dutch higher education system?
3. How is the workload of female academics distributed in the managerial Dutch university?
4. How does this workload differentiation influence their career prospects?

We will address the first two questions by examining secondary sources of data which include a number of European, national and institutional reports, relevant websites as well as pertinent literature. The third and fourth questions will be answered based on a survey conducted among the female academic employees of a particular Dutch university in 2012, complemented with a range of national and institutional documents. Building on these sources, we will organize the chapter in three parts. In the first part we map the changes in higher education policies in Europe with a specific focus on the Dutch higher education system. Further, we discuss the key issues related to the career development of female academic staff and explore the relation between the differentiation of academic roles and gender inequalities in career prospects. The third part will focus on the case analysis of the selected Dutch university. We will study how female academics view their work roles and discuss the implications of the differentiation in their activities for their career development. Finally, we will provide an overall reflection on the changes in teaching-research nexus and career prospects in the light of our findings.

---

[2]The proportion of women in academic top positions in the Netherlands saw an incremental increase from 8 % in 2002 to 13 % in 2010 (European Commission 2012). Further, the Dutch higher education system has a relatively new system of job ranking, creating highly differentiated formal positions in which teaching and research tasks may occur in different proportions while sticking to the traditional Humboldtian model of teaching-research nexus (De Weert 2009: 148).

New Public Management Reforms and Dutch Higher Education System

Managerial control within universities has been strengthened by NPM-inspired governmental policies geared towards establishing the mechanisms of the private sector within the system of higher education, such as increasingly competitive allocation of state funding for universities based on output-oriented performance reviews. As a consequence of these reforms initiated in the 1990s, starting with the UK and gradually spreading into continental Europe (De Boer et al. 2007), universities in Europe have become more autonomous in acquiring and managing their resources and at the same time more accountable to the increasing variety of stakeholders. As part of these processes, universities have tried to modify their organizational structures and have increasingly become more 'corporate' organizations which aim primarily at maximizing their efficiency and effectiveness in order to be able to compete for resources (Leisyte and Dee 2012). These organizational-level changes imply a change in the work conditions of individual academics, in terms of increasing temporary, project-based contracts, the use of performance reviews where research outputs are emphasized, and the division of labor among academics in terms of teaching, research and administration. In particular, this latter development resulted from universities' struggle to increase student numbers, stronger accountability demands to managers and external funders, as well as the need to attract external grants.

The changes in higher education and research organizations in the past decades outlined above are believed to have led to a gradual shift away from the classical Humboldtian model of the teaching-research nexus toward structurally differentiated academic roles in European universities (Leisyte et al. 2009). The Humboldtian ideal, which emphasizes the interrelated unity of teaching and research within the professional role of an academic (Clark 1983), is increasingly put under pressure in the face of the policies that aim at augmenting intra-organizational efficiency and effectiveness. This aim could entail the separation of teaching and research functions by separating personnel categories as well as organizational units and by separate funding for research and teaching (Leisyte 2007; Leisyte and Dee 2012; Leisyte and Hosch-Dayican 2014). Moreover, the massification of higher education can also influence the shift in the teaching-research nexus towards separation since higher teaching workloads may otherwise not be effectively dealt with. The consequence is the transition to the so-called post-Humboldtian model which is characterized by "a differentiation of roles and/or organizations and/or resources for teaching and research" although both roles are still expected of academics at a university (Schimank and Winnes 2000: 398).

These structural shifts have also taken place in the context of the Dutch higher education system as a consequence of the NPM-oriented public sector reforms in the Netherlands; with particular implications for management practices at universities. The increasing performance and efficiency demands resulting from these practices have, in turn, to a large extent modified the formal regulations of work conditions and job descriptions of academics.

Higher Education Reforms in the Netherlands and Management Practices at Dutch Universities

The Dutch government has traditionally played an important role in the coordination of the higher education system. In the Dutch context the higher education reforms in the 1980s strengthened university autonomy and management (De Boer and Huisman 1999). In 1985 the government introduced the concept of 'steering from a distance', under which the universities have been given institutional autonomy in hiring academic staff, raising funds, maintaining their own property and engaging in entrepreneurial activities (Leisyte and Dee 2012). The NPM-inspired reforms of the 1990s echoed this concept as they urged universities to become real corporate organizations which can be prompt in responding to the needs of the labor market and economy overall (Leisyte et al. 2008; Leisyte and Hosch-Dayican 2014).

The implications of the policy changes for Dutch universities have been widely discussed (De Boer et al. 2007). As studies have revealed, managerial power has increasingly shifted to the appointed Executive Boards and deans who have become professional managers. This, in turn, has led to increased administrative hierarchies and professionalization of the human resources departments in Dutch universities. Furthermore, the increasing audit logic in the form of output monitoring and increasing competition for resources have stressed the need to diversify income sources (De Boer et al. 2007). As a result, hiring and promotion criteria in universities have increasingly included numbers of publications in high-ranking journals and success in attracting external research funding (Leisyte 2007; Leisyte et al. 2008). The yearly academic staff performance reviews, from being part of an ad-hoc formality, have increasingly become part of the obligatory organizational routine and have additionally been used to discuss what needs to be achieved in terms of research outputs for the next year, what funding needs to be brought in and what expectations there are towards a contribution to the department to achieve promotion (Leisyte and Dee 2012). One explicit example of the changes has been the introduction of the "tenure-track system" whereby promising staff are hired and their performance expectations are laid down in the time-limited contract. Where the performance is satisfactory the candidates should be promoted to the associate professor and professor levels and are granted tenured (permanent) contracts. In case of failure, they leave the institution (Leisyte and Hosch-Dayican 2014).

The current recession has strengthened managerial levers in Dutch universities towards following stricter rules, more rigid budgeting, a greater use of the non-extension of temporary contracts and hiring freezes. Thus, university human resource policies and procedures have been streamlined and the working conditions and requirements have been increasingly geared towards standardization and performance measurement. In spite of the increasing autonomy of university management in determining their own human resources policies, the employment conditions and benefits for academics are still covered by the "Collective Labour Agreement of Dutch Universities". In addition to employment conditions, the overall division of teaching, research and administration tasks is also centrally defined by this national agreement, which is a particular aspect of the Dutch higher education system that might have specific consequences for the teaching-research nexus.

Teaching-Research Nexus in the Dutch Academic Classification System

The Dutch NPM-inspired reforms in the 1990s changed academic staff employment regulations so that academics were no longer public servants but the employees of universities. This new classification of academic positions (*Universitair Functieordenen* – UFO) was introduced in 2003 and is part of the Collective Labour Agreement of Dutch Universities and features "diversified career patterns in which teaching and research tasks may occur in different proportions" (De Weert 2009: 148). As a result the various roles, tasks and responsibilities to be carried out to achieve specific results have been made explicit by formal criteria that apply to academic employment practices in Dutch universities. This agreement is negotiated between the Association of Universities in The Netherlands (VSNU) representing the 14 Dutch universities and three trade unions (Timmers et al. 2010). It regulates academic as well as non-academic job profiles and salary levels for all Dutch universities.

This new system shifted the focus from years of work experience and performance towards core activities and competencies. The UFO academic profiles are composed mainly of teaching, research and administrative tasks. Depending on the weighting of these tasks within the position the following academic profiles are defined: Lecturers, Researchers, University Lecturers (equivalent to Assistant Professor), Senior University Lecturers (equivalent to Associate Professor), and Full Professors[3] (see Table 5.1). A specified mix of academic activities is foreseen for each one of these positions, which are furthermore broken down into levels differentiated according to the composition of academic activities (Leisyte and Hosch-Dayican 2014).

Table 5.1 reveals first of all that teaching-only (lecturer) and research-only (researcher, post-doc) positions are already a part of the Dutch academic career trajectories (Ibid.). The number of academics in such positions has been increasing substantially since 1990, while a recent study by De Goede et al. (2013) demonstrates

---

[3] In addition to these positions, a common practice in Dutch universities is to employ doctoral candidates as a part of academic staff with employment contracts. The position is called "Research Assistant Trainee" (AiO), consisting mainly of research tasks with approximately 20 % teaching duties (see De Weert and Boezerooy 2007).

Table 5.1 Distribution of tasks among per academic position according to the UFO criteria

	Lecturer	Researcher	Assistant professor	Associate professor	Full professor
Teaching					
Development	±		√	√	√
Execution	√		√	√	√
Examination	√		√	√	
Evaluation	±		√	√	
Coordination				√	
Supervising students	√	√	√	√	√
Acquisition of contracted teaching			±	√	√
Accounting for contracted teaching					√
Supervising PhD students			√	√	√
Teaching total %	**91**	**14**	**54**	**53**	**40**
Research					
Planning/development		√		√	√
Execution		√	√	√	√
Publication		√	√	√	
Coordination		±	√	√	
Accounting for contracted research		±			√
Supervising research related personal		√			
Acquisition of contracted research		±	±	√	√
Dissemination of findings to public			√	√	√
Research total %	**–**	**79**	**38**	**40**	**33**
Administration					
Participating in working groups and commissions	±	±	√	√	√
Administration of teaching and research					√
Administration of human resources					√
Determining long term goals for chair					√
Administration total %	**9**	**7**	**8**	**7**	**27**

Source: VSNU (The Association of Universities in the Netherlands as cited in Leisyte and Hosch-Dayican 2014)

√ means full execution of the described tasks, while ± indicates that the task is optional or might vary according to the level within that position. The total percentages were not included as such in the UFO, but were calculated by the authors based on the list of tasks, where √ was given the weight 1 and ± took the weight 0.5

a steep decrease in the number of assistant professors within the same time span. Furthermore, specific levels within teaching and research are intertwined in separate career tracks in the sense that teaching or research tasks can be carried out only for the duration of a previously arranged period. As a result, the majority of the academics appointed to these positions have temporary contracts (De Goede et al. 2013).

For the remainder of the career profiles – assistant, associate and full professors – the traditional Humboldtian teaching-research nexus appears to have been maintained, since a combination of teaching, research and administrative tasks have been specified for these positions in the job classification system. Even for these positions, however, the nexus can be unbalanced over time for a number of reasons:

1. According to the figures in Table 5.1, there is hardly any balance between research and teaching tasks at mid-career levels, that is, assistant and associate professors. More than 50 % of the contract time of mid-career academics is intended for teaching, while administrative tasks take up roughly another 10 %, leaving no more than 40 % of work time for research activities. Although, formally, both teaching and research qualifications are needed for individual promotion towards professoriate, in the practice, a strong research profile (mostly measured by publications in high impact-factor journals and prestigious external research grants) is largely decisive for the renewal of contracts and promotion to higher career levels (Leisyte and Hosch-Dayican 2014). Lack of such a research profile can create a stumbling-block for career advancement of these academics; especially when the particular forms of the Dutch academic context are taken into account. First of all, although assistant and associate professors generally hold a permanent contract, the number of fixed-term contracts for assistant professors has been increasing in the past decade (Van den Brink 2010). Second, promotion to an upward academic rank is highly dependent on available positions, a unique characteristic of the Dutch academic system. Although there have been attempts to introduce the American tenure track system into Dutch universities in the past years, most positions still become available through formal vacancies (Van den Brink 2010). This means that, even with an excellent performance, promotion to higher ranks is not always an option.

2. Though centrally regulated, the new system defines the composition of tasks per profile as dependent on the purpose and tasks of a group. Thus despite the uniformity of classification criteria, the composition of activities within a profile is determined by factors such as the organizational context within which the profile is embedded (that is, the specificity of the chair group) and the foreseen contribution of this profile towards the organization. Individual development plans are used in which different academic roles are acknowledged including both vertical and horizontal mobility (Leisyte and Hosch-Dayican 2014). Academic staff members can be allocated to specific roles on the basis of an assessment of their qualifications, for example, to be more involved in either teaching or research (De Weert 2009). This can be done on a yearly basis in discussions with the direct superiors (usually the professor in the group) (Leisyte and Dee 2012).

It is observed that the level of competition at all academic levels is quite high, and successful recruitment to a higher position is highly dependent on exceptional research performance as well as the managerial context of the university. Mid-career groups are particularly under pressure due to the workload allocation portrayed above, which is slightly to the disadvantage of research tasks. Furthermore, in the context of the rapidly increasing numbers of students since the introduction of the Bachelor and Master degree system in 2002 in the Netherlands (De Weert and Boezerooy 2007), the formal requirements of teaching for mid-career academics may be easily extended to greater workloads than officially classified to the detriment of research. It is therefore dependent on the negotiations with the Chairs of the groups as to how the balance between teaching and research can be maintained. In such a context, the issue of gender balance in the allocation of teaching and research tasks is highly relevant.

Career Prospects of Female Academics

Despite the increasing number of women obtaining doctoral degrees, and despite the increasing emphasis on gender equality measures at universities, female academics remain a minority among academic staff, being severely under-represented in senior academic positions (Valian 1998; Osborn et al. 2000; Benschop and Brouns 2003; Leisyte and Hosch-Dayican 2014). Today in Europe a "leaky pipeline" is a reality in academia leading to 'a profound gender imbalance in a vast majority of countries' (European Commission 2012); the number of female scientists declines at every stage of the academic career path (Osborn et al. 2000; Rees 2002). For example, in 2009 the Dutch higher education system had 42 % female PhD graduates, 26 % female researchers and 13 % female professors (European Commission 2012). More recent research findings also indicate that the gender gap in employment status with respect to part-time and fixed-term employment contracts is highest in the Netherlands compared to a number of other European countries (Goastellec and Pekari 2013).

It is suggested that the reasons for a strong gender imbalance in academic career progression are complex and multi-faceted (Leisyte and Hosch-Dayican 2014). First of all, a set of institutional arrangements of academic careers shaped by the national reforms coupled with the culturally determined stereotypes of gender roles are very strong determinants of inequalities in academic career progression (Van den Brink 2010). Furthermore, the pre-existing hierarchical structure of an organization plays a crucial role in the likelihood of a new employee reaching the top, which might eventually lead to disadvantaging certain groups. Finally, meritocracy being the key determinant for hiring and promotion – where peer-review is the key selection mechanism – has also been shown to have specific biases towards under-represented groups (Lamont 2009). If transparent recruitment, work organization and promotion procedures are absent. women are more likely to be hindered from ascending to the top of the academe due to unwritten norms and rules which are not necessarily accessible to the female academics (Bain and Cummings 2000; Probert 2005; Timmers et al. 2010).

Taking this into account, the transformation of universities towards more tightly managed corporate organizations – although initially seeming to be 'gender friendly' due to making the promotion criteria explicit and standardized – potentially may reinforce the gendered structure, culture and practices at universities. As discussed earlier, growing workloads due to changes in student numbers, as well as the pressures for performance and accountability stemming from increasing competition in the academic labour markets are the most tangible side effects of the NPM-inspired reforms. We have also shown that this increase in the amount of work may be accompanied with the changing balance between the different roles and tasks of teaching, research and administration. Coupled with the pre-existing gender inequalities in Dutch academe, these changes can lead towards a gendered teaching-research nexus in the Dutch system. As a result, informal discrimination is created in the allocation of academic workload among male and female academics which is based on already existing perceptions as well as practices of gender differentiated roles.[4] This development can lead towards a subtle gender divide in modes of employment and between academic roles and activities, which could hinder career progression of female academics in manifold ways (see Le Feuvre 2009; Barrett and Barrett 2011).

Recent findings suggest that female academics indeed find themselves increasingly disadvantaged in terms of academic work as a consequence of institutional change at European universities. Generally, the NPM reforms are seen as "carriers of masculine discourses, emphasizing competition and instrumental reason that has not been to the benefit of women" (Thomas and Davies 2002; Barry et al. 2012: 54) and are found to have affected women academics more than men. For instance, Barry et al. (2012) have found that women are disproportionately concentrated in teaching roles and pastoral care for students, whereas men predominantly occupy research positions such as lecturer/reader and professor both in Sweden and the UK (both countries have undergone NPM reforms in higher education). Similarly, other studies have shown that female academics perform a disproportionate share of academic departments' care work and emotional labour, such as pastoral care or mentoring (Probert 2005; Barrett and Barrett 2011), especially in higher education systems where the level of transparency of information on workload allocation is low. It was demonstrated that female academics spend more time on teaching (Bird 2011), while male academics are more represented in research-only jobs or in positions where teaching and research are balanced (Barrett and Barrett 2011). There is thus clear evidence of a skewed allocation of different academic tasks between male and female academics (Leisyte and Hosch-Dayican 2014).

[4]Already in the aftermath of World War II, a gendered academic workload division was visible in U.S. colleges and universities: Women were excluded from research-intensive disciplines, while they were over-represented in teaching focused liberal arts colleges (Rosenberg 1988; Bird 2011).

The three primary academic activities – teaching, research and administration – are routinely acknowledged as being of equal importance for faculty excellence in university mission statements, and all three are indeed included in promotion criteria at most universities. However, in practice these tasks are not valued to the same degree; achievements in research remain the dominant requirement in promotion criteria to higher academic levels and are perceived also by the staff as pivotal for promotion (Parker 2008; Barrett and Barrett 2011). Teaching, on the other hand, has fewer measurable outputs and remains less valued in faculty evaluation processes (Blackmore and Sachs 2007). Gender inequalities in teaching-research nexus can thus be of utmost importance for the career prospects of female and male academics and can be considered an essential factor in explaining the leaky pipeline syndrome. The workload imbalance disadvantaging research may mean stagnation or disruption of an academic career path, especially for women in mid-career levels such as assistant and associate professor, where the criteria for career progression are particularly demanding with respect to research outputs.

In the Netherlands, similar to other European countries discussed above, female academics are under-represented in almost all academic positions, with the exception of undergraduate and PhD students (Timmers et al. 2010; Van den Brink 2010; Van den Brink and Benschop 2012) despite policy measures taken at national and European level, The Netherlands still ranks very low with respect to the proportion of female full professors compared to other European countries (European Commission 2012). The demands of accountability and performance in terms of research outputs coupled with the increased competition for resources have possibly led to changing the teaching-research nexus and the disproportionate allocation of different tasks at different career levels for female academics. Given the evidence discussed earlier on the effects of NPM on universities, we may assume that the high percentage of dropouts of female academics at mid-career levels in the Netherlands (the leaky pipeline) is to a great extent associated with the changes in academic workload balance (Leisyte and Hosch-Dayican 2014). Thus we formulate the following hypotheses:

H1: *The teaching-research nexus for female academics in the Netherlands features more involvement in teaching than research.*

H2: *Female academics at mid-career levels (assistant and associate professors) in the Netherlands experience a stronger imbalance in teaching-research nexus compared to female academics at other career levels.*

H3: *Career prospects of female academics are constrained by the imbalanced teaching-research nexus, especially at mid-career levels.*

The Case Study University

We have tested our hypotheses by employing the case study method, whereby we selected a Dutch university which has a low proportion of women in senior academic positions. At the same time, typical Dutch employment procedures and role divisions applied in this university. Our data source was an online survey conducted in February-March 2012, where female employees of the case university were approached by an e-mail request to participate. One hundred twenty-nine employees from different career ranks and faculties returned the survey, which represented approximately 25 % of total female academic staff. However, the analyses in this chapter were based on data from respondents at senior academic levels; doctoral candidates were excluded from the analyses since their task allocation profile with respect to teaching and research activities is distinct from the other academic positions due to their specific status.[5] The remaining 66 respondents consisted of lecturers, researchers, assistant and associate professors as well as full professors. Although the data did not allow for comparisons with male academics with respect to workload balance and career progression prospects, they provided the opportunity to explore the relationship between these two undertakings for female academics in the Netherlands (Leisyte and Hosch-Dayican 2014).

Teaching-Research Nexus Among Female Academics

The online survey contained questions on how much time was spent on average in a week on teaching, research, administrative and other activities and thus enabled the measurement of teaching-research nexus. The respondents were given the opportunity to react to these questions on a 5-point-scale consisting of the following categories: less than 20 %, 20–40 %, 40–60 %, 60–80 %, and more than 80 %. Furthermore, respondents were asked to indicate how they perceived the workload balance between their teaching and research activities on a 5-point scale in a separate question. As we were interested in the balance between teaching and research activities, we used these three variables for our assessment of the teaching-research nexus. A preliminary correlation analysis revealed that all three indicators were strongly and significantly related to each other. The time spent on research was positively correlated with the perceived workload balance among female academics (Pearson's $r = 0.601$), while there was a negative correlation between workload balance and the time spent on teaching (Pearson's $r = -0.625$). This shows that having less time for research than for teaching activities was likely to be regarded as an anomaly among female faculty and had consequences for their satisfaction with their workload balance. We also found a rather strong negative correlation between average weekly time spent on teaching and on research (Pearson's $r = -0.714$), indicating that both activities were competing with each other rather than being complementary (Leisyte and Hosch-Dayican 2014).

How is the teaching-research nexus being experienced among female academics? To evaluate the first two hypotheses, the allocation of weekly work time among different activities and the perceived balance between teaching and research were compared across four different academic career levels: lecturers, researchers

---

[5] See the previous section on teaching-research nexus in the Dutch academic job classification system.

Table 5.2 Descriptive analyses of academic activities and teaching-research nexus among academic ranks

	Lecturer	Researcher	Mid-career	Professors
Perceived workload balance between teaching and research	1.20	3.60	2.55	3.03
Time spent on teaching per week	3.20	1.27	2.45	1.78
Time spent on research per week	1.20	4.13	2.31	3.32
Time spent on administrative work per week	2.20	1.13	1.45	1.29
Time spent on other work per week	1.20	1.07	1.33	1.21
N	5	15	42	4

Entries are means. The response scales for all variables vary from 1 to 5, where the ranking is as follows: For perceived workload balance, 1 indicates no balance at all and 5 refers to full balance. For all variables on time spent for academic activities, 1 refers to less than 20 % of weekly work time spent on activity and 5 refers to more than 80 %. Source: Leisyte and Hosch-Dayican 2014

(including junior and senior researchers and post-docs), mid-career academics (assistant and associate professors) and full professors. As can be seen from the Table 5.2, average weekly time spent on teaching and research activities varied markedly among the different academic ranks. In line with their job status, the weekly working time of lecturers and researchers was devoted predominantly to the respective tasks of teaching and research. Administrative and other duties constituted a minor portion of their academic activities, whereas lecturers appeared to have a much higher administrative load compared to researchers (Leisyte and Hosch-Dayican 2014). The reported time allocated to these activities (more than 40 % of their weekly work time) clearly deviates from the UFO regulation where no more than 9 % administrative work is expected for lecturers (see Table 5.1).

This remarkable finding might have been caused by several factors. First of all, the fact that the administration of teaching requires more time than the administration of research due to the high number of students may have led to the perception of work overload in this task among lecturers. Second, the female lecturers might be more prone to be overloaded by the time-consuming and "low status" administrative tasks. Unfortunately, the data at hand do not allow us to test these assumptions about the causes of this imbalance. Yet its implications are demonstrated clearly by the figures on perceived workload balance among lecturers and researchers. While all of the lecturers surveyed experienced almost no balance at all between academic activities, the researchers were distinctively more positive about their workload balance (Leisyte and Hosch-Dayican 2014).

A comparison of the weekly allocation of academic activities among career groups where the teaching-research nexus is supposed to be more balanced showed that the activities also varied among these groups. Mid-career faculty, i.e. assistant and associate professors, seemed to invest equal time in teaching and research tasks, while teaching activities were slightly more emphasized. Thus there seemed to be a high load of both teaching and research for mid-career groups, which was also reflected in their subjective evaluation of the balance between teaching and research activities. They perceived the workload division between teaching and research to be less balanced compared to researchers and professors. This comparison showed that mid-career groups were worse off with respect to the teaching-research balance; they taught more and did less research compared to more junior researchers and full professors. They were also slightly more loaded with administrative and other activities, but the difference was not very pronounced (Ibid.).

In summary, we could not provide unequivocal evidence for a substantial imbalance in the teaching-research nexus with a tendency towards more teaching among all female academics and thus our first hypothesis cannot be corroborated. Teaching and research tasks seemed to take equal time for female faculty in a week. One major drawback of the survey question on the allocated weekly time for academic activities is, however, that the response scale was presented to respondents in the form of categories. It seems that both teaching and research take 40–60 % of the weekly time of both female faculty in general as well as mid-career female academics (which corresponds to 16–24 h a week), yet this is a large range and the actual hours spent on each activity can vary strongly among respondents who indicated this category. Thus this conclusion should be approached with caution. With respect to hypothesis 2, our analysis provides some support for the assumption that mid-career academics are more prone to be affected by the changing teaching-research nexus, in the sense that they have slightly more teaching duties. Thus they come close to the formal description of their tasks in the UFO criteria (see Table 5.1). However, the same problem with the response scale is also present here, so it is not possible to tell precisely how much time they allocate to each activity.

Workload Allocation and Academic Career Prospects

Academic career prospects are related to practices at several different stages of academic employment, varying from recruitment to evaluation and promotion. Since the survey was aimed at assessing the career progression prospects of female academics, it included a variety of statements on evaluation and promotion criteria and how respondents thought they were being affected by them. Scale analyses were conducted to identify the different aspects of career progression measured by these variables, which revealed that they can be categorized under two dimensions: (1) Transparency of evaluation criteria (Cronbach's Alpha = 0.85), and (2) Promotion procedures and prospects (Cronbach's Alpha = 0.81). Accordingly, two additional indices were built in, based on the results of the scale analyses. Table 5.3 presents the mean positions of each academic career level on individual variables as well as the indices of transparency of evaluation and promotion prospects (Leisyte and Hosch-Dayican 2014). The overall impression gained from the mean scores of the indices is that respondents from all ranks were generally neutral about, or rather satisfied with, evaluation and promotion procedures. Assistant and associate professors also did not deviate from this pattern to a substantial extent. The recognition of academic performance, responsiveness of faculty to promotion needs and the level

Table 5.3 Descriptive analyses of academic career progression prospects among academic ranks

	Lecturer	Researcher	Mid-career	Professors
Congruence between task description and evaluation indicators	2.60 (5)	3.47 (15)	3.40 (42)	3.75 (4)
Clear requirements for a positive job evaluation	3.20 (5)	3.40 (15)	3.19 (42)	3.75 (4)
Transparency of evaluation criteria (index)	**3.20 (5)**	**3.67 (15)**	**3.50 (42)**	**3.75 (4)**
Clear criteria for promotion	2.40 (5)	3.00 (15)	2.93 (42)	3.00 (4)
Positive job evaluation leads to promotion	0.00 (5)	0.20 (15)	0.40 (42)	0.50 (4)
Years since last job promotion	4.67 (3)	2.22 (9)	2.54 (35)	3.50 (4)
Responsiveness of faculty to promotion needs	1.80 (5)	2.80 (15)	2.86 (42)	3.00 (4)
Sufficient guidance and feedback for promotion	2.00 (5)	3.13 (15)	2.55 (42)	2.75 (4)
Recognition of teaching and administrative work for promotion	2.40 (5)	2.60 (15)	2.52 (42)	2.50 (4)
Promotion procedures and prospects (index)	**2.33 (3)**	**3.22 (9)**	**3.26 (35)**	**3.50 (4)**

Entries are means; Numbers of respondents are displayed in brackets. For the variable 'positive job evaluation leads to promotion', where the scale features only two points: 0 (yes) and 1 (no). For all other variables, the response scale varies from 1 (disagree) to 5 (agree). The only exception among these is the variable 'years since last promotion', where 1 refers to less than 1 year and 5 refers to more than 6 years. Source: Leisyte and Hosch-Dayican 2014

of guidance for promotion, however, seem to provide less satisfaction, especially among lecturers and researchers.

How were the career prospects portrayed above associated with the teaching-research nexus in this university? Does the balance between teaching and research relate to the career progression of female academics? In hypothesis 3, we proposed that the shifting teaching-research nexus would have a negative influence on career prospects of female academics, an effect that will be more pronounced for mid-career academics. This hypothesis contains several fundamental assumptions. First, a direct relationship between the teaching-research nexus and career progression prospects is assumed. Second, career prospects are expected to differ among career levels, i.e. between mid-career groups and the rest of the academic staff because of the unequal allocation of teaching and research tasks between these career groups with mid-career faculty having a less balanced nexus. Third, the stress is specifically on female academics suggesting that career prospects of (mid-career) female faculty will be more strongly constrained by the changing teaching-research nexus. These assumptions were tested using bivariate correlation as well as stepwise regression analyses. For testing the second assumption, a dummy variable was constructed in which the academics were divided into two groups consisting of mid-

Table 5.4 Correlation matrix for dependent and independent variables

	Mid-career academics	Gender balanced policies at university	Equal opportunities in department	Transparency of evaluation criteria	Promotion procedures and prospects
Workload balance	−0.444*** (66)	0.210 (66)	0.397*** (66)	0.399*** (66)	0.416** (51)
Time spent on teaching	0.474*** (66)	−0.213 (66)	−0.364** (66)	−0.372** (66)	−0.346* (51)
Time spent on research	−0.564*** (66)	0.206 (66)	0.240 (66)	0.219 (66)	0.263 (51)
Mid-career academics	1	0.009 (66)	−0.007 (66)	−0.080 (66)	−0.019 (51)
Gender balanced recruitment and promotion policies at university	0.009 (66)	1	0.319** (66)	0.093 (66)	0.407** (51)
Dedication for equal opportunities in department management	−0.007 (66)	0.319** (66)	1	0.470*** (66)	0.434*** (51)
Transparency of evaluation criteria	−0.080 (66)	0.093 (66)	0.470*** (66)	1	0.486*** (51)
Promotion procedures and prospects	−0.019 (51)	0.407** (51)	0.434*** (51)	0.486*** (51)	1

Entries are correlation coefficients (Pearson's r); ***$p<=0.001$; **$p<=0.01$; *$p<=0.05$
Number of respondents is displayed in brackets
'Mid-career academics' is a dummy variable consisting of two categories, with 1 being mid-career academics (assistant and associate professors) and 0 covering all other career groups. 'Transparency of evaluation criteria' is an additive index of two items that were found to build a common dimension as a result of the factor analysis (see Table 5.4). The scale of the index varies from 1 (low) to 5 (high). 'Promotion procedures and prospects' is an additive index of two items that were found to build a common dimension as a result of the factor analysis (see Table 5.4). The scale of the index varies from 1 (very negative evaluation) to 5 (very positive evaluation). Source: Leisyte and Hosch-Dayican 2014

career academics and other academics. For the third proposition, we used two survey items as control factors – measuring perceptions of equal opportunities in recruitment and promotion at the department and university levels, since the data contains only female respondents and thus does not allow for a comparison by gender.

Table 5.4 presents the results of the bivariate correlation analyses between the teaching-research nexus indicators, the indices of career prospects and the control variables (Leisyte and Hosch-Dayican 2014). We found that both aspects of career advancement seem to be significantly associated with perceived workload balance and time spent on teaching, whereas the direction of the correlation is different. The more respondents felt that there was a balance between their teaching and research duties, the more positive they were about the possibilities of career progression for female academics at their university. In contrast, the weekly teaching load was negatively associated with these factors, suggesting that efforts made in teaching and related activities were not being regarded by respondents as particularly of avail for their career progression. Finally, time spent on research was found not to be significantly related to any aspect of career progression.

A similar pattern of relationships could be found between career levels and teaching-research nexus variables, indicating that female academics in mid-career groups were more likely to perceive an imbalance between teaching and research duties, and to spend more time on teaching and less on research than academics in other ranks. No relationship was found between academic ranks and career progression as the correlation coefficients turned out to be very weak and not significant.

Last but not least, the control variables showed a mixed pattern in their relation to the dependent and independent variables. Perceptions of both equal opportunities at department level and gender-balanced personnel policies at the university were positively correlated with career prospects, whereas the university-level equality measure bore no relationship with the transparency of evaluation. This is probably due to the fact that staff-evaluation talks are still a matter for the department at Dutch universities and are not yet controlled by the university management as strictly as in other contexts. Only the departmental-level equality policies seem to matter for workload balance and weekly teaching time, implying that the allocation of tasks among academics is influenced by the departmental decision-making to some extent (Leisyte and Hosch-Dayican 2014).

The results of the bivariate correlation analyses provide preliminary insights into the relationships between the teaching-research nexus and academic career prospects. However, more valid conclusions about the strength of influence and direction of causality can be achieved by testing the effects of these variables in stepwise regression models. We conducted separate linear regression analyses for two dimensions of career progression prospects (transparency of evaluation and promotion procedures) as two different dependent variables. Furthermore, we carried out the regression analyses independently for each of the three aspects of the teaching-research nexus: workload balance, time spent for teaching and time spent for research. We preferred this option for a number of reasons. First, as discussed in section "Teaching-Research Nexus Among Female Academics", these variables are highly correlated with each other, suggesting that the odds of cancelling out each other's effects are rather high when they are placed in the same model. Second, each teaching-research nexus indicator is likely to have its own consequences for career prospects and therefore it is worth testing the models for each individual variable.

All in all, this results in six separate regression analyses, each of which is conducted in three steps. Relying on the tentative results from the bivariate analyses we decided to apply the following strategy in the stepwise analysis. In the first model, we tested the independent effects of the respective teaching-research nexus indicator on career progression prospects. In the second model, the mid-career dummy was introduced to see whether and how the initial effect of the teaching-research nexus variable would change. Our assumption that mid-career faculty's career prospects were more strongly constrained by the imbalance in teaching and research tasks would be supported if the initial effect becomes stronger. The third model was the full one in which the control factors were also added to the analysis. We used gender-neutral decision-making procedures as control variables in order to make inferences about gender differences in career progression prospects in the absence of male respondents. The underlying idea was that the teaching-research nexus would have less significance for career prospects (or its effect will diminish) if the department or university management takes precautions to ensure gender-neutral recruitment and promotion, which would matter only if there are strong gendered career advancement procedures (Leisyte and Hosch-Dayican 2014).

The results for the two dimensions of career progression prospects are presented in Tables 5.5 and 5.6. Table 5.5 shows that our expectations have been supported to a great extent in relation to the influence of workload balance and the time spent on teaching on perceived transparency of evaluation criteria. Introducing the mid-career dummy in the second model strengthened the effect of these factors, whereas the coefficient of the dummy variable itself was not significant. This means that being a mid-career academic has only an indirect influence on the transparency of evaluation criteria as viewed by the respondents, which is moderated by workload balance and weekly time devoted to teaching. The introduction of equal opportunities' variables also alters the results in the expected way. The effect of workload balance drops remarkably, and the effect of teaching time diminishes while departmental level equality measures have the strongest significant effect on the dependent variable. Interestingly, time spent for research deviates from this pattern where only the equality policies in the department seem to have an influence on this aspect of career progression. The regression analyses which have promotion procedures and career prospects as dependent variables show a very similar pattern and almost replicate the findings for transparency of evaluation (see Table 5.6). However, university-level gender equality measures also seem to matter for this aspect of career progression, probably because promotion criteria are more centrally determined by the university management. In addition, weekly research time turns out to be a predictor of mid-career academics' promotion prospects, although the effect is not very pronounced. The effects of the teaching-research nexus disappear altogether once controlled by equal opportunity policies at both department and university levels, suggesting that there may indeed be gender disparities in the relationship between the teaching-research nexus and promotion practices at this particular university (Ibid.).

The results of the regression analyses thus strongly support our third hypothesis, i.e. that a high teaching load seems to inhibit career progression of female academics. Further, the findings imply that the unbalanced workload allocation is influencing the career development possibilities for mid-career academics. Finally, we can assume that the relationship between the teaching-research nexus and the prospects for career development is affected by gendered practices in the university which has

Table 5.5 Regression models with the dependent variable transparency of evaluation criteria

	Workload balance			Time spent on teaching			Time spent on research		
	Model 1	Model 2	Model 3	Model 1	Model 2	Model 3	Model 1	Model 2	Model 3
Workload balance	0.349*** (0.10)	0.396*** (0.11)	0.252* (0.12)	–	–	–	–	–	–
Time spent on teaching	–	–	–	−0.378** (0.12)	−0.438** (0.13)	−0.274 (0.14)	–	–	–
Time spent on research	–	–	–	–	–	–	0.185 (0.10)	0.215 (0.13)	0.100 (0.12)
Mid-career academics	–	0.286 (0.30)	0.122 (0.29)	–	0.293 (0.31)	0.123 (0.30)	–	0.151 (0.35)	−0.021 (0.33)
Gender balanced recruitment and promotion policies at university	–	–	−0.092 (0.12)	–	–	−0.094 (0.12)	–	–	−0.081 (0.12)
Dedication for equal opportunities in department management	–	–	0.321** (0.10)	–	–	0.335** (0.10)	–	–	0.389*** (0.10)
Constant	2.573*** (0.30)	2.236*** (0.47)	1.978*** (0.52)	4.377*** (0.29)	4.299*** (0.30)	3.246*** (0.59)	3.043*** (0.30)	2.853*** (0.54)	2.249*** (0.57)
Adjusted R²	0.146	0.145	0.236	0.125	0.123	0.229	0.033	0.020	0.189
N	66	66	66	66	66	66	66	66	66

Entries are unstandardized regression coefficients; ***p<=0.001; **p<=0.01; *p<=0.05

Standard errors are displayed in brackets

'Mid-career academics' is a dummy variable consisting of two categories, with 1 being mid-career academics (assistant and associate professors) and 0 covering all other career groups. 'Transparency of evaluation criteria' is an additive index of two items that were found to build a common dimension as a result of the factor analysis (see Table 5.4). The scale of the index varies from 1 (low) to 5 (high). 'Promotion procedures and prospects' is an additive index of two items that were found to build a common dimension as a result of the factor analysis (see Table 5.4). The scale of the index varies from 1 (very negative evaluation) to 5 (very positive evaluation). Source: Leisyte and Hosch-Dayican 2014 been studied, since an emphasis on equal opportunities was found to alter this relationship to a remarkable extent.

Conclusions and Discussion

The first objective of this chapter was to investigate the extent to which NPM-inspired reforms are changing academic work in universities in general and in Dutch universities in particular. A comprehensive review of the pertinent literature has shown that these reforms as expressed through the increasing quantification of research outputs and increasing student numbers are moving the teaching-research nexus towards a post-Humboldtian pattern. This was further illustrated by the formal regulations on academic task division at different career levels. Lecturer and researcher positions with an emphasis on one of the two tasks (with 80–90 % of contract time devoted to either teaching or research) are already a part of the national academic employment agreement. Despite the challenge of higher teaching loads for mid-career academics, the establishment of these differentiated career paths is already perceived as a rational solution for enabling intra-organisational efficiency, effectiveness and professionalization (De Weert 2009).

However, university career advancement still relies on a tight Humboldtian teaching-research nexus, so that academics are expected to carry out both teaching and research, but where research is given more weight than teaching in the evaluation of academic work. The constraints on research time introduced by the changing teaching-research nexus can hinder the possibilities of career development for academics in general; yet it can be argued that this will have a stronger impact on female academics than their male counterparts. Women are traditionally disadvantaged in academic jobs, especially in the Netherlands where the proportion of female academics in senior positions is dramatically low. Furthermore, our review of the literature on the academic career prospects of women revealed that there is a subtle gender differentiation in the division of teaching and research roles (Bird 2011; Barrett and Barrett 2011). These factors are likely to inhibit the research performance of female academics, particularly of those at mid-career stages where research outputs are crucial for career development (Leisyte and Hosch-Dayican 2014).

We therefore explored the distribution of teaching and research among Dutch female academics and the consequences for their career prospects (research questions 3 and 4). First, we tested the hypothesis that women faculty experience a highly imbalanced teaching-research nexus in the sense that their workload allocation features more teaching than research. As we found that teaching and research took the same amount of time among female academics, this hypothesis could not be corroborated. Yet since the answers were measured on a scale which features large intervals of working hours in each category, we have to approach this finding with caution. Turning to our second hypothesis, we found that female academics at Dutch universities at a mid-career level (assistant and associate professors) are only slightly more overloaded with teaching tasks and have less time for research,

Table 5.6 Regression models with the dependent variable promotion procedures and prospects (index)

	Workload balance			Time spent on teaching			Time spent on research		
	Model 1	Model 2	Model 3	Model 1	Model 2	Model 3	Model 1	Model 2	Model 3
Workload balance	0.319** (0.10)	0.395*** (0.11)	0.228 (0.13)	–	–	–	–	–	–
Time spent on teaching	–	–	–	−0.331* (0.13)	−0.371** (0.14)	−0.111 (0.15)	–	–	–
Time spent on research	–	–	–	–	–	–	0.221 (0.12)	0.261* (0.13)	0.056 (0.13)
Mid-career academics	–	0.497 (0.33)	0.196 (0.33)	–	0.271 (0.33)	−0.036 (0.32)	–	0.258 (0.35)	−0.071 (0.33)
Gender balanced recruitment and promotion policies at university	–	–	0.264* (0.12)	–	–	0.275* (0.13)	–	–	0.284* (0.13)
Dedication for equal opportunities in department management	–	–	0.162 (0.11)	–	–	0.224* (0.11)	–	–	0.246* (0.10)
Constant	2.327*** (0.31)	1.736*** (0.50)	1.071* (0.53)	3.955*** (0.32)	3.837*** (0.35)	1.891** (0.69)	2.657*** (0.32)	2.359*** (0.52)	1.426* (0.54)
Adjusted R²	0.156	0.177	0.271	0.102	0.096	0.227	0.050	0.041	0.222
N	51	51	51	51	51	51	51	51	51

Entries are unstandardized regression coefficients; *** $p <= 0.001$; ** $p <= 0.01$; * $p <= 0.05$
Standard errors are displayed in brackets

'Mid-career academics' is a dummy variable consisting of two categories, with 1 being mid-career academics (assistant and associate professors) and 0 covering all other career groups. 'Transparency of evaluation criteria' is an additive index of two items that were found to build a common dimension as a result of the factor analysis (see Table 5.4). The scale of the index varies from 1 (low) to 5 (high). 'Promotion procedures and prospects' is an additive index of two items that were found to build a common dimension as a result of the factor analysis (see Table 5.4). The scale of the index varies from 1 (very negative evaluation) to 5 (very positive evaluation). Source: Leisyte and Hosch-Dayican 2014 whereas the differences between career groups were not very pronounced. In addition, the use of percentage intervals in the response scale hinders the estimation of actual time spent on each activity. Our second hypothesis was thus supported only to a limited extent. Finally, we proposed that an imbalanced workload division will affect the career prospects of female faculty negatively, and tested this assumption with bivariate analyses as well as regression models. Our findings have provided unequivocal support for this expectation. Both perceived workload imbalance and teaching overload turned out to have constraining effects on the career prospects of female academics, whereas belonging to the group of mid-career academics seemed to strengthen this effect.

These findings show that the preconditions for a change in the teaching-research nexus and the development of new academic career paths with a focus on either research or teaching exist in the Netherlands. Teaching-only and research-only positions are already a part of the national formal job classification system. Moreover, as the analysis of the survey shows, teaching and research tasks are being perceived to be competing rather than complementing, and a high load of teaching is being regarded as a burden for academic work (Leisyte and Hosch-Dayican 2014). Yet more data sources are needed to test whether or not the NPM is gender neutral in its effects, and whether the disruption of the Humboldtian model leads towards social differentiation in academe. In this study we utilized data from a survey which was conducted among female academics at a particular university and in this way we shed light on the state and consequences of the teaching-research nexus for female faculty in one organizational setting. By controlling for the effects of gender-neutral recruitment and promotion policies, we also drew preliminary inferences on whether we can speak of a gendered career development at this particular university.

However, the following questions still need to be addressed: Does the changing teaching-research nexus lead female academics to higher teaching workloads and less time for research than is the case for male academics? To what extent can we speak of gendered academic career progression prospects? And is there a difference between male and female academics with respect to the relationship between career advancement and the changing balance of academic work? To answer these questions it is necessary to compare the allocation of teaching and research duties as well as research productivity and career prospects among male and female academics. Case studies and cross-national studies in this direction are available (see e.g. Bentley 2011; Bentley and Kyvik 2012) but the Dutch case remains to be explored. Comparing different universities with different practices of NPM would help understand how organizational context matters in shaping gendered academic careers across Dutch universities. Therefore, more research in this direction is necessary.

References

Bain, O., & Cummings, W. (2000). Academe's glass ceiling: Societal, professional/organizational, and institutional barriers to the career advancement of academic women. *Comparative Education Review, 44*(4), 493–514.

Barrett, L., & Barrett, P. (2011). Women and academic workloads: Career slow lane or Cul-de-Sac? *Higher Education, 61*(2), 141–155.

Barry, J., Berg, E., & Chandler, J. (2012). Movement and coalition in contention: Gender, management and academe in England and Sweden. *Gender, Work and Organization, 19*(1), 52–70.

Benschop, Y., & Brouns, M. (2003). Crumbling ivory towers: Academic organizing and its gender effects. *Gender, Work and Organization, 10*(2), 194–212.

Bentley, P. (2011). Gender differences and factors affecting publication productivity among Australian university academics. *Journal of Sociology, 48*(1), 85–103.

Bentley, P., & Kyvik, S. (2012). Academic work from a comparative perspective: A survey of faculty working time across 13 countries. *Higher Education, 63*(4), 529–547.

Berg, E., Barry, J., & Chandler, J. (2003). Nice work if you can get it? The changing character of academic labour in Sweden and England. *Comportamento Organizacional e Gestao, 9*(2), 19–37.

Bird, S. R. (2011). Unsettling universities' incongruous, gendered bureaucratic structures: A case-study approach. *Gender, Work and Organization, 18*(2), 202–230.

Blackmore, J., & Sachs, J. (2007). *Performing and reforming leaders*. New York: SUNY Press.

Clark, B. (1983). *The higher education system: Academic organization in cross-national perspective*. Berkeley: University of California Press.

De Boer, H., & Huisman, J. (1999). The new public management in Dutch universities. In D. Braun & F. X. Merrien (Eds.), *Towards a new model of governance for universities* (pp. 100–118). London/Philadelphia: Jessica Kingsley Publishers.

De Boer, H., Enders, J., & Leisyte, L. (2007). On striking the right notes: Shifts in governance and the organizational transformation of universities. *Public Administration, 85*(1), 27–46.

De Goede, M., Belder, R., & De Jonge, J. (2013). *Academic careers in the Netherlands 2013. Facts & figures 7*. The Hague: Rathenau Instituut. www.rathenau.nl.

De Weert, E. (2009). The organized contradictions of teaching and research: Reshaping the academic profession. In J. Enders & E. De Weert (Eds.), *The changing face of academic life. Analytical and comparative perspectives* (pp. 134–154). London: Palgrave Macmillan.

De Weert, E., & Boezerooy, P. (2007). *Higher education in the Netherlands. Country report*. Enschede: Center for Higher Education Policy Studies.

European Commission. (2012). *She figures 2012. Gender in research and innovation. Statistics and indicators*. Brussels: European Commission Community Research.

Eveline, J. (2005). Woman in the ivory tower. *Journal of Organizational Change Management, 18*(6), 641–658.

Goastellec, G., & Pekari, N. (2013). Gender differences and inequalities in academia: Findings in Europe. In U. Teichler & E. A. Höhle (Eds.), *The work situation of the academic profession in Europe: Findings of a survey in twelve countries* (pp. 55–78). Dordrecht: Springer.

Grummell, B., Devine, D., & Lynch, K. (2009). The care-less manager: Gender, care and new managerialism in higher education. *Gender and Education, 21*(2), 191–208.

Lamont, M. (2009). *How professors think: Inside the curious world of academic judgment*. Cambridge: Harvard University Press.

Le Feuvre, N. (2009). Exploring women's academic careers in cross-national perspective. *Equal Opportunities International, 28*(1), 9–23.

Leisyte, L. (2007). *University governance and academic research: Case studies of research units in Dutch and English universities*. Ph.D. thesis, University of Twente, CHEPS, Enschede.

Leisyte, L., & Dee, J. R. (2012). Understanding academic work in a changing institutional environment. Faculty autonomy, productivity, and identity in Europe and the United States. In J. C.

Smart & M. B. Paulsen (Eds.), *Higher education: Handbook of theory and research* (pp. 123–206). Dordrecht: Springer.

Leisyte, L., & Hosch-Dayican, B. (2014). Changing academic roles and shifting gender inequalities. A case analysis of the influence of the teaching-research nexus on the academic career prospects of female academics in The Netherlands. Journal of Workplace Rights, 17(3–4), 467–490. doi:10.2190/WR.17.3-4.m.

Leisyte, L., Enders, J., & de Boer, H. (2008). The freedom to set research agendas – Illusion and reality of the research units in the Dutch universities. *Higher Education Policy, 21*, 377–391.

Leisyte, L., Enders, J., & de Boer, H. (2009). The balance between teaching and research in Dutch and English universities in the context of university governance reforms. *Higher Education, 58*(5), 619–635.

Osborn, M., Rees, T., Bosch, M., Hermann, C., Hilden, J., Mason, J., et al. (2000). *Science policies in the European Union: Promoting excellence through mainstreaming gender equality.* Brussels: European Commission.

Parker, J. (2008). Comparing research and teaching in university promotion criteria. *Higher Education Quarterly, 62*(3), 237–251.

Probert, B. (2005). I just couldn't fit it in': Gender and unequal outcomes in academic careers. *Gender, Work and Organization, 12*(1), 50–72.

Rees, T. (2002). *The Helsinki group on women and science: National policies on women and science in Europe.* Brussels: European Commission.

Rosenberg, R. (1988). The limits of access: The history of coeducation in America. In J. M. Faragher & F. Howe (Eds.), *Women and higher education in America* (pp. 107–129). New York: Norton.

Schimank, U., & Winnes, M. (2000). Beyond Humboldt? The relationship between teaching and research in European university systems. *Science and Public Policy, 27*(6), 397–408.

Thomas, R., & Davies, A. (2002). Gender and new public management: Reconstituting academic subjectivities. *Gender, Work and Organization, 9*(4), 372–397.

Timmers, T. M., Willemsen, T. M., & Tijdens, K. G. (2010). Gender diversity policies in universities: A multi-perspective framework of policy measures. *Higher Education, 59*(6), 719–735.

Valian, V. (1998). *Why so slow: The advancement of women.* Cambridge, MA: MIT Press.

Van den Brink, M. (2010). *Behind the scenes of science: Gender practices in recruitment and selection of professors in The Netherlands.* Amsterdam: Pallas.

Van den Brink, M., & Benschop, Y. (2012). Slaying the seven-headed dragon: The quest for gender change in academia. *Gender, Work and Organization, 19*(1), 71–92.

Chapter 6
Female Academics in Greek Higher Education: Issues of Organizational Change, Economic Crisis and Social Responsibility

Antigoni Papadimitriou

Introduction

In Greece, women appear to have influential and protagonistic roles from antiquity. In the Iliad and the Odyssey Homer referred to Andromache, Nausicaa and several others, while Athenian and Spartan women were also well known for their significant roles. In modern history (1821) Bouboulina had the role of admiral and inspired Byron in more than one instance (see more about Greek Women in Mitchell Carroll). Mothers and grandmothers appear to influence the next generations and almost all school-age children began their education by having female teachers. Elementary and high school female teachers and leaders (principals etc.) are well represented, while this number dramatically drops in higher education professors and university governance bodies. Currently over 50 % of the student body in undergraduate and graduate studies in Greek public universities are female students (Figure A in Appendix). Many women pursue graduate degrees in Greece, however, very few appear in amphitheaters have the role of the professor (higher rank in academia) and very few serve and act as leaders in higher education governance. Nevertheless this is a common issue in several higher education systems worldwide and Greece is not an exception. The glass ceiling, it seems, is still firmly in place. Although, beyond this gap women in Greece appear to have a good representation in the area of Research and Development (Sachini et al. 2014) while academics have an active role and quite good representation in lower rank positions in Greek higher education.

A. Papadimitriou (✉)
Johns Hopkins University, School of Education, Baltimore, MD, USA
e-mail: apapadi1@jhu.edu

© Springer International Publishing Switzerland 2017
H. Eggins (ed.), *The Changing Role of Women in Higher Education*,
The Changing Academy – The Changing Academic Profession in International
Comparative Perspective 17, DOI 10.1007/978-3-319-42436-1_6

119

Greece is a beautiful country in terms of vacationing, history and sightseeing, cuisine, and hospitality, however, the current economic conditions that began in 2009 became a nightmare for its indigenous people that need to survive and excel under economic austerities. This issue was exemplified by Helen Austin, an outspoken activist and proponent of women's right, in her recent book. She mentions "My beloved Greece has been very much in my mind these days. Greece's economy is suffering badly, and one senses the desperation among most of the Greeks I have spoken with in recent months. Their pensions are cut by 40 percent, the taxes have almost doubled, and the unemployment for those in their twenties has climbed to around 60 percent" (Austin-Stavridou 2014, p. 166). The domino effect due to the economic crisis creates also problems to academia, which includes both students and faculty members.

Papadimitriou (2015) provided a picture about economic crisis and academic challenges in Greek higher education, using interviews that took place in 2012 with 23 academics from one big university and among them only 5 out of 23 were women. Understanding contemporary changes and challenges in academic work requires systematic empirical studies (Papadimitriou 2015). There is research especially in women's studies that provides information about Greek women in academia. To mention a few, in 1991 Eliou focused in the academic profession of women in Greek higher education. Karamesini (2004) presented a paper with women's representation and progression in science careers in Greece, where she discussed data until 2003. More recent Assimaki et al. (2012) discuss female faculty members in the field of electrical engineering. Platsidou and Diamantopoulou (2009) studied professors' job satisfaction from four universities located in Northern Greece where less than 25 % in their study were female professors. Florou (2014) presented a study of mostly proportions about female university staff in Greek and Turkish higher education. While the most recent was from November 2014, Sachini and her co-authors reported about the participation of women in Research and Development in Greece for the year 2011 (Sachini et al. 2014). That report includes data from higher education as well.

However, there are no current empirical studies that investigate contemporary challenges due to organizational changes (legal and economic issues) about Greek women in academia, their triple role (i.e. teaching, research and services), their job satisfaction and their motivation. Therefore, the current study exclusively deals with this topic. It is also important from organizational perspectives to understand how female academics deal with the implementation of radical change and illuminate the change role that women as (change agents within the organization) play therein. The data consist of legal documents, national data, and interviews with 25 Hellinides (Greek women) academics (n = 25) from various disciplines in 10 out of 20 public universities. This study is focused on Greek women academics, however similar issues might are faced in other countries (European and global), as several higher education systems are under some financial stress, therefore, the author hopes that a look of the Greek case might provide a window for understanding what could happen elsewhere.

Background Information About Greek Higher Education

Over the last few years, higher education in Greece appears to have settled into two separate sectors: nationalized and centralized. In 2009 these sectors included 22 public universities (not including the online Open University and the International University that offers graduate studies in English) as well as 16 technological education institutions (not discussed in this chapter). While currently in Greece (2015, the year that this study took place) the 22 public universities became 20. The most recent series of Greek higher education reforms have occurred since 2005 (see for more information Papadimitriou 2011, 2015). The paradox that elections in Greece take place very often and the new Minister proposes new laws creates an unfavorable climate within the academia. During the writing of this study, the universities in Greece operated under the law 4009/2011 that introduced substantial changes to the structure of higher education with the intent to restructure the whole higher education system (universities and technological institutions). Under the law 4009/2011, as well as the previous law, all universities in Greece operated in a similar manner since they all had to adhere to specific rules and national regulations. Under those laws (both past and present), the Ministry of Education determines the number of teaching positions to be filled each year and checks the legality of the academic staff selection process. The latest 2011 legislation divided the regular teaching academic staff into three main ranks: professors, associate professors, and assistant professors. The lecturer rank has disappeared; however, those lecturers with tenure appeared to work as lecturers until their retirement. Universities, apart from their regular personnel, employ academics on limited duration contracts (adjuncts), which are related to the budget that the Ministry of Education allocates to each university for open positions. Figure 6.1 provides an overview of academics in Greek public universities beginning of the academic year 2013 (the most recent available data in order to develop the overview). In this Figure I took into consideration only academics working in the public universities excluding the academics working at the Open University and the International University – as technically those academics could be members also in any public university.

Additionally Fig. 6.2 presents the age of academics for the academic year 2012.

Academic performances such as teaching, research, and services are stipulated by the Greek legislation. This adherence to a set of common regulations can lead to uniformity among Greek academics (Papadimitriou 2015). Additionally, the quality assurance law that was finally passed almost a decade ago (2005) was still active during the academic year 2009–2010 and therefore academics were still required to participate in additional administrative work as required by the quality assurance law. Failure to meet quality assurance requirements resulted in sanctions targeted at funding and human resources. In addition, all universities require following specific regulations and processes regarding quality assurance matters.

Another core change, due to the latest (?) (2011) higher education law, is a change in the election process of rectors. Universities are required to select board members from both internal (professors in the same university) and external

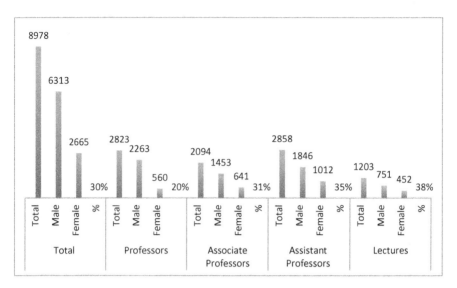

Fig. 6.1 Overview of academics representation in Greek public universities beginning of the academic year 2013 (Source: Data provided by the Greek Statistics figure designed by the author)

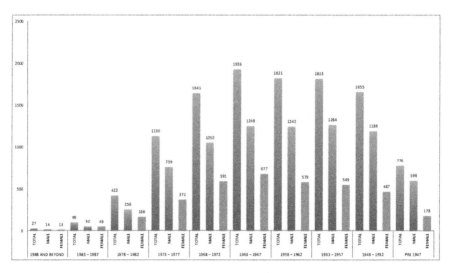

Fig. 6.2 Age of Greek academics in 2012 (Source: Data provided by the Greek Statistics figure designed by the author)

(academics or other individuals working in Greece or abroad). The new legal framework introduces a council responsible for appointing rector (similar to board of trustees). This governance model for board members has been very instrumental for selecting responsible rectors who are represented by university academics rather than by students and by non-invested employers as had previously happened with earlier Greek State regulations. However, as Papadimitriou and Nyctopoulou (2015) noted, this governmental model was under consideration by the Minister of Education that was elected in January 2015 and currently (October 2015). After another election, the newest minister remains to decide about the existence or lack thereof of that model.

As an interjectory note, one must mention that universities in Greece are entitled to financial support by the state; however, the Greek legislation now allows universities and their academics to develop entrepreneurial activities in both research and services within the private sector. The Ministry of Education and the Ministry of Economy and Finance provide financial support to all universities. Thus, the Ministry of Education directly controls the salaries of all academics and administrators as well as finances for universities' operations. The amount covering salaries is an annual, fixed, and defined rate; therefore, wages of each employee at all universities are determined by rank, years of service, and marital status as per the current and past laws as well. Resultant from current and past laws, universities have no authority to negotiate salaries with any of the academics. Moreover, during the years of the economic crisis (from 2009 to present) educational spending decreased enormously; meanwhile, universities and their employees faced severe losses of their income. From personal conversations with several Greek academics, I noticed that since 2009, the budgets for Greek universities were cut more than 23 %, meaning no funding was available for basic needs such heating or educational facilities, while for some others, those budget cuts eliminated basic academic needs such as buying photocopy paper, cleaning materials, and funds for custodial staff.

Moreover, the Ministry of Education not only regulates undergraduate students' access to higher education through PanHellenic exams, but it also decides on the number of undergraduate students who are accepted and distributes them among the 20 public universities (except for the Open and International Universities). The Ministry of Education assigns a specific student allotment to the academic departments; however, the Ministry of Education never takes into account the rectors' requested number of students that academic departments could accommodate. Consequently, too many students are assigned to already overloaded departments. Although this student overload has sparked a lively debate, specifically between the academic departments located in universities in Athens and Thessaloniki (urban cities), a feasible solution does not yet exist. A spin-off from this overcrowding, as reflected in the data found by this author, indicated that the increased number of students did not go hand-in-hand with the decreased number of academics. To make matters worse regarding overcrowding in the two major urban centers, the Ministry of Education also regulates the transferability of students within similar departments across all academic departments and across all universities. Thus, students may appeal to the Ministry of Education for transfers whose approvals mostly reflect social reasons (low income families, sick students, or students having siblings studying in universities). As a result, students frequently request a transfer from the peripheral universities in order to attend the urban ones. Many students take advantage of the transfer option, thus one frequently finds peripheral university academic departments nearly empty. Consequently, the negative impacts upon the urban academic departments are that they remain severely overcrowded, have fewer available professors and administrators, and most importantly, the smaller facilities and infrastructure cannot possibly support the student overload. These negative impacts are, however, not any consideration of the existing laws because the laws regulate wages for university employees (academics and administrators) regardless of the student population. Lastly, the Ministry of Education also sets the university's budget at the beginning of the academic year, well in advance of the student assignments. Herein lies another paradox: following the student assignments, many of them request a student transfer, which is granted. However, the budget, already having been fixed, remains untouched and unchanged. Thus, peripheral universities' budgets neither reflect the loss of students nor a reduction in their budgets. Likewise, urban universities' budgets neither reflect their increased student census nor an increase in their fixed department budgets. This paradox, as the data indicate, may account for the loss or attrition of academics who suffer from, not only from budget cuts based upon government austerity programs, but also the huge size of urban universities' classes have engendered a significant crisis in Greek higher education.

Compounding this crisis is overcrowding, budget cuts, and student census per class, not to mention the ongoing economic crisis in Greece; these elements have spurred the Ministry of Education to introduce mergers in its higher education system at the beginning of academic year 2013–2014. Greece currently has 20 public universities and 261 academic departments (Open University and The International University are still operating, however not take into consideration for this study). These mergers resulted in the distribution of students and faculty to other similar departments within other Greek universities. This sudden distribution took place for the academic year 2014–2015, and required many adjustments and changes causing many academic programs to suddenly expand in order to accommodate the new student and faculty assignments. In addition to the mergers, the Ministry of Education in cooperation with the Ministry of Economics followed the directives from "Troika" (*The term troika has been widely used in Greece and Cyprus Ireland, Portugal and Spain to refer to the presence of the European Commission, European Central Bank, and International Monetary Fund in these countries since 2010 and the financial measures that these governments have taken*) that forced adoption of regulations to reduce redundancies in administrative staff in the public sector, including universities. Although these regulations affected several universities within the Greek higher education system, each was affected to a different degree. For example, one university lost more than 15 % of its administrative staff while other universities were not affected at all. In addition, The Ministry of Education decided to purge 40,000 inactive students from university registry files who had not participated in taking course exams in the past few years, yet who had registered as students more than 10 years ago without having completed their studies (within Greek culture such students have a name: students for ever (*aionioi*).

General knowledge within Greece is that policy making is top-heavy because higher education reforms originated from the Ministry of Education, which retains the formal authority in policy decision-making; however, many of those decisions appear to lack any support from evidence-based studies. Further complicating the decisions in policy making have been politically charged issues and a very weakly supportive central government from which the Minister of Education was appointed. During the beginning of the writing of this study (January 2015), a new government was elected in Greece (January 25, 2015) and again, for one more time the Minister of Education changed as well the name of the Ministry of Education, which is now called, "Ministry of Culture, Education and Religious Affairs". That time (January 2015), announced appeared on television channels and in newspapers that the Ministry of Education will rehire administrators who had lost their jobs and re-register the students who were recently purged from the registry. Although during the completion of this study (October 2015) gain elections took place in Greece (September 2015) and the Ministry change name to "Ministry of Education, Research and Religious Affairs" as well we are waiting to listen the newest announcement of the current Minister of Education.

The plethora of elections, laws, and regulations, which if not already confusing/conflicting/contradicting, now require additional organizational changes within the universities. What is missing in these many and often too frequent changes is a compass that defines true North: a master plan for policy founded upon an evidence-based platform, and an insulation of the Minister of Education from the ever shifting political winds of change. Under this jeopardy of political/legal, economic (crisis), and socio/cultural changes the following section explains the methodology used for this study.

Methodology

In this study personal experiences and previous research on higher education personnel provided a useful mechanism for developing a list, which included more than 200 telephone numbers of women academics. These women were the potential study participants in Greek public universities. Whereas this approach to sampling has come under heavy criticism (Creswell 1998), the cost, geographical range and time constraints of the study meant that it was the best option. Yet, the author also acknowledges that it does impose certain limitations on the generalizability of the findings.

Data for the current study derived from 25 interviews. In order to investigate contemporary challenges I employed a small-scale study (N=25), where I interviewed women academics in 10 out of 20 universities in Greece. I used telephone interviews. The same methodology was also used by Assimaki et al. (2012), these authors mentioned reasons such as the great geographical distance between the universities, as well as the advantage of the telephone interview – in which there is no visual contact between interviewer and interviewee and this makes it easier to speak for "sensitive" issues, and also permits the research subjects to speak more freely

(Mertens 2009; Sturges and Hanrahan 2004). Trier-Bieniek (2012) mentioned that contend that being interviewed over the phone may result in more honest data as people have become more accustomed to 'virtual' communications, serving to benefit to both the participant and researcher. The author also noted that "conducting interviews over the telephone with people who are strangers can lead interviews that are rich in data, allowing [her] to contact and interview women who [she] should never have been able to access using in-person interviews" (Trier-Bieniek 2012, 642). Trier-Bieniek (2012) suggests that qualitative telephone interviews can be used when studying sensitive subjects, and can be developed through a combination of semi-structured interviews and feminists approach to research. Moreover "this blend allows the researcher to re-define relationships between researcher and participant, particularly when considering the "sender-receiver" dynamic (Shuy 2002), or the ways that questions are asked and responded to. Trier-Bieniek (2012) also noted data collected over the phone can be used when dealing with traumatic or sensitive topics and can result in rich data.

The telephone interviews for my study took place during October–November 2014, weekdays and mostly around 12.00–16.00 due to the time difference between US (author's location) and Greece. All interviews were in Greek. A limitation of this study might be that the time difference caused the inability to make phone calls early in the morning that might have provided the inclusion of more opinions.

In order to learn about conditions of employment of women academics (professors, associate professors, assistant professors, and lecturers), I used a similar questionnaire that was used in my previous study (Papadimitriou 2015). This questionnaire included open ended and semi-structured questions. Besides demographic characteristics, I asked questions about respondents' academic rank, discipline, and years in academia. I asked academics to report estimates for two separate time periods: during 2009 (before the crisis) and current situation in 2014 (beginning of academic year 2014–2015).

Bentley and Kyvik (2012, 533) stated, "given the professional autonomy academics have beyond teaching and administrative hours, self-reports seem appropriate when estimating typical working hours in academia" (for more information about methodological problems see Bentley and Kyvik 2012 and Kyvik 2012). Also Kyvik (2012, 5) noted that "the methodology used in the surveys by Bentley and Kyvik (2012), has its limitations. In the first three surveys, staff members were asked to estimate the approximate allocation of their time in the previous year, while in the latest survey they are asked about the current academic year. These surveys involved drawing on memories of working life in the past and such self-estimates of typical working hours are subject to errors or recall". A similar problem could arise in my research as well; however, I perceive that women academics under these difficult circumstances in Greece have clear memories about their working conditions before and after the economic crisis.

Sample

The demographic data of interviewees was wide ranging. The 25 individuals belong to the academics of 10 out of 20 universities located in Thessaloniki, Ioannina, Corfu, Athens, Piraeus, Volos, and Korinthos. Twelve were professors, five associate professors, seven assistant professors and one lecturer working for 34 years. Academics employed in 14 different disciplines: Agriculture, Archaeology, Biology, Economics, Business, Marketing, Italian, Education, Pharmacy, Primary Education, Medicine, Physiology, Dietetics and Nutritional Science, Social Anthropology, Music.

The professors worked at the university between 10 and 43 years (an average 27 years of employment) and they reported working as a professor from 2 to 15 years (an average of 5.8 years). Their age ranged from 40 to 66 as 67 is the age of mandatory retirement.

Associate professors worked at the university between 6 and 34 years (average 15 years of employment) and also reported that they worked in the associate professorate rank between 1 and 2 years (average 1.6 years). Their age ranged from 40 to 60.

Assistant professors worked at the university between 3 and 42 years (average 15 years of employment) and also reported that they worked in the assistant professorate rank between 3 and 5 years (average 4.28 years). Their age ranged from 30 to 60 plus.

Only one respondent was a lecturer for 34 years and she was over 60 years old.

In relation to having children 14 stated that they have between 1 and 4 children and 11 mentioned no children. Out of 14 with children only 6 noted that their children's age ranged from 1 to 15 years old.

Regarding leadership positions two mentioned that they were elected as university internal board members, one as a dean, three department heads, one deputy department head, one graduate studies director, and one program coordinator.

Results

Changes in the Way of Teaching

Concerning changes in the way of teaching **due to the quality assurance law** women academics did not observe changes in their way of teaching. Moreover, several noted that they are more satisfied due to the quality assurance law that requires reporting their teaching methods, and that their teaching techniques received visibility, as they have to report them. Several noted "they always try to improve their way of teaching not because of the required evaluation; but because they care about their students' well-being". Another also noted that "I always look at what students commented in their evaluations, then I try to change the way of my teaching in order to meet students' needs". While another professor and member of the university board highlighted that "we always try to improve our teaching, however the quality assurance process most of the time remains on paper and there is no appropriate analysis of the students' comments". While another assistant professor noted "I used to work abroad and students were required to participate in classes, here students are coming mostly on a volunteer basis, and some time they participate in the course evaluation even when they have attended less than 50 % of the regular classes".

Concerning changes in teaching **due to the new law** four women academics did not report changes as they were board members, dean or department heads. Almost all of them noted "so far mergers were not an issue in my department therefore I do not have to mention changes, however, I know colleagues from merged departments who are dealing with many problems and also several professors who have to teach more courses". Additionally they noted that the new law requires additional teaching hours but not for those that serve in leadership positions. The remaining 21 women academics noted that they have to teach more hours following the requirements of the new higher education law.

Six women academics mentioned that the law about mergers affected their department as they needed to reorganize their entire curriculum. More specifically one associate professor who was also the program coordinator noted: "I worked for several months and for several hours as we had to reorganize our curriculum for both undergraduate and graduate studies. During those changes we had to take into consideration subjects that taught by incoming academics. At the same time we have to provide courses for students in transition that came from another department that currently does not exist". Another professor of marketing mentioned "now I need to teach more than 300 students, previously the department had about 70, and I have to change my teaching methods in order to be appropriate for large size classes". Another associate professor from the same department noted that due to recent mergers she needs to teach more courses. Another professor mentioned that "as these changes just happen we are ready for "everything" this academic year is a transitional one". Another professor from the agricultural university mentioned characteristically: "we were waiting for those changes 10 years; the academic profile of the curriculum is totally changed. Students in agriculture have to study the first 3 years core courses then the last 2 years we added a thesis and specific minors and concentrations. Greece is an agricultural nation we needed those changes".

Due to the economic crisis, six did not observe changes in their teaching approach while 19 noted YES. Academics who observed changes in their teaching approach mostly belonged in the disciplines that require laboratory and hands-on exercises. Most of those professors noted that every year the Ministry of Education accepts more students to their departments while at the same time decreases their budget. The last few years the student body in several departments especially in Athens and Thessaloniki appeared to have doubled. One lecture said: "I use to teach a small number of students, currently I am teaching the same course for more than five times per week as the student body of 50 students became 200 – all those students need to use laboratories and we really have a hard time to educate all appropriately as our laboratories have a limited capacity of 30 students– I am teaching 30 years, I really want to help students however there is no available time during the week". Retirement of supporting staff and budget cuts did affect supplies and the infrastructure; these created challenges in maintaining positive experiences in lab courses. Several respondents noted an inability to support their students with photocopies and almost all respondents started to use the online repository to help students with extra resources. In difficult situations, it seems that new technologies provide help. Skype became a common practice and is used by several professors to increase their communication with students. A professor from a peripheral university noted that students have a difficult time to pay rent therefore they attend universities only during the examination period. The professor said: "I feel responsible for them therefore I developed on line teaching by using Skype – actually this became one on one teaching, and therefore I spend more hours working– I really need to help those students to complete their studies- someone has to care about students". Another academic with more than 30 years of work experience said: "I care about students, a few years ago I was able to retire however I am staying even as I have lost some of my privileges – I care about the university – about the students – someone needs to be responsible for them (students)".

Changes in Research

All women academics noted no changes in **research due to the quality assurance law**. Several commented: "they always wanted to publish in high quality journals" and "our department introduced high standards in research and publications before the evaluation law". One professor was "very angry with the colleagues who expected the evaluation process to motivate them for high quality research and publications". While a music professor said: "The quality assurance law does not suggest changes, but it simply reassures the reason of my existence idealistically".

Concerning changes in research **due to the new higher education law**, only one answer was positive. A professor from a department that have been merged noted: "I really enjoy the cooperation with others professors, this might be the only positive outcome due to mergers".

Regarding changes in research **due to the economic crisis**, four mentioned that until now the crisis did not affect their research, almost all of them mentioned: "I never have money for research, prior or post the crisis I had to conduct research and publish with limited or no resources, therefore I do not feel that the crisis created a difference". One of them also noted: "You know, I do not have kids therefore I can spend money out of pocket for my research, participate in conferences and buy books. I do not know if I could have afforded all of that, if I had family and kids". These academics were employed in social sciences and education, where it is very common to do research without extra resources. On the other side one professor from Dietetics and Nutrition science noted "even with the economic crisis my research projects were not affected because my research results are directly connected to the market needs. The private sector provided some financial support". While another professor noted that the use of technology for teleconferences is "better than nothing", she simply said "I need to make use of all available resources".

Almost all women noted that they have limited or no resources to participate in international conferences. One professor said, "it is sad as we cannot invite researchers from abroad to participate in collaborative projects or to teach as visiting scholars in our programs". Another professor noted that "a few years ago she received a small amount of money due to an excellence award in publishing – currently this little amount has also disappeared".

Additional explanations from the 21 academics that mentioned changes in research due to economic constraints are stated as follows:

- More work on proposal development (for research grants) vs. research per se. It is very challenging to find financial support
- Need to improve our skills in order to develop cooperation with international colleagues and to publish together
- It is very hard to find resources for experiments; I really do not know what to do and mostly how to help students in order to participate in those laboratories.
- These days we have to look for research money in private sources; that was not a case few years ago
- No resources for supplies- we try very hard at least to help our PhD students to complete their experiments
- The problem is not only the money, we lost our trust abroad, even if we have the money to pay for materials and supplies the order process is very complicated and these enterprises require first to deposit the money and then deliver the materials
- The situation is hard as most of our research money is derived from our bonds; however, now we lost most of them due to PSI.
- Hard to invite and cooperate with colleagues from abroad – now we need invitations and is not fair only to visit other universities without having money to invite them
- It is hard to participate in conferences as there is no money for that- previously we self-funded conferences but now due to the crisis and salary cuts participation in conferences is a "luxury"
- Our main external resources derived from pharmaceutical companies that also have serious problems with the current economy – therefore we need to try hard to develop appropriate, and attractive research proposals

Changes in Services

Five women academics, mostly working few years in peripheral universities or with more than 30 years in Athenian universities reported no changes in administrative services **due to quality assurance**, while 20 reported yes. Most of the academics

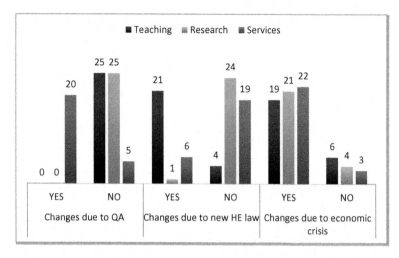

Fig. 6.3 Greek female academic's task and changes overview

that indicated changes were mostly board members either in their department quality assurance committee or in the university's quality assurance unit. Several professors noted that the quality assurance law requires a lot of paperwork and bureaucracy and the lack of appropriate administrators results in spending an enormous amount of time to complete reports and quality assurance requirements. Concerning changes in services **due to the new law (mergers)** the same six women academics who were affected by mergers reported an increased workload while the other 19 women academics did not report changes.

About changes in services **due to the economic crisis**, only 3 reported no changes while 22 replied that they observed changes as they have to spend an enormous amount of time because mostly "administrators and other professors retired without replacement". One professor from Athens and university board member noted "the problem is not always the lack of administrators but the reorganization of the administration and the power that the administrators have. The system evaluates professors for their services however it does not evaluate the administrators. We need to develop an effective administrative operation in order to benefit the entire university". Another one also from Athens had the same opinion: "we always had lot of administrative work even before the number of administrators was reduced; the problem was related to the administrative tasks' proper allocation".

Figure 6.3 presents an overview of the changes or not due to the quality assurance law, to the new higher education law and due to the economic crisis. Data revealed that most changes reported in services due to quality assurance. Due to the higher education law most changes related to teaching, while due to the economic crisis changes reported in all areas (teaching, research and services). Overall fewer changes were reported due to the quality assurance law in teaching and research and almost no changes at all due to the new higher education law especially in research.

Workload and Working Time Due to Economic Crisis

Interview data indicate that the average number of weekly hours these professors worked were 49 (average) before the crisis and 59 after the crisis. Data indicate that teaching hours increased due to the new law requiring teaching additional hours per week (from 6 to 8) and also the need to teach several subjects due to retirement of professors without replacement. Participants in this study reported huge differences in their administrative work. Most of the academics noted that they work several hours for administrative purposes and also have work at home. Additionally almost all of them noted that there is reduction in the time they spend on research. Most of them had difficulty to calculate the exact hours per week for each of the 3 areas (teaching, research and services), therefore I did not present data for each subject. One professor told me "I simply work and I am doing research during nonexistent time, I am optimistic that better days will come".

After the crisis the lecturer worked 50 h per week. Assistant professors seem to have worked less on average (51 h per week) than the associate professors (64 h). Associated professors seem to have worked more on average than the professors (60 h per week). Only three women noted that they work the same amount of time pre and post crisis and two of them have more than two children less than 12 years old. Data show that women academics mostly professors, with more than 25 years of work at this university, (also including associate, assistants professors and lecturer) work hard (average 62.2 h per week).

Working Outside of the University

Only six women academics currently work in other universities (Open University – public distance learning); however, half of them mentioned that they taught at the Open University before the crisis.

Satisfaction-Dissatisfaction

Eight women academics reported dissatisfaction with their working environment; five found their working environment neutral and a majority of the sample (n = 12) commented that the working environment was satisfactory. Dissatisfied academics noted many problems in the infrastructure and administrative staff (due to retirement and not replacement) which do not allow them to work properly. Satisfied professors simply noted their satisfaction without additional comments. One professor and board member said: "I have accepted all those difficulties I am a tough person, I am looking ahead I do not let myself to go down".

Motivation

Under these circumstances, even academics that reported dissatisfaction with their working environment frequently mentioned factors that reflected self-motivation. One professor said: "I am in love with my research and I want to be ok with my conscience". Sources of motivation were mostly reported as a personal desire for research and respect for their profession. The analysis of answers shows that women academics focus on their students' success and accomplishment. Although the most common factor related to their motivation came from their students and their desire to teach them. One professor said: "my motivation is the quality of our students, almost every year better students are coming to our department (biology) and we need to offer them quality education even under these circumstances". Others more precisely said: "we need to respect our students and help them to complete their studies and to help our university to remain open". Several also noted that in this difficult time "we need to show our patriotism" while others said we work because we have "filotimo" (pride). One professor said: "currently we do not have motivational factors- only luck of motivation- we work only for filotimo". The music professor noted, "I love my discipline and I am responsible for others". Several professors having administrative positions reported that they feel responsible and their work reflects social responsibility. One professor and board member said: "I remember my own professors, now I feel that I have to support Greece, I need to offer a sense of education as a common good". A professor from health science with 34 years of experiences said: "This university is like my home, my salary has been decreased 40 %, however I like my work". Another professor also noted: "I will retire in 6 years, I would like my students to remember me as a good teacher, I am working only for self-esteem and filotimo". While another professor and dean said: "My motivation is that I have the feeling that I fulfill a higher purpose towards the young students and colleagues and I hope that I contribute to the common good and this is an example to the new generation of academics".

Gender Issues

In this study I only asked one question whether gender makes any difference in the current situation. I did not pose questions about career opportunities and promotion or about performance attribution. Most of the respondents in the sample did not distinguish between the sexes in respect to the challenges regarding legal and current economic conditions in Greece. Professors think that successful performance in academia for both men and women is generally attributed to the same causes: ability and effort. One professor and board member noted: "I do not believe that gender makes a difference – I believe that women professors need to show professionalization when interacted with male dominated market and Greece is still male dominated.

Professionalization is the key of the success". Another said: "Art does not recognize genders". Few academics noted that the economic crisis and legal issues in Greece are gender free- however they highlighted that women are promoted less rapidly than comparable men in several disciplines. Data in my study shows that a professor with 40 years of experience appeared in the professorate rank only in the last 3 years. National data also show that within the professorate rank only 20% are women, while in antithesis the percentage in lecturers is 38%. Some of the professors noted that their promotion was normal. It should be noted that the purpose of my study was not to find explanations regarding promotion and leadership position in Greek universities.

Conclusion

At the national level this study provides an understanding of women academics in Greece in the context of the economic crisis as it affects higher education policy changes. Under such changing circumstances, the study shows that professors, with more than 25 years of work experience (including associate, assistant professors and lecturer) are devoted (average 62.2 working hours per week) and this might indicate an effort to keep the university open and help students to complete their degree. Bentley and Kyvik's (2012) study shows that full-time academics at universities across countries worked 48.4 h per week during the teaching semester. Perhaps this study can account for limitations and reveal a paradox about women academics working more than 60 h per week. It is also possible that a limitation is that I interviewed "work-alcoholics" and passionate academics. Although, during my previously study (Papadimitriou 2015) similar findings were discovered, when I included male and female academics from only one Greek large university.

In Greece, academics deal with an increased number of students at all levels (undergraduate, graduate, and PhDs) while data revealed a decreased number of academics both female and male. Most of the professors noted that they try to help students to complete their degree and highlighted their social responsibility as academics. In Greece, undergraduate and PhD students do not pay tuition, however several graduates students in master's degree programs pay tuition. Data also revealed that academics are productive in publications, however in this study I cannot present separate results for women academics. Taking into consideration that academics in Greece have to publish for promotion and evaluation the law is equal for both genders. The number of students, as well as the number of publications is an attempt to explain that academics in Greek universities still maintain many hours for teaching, research, and services. When I asked academics to count their working hours by activities (teaching, research, and services) before and after the economic crisis, several of them had difficulty to account specific hours per subject, however in total they noted that they work more than 25% additional hours than prior to the crisis. Some academics took for granted their duties because they never used a paper and pen to account for actual hours worked per duty. Then the "moment of truth" came when I asked them about their motivation. It was very idealistic to hear self-esteem, pride, social responsibility and patriotism.

Academics in Greece face economic problems from 2009, more than 5 years and they still work while the country remains under the same situation. In order to be productive and effective, academics around the world expect and assume a relative stable and healthy professional environment. Without a stable economic and political environment, universities cannot effectively and efficiently actualize a plan and operationalize it; therefore, all stakeholders' interests are depreciated. Productivity is generally linked to satisfied staff that are confident within economic stability. Maslow's hierarchy of needs[1] speaks to the basic human psychological need for shelter, food, and water. Next step up is security, which includes employment, resources (income), and health. Academics certainly require these two levels before they can feel motivated to be productive and creative. In the Greek case, distractions about the stability of an income are reflected in several comments. This instability signals that more changes are coming in Greek higher education. In this small study women academics noted social responsibility as a motivation; however, if Maslow's needs cannot be met at the lowest level, social responsibility alone cannot suffice basic human needs nor can this responsibility provide the sufficient resources for effective and efficient operation of the universities. Similar results I discovered few years ago and I suggested that a national survey could provide adequate data to explain the Greek paradox: not only working for less but working for "nothing", or working because they have "filotimo" and social responsibility. Women academics from both departments with a few students and from departments with double the number of students demonstrated the same responsibility. A national survey might provide a different picture – until then we could remain thankful for those academics that remain and protect Thermopiles.[2]

Study Significance

There are no current empirical studies that investigate contemporary challenges due to organizational changes (legal and economic issues) about Greek women in academia, their triple role (i.e. teaching, research and services), their job satisfaction and their motivation. Therefore the current study exclusively deals with this topic. It is also important from organizational perspectives to understand how female academics deal with the implementation of radical change and illuminate the change role that women as (change agents within the organization) play therein. Thus this study contributes to the growing discourse on women in higher education (in Greece and beyond) and from methodological point of view to the utility of qualitative telephone interviews (Trier-Bieniek 2012).

---

[1] http://www.netmba.com/mgmt/ob/motivation/maslow/
[2] https://en.wikipedia.org/wiki/Battle_of_Thermopylae

References

Assimaki, A., Koustourakis, G., & Papaspyropoulou, K. (2012). Female faculty members in the field of electrical and computer engineering: The case of Greek Universities. Problems of education in the 21st century (Vol. 39, pp. 15–28).

Austin-Stavridou, H. (2014). *The road from Serres. A feministic Odyssey*. LA: Marcovaldo Productions, Inc.

Bentley, P. J., & Kyvik, S. (2012). Academic work form a comparative perspective: A survey of faculty working times across 13 countries. *Higher Education, 63*, 529.

Creswell, J. W. (1998). *Qualitative inquiry and research design: Choosing among five designs*. Thousand Oaks: Sage.

Florou, G. (2014). Female university staff in Greece and Turkey. *Procedia Economics and Finance, 9*, 342–348.

Karamessini, M. (2004). *Women's representation and progression in science careers in Greece*. Athens: KETHI Research Centre for Gender Equality.

Kyvik, S. (2012). Academic workload and working time: Retrospective perceptions versus time-series data. Higher Education Quarterly, pp. 1–12! doi: 10.1111/hequ.12001

Mertens. (2009). *Transformative research and evaluation*. New York: The Guilford Press.

Papadimitriou, A. (2011). *The enigma of quality in Greek higher education: A mixed methods study of introducing quality management into Greek higher education*. Enshcede: University of Twente, CHEPS.

Papadimitriou. (2015). Coping with the crisis: Academic work and changes in Greek higher education. In William K. Cummings & Ulrich Teichler (Eds.), *The relevance of the academy* (pp. 40–57). Basel, Switzerland: Springer.

Papadimitriou, A., & Nyktopoulou, M. (2015, September). Positioning for prestige: Diversity, isomorphism and social capital among Greek and US university trustees. In *EAIR 37th Annual Forum*, Daube University Krems, Austria.

Platsidou, M., & Diamantopoulou, G. (2009). Job satisfaction of Greek university professors; is it affected by demographic factors, academic rank and problems of higher education? In G. K. Zafiris (Ed.), *Educating the adult educator: Quality provision and assessment in Europe, Conference Proceedings, ESTEA-ReNAdET* (pp. 535–545). Thessaloniki: Grafima Publications.

Sachini, E., Malliou, N., & Samara, M. (2014). *The participation of women in research and development in Greece of the 2011*. Athens : Greek National Documentation Center (in Greek).

Shuy, R. W. (2002). In-person versus telephone interviewing. In J. F. Gubrium & J. A. Holstein (Eds.), *Handbook of interview research: Context and method* (pp. 537–555). Thousand Oaks: Sage.

Sturges, J. E., & Hanrahan, K. J. (2004). Comparing telephone and face-to-face qualitative interviewing: A research note. *Qualitative Research, 4*(1), 107–118.

Trier-Bieniek, A. (2012). Framing the phone interview as a tool for qualitative research: A methodological discussion. *Qualitative Research, 12*, 630–644.

Chapter 7
Managing Modern Malaysia: Women in Higher Education Leadership

Louise Morley, Madeline Berma, and Bahiyah Dato' Hj. Abdul Hamid

Higher Education in Malaysia

Higher education (HE) in Malaysia is characterised by expansion, internationalisation, transnational education and privatisation. This is the Asian Century, with the continent seeing the highest growth rate in HE enrolments globally. The gross undergraduate enrolment ratio of men in the Asia Pacific region increased from 11 % in 1970 to 26 % in 2009. The ratio for women in the same period tripled from 8 to 28 %, now exceeding male participation (Morley 2013). Malaysia has been a key player in neo-liberal reform including market-led expansion. Demand for higher education has come from a population keen to be part of the global knowledge economy, and a desire by the state for national competitiveness in the global academic arms race (World Bank 2007). The Ministry of Higher Education was established in 2004, and in 2007, it formulated the policy the *National Higher Education Strategic Plan* to develop access, internationalisation, quality assurance- especially of teaching and learning, lifelong learning, research and innovation, and institutional strengthening (Azman et al. 2013; Malaysia Government 2007). Higher education has been overtly linked to economic growth. Recently, the Malaysian Prime Minister called upon universities to play 'a more proactive role in efforts to boost the country's wealth' (Abas and Idris 2014:2). Malaysia has emphasised the imperative to build a competitive and knowledge-oriented economy and has undertaken a range of neo-liberalised reforms (Henderson and Phillips 2007). Neo-liberalism and

L. Morley (✉)
Centre for Higher Education and Equity Research (CHEER), University of Sussex, Sussex, UK
e-mail: L.Morley@sussex.ac.uk

M. Berma • B.D.H. Abdul Hamid
University of Kebangsaan, Bangi, Selangor, Malaysia
e-mail: madeline.berma@gmail.com; Bahiyahabdulhamid@gmail.com

© Springer International Publishing Switzerland 2017
H. Eggins (ed.), *The Changing Role of Women in Higher Education*,
The Changing Academy – The Changing Academic Profession in International
Comparative Perspective 17, DOI 10.1007/978-3-319-42436-1_7

feminism are not natural allies. However, competitiveness is promoted, in part, by enhancing women's participation in the labour force (Malaysia Government 2005:281). Hence the important role that access to HE plays both for women and for the state. It could be argued that gender equality is being instrumentalised for economic purposes (Berma 2014), and there are questions about how HE systems and structures have responded to new constituencies. There are also questions about why, when higher education participation rates for women have increased so dramatically, that the overall female labour force participation rate in Malaysia has remained at 44 % in the period 2009–2012 (Elias 2011). In its 2012 report, the World Bank observed that Malaysia's female labour force participation was only at 46 % and lower than the middle-income country's neighbours including Singapore (60 %) and Thailand (70 %), and significantly lower than high-income countries like the UK (70 %) and Sweden (77 %) (World Bank 2014). Malaysia is currently an upper middle-income country with a goal to transform itself into a high-income country by the year 2020 (Lee 2004). State financing and provision alone have been insufficient to meet the growing demands for HE. Hence, Malaysia has looked increasingly to the market and the private sector to augment its provision of higher education places (Mok 2008). Consequently, there are now 79 private universities and 20 public universities in the country (Malaysia Government 2012). Off-shore universities are counted as private and approximately 90 % of private higher education institutions are reportedly for-profit.

In terms of internationalisation, Malaysia has transformed itself from a provider of international students to HE markets in the Global North such as the UK and Australia, to a provider of higher education to incoming students. Malaysia provides a Muslim friendly environment for students where values and practices are understood and respected, for example the availability of a Halal diet and easy access to places of worship. International students come to Malaysia from countries including Indonesia 14 %, Iran 11 %, Yemen 5 %, Bangladesh 3 %, Sudan 2 %, Pakistan 2 %, Iraq 2 % (Saraswathi 2014; UNESCO 2014). Additionally, Malaysia's colonial legacy means that many of its educational qualifications are recognised internationally and the English language is Malaysia's second language and hence, understood and widely spoken in Malaysia.

Another form of internationalisation has been the spectacular rise in transnational education (TNE). World-class universities from around the globe now have off-shore campuses in Malaysia including the University of Nottingham from the UK, and Monash and Curtin from Australia (Ball 2007). Malaysia has 9 foreign university branch campuses. Singapore currently has the highest number of international branch campuses in Asia with 16 campuses followed by China with 13 (UNESCO 2014). It is argued that these campuses have enabled people to participate in HE who previously would not have been able to afford the costs of studying overseas (Mok 2008; Wilkinson and Yussof 2005). However, it is also argued that these are examples of the commercialisation and commodification of HE on the global market, with increasing hybridization between the public and private sectors (Ball 2007).

Malaysia is characterised by complex intersectionalities – especially in relation to ethnicities (Berma 2003). Mohamad et al. (2006) describes Malaysia as a mosaic of state-driven democracy, identity politics and multiculturalism. Diversity is a much-reported feature of Malaysia (Berma 2014). This has given rise to affirmative action programmes (Berma 2003). For example, until 2002, Malaysia had an ethnic quota system (in favor of the Bumiputera) population for admission to public universities (Lee 2007). The Malay term *Bumiputera* or *Bumiputra* is widely used in Malaysia to embrace the Malays, the indigenous peoples of the Malay Archipelago (including the Orang Asli of Peninsular Malaysia and the native peoples of Sabah and Sarawak), the Muslim Indians, and the Kristang peoples of Malacca (with Portuguese lineage). The term comes from Sanskrit *bhumiputra, which* literally means "son of the earth/land" (bhumi = earth/land and putra = son). The term is frequently translated as 'son of the soil' (Bahiyah 2008). The 10th Malaysia Plan reconfirms the state's commitment to, protecting the status of the Bumiputera population (Malaysia Government 2010: 165–173). It has recently been reported (New Straits Times 2014) that 286 Orang Asli (indigenous peoples of Peninsular Malaysia) are now enrolled in Malaysia's public universities, exceeding the ministry's target of 239 for 2014.

Malaysia aspires to mark its success in the global prestige economy by securing a place in the top 100 – *Times Higher Education (THES) World University Rankings* (Azman et al. 2010). Currently, it only features in the global rankings for universities less than 50 years of age, with one Malaysian university at position 98 (THES 2014). A challenge is that despite Malaysia's recent economic growth (Yusof and Bhattasali 2008), the Gini Coefficient Index, which measures the degree of inequality in the distribution of income (0 = equality and 1 = Inequality) places Malaysia at 0.431 compared with other countries in the region such as Indonesia at 0.37 and India 0.33 (Malaysia Government 2010).

Women in Malaysian Higher Education; Students and Academics, but Rarely Leaders in the Knowledge Economy

It is pertinent to pose questions about the implications for women in the expanded, marketised and neo-liberalised higher education sector in Malaysia. Women seem to have been some of the main beneficiaries in terms of student enrolment. However, there is still some horizontal segregation in Malaysia, with women comprising 66 % of humanities and social science students in 2011 in public universities (Wan 2012).

Gender equality legislation and policy initiatives, changes in socio-economic gender relations, aspirations and global expansion of higher opportunities have all contributed to increasing numbers of women undergraduate students globally (Leathwood and Read 2009; Morley 2011). An estimated 138 million students enroll in tertiary education each year, 45 million more than in 1999 (UNESCO 2009). Female enrolment ratios now exceed those of men in two out of every three countries with data and the number of women enrolled in tertiary institutions has grown almost twice as fast as that of men since 1970 (UNESCO 2010). The Global

Gender Parity Index of 1.08 means that there are now slightly more women under-graduates than men enrolled in higher education worldwide. Globally, the number of female students rose sixfold from 10.8 to 77.4 million between 1970 and 2008 (UNESCO 2010). However, the enhanced participation of women in higher educa-tion is not in itself an indicator of women's participation in wider civil society. Women comprise a large part of the academic labour market in Malaysia, of which 26.2%, or 511 out of 1953 in 2012 are professors in public universities (Malaysia Government 2013:60). It is important to note, that in Malaysia, like many other countries in Asia, the posts of Vice-Chancellor and Deputy Vice-Chancellor are political appointments. Women are noticeably absent from senior leadership posts. At the time of us conducting this research, there were four women Vice-Chancellors of public universities. Two have now retired and have been replaced by male Vice-Chancellors, and one has been promoted to another post. Just one female Vice-Chancellor remains in the International Islamic University Malaysia (IIUM).

A question relates to what level of work is available to women in Malaysia's knowledge economy- especially when there is a policy to have women occupying 30% of decision-making positions (10th Malaysia Plan). Again, Malaysia is follow-ing a global trend. High rates of women's participation in higher education have yet to translate into proportional representation in the labour market or access to leader-ship and decision-making positions (OECD 2010). From the limited statistical data on the topic (e.g. EC 2011; Lund 1998; Singh 2003, 2008; She Figures 2003, 2006, 2009, 2012), it appears that a global gender gap remains in the leadership of higher education. She Figures (2012) reported that, in 2010, on average throughout the EU-27, 15.5% of institutions in the Higher Education Sector were headed by women, and just 10% of universities had a female rector. This under-representation reflects not only continued inequalities between men and women, but missed oppor-tunities for women to contribute to solving the most pressing problems facing humankind and the future of universities. There is a business case e.g. skills wast-age, a social justice case e.g. removing exclusionary structures, processes and prac-tices, and a cognitive errors case e.g. gender bias in knowledge, technology and innovation for investigating and overturning this state of affairs (EC 2011).

Women's absence from senior leadership is a recurrent theme in studies in the Global North (e.g. Bagilhole and White 2011). It has also emerged as a theme in studies from the Global South in the past two decades for example from Ghana (Ohene 2010); Kenya (Onsongo 2004); Nigeria (Odejide et al. 2006); Pakistan (Rab 2010); South Africa (Shackleton et al. 2006); and Sri Lanka (Gunawardena et al. 2006). However, Malaysia seems to fall between the gaps in scholarship. Gender is largely absent from studies on higher education in the country. For example, a major international study on the *Changing Academic Profession* included a chapter on Malaysia, but did not take any consideration of gender into account (Azman et al. 2013; Teichler et al. 2013). Global studies on women and leadership rarely include Malaysia as a site of inquiry. Singh, however, did include it in her 2003 and 2008 reports and found that among the East-Asian countries surveyed, only in Malaysia was there an appointment of a woman Vice-Chancellor (9.1%) out of a total of 11 Vice-Chancellors in 2006 (Singh 2008:11–12) confirming that Executive Head positions which include Vice-Chancellors, Rectors and Presidents continued to be offered to men in the academy.

Despite, its high rates of literacy – 92.1 % in 2012 (Malaysia Government 2013:55), and high enrolment of women in higher education, Malaysia does not score highly in international indices of gender equality. For example, the 2013 Global Gender Gap Index which seeks to measure the relative gaps between women and men, across a large set of countries and across four key areas: health, education, economics and politics ranks Malaysia at 102 out of 136 countries.

Rejection, Reluctance and Refusal: Why Bother?

The above concerns – especially about women's under-representation in leadership positions prompted the Ministry of Women, Families and Community Development and the former Vice-Chancellor of Universiti Kebangsaan Malaysia – Professor Tan Sri Dato' Sri Dr Sharifah Hapsah binti Syed Hassan Shahabudin – to set up the *Tun Fatimah Hashim Women's Leadership Centre*, directed by Madeline Berma and co-directed by Bahiyah Dato' Hj Abdul Hamid. Louise Morley was the Inaugural Professor in the Centre for 2013–2014. The Centre conducted a Focus Group with 8 women and distributed 160 open-ended questionnaires and 36 were returned from 3 professors, 12 Associate Professors, 11 Senior Lecturers, 9 Lecturers + 1 Tutor. The research site was one public university in Malaysia and the study was designed to ascertain the following:

- Enablers and impediments to women entering higher education leadership
- What makes senior leadership attractive/unattractive to women in higher education?
- What are the consequences of women's under-representation in senior leadership positions in higher education?
- Recommendations for specific actions, strategies, initiatives and interventions to support more women to enter higher education leadership?

A major finding was how women expressed a tension between the modernisation agenda of the knowledge economy and traditionalist discourses of gender appropriate work and lifestyles. When asked about what enables and impedes women's entry to senior leadership positions in higher education, responses included: the power of the socio-cultural; personal/psychological attributes and qualities; academic capital; skills, competencies and dispositions; power relations; affective load; social relations and social capital and structural factors. Many of the enablers were also constraints e.g. family support was seen as an enabler, but family responsibilities were seen as an impediment (Stivens 2006). The power of the **socio-cultural** was a dominant concern. A major problem for many of the women in the study was that women's socially reproductive responsibilities were normalised and naturalised, leaving them few opportunities for alternative lifestyles. Women were sealed into a reified maternal identity and socio-cultural traditions including extended family commitments were often seen as solely the women's responsibility. A socio-cultural topic that attracted considerable attention was the **Gendered Division of Labour** – both in wider society and within institutions themselves. A Senior Lecturer suggested that women were thought to prioritise their families, rather than their professions: *The general view that woman is not able to always be available due to her commitment to her family.* Another Senior Lecturer thought that women themselves might sometimes have a: *Priority for the other things- e.g. family, stress free-life, time for oneself.* These views articulate with those of Elias (2011: 531) who argues that in Malaysia:

> Women's productive roles are constantly brought into tension with embedded social structures, which include localised understandings of appropriate gender roles shaped through their intersection with other sets of social norms such as those relating to ethnicity, religion and national identity.

The Gendered Division of Labour is a major theme in the global literature. Leadership is often perceived to be at odds with the demands of motherhood, domestic responsibilities and work/life balance (Grummell et al. 2009). Lynch (2010) suggested that the academy is constructed as a 'carefree zone' that assumes that academics have no relations other than to their profession. The senior manager is constructed as a zero-load worker, devoid of familial and care responsibilities (Grummell et al. 2009). Runte and Mills (2004) claimed that as it is women who invariably 'navigate between parental and employee roles, it is women only who pay the "toll" for crossing the boundary between work and family' (p. 240).

A dominant view is that time expended on role performance in one domain depletes time available for the demands of the other domains (Runte and Mills 2004). Research has indicated that given the moral imperative on women to care for children, the sick and elderly, women have a form of negative equity in the workplace (Guillaume and Pochic 2009; Lynch et al. 2009; O'Brien 2007). While the gendering of primary care responsibilities is a major consideration, it does not account for why some women who are single, child-free, or whose children have grown up, are also absent from senior HE leadership positions (Currie et al. 2002). The gendered division of labour, and horizontal segregation were also seen to relate to different roles and responsibilities within universities as a Professor noted: *A woman is always being given an operational task rather than a strategic one.* Women in this study noted how they were often responsibilised with teaching and student support activities, rather than research or leadership opportunities. For some, this was because women were not seen as equal to men, as a Lecturer commented: *The men need to see the women as equal colleagues and not just some doll.*

The socio-cultural was also seen to determine what is gender appropriate, with the symbolic gender order requiring women to be led by men rather than to be leaders themselves. An Associate Professor berated those: *Women and men who consider 'ambitious' as a dirty word.* An Associate Professor also commented on the power of the socio-cultural to impede women: *Socio-cultural constraints, such as stereotypes and prejudices as well as familial roles and functions.* Prejudices were thought to flourish as a consequence of gender bias and lack of transparency in selection and promotion processes. The misrecognition of women's leadership potential was noted by a Professor:

> The mind setting of recruiters who normally find/conclude that a high- calibre woman with some Islamic Principles as her way of life, though well- equipped with merits, is not capable enough to lead.

These observations correspond to research findings in Europe. Van den Brink et al.'s (2010) study of 13 universities in the Netherlands revealed a range of casual discriminatory practices in the appointment of professors that eluded formal protocols and objective criteria. Women can still be perceived as 'risky' appointments to senior positions (Ibarra et al. 2010).

The association of men, rather than women, with leadership authority and the internalised oppression that meant that women did not always value other women was reported by a Senior Lecturer who believed that there is a: *Preference towards having male bosses than female ones.* Another Senior Lecturer highlighted the socio-cultural devaluation of women as a major impediment: *Cultural – perception that women make less efficient leaders.* Femaleness is often perceived as irreconcilable with intellectual and managerial authority – a theme explored in Pakistan by Shah (2001) and Smit in South Africa (2006), and theorised by scholars in the Global North including Eagly et al. (1992) and Valian (1999). These studies suggest that woman leaders challenge a gender stereotype. The concept of social cognition suggests that we 'think gender' and that we have deeply embedded notions of gender-appropriate behavior and roles. When we think 'manager', we think 'male' (Sinclair 2001). A conventional view is that the skills, competencies and dispositions deemed essential to leadership including assertiveness, autonomy and authority are embedded in socially constructed definitions of masculinity (Knights and Kerfoot 2004).

While some respondents focussed on external socio-cultural factors, others believed that the enablers and impediments resided in women themselves, with their internal narratives working against them. A range of **personal and psychological** factors were discussed including women's agency, or lack of it, integrity, and aspirations. Self-efficacy was emphasised, as one lecturer observed: *Women need to believe in themselves.* Women were also positioned as reluctant to opt for high-profile positions and an Associate Professor was critical of: *The women that hide themselves from visibility.* Another Associate Professor thought that leadership was not an object of desire: *The women themselves are reluctant to be a leader.* Women's internalised narratives of lack and deficit were mentioned by one Senior Lecturer:

> Some women tend to think that they are not good enough for senior posts/ setting too high standards for themselves.

Emotional capital such as charisma, self-confidence, being thought of as trustworthy were also thought to be important enablers. Charisma was defined by a member of the Focus Group as: *Not too open and not too close to you.* The demographic variables of seniority and maturity were cited as enablers, reflecting cultural traditions of respecting age in the region.

Academic capital was thought to carry considerable weight including qualifications- especially a PhD, knowledge, job track performance, merit, academic reputation, being a professor, experience, leadership credibility, research experience and publications. A finding in the global literature suggests that leaders need to have also demonstrated excellence in publishing and research (Fletcher et al. 2007). The under-representation of women in the global research economy is a structural barrier to leadership. Women account for only 29% of the world's researchers (UNESCO 2010). Globally, women are less likely to be journal editors or cited in top-rated academic journals (Wilson 2012), principal investigators, and are under-represented on research boards and peer review structures that allocate funding (EC 2008, 2011). They are also awarded fewer research prizes (Nikiforova 2011), and are less likely to be keynote speakers at prestigious academic conferences (Schroeder et al. 2013). Hence, a vicious circle develops in which research success generates more success. A member of the Focus Group identified parallels between the research economy and the wider global economy:

> Capitalism. It is like capitalism. Because the more money you have, the more ability you get… Because, if you are junior, you get nothing.

It is questionable why women are faring so badly in the global research economy. One explanation is that there is prejudice against women. Rees (2011) identified that gender bias exists in judgements of excellence – even by peers. Hence the importance of reviewing research resource allocation processes (Wenneras and Wold 1997; Husu 2014). In spite of their exclusion from many research opportunities, some women in the study felt that they had entered the academy as intellectuals and researchers, not as administrators. Leadership was perceived as a diversion from their scholarship, as a Senior Lecturer suggested, her priority was: *fulfilling publications and research KPIs*. Leadership requires a completely different skill set and it is questionable how successful many academics are in making the transition from scholar to chief executive of large institutions.

Power Relations and engagement with power were frequently cited in the questionnaire responses. Sponsorship and recognition from top management were also mentioned, with impediments sometimes located in micropolitical power relations including favoritism and sponsorship. Some believed that enablers related to social capital in the form of networks and political connections. A lecturer commented: *Personal and professional achievement alone will not enable them to enter the position without political recognition*. It was also suggested that only those who share the values of the new neo-liberal university were likely to access senior leadership. A Senior Lecturer emphasised the need to be aligned with the organisational culture: *Personal attributes that are in line with the organisation's culture*.

Particular **skills and competencies** were highlighted by some respondents including interpersonal and communication skills, management skills and the ability to administer. Some respondents believed that certain dispositions and personality traits were important including a high-level of commitment to the job, determination, passion, personal aspiration and the ability to establish a good work/life balance. Communication skills were emphasised by members of the Focus Group:

> I would like my leader to have good communication skills…It means that, I feel that I can talk to her without being afraid, she will judge me in a negative way, you know.

For many women, the **affective load** of leadership was a major deterrent. Lack of women in senior posts means that those who do enter seniority are often perceived as 'other'. This can place an additional burden on women and can produce a sense of isolation, and a Senior Lecturer suggested that: *Fear of being alone at the top* was a most unattractive prospect. Women's refusal to take on the additional burden of leadership was noted by one Senior Lecturer:

> Avoiding extra responsibilities- being an academic without administrative post is already demanding, why bother to take more responsibilities?

Other women discussed how structural factors operated as both enablers and impediments including government quotas of 30 % women in senior positions. This was seen as beneficial to women by some, but as a contradiction to merit-based career progression by others. A major structural observation was that there was a lack of professional development opportunities for women including mentorship and leadership training.

What Makes Leadership Attractive/Unattractive to Malaysian Academic Women?

The main aspects of leadership that were thought to be attractive related to power, reward and recognition. The unattractive side related to the long working hours' culture, the affective implications of being in a minority, toxic social relations, and incompatibility with women's family responsibilities. Access to **power** was a major attraction in terms of status, financial rewards, influence, authority, and social capital as a Senior Lecturer suggested:

> Attractive for those who get motivation from having power and extra responsibility, as well as those who enjoy networking and meeting people.

However, power was also constructed as unattractive and seen as resulting in a heavy bureaucratic burden and the imperative to re-signify oneself as an authority figure, as a Senior Lecturer describes:

> Unattractive for those who don't like going to meetings all day long. Also the fact that once one is in leadership position, she might have to change her ways of doing things and be more strict and demanding (perhaps?).

The affective load of leadership was also discussed in the Focus Group, suggesting that fear is a dominant factor in leadership roles:

> Sometimes the leader tries to control us. At time we are scared, just respect him because of their position…because they have power to punish.

Occupational stress, competition and negativity from colleagues were frequently cited as off-putting for women. A Professor noted the long-hours' culture and the affective load of dealing with toxic social relations: *Crazy hours, back-stabbing.* There were numerous examples of toxic social relations and negative micropolitical activities to block women's thriving. An Associate Professor recalled: *When female colleagues ganged up together to exclude me in decision-making.* Another Associate Professor described how: *My superior did not want to have two women as his deputies – therefore my nomination was not supported by him.* A Senior Lecturer complained that she was given all the: *bad postgraduate students.* Another Senior Lecturer reported the precariousness of the promotions' procedures:

> I submitted my application for Assoc. Prof which met all the requirements and conditions at the time of submission of the application. I was told my application will not proceed since they had new ruling as to the requirements and conditions for the post.

Managing identity, discrimination and other people's negativity can be an additional affective workload which deters women from applying for highly visible senior positions (Kram and McCollom Hampton 2003; Morley 1999). Stress, well-being, work/life balance and sustainability are concerns in academic life (Barrett and Barrett 2007; Kinman and Jones 2008). HE leaders are under increasing pressure to succeed in competitive, performative audit and austerity cultures (Lynch 2006; Morley 2003).

The construct of **Greedy Institutions** was also relevant to this study. Many women perceived leadership as an all-consuming activity. The conflict with domestic responsibilities and the high expectations made senior leadership unattractive to many women. An Associate Professor commented: *Long hours outside, family is more important.* Leadership was frequently conceptualised in terms of loss and sacrifice. A Lecturer observed that leadership means: *The personal sacrifices that have to be made (children, family, friends).* Another Lecturer also referred to the totalising commitment that was required:

> Unattractive because the position warrants total commitment and sacrifices, which sometimes is problematic since there are family matters to think of.

A Lecturer invoked the power of the socio-cultural to make leadership unattractive to women: *The stigma of neglecting your family and being so called career driven.* These views are supported by findings in the global literature- especially that on greedy institutions. Devine et al. (2011:645) claimed that:

> Effective senior management required relentless commitment to the strategic goals of the organization and an implicit assumption of their 24/7 availability to their management roles.

Fitzgerald (2011) described leadership as exhausting, with unrelenting bureaucratic demands and institutional pressures. Universities' leadership involves multiple, complex tasks and responsibilities including management of staff, strategy, finances and resources, operational planning, policy development, quality assurance processes, improving student outcomes and engaging with community and the professions and industry (Currie et al. 2002). Women HE managers in Woodward's UK study (2007) reported 'unmanageably large workloads' (p. 11). These observations have led to leadership being described as 'greedy work' (Currie et al. 2002; Gronn and Lacey 2006). Devine et al. (2011), in their Irish study, discussed leaders requiring 'an elastic self' in the context of new managerial reforms of higher education, and 'a relentless pursuit of working goals without boundaries in time, space energy or emotion' (p. 632). Work intensification is partly the result of neo-liberalisation in which all organisational members have to constantly demonstrate their worth. Elias (2011: 547) observed that:

> Women are increasingly constructed as flexible neoliberal subjects in Malaysia's pursuit of national competitiveness.

While neo-liberalism was not mentioned by name in this study, many of the functionalities such as accountability, performance management and the financialisation of higher education (Blackmore 2014) were cited as features that made many academic women in Malaysia reluctant to take on senior leadership posts.

Consequences of Women's Absences: Representation of Interests and Reproduction of Male Dominance

The dominant narrative regarding the consequences of women's absences from senior leadership related to fears that women's voices, interests and concerns would not be represented in decision-making. There were numerous comments on this topic. An Associate Professor observed that, without women, there were dangers of: *Little voice in terms of fighting for women employees' needs.* A Senior Lecturer also suggested:

> Women's under representation in senior leadership positions in higher education might lead to fewer women in decision-making positions. Thus women's issues might be less considered.

It was feared that matters that relate largely to injuries done to women including sexual harassment would not be taken seriously by male leaders, as a Senior Lecturer suggests: *Rising numbers of issues affecting women's rights and dignity such as sexual harassment.* A Professor was concerned that: *Decision-making is based on males' perspectives.* An Associate Professor commented on the danger of male bias reproducing itself in the absence of women. *It may affect decision-making and policies- seen only from males' perspectives.* A Professor warned that lack of women in senior leadership would result in: *Lack of gender sensitive policies.* Fears of imbalance- especially in policy were expressed by a Senior Lecturer: *Imbalanced rights in policy – biased towards men.* A Professor was concerned about women students:

> Issues of majority female students will not receive proper attention. Some issues might be overlooked which might effect the performance of higher institutes since it is well- known the percentage of female students is much higher than male students.

Some respondents focussed more on human capital inspired views about wasted talent, or the reproduction of male dominance, as an Associate Professor suggested that without women: *Weak and corrupted men remain in power.* Lack of women in senior positions was thought to demoralise other women in the organisation. An Associate Professor believed that the presence of more women in leadership would shift the culture:

> Workplace ambience – depending on culture in the country i.e. the reservation and distance between female and male staff towards male superiors as compared to female superiors, female staff may be more open towards female superior.

While the strength of feeling about lack of representation is noteworthy, these somewhat essentialised views imply that counting more women into male-dominated systems will in itself be transformative. The above comments assume that women in senior leadership positions will champion the rights of all women in the organisation and will be gender sensitive (Billing and Alvesson 2000). Not all women are feminists. Indeed, one of the female respondents, a Lecturer stated: *Women should not be a leader… I personally do not favour women becoming leaders.*

Recommendations

Women in this study were quite clear that they wanted change. Their recommendations focussed on the re-distribution of resources via more investment in their training and professional development. It was proposed that more resources need to come from the state and a Professor called for: *Government support.* An Associate Professor called for: *Academic leadership, and management programmes.* A Professor suggested: *A specific program to identify potential women leaders.* A Lecturer proposed: *Set up modules/courses/programmes specifically for women academics & academic and leadership management programmes.* Mentorship and coaching were also seen as silver bullets by many women. An Associate Professor made the plea: *I'm going to retire next year but my wish for younger women academics is that the institutions provide them with mentor and better support.* A Senior Lecturer said: *I would like to see more mentoring efforts specifically for women academics.* Support to help women manage work/life balance challenges was highlighted by an Associate Professor:

> By nature women's responsibilities, personality, family commitment etc. differ from those of the males. Thus, such women need coaching and training on how to deal with all these entities.

Networking was seen as a mechanism for increasing collectivity, as an Associate Professor suggested:

> Perhaps we can form a network or a body that can fight the cause in an intense and policy-implicating manner- need a strong collective voice and champion for this.

A Lecturer called for the formation of a: *support group and an association/ society to fight/protect with women' issues/rights.*

When asked about recommendations for change, women shifted discourse from their earlier descriptions of impediments and obstacles. Having previously described the irrationality of organisational life in terms of complex micropolitics including favouritism, backstabbing, ganging up, blocking, they proposed rational interventions for change such as the redistribution of knowledge via mentoring and coaching and the input of professional development programmes. Manfredi et al. (2014) found that in the UK, women who had received professional development in the form of the *Leadership Foundation for Higher Education's Top Management Programme* were 2.5 times less likely than their male counterparts to enter senior leadership roles after completion of the programme. This suggests that rational, linear models of change are disrupted by the irrationalities of sexism and prejudice against women leaders. In spite of the backstabbing that was reported, there was still a belief in the altruism and willing re-distribution of knowledge involved in mentoring others in a knowledge economy that is defined by its differentiation and competition.

Conclusion

Lack of women in senior positions means that women are under-represented across all-decision making fora, including committees, boards, recruitment panels and the executive. This means that currently the expertise and skills of a significant part of the HE workforce are being under-utilised. It would be misleading to construct women as victims in all-powerful patriarchal organisations of knowledge production. Women are entering leadership positions- especially as deputies, assistants and adjuncts- and are being creative and innovative (Bagilhole and White 2011). However, the empirical data from this Malaysian study and much of the global literature suggests that women and men in higher education are largely placed differently, with differential access to leadership, and hence to influencing meanings, discourses and practices (Manfredi et al. 2014; Marshall 2007).

The women in this study berated and mourned the lack of women in senior leadership positions in higher education. However, none of them actually wanted to be a Vice-Chancellor or even a Deputy Vice-Chancellor. These posts were perceived as onerous, incompatible with a healthy life/work balance and necessitating the living of unliveable lives (Butler 2004). Counting more women into posts is important, but the liberal feminist strategy to increase representational space cannot be the only goal for gender equality (Bonner 2006; Neale and Ozkanli 2010). It is the gendered world itself that represents the problem, not simply the exclusion of women or the existence of the male norm (Billing 2011; Verloo and Lombardo 2007). Leadership roles appear to be so overextended that they represent a type of virility test, and as such were seen as highly unattractive to the women in this study. What is clear from these data is that gendered change is not just about counting different bodies into leadership positions, but about changing the values that inform and drive leadership in today's neo-liberalised higher education sector. We need to ask how leadership practices can become more sustainable, with concerns about wellbeing as well as competitive advantage in the global academy.

Acknowledgements Thanks to the Ministry of Women, Families and Community Development in Malaysia for funding the research, and to the University of Sussex for Louise Morley's time and to Hidir Mohamed for research assistance with this paper.

References

Abas, A., & Idris, A. (2014, September 3). Dons must be proactive. *New Straits Times.* p. 2.

Azman, N., Jantan, M., & Sirat, M. (2010). The transformation of the academic profession in Malaysia: Trends and issues on institutional governance and management. *Journal of the World Universities Forum, 2*(5), 123–138.

Azman, N., Sirat, M. B., & Samsudin, M. A. (2013). An academic life in Malaysia: A wonderful life or satisfaction not guaranteed? In P. J. Bentley, H. Coates, I. R. Dobson, L. Goedegebuure, & V. L. Meek (Eds.), *Job satisfaction around the academic world.* Dordrecht: Springer.

Bagilhole, B., & White, K. (Eds.). (2011). *Gender, power and management: A cross-cultural analysis of higher education.* London: Palgrave Macmillan.

Bahiyah, A. H. (2008, October 26). Malaysian women in S & T: Opportunities, choices and challenges. Paper Presented at the ICWS- International Conference on Women Scientists, National Yang-Ming University Taipei, Taiwan, Republic of China.

Ball, S. J. (2007). *Education plc: Understanding private sector participation in public sector education.* London: Routledge.

Barrett, L., & Barrett, P. (2007). Current practice in the allocation of academic workloads. *Higher Education Quarterly, 61*, 461–478.

Berma, M. (2003). Towards the national vision policy: Review of the new economic policy and new development policy among the Bumiputera of Sarawak. *Kajian Malaysia, XXI*(1), 221–256.

Berma, M. (2014, July 15). Gender perspective in development tranformation. Paper presented at the *Intellectual Discourse Series, Sabah State Legislative Assembly.*

Billing, Y. (2011). Are women in management victims of the phantom of the male norm? *Gender, Work and Organization, 18*(3), 298–317.

Billing, Y. D., & Alvesson, M. (2000). Questioning the notion of feminine leadership. A critical perspective on the gender labelling of leadership. *Gender, Work & Organization, 7*(3), 144–157.

Blackmore, J. (2014). 'Wasting Talent'? Gender and the problematic of academic disenchantment and disengagement with leadership. *Higher Education Research and Development, 33*(1), 86–99.

Bonner, F. B. (2006). Gender diversity in higher education: 'The Women are Fine, but the Men are not?'. In W. R. Allen et al. (Eds.), *Higher education in a global society: Achieving diversity, equity and excellence. Advances in education in diverse communities: Research, policy, and praxis* (Vol. 5, pp. 159–180). Bingley: Emerald Group Publishing Limited.

Butler, J. (2004). *Undoing gender.* New York: Routledge.

Currie, J., Thiele, B., & Harris, P. (2002). *Gendered Universities in globalized economies: Power, careers and sacrifices.* Lexington: Lexington Books.

Devine, D., Grummell, B., & Lynch, K. (2011). Crafting the elastic self? Gender and identities in senior appointments in Irish education. *Gender, Work and Organization, 18*(6), 631–649.

Eagly, A. H., Makhijani, M. G., & Klonsky, B. G. (1992). Gender and the evaluation of leaders: A meta-analysis. *Psychological Bulletin, 111*(3–2), 3–22.

Elias, J. (2011). The gender politics of economic competitiveness in Malaysia's transition to a knowledge economy. *The Pacific Review, 24*(5), 529–552.

European Commission. (2008). *Mapping the maze: Getting more women to the top in research.* Brussels: EC.

(EC) European Commission: Directorate-General for Research and Innovation. (2011). *Structural change in research institutions: Enhancing excellence, gender equality and efficiency in research and innovation.* Brussels: European Commission.

Fitzgerald, T. (2011). *Troubling leadership? Gender, leadership and higher education* (Paper presented at the AARE Conference). Australia: Hobart. 30 November.

Fletcher, C., Boden, R., Kent, J., & Tinson, J. (2007). Performing women: The gendered dimensions of the UK new research economy. *Gender, Work & Organization, 14*(5), 433–453.

Gronn, P., & Lacey, K. (2006). Cloning their own: Aspirant principals and the school-based selection game. *Australian Journal of Education, 50*(2), 102–121.

Grummell, B., Devine, D., & Lynch, K. (2009). The careless manager: Gender, care and new managerialism in higher education. *Gender and Education, 21*(2), 191–208.

Guillaume, C., & Pochic, S. (2009). What would you sacrifice? Access to top management and the work–life balance. *Gender, Work & Organization, 16*(1), 14–36.

Gunawardena, C., Rasanayagam, Y., Leitan, T., Bulumulle, K., & Abeyasekera-Van Dort, A. (2006). Quantitative and qualitative dimensions of gender equity in Sri Lankan Higher Education. *Women's Studies International Forum, 29*(6), 562–571.

Henderson, J., & Phillips, R. (2007). Unintended consequences: Social policy, state institutions and the "stalling" of the Malaysian industrialisation project. *Economy and Society, 36*(1), 77–101.

Husu, L. (2014). *Research funding gap: Her excellence dwarfed by his excellence.* http://eurosci-entist.com/2014/06/research-funding-gap-excellence-dwarfedexcellence/#sthash.aMIyrJ3S.dpuf. Accessed 8 July 2014.

Ibarra, H., Carter, N. M., & Silva, C. (2010). Why men still get more promotions than women. *Harvard Business Review, 88*, 80–85. September.

Kinman, G., & Jones, F. (2008). A life beyond work? Job demands, work-life balance, and wellbeing in UK academics. *Journal of Human Behavior in the Social Environment, 17*(1–2), 41–60.

Knights, D., & Kerfoot, D. (2004). Between representations and subjectivity: Gender binaries and the politics of organizational transformation. *Gender, Work & Organization, 11*(4), 430–454.

Kram, K., & McCollom Hampton, M. (2003). When women lead: The visibility-vulnerability spiral. In R. Ely, E. G. Foldy, & M. Scully (Eds.), *Reader in gender, work and organization* (pp. 211–223). Oxford: Blackwell Publishing.

Leathwood, C., & Read, B. (2009). *Gender and the changing face of higher education: A feminised future?* Maidenhead: McGraw-Hill, Open University Press.

Lee, M. (2004). *Restructuring higher education in Malaysia.* Penang: School of Educational Studies, Universiti Sains Malaysia.

Lee, M. (2007). Higher education in Southeast Asia in the era of globalization. In J. F. Forest & P. G. Altbach (Eds.), *International handbook of higher education* (pp. 539–555). Dordrecht: Springer.

Lund, H. (1998). *A single sex profession? Female staff numbers in Commonwealth Universities.* London: Commonwealth Higher Education Management Service.

Lynch, K. (2006). Neo-liberalism and marketization: The implications for higher education. *European Educational Research Journal, 5*(5), 1–17.

Lynch, K. (2010). *Carelessness: A hidden doxa of higher education CHEER/ESRC seminar series 'Imagining the University of the Future'. seminar 2: What are the disqualified discourses in the knowledge society?* Centre for Higher Education and Equity Research (CHEER), University of Sussex. http://www.sussex.ac.uk/education/cheer/esrcseminars/seminar2. Date accessed 5 Sept 2012.

Lynch, K., Baker, J., & Lyons, M. (2009). *Affective equality: Love, care and injustice*. London: Palgrave Macmillan.

Malaysia Government. (2005). *Ninth Malaysia plan 2006–2010*. Kuala Lumpur: Government Printers.

Malaysia Government. (2007). *National higher educational strategic plan 2007–2010*. Putrajaya: Ministry of Higher Education, Malaysia.

Malaysia Government. (2010). *Tenth Malaysia plan 2011–2015*. Putrajaya: Economic Planning Unit.

Malaysia Government. (2012). *National education statistics: Higher education centre*. Putrajaya: Planning, Research and Policy Coordination Division.

Malaysia Government. (2013). *Statistics on women, family and community Malaysia*. Putrajaya: Ministry of Women, Family and Community Development.

Manfredi, S., Grisoni, L., & Handley, K. (2014). Gender and higher education leadership: Researching the careers of top management programme alumni. http://www.lfhe.ac.uk/en/research-resources/published-research/research-bytheme/leading-equality-and-diversity/gender-and-higher-education-leadership.cfm. Accessed 2 Sept 2014.

Marshall, J. (2007). The gendering of leadership in corporate social responsibility. *Journal of Organizational Change Management, 20*(2), 165–181.

Mohamad, M., Ng, C., & Hui, T. (2006). *Feminism and the women's movement in Malaysia: An unsung (R)Evolution*. London: Routledge.

Mok, K. H. (2008). Varieties of regulatory regimes in Asia: The liberalization of the higher education market and changing governance in Hong Kong, Singapore and Malaysia. *The Pacific Review, 21*(2), 147–170. May 2008.

Morley, L. (1999). *Organising feminisms. The micropolitics of the academy*. Basingstoke: Macmillan Press.

Morley, L. (2003). *Quality and power in higher education*. Buckingham: Open University Press.

Morley, L. (2011). Misogyny posing as measurement: Disrupting the feminisation crisis discourse. *Contemporary Social Science, 6*(2), 163–175.

Morley, L. (2013, March). Absent talent: Women's participation in higher education leadership and research. Paper presented at the Going Global 2013 Conference in Dubai.

Neale, J., & Ozkanli, O. (2010). Organisational barriers for women in senior management position: A comparison of Turkish and New Zealand Universities. *Gender and Education, 22*(5), 547–563.

New Straits Times. (2014, August 30). 286 Orang Asli enroll into public institutions, p 5.

Nikiforova, I. (2011). Merit & occupational attachment of women in computer science. In S. Sofia & L. Husu (Eds.), *GEXcel work in progress report volume XVII. Proceedings from GEXcel Themes 11–12: Gender Paradoxes in Changing Academic and Scientific Organisation*. http://www.genderexcel.org/?q=webfm_send/99. Accessed 17 Sept 2014.

O'Brien, M. (2007). Mothers' emotional care work in education and its moral imperative. *Gender and Education, 19*(2), 159–177.

Odejide, A., Akanji, B., & Odekunle, K. (2006). Does expansion mean inclusion in Nigerian Higher Education? *Women's Studies International Forum, 29*(6), 552–561.

OECD. (2010). *Atlas of gender and development: How social norms affect gender equality in non-OECD countries*. Paris: OECD.

Ohene, I. (2010). *Gender and leadership in higher educational institutions: Exploring perceptions and practices in University of Cape Coast, Ghana*. International EdD Thesis, University of Sussex.

Onsongo, J. (2004). *Factors affecting women's participation in University Management in Kenya*. Addis: Organisation for Social Science Research in Eastern and Southern Africa.

Rab, M. (2010). *The life stories of successful women academics in Pakistani public sector universities*. EdD Thesis, Institute of Education, University of London.

Rees, T. (2011). The gendered construction of scientific excellence. *Interdisciplinary Science Reviews, 36*(2), 133–145.

Runte, M., & Mills, A. J. (2004). Paying the toll: A feminist post-structural critique of the discourse bridging work and family. *Culture and Organization, 10*(3), 237–249.

Saraswathi, M. (2014). *Malaysia fast becoming preferred destination for higher education among Pakistan students – consul general.* 25 Aug. http://www.bernama.com.my/bernama/v7/ge/newsgeneral.php?id=1063165. Accessed 30 Aug 2014.

Schroeder, J., Dugdale, H. L., Radersma, R., Hinsch, M., Buehler, D. M., Saul, J., Porter, L., Liker, A., De Cauwer, I., Johnson, P. J., Santure, A. W., Griffin, A. S., Bolund, E., Ross, L., Webb, T. J., Feulner, P. G. D., Winney, I., Szulkin, M., Komdeur, J., Versteegh, M. A., Hemelrijk, C. K., Svensson, E. I., Edwards, H., Karlsson, M., West, S. A., Barrett, E. L. B., Richardson, D. S., van den Brink, V., Wimpenny, J. H., Ellwood, S. A., Rees, M., Matson, K. D., Charmantier, A., dos Remedios, N., Schneider, N. A., Teplitsky, C., Laurance, W. F., Butlin, R. K., & Horrocks, N. P. C. (2013). Fewer invited talks by women in evolutionary biology symposia. *Journal of Evolutionary Biology, 26,* 2063–2069. doi:10.1111/jeb.12198. Accessed 29 September 2014.

Shackleton, L., Riordan, S., & Simonis, D. (2006). Gender and the transformation agenda in South African higher education. *Women's Studies International Forum, 29*(6), 572–580.

Shah, S. (2001). Tertiary colleges in Pakistan: Gender and equality. *The School Field, XII*(3/4), 49–70.

She Figures. (2003). *Statistics and indicators on gender equality in science.* Brussels: European Commission.

She Figures. (2006). *Statistics and indicators on gender equality in science.* Brussels: European Commission.

She Figures. (2009). *Statistics and indicators on gender equality in science.* Brussels: European Commission.

She Figures. (2012). *Statistics and indicators on gender equality in science.* Brussels: European Commission.

Sinclair, A. (2001, June 22–29). The body and management pedagogy. Proceedings of the *Gender, Work & Organization* Conference, Keele.

Singh, J. K. S. (2003). *Still a single sex profession? Female staff numbers in Commonwealth Universities.* London: Association of Commonwealth Universities.

Singh, J. K. S. (2008). *Whispers of change. Female staff numbers in Commonwealth Universities.* London: Association of Commonwealth Universities.

Smit, P. (2006). *Leadership in South African higher education: A multifaceted conceptualisation.* PhD Thesis, Institute of Education, University of London.

Stivens, M. (2006). Family values and Islamic Revival: Gender, rights and state moral projects in Malaysia. *Women's Studies International Forum, 29*(4), 354–367.

Teichler, U., Arimoto, A., & Cummings, W. K. (2013). *The changing academic profession: Major findings of a comparative survey.* Dordrecht: Springer.

THES. (2014). *THE 100 under 50 universities 2012.* http://www.timeshighereducation.co.uk/world-university-rankings/2012/one-hundred-under-fifty. Accessed 30 Aug 2014.

UNESCO. (2014). *Higher education in Asia: Expanding out, expanding up.* Quebec: UNESCO Institute of Statistics. http://www.uis.unesco.org/Library/Documents/higher-education-asia-graduate-university-research-2014-en.pdf. Accessed 3 Sept 2014.

UNESCO Institute of Statistics. (2009). *Global education digest 2009: Comparing education statistics across the world.* Montreal: UNESCO Institute of Statistics.

UNESCO Institute of Statistics. (2010). *Global education digest 2010: Comparing education statistics across the world (a special focus on gender).* Paris: UNESCO.

Valian, V. (1999). *Why so slow? The advancement of women.* Boston: MIT Press.

Van den Brink, M., Benschop, Y., & Jansen, W. (2010). Transparency in academic recruitment: A problematic tool for gender equality? *Organization Studies, 31*(12), 1–25.

Verloo, M., & Lombardo, E. (2007). Contested gender equality and policy variety in Europe: Introducing a critical frame analysis approach. In M. Verloo (Ed.), *Multiple meanings of gender equality. A critical frame analysis.* Budapest/New York: Central European University Press.

Wan, C. D. (2012, December). *Bulletin national higher education research* (pp. 3–7), No 20. National Higher Education Institute (IPPTN).

Wenneras, C., & Wold, A. (1997). Nepotism and sexism in peer review. *Nature, 387*, 341–343. 22 May.

Wilkinson, R., & Yussof, I. (2005). Public and private provision of higher education in Malaysia: A comparative analysis. *Higher Education, 50*, 361–386.

Wilson, R. (2012, October 22). Scholarly publishing's gender gap: Women cluster in certain fields, according to a study of millions of journal articles, while men get more Credit. *The Chronicle of HigherEducation.*http://chronicle.com/article/The-Hard-Numbers-Behind/135236/?cid=wb&utm_source=wb&utm_medium=en. Accessed 26 Oct 2013.

Woodward, D. (2007). *Work-life balancing strategies used by women managers in British 'Modern' universities.* http://www.emeraldinsight.com/doi/full/10.1108/02610150710726507. Accessed 18 Sept 2014.

World Bank. (2007). *Malaysia and the knowledge economy: Building a world-class higher education system.* Washington, DC: The World Bank. http://siteresources.worldbank.org/INTMALAYSIA/Resources/Malaysia-Knowledge-Economy2007.pdf. Accessed 30 Aug 2014.

World Bank. (2014). *Labor force participation rate female (% of female population age 15+) (modelled ILO estimated).* Washington, DC: The World Bank. http://data.worldbank.org/indicator/SL.TLF.CACT.FE.ZS. Accessed 4 Sept 2014.

Yusof, Z. A., & Bhattasali, D. (2008). *Economic growth and development in Malaysia: Policy making and leadership* (Commission on Growth and Development Working Paper No. 27). Kuala Lumpur: Commission on Growth and Development.

Chapter 8
Women of Color Advancing to Senior Leadership in U.S. Academe

Belinda Lee Huang

Introduction

Today, educational trends indicate that each generation of younger women is attaining higher levels of postsecondary education in the U.S. (Jaschik 2010; Ryu 2010). Since the baby boom generation, women are surpassing men in educational attainment and the gap between them is getting larger (Boushey and O'Leary 2009; Ryu 2010). More women complete high school, enroll in and graduate from college, and complete advanced degrees at the master's and doctoral level; however, men still outnumber women in doctoral degrees conferred in typically male dominated fields (i.e., business/management, engineering, and law) (Bell 2010; Ryu 2010). New data from 2013 revealed that women were 57.1 % of all first time graduate students, and men were 42.9 % (Alum et al. 2014).

In this chapter the use of the term academe includes doctoral granting, master's, bachelor's, associate colleges and universities. Although the numbers of women faculty in the U.S. have been slowly increasing in the last decade, women continue to lag behind men in status, salary, and leadership positions (White House Project Report 2009). Data indicates as the prestige of the institution increases women fall significantly behind (Bach and Perucci 1984; Konrad and Pfeffer 1991; Kulis 1997; Tolbert and Oberfield 1991). Women are only 30 % of the faculty at research universities, 40 % of the faculty at master's degree granting institutions, 42 % of the faculty at private liberal arts colleges, and 49 % of the faculty at public 2-year institutions (The White House Project Report 2009). As faculty rank increases the number of

B.L. Huang, Ph.D. (✉)
Visiting Assistant Professor, Higher Education Administration,
Graduate School of Education and Human Development,
George Washington University, Washington 20052, DC, USA
e-mail: bjhuang98@outlook.com

© Springer International Publishing Switzerland 2017   155
H. Eggins (ed.), *The Changing Role of Women in Higher Education*,
The Changing Academy – The Changing Academic Profession in International
Comparative Perspective 17, DOI 10.1007/978-3-319-42436-1_8

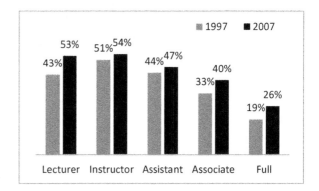

Fig. 8.1 Women Faculty By Rank, 1997 and 2007 (Adapted from M. Ryu (2010). Minorities in higher education: Twenty-fourth status report. p. 114–117. Copyright 2010 by the American Council on Education)

women steadily declines (Ryu 2010). Among full-time professors, 85 % were White (60 % were White males and 25 % were White females), 4 % were Black, 3 % were Hispanic, 8 % were Asian/Pacific Islander, and less than 1 % were American Indian/Alaska Native (NCES 2014).

In fall 2011, women had the largest representation among instructors (64 %) and lecturers (63 %) (NCES, 2014 (see Fig. 8.1). There is a considerable decline in representation from assistant (63 %), to associate (54 %), to full professor rank (38 %). In each of these ranks, women faculty representation has increased from 1991 (Ryu 2010). However, women who are full professors at public universities are still a small percentage: 19.2 % at doctoral granting institutions; 28.7 % at masters, 31.3 % at bachelor, and 52.9 % at associate institutions (West and Curtis 2006). The small numbers of women faculty who reach full professor rank affect the pipeline to the university presidency since the traditional pathway to the presidency is from tenured full professor positions to senior level administrative positions such as dean and chief academic officer (King and Gomez 2008).

The American Council on Education's *The American College President 2012* revealed that only 13 % of the nation's college and university presidents are persons of color. Women presidents increased 3 %, from 23 % to 26 % in 2011. For the last 10 years, the number of female presidents has remained at about 500 out of approximately 4,000 postsecondary institutions (The White House Project Report 2009). Women presidents are more likely to be presidents at private doctoral granting universities (24 %) than public doctorate granting institutions (21 %) (ACE 2012). At master's and bachelor institutions, the share of women presidents is 23 %; the largest share of women presidents are concentrated at community colleges (33 %) and less at doctorate granting institutions (19 %) (ACE 2012).

On the Pathway to the Presidency (2008) report indicated that presidents are most likely to advance from academic positions. Of the current presidents, 40 % came from the chief academic officer or provost position. Prior to becoming chief academic officer 85 % had served in a faculty or academic administrator position (King and Gomez 2008). Twenty-three percent of first-time presidents came from non-academic areas such as finance, development, or student affairs. Prior positions held by presidents included: senior administrator officers (20 %), deans (17 %), chief student affairs or enrollment management officers (13 %), chief of staff (5 %), and chief diversity officer positions (2 %) (King and Gomez 2008).

Women of color are less likely to emerge from senior academic positions. They comprise only 3 % of chief academic officers compared to 6 % men of color and 35 % White women (King and Gomez 2008). They are 7 % of all senior administrators compared to 9 % men and 38 % white women. At the time these data were collected there were no women of color chief academic officers in the doctoral granting public university system; within master's public universities, there were 7 % African-American women and 1 % Latinas; within public baccalaureate universities, there were less than 1 % Asian American Pacific Islander women and Latinas (King and Gomez 2008).

Since 40 % of current presidents ascended from chief academic officer positions, the lack of women of color in chief academic officer positions is a cause for concern (King and Gomez 2008). However, if other senior academic positions (e.g., chief diversity officers) were considered as possible pathways to the presidency, significant possibilities emerge given that women of color are better represented in these positions.

King and Gomez (2008) asserted that academe should consider non chief academic officer positions when searching for future presidents and tap into the pool of African American and Latina chief diversity officers. African-American women held 42 % of chief diversity officer positions at public doctoral granting institutions, Latinas held 4 %, Asian American Pacific Islanders held 2 %, compared to 8 % White women (King and Gomez 2008). The majority of senior administrator positions held by Asian American Pacific Islanders and Latinas were between 1 and 2 % at public and private baccalaureate institutions (King and Gomez 2008). At public baccalaureate institutions African Americans held 7 % of chief student affairs enrollment management positions, Asian American Pacific Islanders held less than 1 % and Latinas held 1 % compared to 35 % White women. In chief of staff positions, Asian American Pacific Islanders and Latinas held 7 % compared to 63 % White women at private doctoral granting institutions. At the doctoral granting and baccalaureate granting universities, the number of women of color senior administrators is very small (King and Gomez 2008).

The question of why there are so few women of color at the highest level of administration in U.S. academe concerns scholars and policy makers in higher education. Literature has documented the slow growth of diversifying the leadership pool, but attempts to understand why women lag behind in status, representation, and leadership are not well understood. Bridges et al. (2008) cited biased perceptions of women and candidates of color and their capacity to lead; this is often the result of conscious or unconscious reliance on existing stereotypes (Ridgeway 2001). Women of color in U.S. academe report tokenism and stereotyping as contributing to isolation, loneliness, and burnout (Edwards and Camblin 1998; Hune 1998; St. Jean and Feagin 1998; Turner and Myers 2000).

Barriers to advancement for women in U.S. academe include the chilly climate for women, structural characteristics, leaky pipeline, and socialization experiences (Fairweather and Rhoads 1995; Konrad and Pfeffer 1991; Sandler 1986). The low numbers of women of color in senior level administrative positions suggest that more research is needed to understand why women of color are underrepresented. Whether women of color are not being tapped for senior leadership positions or choosing not to take on these roles requires further inquiry. Research may suggest ways to improve the institutional climate, structural hiring, and resources to improve women of color retention and increase their advancement.

Purpose of the Chapter

Drawn from a larger research study which investigated how women of color navigate power and politics to arrive at senior levels of U.S. academe, this chapter focuses on the research question: what factors do they (women of color senior leaders) perceive as contributing to their advancement to senior level positions? Senior level administrators include women at the cabinet level (i.e. chief of staff, executive vice president, chief academic officer/provost, dean of academic college, chief student affairs officer). Women of color senior leaders, who served at doctoral granting and baccalaureate granting universities, were selected because of the complexity of governance and organizational systems at these type of institutions, and because few women of color hold senior level administrative positions at these institutions.

Key Terms

In this chapter, I utilize the term 'women of color' senior leader to describe women who are African American or Black American, Asian American Pacific Islander, American Indian and Latina heritage. The descriptor 'women of color' is used in this chapter rather than minorities because of inherent implied positionality, power, and status. By 2050, the U.S. census predicts non-Hispanic Whites will no longer be the majority.

In this chapter the term 'African American' references Black Americans or Afro-Americans as citizens or residents of the United States who have origins in any of the Black populations of Africa (U.S. Census 2000). The term 'Asian American Pacific Islander' is used to denote persons of Asian/Pacific Islander American heritage. Within this chapter, Asian American Pacific Islander encompasses individuals of East Asian, South East Asian, South Asian, Hawaiian, Guamanian, Samoan, and other Pacific Islander descent living in the United States (U.S. Census 2000). The term 'Latina/o' recognizes persons of Latin American descent living in the United States. Latina encompasses individuals who are Mexican Americans, Chicanas, Cuban Americans, Argentinean Americans, Colombian Americans, Dominican Americans, Puerto Rican Americans, Spanish Americans, and Salvadoran Americans. The term American Indian and Alaskan Native refers to individuals having origins in North and South American (including Central America) and who maintain tribal affiliation or community attachment (U.S. Census Bureau 2008).

Why So Few Women of Color Senior Leaders?

Though U.S. academe has seen an increase in the pool of available women and persons of color at the presidency level, there is still a dearth of women of color presidents (American Council on Education 2012; White House Project 2009). In 2009, 22 % of the nation's historically/predominantly Black institutions were led by African American women, but only eight of the predominantly White, 4 year institutions were led by African American women (Bower and Wolverton 2009). *The American College President: 2012 Edition* report indicated there are 4.8 % African American college presidents, 1.4 % Asian American Pacific Islander, 2.8 % Latina/o, and 0.9 % American Indian; of these presidents the percentage that are women include 5 % African American, 4.3 % Latina, 0.7 % Asian American, and 0.7 % American Indian. At the time of this study, there was only one American Indian woman president of a baccalaureate institution outside of the tribal college system in 2012. Therefore, even though the *Minorities in Higher Education, Twenty-fourth Status Report* (2010) indicates that the share of presidential positions filled by women of color increased from 8 to 13 % in the last two decades and the numbers of Latina and Black women presidential appointments nearly doubled (Harvey and Anderson 2005), in fact, in the last 25 years few women of color have attained the presidency level in U.S. higher education institutions.

Research Design

This chapter is based on a research study of individual case studies of nine women of color at nine U.S. higher education institutions. The "unit of analysis" (Merriam 2009) was each individual woman of color, while the U.S. institution was the context of the bounded system (Smith 1988). Case study methodology enabled unique cases to be examined while conducting cross-case analysis to see whether intragroup (e.g., African American, American Indian) or intergroup similarities or differences were revealed.

Nine participants were selected: three African Americans, two Asian American Pacific Islanders, two Latinas, and two American Indian women at a doctoral or a baccalaureate granting university. Each woman was interviewed for 60–90 min in her office at her home institution or off site. To support credibility, member checks and triangulation were conducted. Denzin (1989) defined triangulation as using multiple methods, multiple sources of data, multiple investigators, or multiple theories to confirm emerging findings.

For this study, triangulation included reviewing primary and secondary documents including websites for information about each participant's status/statistics at the university, organizational charts, newspaper articles, and university publications. In addition, the researcher utilized direct observation of the administrator's office (including location and spatial layout of the office), and took photographs of conference rooms, waiting areas, and the senior leader's office. Member checks added to the validity of the study by asking the participant to provide feedback on the emerging findings (Maxwell 2005). Leaving an audit trail authenticated the findings of the study because the researcher described in detail how the data were collected, categories decided, and decisions made (Goetz and LeCompte 1984).

Theoretical Frameworks

This chapter's research question focuses on what factors women of color perceive as contributing to their advancement to senior level positions in U.S. academe. Three theoretical frameworks helped inform this study's domains of race, gender and leadership: critical race theory (CRT) and Lipman-Blumen's (1992) connective leadership, and Dill and Zambrana's (2009) intersectionality. Using only one theory would not have allowed for an intersectional analysis of the experiences of women of color senior leaders.

Critical race theory (CRT) examines existing entitlements, and how women of color resist racism and oppression in academe. A critical contribution of CRT is it allows women of color senior leaders to name their own reality, in their voice, while affirming their experiential knowledge. Using CRT enables an interdisciplinary examination of participant's experience, where disciplines such as women's studies, sociology, and Lesbian, Gay, Bi-sexual, Transgender, Queer (LGBTQ) studies can be used to illuminate analysis of the data.

Lipman-Blumen's (1992) connective leadership model connects individuals to their tasks and ego drives. Through this model, women of color's leadership style is based upon the "premise of connection" (Gilligan 1982), and described by these achieving styles: direct, instrumental, and relational. Women of color senior leaders were most closely matched to instrumental and relational achieving styles.

Intersectionality, (Dill and Zambrana 2009) which draws upon knowledge developed by the experiences of previously excluded communities—Black, Latina/o, Asian American, and American Indian—is derived from people of color's counter histories and counter narratives to narratives of the experiences of social elites. Intersectional analysis reveals how oppression is "constructed and maintained through multiple aspects of identity simultaneously" for the women of color senior leaders in this study (Dill and Zambrana 2009, p. 7). This framework examines how structural, disciplinary, hegemonic, and interpersonal domains of power affected women of color senior leaders who experienced discrimination because of combinations of race, class, gender, sexual orientation, ethnicity, and other aspects of difference (Dill and Zambrana 2009).

Advancing Women Through Opportunity and Experience

Each woman of color in this study credited individuals in their lives that helped them become the leaders they are today. While leadership is often thought to be a position, these women proved it was a process by which they learned by trial and error how to navigate their surroundings. Their families influenced them in their developmental years; spouses and partners were critical support systems; and mentors and guides propelled them forward.

Parental Influence

Many of the senior leaders spoke of the enduring effects of parental influence. Parents were instrumental in teaching values, and their sacrifices and support motivated them to achieve senior level positions. Often their encounters with racism or bias could be difficult. However CRT asserts that the experiential knowledge of people of color is legitimate. It describes the importance of the counter story: parents teach their children to remember family histories, testimonies (testimonials), dichos (proverbs) and chronicles:

> And she was constantly trying to instill that in us to be able to say you need to listen closely to what people say and not what you hope they're saying. Think about the words they're using, you know. If people tell you something that is different than what you know about who you are, you need to go with what you know about yourself, especially when you get that reinforced by others who know and love you.

This woman of color senior leader cited these teachings as helpful when she faced racism in her graduate program or when advancing to senior leadership positions. The use of CRT and intersectionality as frames of reference inform our understanding of how parents of women of color senior leaders schooled and prepared them for the challenges they would face because of their race and racism in the outside world. Literature confirms that family gave African American women leaders a strong self-concept and strength to compete in the White academic environment (Benjamin 1997; Gregory 1995; Hughes 2009). In dominant majority environments, women of color were often embattled and their struggles might lead them to question their abilities. Therefore, family members played a critical role in validating women of color and helping them overcome self-doubt.

Despite obstacles encountered, parents of color pushed their daughters to go out and be bold. While one might encounter setbacks, one mother told her daughter: "Don't sit and cry over spilled milk. There's much more work to be done out there."

Faced with challenges, women of color questioned whether they should continue. A mother advised her daughter, "You can say it's hard, but you can't say you can't do it." Parents admonished them to keep going despite the challenges they faced. Literature referred to family as an important influence and motivator (Knowlton 1992; Manuelito-Kerkvliet; Rodriguez 2006; Schilling 2009; Valdata 2008).

Parents and leaders of color taught women of color that if they were given a position of leadership, they had a responsibility toward their ethnic community. One Latina senior leader recalled an African American board member chastising her for being tired of having to speak up for all Hispanics: "As long as you're the only woman or the only Hispanic on that Board, your responsibility is to speak for them and your job then is to open that door so that there'll be others on that board." Thus, in addition to reminding her of her cultural heritage, family also instilled beliefs about ethical values. Being a leader was not about one's position, but also about how to do the right thing for one's community. This same leader also commented that one must have a "respectful way of leading, and if you go from ego you can really harm."

Parents of women of color taught them to be resilient, gave them a strong sense of self, and taught them to remember who they were. Yet, some participants faced discrimination because of their race/ethnicity and had the additional burden of negotiating two cultures and two languages. Nieves-Squire (1994) and Padilla (2003) confirmed that Latinas experience "double discrimination" and "double minority" status. A Latina senior leader recalled how her mother had missed being valedictorian by a fraction of a point:

> Mother didn't have a bitter bone in her body. She just said "That's why you have to be smart. Because it's always gonna happen to you and you have to be smart in two languages and so you'll be smarter than they because you will be able to perform the same job but in town languages and so that'll be a one-up for you.

Literature confirms that faculty of color who were non-native speakers experienced language and cultural bias; they were critiqued for their accents and ridiculed by some of their students for being non-native speakers (Huang 2013). To combat these challenges, parents encouraged them to work harder and not be distracted by negative remarks. Women of color senior leaders carried these teachings into their work as leaders, so they were not discouraged by the challenges they faced or the resistance they experienced.

Parents emphasized education and set the expectation that women of color leaders could achieve anything they wanted. Family supported and sacrificed for participants to get the education necessary to make it possible for them to attain senior leadership positions even though some parents had low levels of education. Even though some of these women of colors' parents might have had a grade school education, they believed that education was the social elevator that could elevate their daughters to careers that surpassed their own station in life. Other parents believed there were no gender differences and expected that their daughters would go to college. Just because they were girls did not mean that they should not have careers. Their parents believed strongly that they could achieve anything they wanted to.

Recalling her family's sacrifice for her to obtain an education, especially since few in her community were able to obtain an education, this American Indian senior leader remarked:

> Tremendous sacrifices were made for me to be in my role…. All those people and all those prayers and all those songs and all those ceremonies, they sacrificed….for me to know them today, that's my foundation. And at the same time, my parents, my grandparents sacrificed a lot for me to get an education.

This participant was indebted to her family for how they had supported her education and she retained the values of family, community, and spirituality in her senior leadership role. Much of the literature on women of color cites family influences, particularly mothers who taught them the value of hard work and expected them to pursue higher education (Schilling 2009; Valdata 2008). Other literature of an African American president cited her father who set the expectation that she should "do something and not be shy about it" (Moses 2009, p.5). Family expectations that they would achieve in their careers pushed women of color to get their education and use it for their community.

Partner Influence

Several women described their marital status and partner influence as instrumental in their career success. Partners pushed them to take risks and saw their potential before they recognized it. Partners were supportive of their careers, and encouraged them to interview for senior level positions. In the literature, African American women presidents had husbands who were supportive of their careers, had flexible work, or were retired (Moses 2009; Tatum 2009). Their husbands were able to relocate and actively raise their children (Moses 2009; Tatum 2009). Literature on Latinas cited the powerful influence of family and having husbands that helped them pursue careers at the university (Cipres 1999; Rodriguez 2006). This woman of color described her reticence in pursuing a presidency and her husband's encouragement:

> … I said, "The presidency?" I went back home and talked to my husband, I said, "What is this?" And he said, "Go for it. Whatever it is – you can always say, 'I don't want it.'" Because truthfully, I had never heard of _____. And I wouldn't tell him that but I hadn't. And so I went down and I met with the people, and whatever it was that I got at those other – working with those organizations and being at the_____school, I think convinced them that I could work in a different environment because in a _____ school, did you know Ph.Ds don't count?

Other senior leaders commented that they lacked confidence, but their partners told them to apply for positions. They encouraged them to investigate positions and not be shy about pursuing opportunities. Without their partners' support, many of these women of color might not have become senior leaders. Literature confirmed that women of color presidents attributed marrying the right person, one who was able to see their potential career and supported them in times of self-doubt, as critical to their pathway to the presidency (Turner 2007).

Many women of color disclosed they had not considered becoming a president or senior leader. One was nominated by a fellow classmate at the Harvard Institution for Education Management (IEM) program; another was asked to apply for a presidency by a search firm because she had done well in a Dean search; another was encouraged by her president to apply for a vice-provost position. These findings confirm a study by Benjamin (1997) that African American women presidents did not plan to pursue the presidency position; others nominated them or asked them to apply (Turner 2007). It is interesting to note that women of color, although credentialed and highly respected did not see themselves as others – search firms, partners, presidents – viewed them and would not have applied for the presidency or senior level position without prodding by others. Perhaps this speaks to women of color not seeing themselves in the senior leader role or having few women of color role models who had achieved the senior leader position. Is it women of colors' self-concept that was lacking, or society that had promoted so few women of color into senior leader positions? These women of color were not the first women to rise to senior leader positions in U.S. academe, but they were the first women of color to retain their cultural heritage, language, and ethnicity in their senior level positions, aspects which they cited as being integral to their leadership.

Connections and Class Privilege

Advancing to senior level positions is often based upon having connections with individuals with hiring authority. However, women of color did not have the advantages of being part of the old boy's network. Within their social networks, sometimes women of color leaders were frustrated that colleagues did not consider them for positions. One participant cited her frustration that a former supervisor asked her to recommend a woman of color for a position, yet did not consider her as a potential hire:

> You just make me mad. How come you don't even invite me? He said you just went to
> _____. I didn't think you'd want to come. I said well, maybe not but I want to be invited.
> He said, okay, I'm inviting you.

If this senior leader had not spoken up she would have missed an opportunity to work for a national organization, which led to other senior opportunities. She commented that advancing to senior level positions had a lot to do with one's connections.

Another finding was the privilege of one's marital status as a senior leader. One woman of color senior leader, who was unmarried, remarked that in advancing to higher level positions, having a partner gave a certain social status. The position and title of partners and how willing they were to be involved in campus life could be an asset to a senior leader. In this study, the majority of women were married or partnered. A few were divorced and one remarried. In the American Council on Education's *The American College President: 2012 Edition*, only 72 % of women presidents were married, compared with 90 % of their male colleagues. This has significantly increased from 1986, when only 35 % women presidents were married. Women presidents who were divorced, separated, or widowed have decreased from 19 % in 2006 to 16 % of women presidents in 2011 (ACE 2007, 2012). The statistics of women senior leaders in this study who were married or partnered is similar to *The American College President: 2007 Edition* study.

Whether marital status affects the selection or advancement of senior leaders is a factor which requires further investigation. As discussed by Dill and Zambrana (2009) one's multiple aspects of identity can extend privilege or perpetuate inequality because of social identity. Therefore a woman of color who was divorced or single could experience inequality because of her social status. This woman of color describes the challenges of moving up without a partner:

> I mean whether or not you're in a partnered relationship and you're in some senior positions, your partner's station in life.... and role they're willing to play...... makes a difference to some positions. You know I'm a single—I was a single mom....I think that there are some issues that maybe not intentionally get played out that affect..... how successful you can be or how—maybe not how successful, how difficult it can be, how challenging it can be for you.

When ascending to the role of the presidency, women of color who were divorced or single did not have the same social status and advantage as having a partner. Having a partner who would play a spousal role and accompanying duties could impact on one's success.

Class privilege was another social identity that impacted on advancing to senior leadership. One president, who was from a working class background, said that without a fellowship from the Ford Foundation she would not have made it to the presidency, because it helped pay for her graduate education. She was the only senior leader that acknowledged her class background and breaking through the class barrier. Viewed through an intersectional lens, the fellowship mitigated her working class background by providing her equal opportunity to benefit from graduate study (Dill and Zambrana 2009).

Opportunities to Lead

Women of color were able to advance to senior leadership roles through opportunities to lead. Turner (2007) confirmed that for women of color presidents "individual validation with institutional opportunities critical to growth and development, personally and professionally" (p. 17). When asked if she encountered any obstacles to being one of the first women of color in senior leadership, one woman of color said that being the first woman of color had the potential to open doors:

> Not a negative factor. I think because at my age I would have been one of the first, see. So it opened doors for me instead of [closing] them, but at a time when this country was looking to open some doors.

This woman of color had multiple opportunities to advance through personal connections. She welcomed the opportunities and stressed that if women desired to advance they had to be willing to move to other places in the country. Being in the right place presented opportunities for women of color senior leaders, and as the first woman of color, it established the way for others to follow.

Learning and Preparation

Women of color senior leaders stressed the importance of learning new skills and preparing to advance to senior leader positions. They recommended learning a new discipline, rounding out one's knowledge base by learning about new areas of administration, attending seminars to expand one's skill set, observing others, and taking on additional roles and responsibilities. All women of color senior leaders participated in professional development programs including the Harvard Institute of Education Management (IEM), American Association of State Colleges and Universities (AASCU) training for new presidents, Council of Independent Colleges New Chief Academic Officers Seminar, and the American Council on Education (ACE) New Chair's Workshop. Other leaders received American Council on Education and Ford Fellowships. One woman of color who participated in new president training credited it with helping her be successful in her first year:

> In (the) new president's boot camp it's run by AASCU, the American Association of Colleges and Universities. They tell you to think deeply about your first year not about your presidency, that first year. What things do you want to accomplish in that first year because that sets a real tone for your presidency and a lot of people make strategic mistakes in their first year and they can't come back from it. So in that boot camp, in those classes I really thought about what I was going to do and one of the decisions that I made was that I would study my team and give them the year to work with me. Instead of making the decision up front about who should go, who should stay when…

She emphasized how critical it was to have the right team in place, and as president to be matched to the right institution. In configuring her team, she chose three or four people whom she trusted for their intelligence, who brought different strengths to the discussion and who were committed to the mission of the university. Other presidents added that having the right team in place included advisors that helped them be successful in their presidencies.

Within baccalaureate and doctoral institutions, women of color stressed taking advantage of opportunities to develop one's skills and broaden one's network. Senior leaders explained that they advanced in their careers by working hard, volunteering in committees, and preparing for what would come next:

> And I don't know if that's a common thing but I find the more you learn from different people, the more you are knowledgeable …… leadership takes broad understanding, cannot

be too narrow. So you have to know other department (s), other program (s), (the) academic side.....volunteer in academic committee or something if possible, when you have time. If you don't have time, don't do it. Teach a course ....So it's to prepare yourself into all directions.

Thus, preparation included knowing both student affairs and academic administration. By learning new areas and developing new skills, senior leaders stated they met more people which added to their network and contributed to their understanding of multiple areas on campus. This knowledge of student affairs and academic administration helped prepare them for senior leadership positions. Literature cited senior leaders developing competence through experience and learning everyone else's job which developed their breadth of exposure and substance (Austin 2009; Hughes 2009; Moses 2009).

Communication skills were frequently cited in the literature as contributing to senior leaders' success. African American women presidents recognized the importance of being able to communicate effectively—articulating their message, and crafting it for different purposes (Moses 2009). Two women of color emphasized developing skills of argumentation, a divergence from the literature in that effective communication skills (Darden 2006) are stressed, not argumentation. One woman of color senior leader president participated in debates during college and reflected on how she benefited from this skill in her current situation (she was 1 of 2 women out of 15 presidents in her university system):

As it turned out, I debated in college and in those days when you debate women debated against women, men debated against men. Now it sounds kind of funny but that's how it was. But if you were a mixed team, boy and girl, you had to debate in the men's division. Well, it turned out I had a boy as a partner so I always debated in the men's division and I cannot help but think that growing up with boys and debating in the men's division all was some sort of preparation for what my world was to be.

As a woman of color working with White males she used her debate and argumentation skills, and unwittingly, she prepared for it in college. Woman of color senior leaders participated in a predominantly male context, with very few women at the highest level. In these environments, senior leaders had to negotiate hierarchy and privilege daily in academe.

Mentoring

As an analytical framework, intersectionality (Dill and Zambrana 2009) helps us understand the particular nature of inequalities derived from the intersection of race, ethnicity, class, and gender. Placing specific groups in a privileged position with respect to other groups offers individuals unearned benefits or group membership. Hence, participants were challenged in the academic arena by negotiating environments where race, class, and gender intersected with structures of power and privilege. The women in this study emphasized the importance of navigating the environment with a guide (mentor). Participants recommended assigning mentors right away to junior faculty or administrators, after they joined the university. In the literature, mentoring was a strategy that facilitated the professional growth, job satisfaction, and advancement of African American faculty in predominantly White institutions (Crawford and Smith 2005); it also helped them navigate the complexities of higher education in their early years as tribal college administrators (Manuelito-Kerklviet 2005). As a newcomer the effort to find one's way in the challenging terrain of the institutional environment required having someone who could guide you:

> I would never bring women period and particularly women of color in without - I think they need to have mentors assigned when they come in. It's a hard place to be when you're here by yourself and nobody is telling you what the game rules are that have existed.

This participant refers to the rules that individuals adhere to but are not formally disclosed. Without someone to explain this to them, women of color can get lost in the university system. Literature confirmed mentoring counteracts the difficulty of navigating this terrain by providing networks, and guidance to persevere in academe (Fries Britt and Kelly 2005; Gregory 1995; Huang 2013; Hune 1998; Murata 2006; Turner and Myers 2002). Also informal mentoring was helpful in navigating the complexities of higher education (Manuelito-Kerkvliet 2005; Schilling 2009; Valdata 2008).

Mentors provided social and cultural capital. Women of color were advanced, on mentor's recommendations, allowed to attend senior level meetings, and invited to shadow them in their presidencies. Literature found that obstacles for Latina/o community college presidents included a lack of cultural capital (Mata 1997). One participant commented that though she wished for a woman of color coach there were too few women of color senior leaders. Consequently, many of their mentors were White males: supervisors, deans, or presidents who advised and prepared them for leadership. Stanley and Lincoln (2005) confirmed that cross race mentoring was helpful. White males, because of the privilege that accompanied their race and gender, were able to use their status and social capital to advocate for participants. Some were also influential and powerful behind the scenes. One senior leader described how a White male mentor helped her understand the subtext of statements people made in meetings:

> He would tell me what the intent of the person was. Which I could never have figured out. So what a person says in a meeting is not exactly what is on their mind. That there's something behind the statement and that training I got has served me well.

This participant described how this skill assisted her in her presidency, as she and her staff would often debrief after meetings and discuss the content and intent of what had been said. If necessary they would inquire from others close to that person about that person's position on the issue. Understanding the subtext of people's statements provided information about their perspectives, whether antagonistic or uncooperative, that could be helpful in a negotiation.

Mentors cautioned women of color senior leaders against serving on too many committees while working towards tenure. They pointed out which publications would enhance their portfolios, and negotiated their job placements. Literature on mentors confirmed they helped protégés navigate and maneuver through the system (Huang 2013; Valdata 2008); told them what the rules were; showed them how to develop political skills, provided venues for them to showcase their work and nominated them for senior positions (Benjamin 1997; Kanter 1983). Mentors noticed their potential. One women of color president took an interest in an Asian American leader's career and propelled her into senior leadership positions. This leader acknowledged she would not be in her current role without that sponsorship (Hune 1998; Murata 2006; Yamagata-Noji 2005).

Participants did not mention who their current mentors or sponsors are now that they are senior leaders. Some participants mentioned how lonely it is to be in senior leadership and have few individuals to discuss issues with.

Conclusion

This chapter prompts the question: how can we cultivate more women of color senior leaders in U.S. academe? From this study's findings, women of color cited parental and partner influences, mentoring and leadership preparation as pivotal to their ascending to senior leader positions in academe. These findings speak to influences at the personal level and do not attempt to construct what systemic changes are needed to increase women of color in U.S. higher education.

The findings also reveal women of color benefited from strong teaching from their parents to disregard external influences and to listen to internal knowledge of their sense of self. Cultivating a strong sense of self, women of color were able to manage discrimination they faced in academe due to racism, sexism, language bias, and homophobia. In addition their partners and spouses instilled encouragement and recognition of their abilities which boosted their confidence to apply for senior level positions. Mentors, who were mostly White male, also supported them and opened doors for them, using their social and cultural capital. Today, one should find cross –race mentors and gender, to provide career guidance and to explain the system of higher education. Women of color senior leaders in this study spent a great deal of time attending leadership development programs; thus if one is seeking a senior leader position, attending a leadership development program and volunteering on various committees on their campus enhanced one's preparation for the senior leader role.

Reaching a presidency, provost or other senior level position in U.S. higher education, requires great discipline, fortitude and commitment. The women of color in the study demonstrated that it is possible to reach the senior level positions while staying true to their language, culture and heritage. Following ethical principles and cultural values, they are role models for the next generation of women leaders.

References

Alum, J., McCarthy, M., & Kent, J. (2014). *Understanding PhD career pathways for program improvement*. Washington, DC: Council of Graduate Schools.

American Council on Education. (2007). *American College President Study* (2007th ed.). Washington, DC: American Council on Education.

American Council on Education. (2012). *The American College President 2012*. Washington, DC: American Council on Education.

Austin, D. (2009). Being okay with me. In B. Bower & M. Wolverton (Eds.), *Answering the call African American women in higher education leadership* (pp. 9–24). Sterling: Stylus Publishing, LLC.

Bach, R. L., & Perucci, C. C. (1984). Organizational influences in the sex composition of college and university faculty. *Sociology of Education, 57*(3), 193–198.

Bell, N. (2010) Graduate enrollment and degrees: 1999 to 2009. Washington, DC: Council of GraduateSchools.

Benjamin, L. (Ed.). (1997). *Black women in the academy promises and perils*. Gainesville: University Press of Florida.

Boushey, H., & O'Leary, A. (Eds.). (2009). *The Shriver report a woman's nation*. Retrieved from: http://www.americanprogress.org/issues/2009/10/womans_nation.html

Bower, B., & Wolverton, M. (Eds.). (2009). *Answering the call African American women in higher education leadership* (pp. 59–76). Sterling: Stylus Publishing, LLC.

Bridges, B., Eckel, P., Cordova, D., & White, B. (2008). *Broadening the leadership spectrum: Advancing diversity in the American college presidency*. Washington, DC: American Council on Education.

Cipres, E. (1999). *A case study of perceived characteristics and life events that enabled Latinas to become California community college presidents*. Doctoral dissertation. Retrieved from ProQuest. (AAT 9960957).

Crawford, K., & Smith, D. (2005). The we and the us mentoring African American women. *Journal of Black Studies, 35*(1), 52–67. doi:10.1177/0021934704265910.

Darden, M. L. (2006). *Women presidents in four-year college and universities and analysis of reported changeable attributes contributing to their success*. Unpublished doctoral dissertation, Baylor University, TX.

Denzin, N. K. (1989). *Interpretive biography*. Newbury Park: Sage Publications.

Dill, B., & Zambrana, E. (Eds.). (2009). *Emerging intersections race, class, and gender in theory, policy, and practice*. New Brunswick: Rutgers University Press.

Edwards, J., & Camblin, L. (1998). Assorted adaptations by African American administrators. *Women in Higher Education, 7*(11), 33–34.

Fairweather, J., & Rhoads, R. (1995). Teaching and the faculty role: Enhancing the commitment to instruction in American colleges and universities. *Education Evaluation and Policy Analysis, 17*(2), 179–194.

Gilligan, C. (1982). *In a different voice: Psychological theory and women's development*. Cambridge, MA: Harvard University Press.

Goetz, M. D., & LeCompte, J. P. (1984). *Ethnography and qualitative design in educational research*. Orlando: Academic.

Gregory, S. (1995). *Black women in the academy: The secrets to success and achievement*. Lanham: University Press of America.

Harvey, W. B., & Anderson, E. L. (2005). *Minorities in higher education: 2003–2004; twenty-first annual status report*. Washington, DC: American Council on Education.

Huang, B. (2013). Revolving doors and a chilly climate: Asian American Pacific Islander Junior faculty and the tenure review process. In S. Museus, D. Maramba, & R. Teranishi (Ed.). *Asian Americans in higher education*. Sterling: Stylus Publishing LLC.

Hughes, M. (2009). Finding purpose through meaningful leadership. In B. Bower & M. Wolverton (Eds.). *Answering the call African American women in higher education leadership* (pp. 39–58). Sterling: Stylus Publishing, LLC.

Hune, S. (1998). *Asian Pacific American women in higher education: Claiming visibility and voice*. Washington, DC: Association of American Colleges & Universities.

Jaschik, S. (2010, September 14). Women lead in doctorates. *Inside Higher Education*. Retrieved from: http://www.insidehighered.com/layout/set/print/news/2010/09/14/doctorates

Kanter, R. (1983). *The change masters innovation and entrepreneurship in the American corporation*. New York: Simon and Schuster.

King, J., & Gomez, G. (2008). *On the pathway to the presidency characteristics of higher education's senior leadership*. Washington, DC: American Council on Education.

Knowlton, L. (1992). *Leadership in a different voice: An ethnographic study of a Latina chief officer in a California community college*. Doctoral dissertation. Retrieved from ProQuest (AAT 9304533).

Konrad, A. M., & Pfeffer, J. (1991). Understanding the hiring of women and minorities in educational institutions. *Sociology of Education, 64*(3), 141–157.

Kulis, S. (1997). Gender segregation among college and university employees. *Sociology of Education, 70*(2), 151–173.

Lipman-Blumen, J. (1992). Connective leadership: Female leadership styles in the 21st-century workplace. *Sociological Perspectives, 35*(1), 183–203.

Manuelito-Kerkvliet, C. (2005). *Widening the circle: Mentoring and the learning process for American Indian women in tribal college administration*. Doctoral dissertation. Retrieved from Proquest. (AAT 3181109).

Mata, D. (1997). *A profile of Latino community college presidents: A multi-method study of leadership development and functioning*. Doctoral dissertation. Retrieved from ProQuest. (AAT3259056).

Maxwell, J. A. (2005). *Qualitative research design: An interactive approach* (2nd ed.). Thousand Oaks: Sage Publications.

Merriam, S. B. (2009). *Qualitative research a guide to design and implementation*. San Francisco: Jossey-Bass.

Moses, Y. T. (2009). Making things happen. In B. Bower & M. Wolverton (Eds.), *Answering the call African American women in higher education leadership* (pp. 59–76). Sterling: Stylus Publishing, LLC.

Murata, A. (2006). Bridging identities making sense of who we are becoming to be. In T. Berry & N. Mizelle (Eds.), *From oppression to grace* (pp. 24–33). Sterling: Stylus Publishing, LLC.

National Center for Education Statistics. (2014). *The condition of education*. Retrieved from: http://nces.ed.gov/programs/coe/indicator_cuf.asp

Nieves-Squire, S. (1994). *Hispanic women: Making their presence on campus less tenuous*. Washington, DC: Association of American Colleges, Ford Foundation.

Padilla, R. (2003). Barriers to accessing the professoriate. In J. Castellanos & L. Jones (Eds.), *The majority in the minority* (pp. 179–206). Sterling: Stylus Publishing.

Ridgeway, C. (2001). Gender, status, and leadership. *Journal of Social Issues, 57*(4), 637–655.

Rodriguez, S. (2006). *The career paths of California community college presidents*. Doctoral dissertation. Retrieved from ProQuest. (AAT 3208933).

Ryu, M. (2010). *Minorities in higher education twenty-fourth status report*. Washington, DC: American Council on Education.

Sandler, B. R. (1986). *The campus climate revisited: Chilly for women faculty, administrators, and graduate students*. Washington, DC: Association of American Colleges.

Schilling, V. (2009). AIEHEC CEO Carrie Billy explains what drives her as public servant, mother. *Tribal College Journal, 20*(4), 28–29.

Smith, H. (1988). *The power game*. New York: Random House.

St. Jean, Y., & Feagin, J. (1998). *Black women and everyday racism*. Armonk: M. E. Sharpe.

Stanley, C. A., & Lincoln, Y. S. (2005). Cross-race faculty mentoring. *Change, 37*(2), 44–50.

The White House Project. (2009). *The white house project report: Benchmarking women's leadership*. New York: The White House Project. Retrieved from: www.thewhitehouseproject.org.

Tolbert, P. S., & Oberfield, A. A. (1991). Sources of organizational demography: Faculty sex ratios in colleges and universities. *Sociology of Education, 64*(4), 305–315.

Turner, C. S. (2007). Pathways to the presidency: Biographical sketches of women of color firsts. *Harvard Educational Review, 77*(1), 1–38.

Turner, C., & Myers, S. (2000). *Faculty of color in academe: Bittersweet success*. Boston: Allyn and Bacon.

U.S. Department of Commerce, U.S. Census Bureau. American community survey. 2008.

Valdata, P. (2008). Returning home. *Diverse: Issues in Higher Education, 25*(3), 22–24.

West, M., & Curtis, J. (2006). *AAUP Faculty Gender Equity Indicators 2006*. Washington, DC: American Association of University Professors.

Yamagata-Noji, A. (2005). Leadership development program in higher education: Asian Pacific American leaders in higher education—An oxymoron? *Diversity in Higher Education, 5*, 173–206.

Chapter 9
Women's Place in Academia: Case Studies of Italy and Switzerland

Gaële Goastellec and Massimiliano Vaira

Introduction

During the last few decades, massification of the higher education systems in Europe has given women access to the academic profession. This quantitative improvement of access for women has been widely emphasized (Carnegie 1992 survey, Altbach 1996; Kogan and Teichler 2007, etc.), but important differences remain regarding the levels of status achieved (in other words, where women stand in the academic hierarchy) and the types of professional activities (the gendered division of work) (Goastellec and Pekari 2014; Fumasoli & Goastellec 2015; Goastellec and Crettaz Von Rotten forthcoming, 2016). Globally, large differences remain between academic markets and the dependent societies. Based on the EuroAC survey[1] and additional research, this chapter is an attempt to reveal some of the mechanisms favouring

---

[1] The EuroAC research – "The Academic Profession in Europe: Responses to Societal Change" took place between 2008 and 2011 in 10 European countries. A survey that was common across these counties was undertaken to characterise the academic profession. In the case of Switzerland, an online questionnaire was conducted in February and March on the basis of the questionnaire that has been used 2010. The questionnaire was constructed in the CAP ("Changing Academic Profession") project which has been slightly adapted to the Swiss context. All Swiss universities and universities of applied sciences (including universities of teacher training) were asked to participate in the project and the questionnaire was sent out to approximately 18,000 academics. A total of 1471 questionnaires were completed. In addition, 2206 questionnaires were started but not fully completed. After a detailed check of the completed questionnaires, 1424 of them were considered for further analysis. In the case of Italy, the "Changing Academic Profession" (CAP) data survey referred to the years 2007–2008 conducted on a sample of 1716 academics.

G. Goastellec (✉)
OSPS, Faculty of Social and Political Sciences, University of Lausanne,
Lausanne, Switzerland
e-mail: gaele.goastellec@unil.ch

M. Vaira
CIRSIS, Department of Political and Social Sciences, University of Pavia, Pavia, Italy

© Springer International Publishing Switzerland 2017
H. Eggins (ed.), *The Changing Role of Women in Higher Education*,
The Changing Academy – The Changing Academic Profession in International
Comparative Perspective 17, DOI 10.1007/978-3-319-42436-1_9

gender (in)equality in the academic profession by comparing women in the Italian and Swiss University academic contexts.

In order to make a comparison between countries characterised by different academic career systems and organisations, this research focuses on the "traditional" academic profession (i.e. academics working in one institution for at least 50 % of their time). The categorisations of different types of academic status used a binary category, differentiating senior academics (those with a permanent position equivalent to a professorship) from junior academics (those who were not necessarily permanent). Furthermore, since the Swiss Higher Education system is composed of different types of institutions, the comparison focuses on university academics in order to allow for cross-country comparison.

This chapter is structured into three parts. The first section depicts the gender distribution among students and within the academic profession, its evolution over time, and the probability of women progressing in their academic careers. This first section also questions the gender imbalance in Italy and Switzerland. The second section analyses gender-related professional behaviour to grasp the link between women's representation and women's professional activities, in relation to the national context. Lastly, the conclusion raises some questions about the structural and organisational dimensions of academic systems and identifies the mechanisms at play in the reproduction of male domination in academia.

Gender Distribution: A Pyramidal Structure

To understand women's careers in academia, it is important to keep in mind their participation in higher education studies, as it allows us to reveal the existence of a leaky pipeline.

Women and the University: Background Data on Students

The second half of the twentieth century has witnessed a silent revolution regarding access to higher education. Women's access to higher education has increased to the extent that, today, they exceed the number of male students in a large number of Western countries. In 1952, the number of women enrolled in Italian universities was only 25 % of the total; 20 years later, their presence had grown to 38 % and in 1994, they surpassed the number of men, making up 53 % of total enrolled students. In 2002, women graduates constituted 56 % of the total and 54 % of the freshers (Bianco 2002, 2004). In the academic year 2009–2010, women accounted for 57 % of total number of enrolled students (Ministry of Education, University and Research – Office of Statistics website). The history of women students in Switzerland is, by comparison, quite unusual; in 1906, women accounted for 25 % of the student population, but 90 % were foreigners. This shows that for more than a century, the internationalisation process has been a most significant aspect of the Swiss higher education system. The First World War generated a decrease in the level of internationalisation, and the proportion of women was reduced to 10 %. However, in 1973, women again composed one-quarter of the student body, with a proportion of 70 % of Swiss women (Commission fédérale pour les questions féminines 1998). In 1990, women constituted 38.8 % of the student body and, in 2011, they became a majority with 50.1 % of the registered students (2012), which is about 7 % less than in Italy.

However, this majority of women accessing higher education hides a disparity that is both disciplinary and degree-related. In Italy, since 1991, the number of female graduates has matched the number of males and since then, women have outnumbered men. In 2000, 55.5 % of the total number of graduates were women and, 10 years later, this proportion had risen to almost 60 % (58.5 %).

In Switzerland, in 2010, women constitute 51.8 % of the new university graduates with a bachelor degree, 48.9 % of those with a master degree, and 43.9 % of those who have completed a PhD (OFS 2011). Disciplinary wise, women represent 72.9 % of social sciences bachelor graduates compared with 19.1 % in hard sciences. Indeed, disciplines are still strongly gendered.

In Italy, growth in women's representation has taken place, and still takes place, in all disciplinary fields, even those – like medicine, law and science which were traditionally masculine (females make up more than 50 % of total students and graduates). However, there is the exception of engineering, where the female presence among enrolled and graduate students is around 30 % for both categories, and of economics, where the enrolled female students are 48 % of the total and graduates are only 26 % of the total. It must be noted that while engineering and economics are perceived to be masculine fields, humanities is a female-dominated one, as 77 % of the enrolled students and 79 % of the graduates are women. Rather interesting is the field of law, which for a long time has been male-dominated and now is female-dominated, as 60 % of the enrolled and graduate students are women (personal elaboration on data related to 2010 by Ministry of Education, University and Research – Office of Statistics).

Generally, in the last 20–25 years, female students have performed better than their male colleagues. They attended their courses more regularly, they received better marks, and they graduated more frequently in the expected time with higher marks. The same dynamic has been observed for doctoral degrees. From 1987 to 1996, men were the majority who received the degree (57 % was the average of the period); since 1997 and up to 2006 (latest data available), women surpassed the proportion of men with 51.5 % (average of the period) (Istat 2001 for data up to 1997, Ministry of Education, University and Research – Office of Statistics, for data from 1998 to 2006). This trend is obviously linked to the transformation of the student body. Since there are more women than men and more female graduates than male graduates, it is not surprising that women are gaining ground also in doctoral courses. On the whole, women have become the majority in university study courses.

In Switzerland, disciplinary fields are also a determining factor. Women repre-sent 67.1 % of the registered university students in social and human sciences; 60.7 % in medicine and pharmacy; 56.6 % in law; 38.1 % in natural sciences; 33.5 % in economic sciences; and 27.7 % in technical sciences.

By comparison, women appear to have a higher representation in Italian higher education and within different disciplinary fields. The feminisation of the student body thus appears slightly more important in Italy. The same is true when it comes to the academic professions (faculties).

Academic Women's Place

The comparison of female representation among students and academic staff reveals a highly different picture. If women have become the majority of the student body, they still represent only a minority of the academic profession. In Italy, women compose 24 % of senior academics and 46 % of junior academics. In Switzerland, the situation is even worse; women represent just 17 % of senior academics, com-pared with 40 % of juniors. The Italian academic profession is thus slightly more feminised, which is consistent with the fact that the student body comprises a larger proportion of females in Italy than in Switzerland.

Interestingly, this larger representation of women in Italian universities, com-pared with Swiss universities, is not associated with a disciplinary over-representation at the higher education system level. Women appear to be much more represented in Switzerland in social and human sciences, where they compose more than a half of the academic population (52 %, compared with 45 % in Italy), as well as in medicine and physics, where they represent 43 % (33 % in Italy) and in business and law (35 % in Switzerland and 26 % in Italy). In contrast, in Italy, the proportion of women is higher in physics and engineering, which are, historically, the most mas-culine disciplinary groups, in comparison with Switzerland (27 % in Italy, com-pared to 20 % in Switzerland).

Contracts of Employment

In Italy, nearly all positions appear to be full-time ones, while the situations in Switzerland vary greatly, depending on the level of position (junior/senior). This differentiation between full-time and part-time contracts can create, in Switzerland, a differentiation between men and women. Women often have less access to full-time positions, in comparison to men, and the gap is biggest among juniors, suggesting possible handicaps for the future of women regarding their careers (Table 9.1).

Table 9.1 Percentage of full-time employment by gender, country, status and type of institution

Academic Rank	Gender	CH	I IT
Senior at universities	(M) Male	92	96
	Female	86	98
Junior at universities	Male	66	97
	Female	42	98

Question: "What is your employment situation in the current academic year at your higher education institution/research institute?"

Table 9.2 Logistic regression – full-time employment by country Switzerland, Italy

Gender (man)		0.43***	1.35
Age		1.02*	0.98
Marital status (single)		1.1.06	0.66
Children at home (no)		0.68*	0.88
Father tertiary educ. (No)		0.77*	1.41
Academic rank (junior)		3.62***	1.24
University/other (other)		1.37*	
Business and Law (SHS)		1.56*	0.19**
Life Science and Medicine (SHS)		2.04***	1.75
Physics and Engineering (SHS)		2.81***	0.71
Costant		0.49	119.21***
Pseudo R2 (Nagelkerke)		0.19	0.08

*p<.01 ** : p<.05 *** : p<.10

In order to understand the effect of gender on access to full-time employment in Switzerland, a logistic regression is created and controls for variables such as age, marital status, children, father's education, academic rank, discipline, and internationalisation of career (Table 9.2).

Italy exhibits no gender differences due to the fact that a part-time contract is very unusual. However, in Switzerland, where everything else is equal, women have a much lower probability of being full-time employees than men.

A Historical Perspective

In Italy, although the academic workplace remains strongly gendered, the last 13 years (from 1997 to 2010, the last period of official data collection) an outstanding growth regarding women's presence in academic ranking has been seen. In absolute and relative terms there are still fewer women than men in the profession, especially in the higher rank positions (see Table 9.3). Nonetheless, women's growth rate has

Table 9.3 Women's presence in Italian academic rankings, 1997–2010 (totals and female percentage)

	Position	M	F	Total	F%
1997					
	Full professor	11,877	1525	13,402	11.4
	Associate professor	11,545	4073	15,618	26.1
	Researcher	12,191	7976	20,167	39.5
	Total staffed academics	35,613	13,574	48,187	28.1
2010					
	Full professor	12,671	3182	15,853	20.1
	Associate professor	11,139	5814	16,953	34.3
	Researcher	13,647	11,285	24,932	45.3
	Total academic staff	37,457	20,281	57,738	35.1

Source: Ministry of Education, University and Research – Office of Statistics

been far higher than that of men. The number of full-time male professors has grown by less than 6 % in this period, while the number of female professors has increased by almost 109 %, more than doubling their number. In associate professor positions, males show a negative growth (-3.5 %), while the number of women grew by almost 43 %. Lastly, in researcher positions, the number of men has increased by 12 %, and the number of women has increased by 41.5 % (Personal elaboration on Ministry of Education, University and Research – Office of Statistics data related to 2010).

These figures are impressive if compared to the statistics from decades ago. In 1954, women made up less than 2 % of full professors, 7 % of Associate professors, and 15 % of researchers. Ten years later, those percentages were 2 %, 10 %, and 19 %, respectively. At the end of the 1980s, the percentages were 9 %, 24 %, and 41 % (Bianco 2002; Istat 2001). This development suggests that women had started to gain ground, slowly but constantly, in the academy, particularly at a precise point in time – that is, when the university started to became a mass system in the second half of the 1960s.

Although data show that women have been enjoying better conditions while entering their professions and developing their careers, the gap between genders in the Italian university is far from being closed, albeit conditions are more favourable now than in the past. Nonetheless, they are still rather adverse for women.

To a large extent, women's presence in the academic profession has been characterised by a rather similar trend that is detectable in other professional fields. While there is a significant increase in their presence, it is paralleled by continuing differences in the structures and pathways of their careers. Generally, women's careers progress more slowly and are largely confined to middle positions in the organisational ranks.

In Italian universities, academic women's distribution is a pyramid-shaped one; it has a large base, which increasingly narrows towards the middle and top strata, while men are almost equally distributed in the three positions (cylinder-shaped distribution), as Table 9.3 shows. Thus, considering data related to 2010, for 100

Table 9.4 Women's presence in each academic rank, Swiss university sector 1997–2010

	Position	M	F	Total	F%
1997					
	Professor	2481	192	2673	7.2
	Other teachers	4704	1117	5821	19.2
	Assistants and scientific collaborators	15,036	6074	21,110	28.8
2010					
	Professor	3050	626	3676	17
	Other teachers	6822	2330	9152	25.5
	Assistants and scientific collaborators	15,669	10,889	26,588	41

women in research positions (the lowest status in the hierarchy), there are about 50 women in associate professor position, and only 28 in full professor positions, while men are more equally distributed among the different positions, at a little less than 1 to 1.

These features are meaningful with regard to gender inequalities in careers. Data presented above, which show the number and performance of women in the university study courses, suggest that a theoretical distribution should show the prevalence of women over men in the ranks of the academic profession, both in terms of total numbers and in the distribution in different positions (Bianco 2002). It is not easy to ascertain and to agree on the determining factors and/or mechanisms that influence this current situation, as we discuss later on.

In Switzerland, female representation has increased from 192 professors in 1997 to 626 in 2010 (7–17 % of the professors); from 1117 "other teachers[2]" to 2330 (19.2–25.5 %); and from 6074 assistants and scientific collaborators to 10,889 (28.8–41 %). Even if women remain underrepresented, particularly at the highest levels (similar to the trend in Italian universities), the growth has still been greater than for men. The increase in men's representation among professors is 22 %, while it is 226 % for women. Unfortunately, available data only allow for a very broad categorisation of academic staff and do not permit us to question precisely the gender bias at the different stages of an academic career (Table 9.4).

Questioning Equality in Academic Careers

If we look beyond the percentages and growth rates and analyse academic opportunities regarding careers for women, in terms of probability, we find some unexpected results. In this analysis, for Italy, we follow the study carried out by the

---

[2] The category « other teachers » is employed by the Swiss Federal Office for Statistics to cover the heterogeneity of non-professorial academic statuses in Swiss Universities. Those are characterised by the fact that they tend to work part time (less than 50 %) and on teaching-oriented contracts.

Italian National Statistics Institute (Istat) on women in the university, which was published in 2001 and based on data from 1999 (Istat 2001), repeated by Bianco in 2001 (Bianco 2002). The methodology is rather simple; it is to calculate the probability of women entering an academic career (researcher position) in a given year. One must take the number of men and women graduates 8 years before the chosen year and the number of male and female researchers in that year. Then, one must find an odds ratio within each gender between researchers and graduates, as well as another odds ratio between the former odds ratio for women and for men.[3]

Pwomen Res = Odds ratiowomenRes / women grad × 100 / Odds ratiomen Res / men grad × 100 × 100;

To calculate the probabilities of career advancement from a research position to an associate and from an associate to a full professor, the logic followed is the same, except one must consider the number of men and women in each position 3 years before the chosen year.

Pwomen Associate =

Odds ratiowomen Associate / women Res × 100 / Odds ratiomen Associate / men Res × 100 × 100

Pwomen Full =

Odds ratiowomen Full / women Associate × 100 / Odds ratiomen Full / men Associate × 100 × 100

This methodology does not permit an objective and precise result because many variables could intervene and distort the normal distribution of probabilities. Nonetheless, the methodology gives us more than an impressionistic idea about gender differences in career paths. For this purpose, we consider the following data:

• Graduates in 2000 and researchers in 2008 to analyse the probability of women entering an academic career;
• Researchers in 1999, 2003, and 2006, to analyse the probability of women changing careers from researcher positions to associate professor positions in 2001, 2005, and 2008;
• Associate professors in 1999, 2003, and 2006 to analyse the probability of women changing careers from associate professors to full professors in 2001, 2005, and 2008.

All calculated data will be crossed by 7 disciplinary fields out of 14, namely: mathematics, engineering/architecture, medicine, economics/statistics, law, political sciences/sociology, and philosophy/pedagogy/psychology.

The reason for confining the data analysis to 2008 is due to two facts. First, 2008 was the last year in which competitive examinations for recruitment and career

---

[3] An odds ratio is the probability of occurrence of an event to that of the non-occurrence of the event i.e. the rates of the probability of something that is true to the probability that it is not true.

Table 9.5 Probabilities of graduate women in 2000 becoming researchers in 2008 – Italy

Disciplines	Probabilities in %
Mathematics	15.6
Engineering/architecture	207.5
Medicine	59
Economics/statistics	66.7
Law	70.8
Political sciences/sociology	75.6
Philosophy/pedagogy/psychology	22.2

Source: Personal elaboration on data of Ministry of Education, University and Research – Office of Statistics

advancement were held; since then, examinations have been blocked and still are, due to a 2010 university reform. This reform changed the juridical status and the recruitment procedures of academics. Second, this period has been characterised by a favourable legal framework for recruitment and career advancements, created by the 1998 reform and by financial resources and available positions. These resources created better conditions for career dynamics, which will be discussed later in this chapter as one of the explanations regarding differences in career path.

Table 9.5 lists the probability of women achieving a position as a researcher which is the first stage in an academic career for each of the seven disciplines:

As mentioned above, the data show a rather surprising scenario: women have greater chances of entering researcher positions not in the most feminised disciplines, such as philosophy/pedagogy/psychology, but in the most masculinised one – engineering/architecture, where such a probability is almost ten times greater than in the humanistic disciplines and more than double that of men. In mathematics, another feminised discipline, the probability is even worse than in humanistic discipline. The first conclusion is that in the most feminised fields, women are far more disadvantaged in their access to the academic career. Why? Both Istat (2001) and Bianco (2002) explain the results in the following argument: graduates in engineering/architecture find it more prestigious and profitable, in terms of monetary income, to develop their career outside the academy. Since outside professional careers are largely dominated by men, women have a greater chance of entering the academic profession, given the "vacant posts" left by men. In contrast, in the mathematics and philosophy/pedagogy/psychology fields, where the outside professional opportunities (e.g., teaching in secondary schools) are far less prestigious than academic ones, male graduates in such fields tend to enter the academic profession, and women are more disadvantaged. Bianco (2002), basing her analysis on data related to 2001, gives the same explanation, even for economics/statistics.

This conclusion is suggestive, but it does not seem to be generally applicable. Actually, it does not explain why in disciplinary fields such as law and medicine, where the outside professions (e.g., lawyer, judge, notary; physician) are far more prestigious, remunerative and male-dominated we do not see similar probabilities in the case of engineering/architecture. Furthermore, the conclusion does not explain why in the past 7 years, the probability of women entering a researcher position in economics/statistics has deteriorated so much. In 2001, women had a fairly good chance of entering the academic profession. Indeed, outside jobs in economics/statistics are more attractive than those in the academic profession. Further, it does not explain the similarity of probability values between political sciences/sociology and law, both feminised but very different, in terms of outside professional opportunities, prestige and remuneration. Finally, the conclusion does not explain the differences of probability values between medicine and law; both are feminised fields of studies but are male-dominated professional fields outside academia.

Studies that take into consideration these kinds of problems have not yet been undertaken, at least to our knowledge. It could be hypothesised that such differences might be explained by referring to disciplines' organisational and cultural features. Such a hypothesis has been advanced, but not empirically verified, by Facchini (1997). This hypothesis highlights how in the hard sciences, the organisation of work is more rigid, more likely to be undertaken in a routine manner (e.g., laboratory work) and often more collaboratively than in the soft sciences, which are more flexible (e.g., a good part of the work could be done at home) and individually carried out. In the former case, women could be more advantaged by the more "rigid" work organisation, while in the latter, women could encounter more problems because the work time has to be added to everyday activities.

However, this hypothesis cannot completely account for the differences we have seen. In our opinion, the explanation should consider the hypothesis related to the role of more subtle cultural factors, such as expectations and conceptions of academic work; these factors make women seem not as fully "reliable" researchers and academics, given they could be "at risk" of interruptions, such as motherhood and other family responsibilities. This hypothesis seems to be quite valid if we consider that the committees evaluating the candidate's suitability for a post are male-dominated; men are the large majority of academics in the middle and top positions, from which members for recruitment evaluation committees are selected and appointed as members of an examination board. Men bring with them in their evaluations – if not intentionally, at least in a tacit and taken-for-granted way (Bourdieu 2001) –the expectations and conceptions that can well penalise female candidates.

Let us turn our attention now to career development after a researcher position. Table 9.6 presents longitudinal data in this regard, comparing probabilities of women gaining associate and full professor positions in the seven chosen disciplinary fields in the years 2001, 2005, and 2008.

Starting from the general data (last columns and rows), it is clear that the opportunities for career progression from associate to full professor positions are higher than from researcher to associate professor, both within disciplines and on the whole. This could mean that the selection of women, after they obtain the researcher positions, is taking place at the middle of the career path; for the women who have gained the associate position, it becomes relatively easier to enter the full professor position. This is true for all of the disciplines considered here except for mathematics, where the probability of obtaining the position of full professor is lower than

Table 9.6 Women's career probability by position and discipline in Italy (% values)

	2001	2005	2008	Discipline average
From researcher to associate professor				
Mathematics	45.5	60.7	56.4	*54.2*
Engineering/architecture	75.5	81.2	94.1	*83.6*
Medicine	59.5	63.4	66.2	*63*
Economics/statistics	51.8	60.5	69.4	*60.6*
Law	61.6	65.6	59.8	*62.3*
Political sciences/sociology	69.9	112	66	*82.6*
Philosophy/pedagogy/psychology	77.3	89.1	81	*82.5*
General average	69.8			
From associate professor to full professor				
Mathematics	32.5	52.7	33.1	*39.4*
Engineering/architecture	78.7	110.1	77.4	*88.7*
Medicine	67.2	81.2	66.7	*71.7*
Economics/statistics	98.6	79.2	64.7	*80.8*
Law	103.4	102.8	82	*96.1*
Political sciences/sociology	89.2	76.6	79.6	*81.1*
Philosophy/pedagogy/psychology	91.3	106.5	84.9	*94.2*
General average	*79*			

Source: Personal elaboration on data of Ministry of Education, University and Research – Office of Statistics

that of the associate position. It is not easy to find an explanatory hypothesis for this anomalous case and it could be an interesting one on which to work. Thus, in general, data seem to corroborate the previous hypothesis that women do suffer from the deep-seated expectations and conceptions about their ability to perform academic work as effectively as men. The more they advance in academic rank, the more they prove themselves to be as reliable as male academics in being able to meet those conceptions and expectations – largely constructed by men – that characterize the academic world.

On average, women enjoy almost equal opportunities to gain associate positions in engineering/architecture, philosophy/pedagogy/psychology, and political sciences/sociology. However, in medicine, law, and economics/statistics, women's chances are two-third of men's chances. Furthermore, in mathematics, women have only about half the chance of men. The chances of gaining full professor positions are on average almost equal in philosophy/pedagogy/psychology, engineering/architecture, political/sciences/sociology, and economics/statistics. In law, the chances increase to almost three quarters, and in mathematics, the chances drop to less than one-fifth.

The average data, however, hide different dynamics in the disciplines through the three specific years, as Table 9.6 shows. In some disciplines, the chances have grown over time. In the associate positions in engineering/architecture, medicine, economics/statistics, women experienced a constant growth of their chances of promotion, while in other disciplines, where there has been growth followed by contraction, there has been a sort of pendulum effect. For full professor positions, only in political science/sociology the growth has been constant, while in other disciplines, we can observe the pendulum effect.

When Bianco (2002, see also Facchini 1997, in relation to the early 1990s situation) explained women's chances of preferment in 2001, she highlighted the double effect created by a significant growth of the financial resources for recruitment/career advancement and the availability of a better number of entry positions available (up to three for each advertised competitive examination), as the 1998 recruitment system reform specified. In other words, the resources available were greater than before, and women took advantage of this, thereby increasing their career chances, in a "trickle-down" effect. This was the situation until 2005, when the legal framework changed; the number of entry appointments per competition was reduced to two and in 2008 to only one. The financial resources shrank both at the central level and for the individual institutions. This could explain, at least partially, the pendulum effect between 2005 and 2008. As the available resources were reduced, women's career chances decreased. However, as mentioned, this explains only those cases in which their chances *did* decrease; why, in some disciplines, did this decrease not occur? The most plausible explanation is that those disciplines, mainly at a national level but also in individual institutions, had more resources than the others – especially financial ones – to support a constant growth in career advancement opportunities over time.

The conclusion we can draw from this analysis is the following: when the available resources are enough to allow an expansionist policy for career advancement, women experience a trickle-down effect, which increases their chances; when resources shrink, women's chances deteriorate, and men get the larger part of the stake. Bianco (2002) and Facchini (1997) developed a similar argument that mirror's the previous one. When resources are relatively abundant (in terms of finance and number of available posts) the recruitment/career advancement logic becomes more "universalistic", favouring women who would otherwise be a disadvantaged group; when resources shrink, stricter selective criteria are applied, thereby reinforcing the disadvantage.

We have applied the same type of calculation for Switzerland. However, because academic status depends on universities, national statistics only allow us to distinguish between assistants and scientific collaborators, as well as other teachers and professors. As a result, and to take into account the very slow progression within academic careers, as a starting point we have referred to the number of PhD graduates in 1990, the number of other lecturers in 2001, and the number of professors in 2010. Because female representation was so low in 1990, and because of the broad categories used, these statistics provide an optimistic view of women's careers.

Nevertheless, these results reveal that the move from the PhD to the status of "other teacher" is easier for women in the human and social sciences, technical sciences, economy and law, by comparison with medicine and the pure sciences. However, a very different picture is depicted when looking at the move from "other teachers" to "professors"; the probability for women becomes low in the human and

Table 9.7 Women's career probability in Switzerland

	Oddwomen/oddmen/Ph.D. graduates/other teachers 1990–2001	Oddwomen/oddmen/o other teachers/prof 20 2001–2010
Humanities/social sciences	125	60
Economics	227	101
Law	111	131
Exact and natural sciences	53	119
Medicine/pharmacy	40	79
Technical sciences	178	74

Source: Own calculations on the basis of FNS data: "Doctoratselon le domained'étudeset le sexe, 1990. OFS, Encyclopédiestatistique de la Suisse, Education et Science, 15.2.2.5. Degrétertiaire: hautesécolesuniversitaires

social sciences and decreases in the technical sciences. Nevertheless, the probability remains high in economics, law, and the pure sciences. Lastly, the probability improves in medicine and pharmacy but there remains a disadvantage for women.

As a result, it appears that the disciplines in which women are the most numerous (human and social sciences) are also the ones in which it is the most difficult to become a professor (Table 9.7).

Gendered Activities?

Italian academic women are less research-oriented, especially when junior academics are considered, by comparison with Swiss academic women (71 % versus 79 %) (Table 9.8).

Gender differences regarding the primary focus of interest (research or teaching) are much higher in Italy, where women are less likely to prioritise research than men. There are two exceptions, physics and engineering, in which Switzerland appears to be more gendered. It is interesting to note that these are the only fields that are more feminised in Italy than in Switzerland (Table 9.9).

Senior women appear to teach an average of 4 h more per week than men do in both countries. As for juniors, differences in teaching load are country-related more than gender-related. In the Italian context, juniors teach more than twice as many hours as Swiss juniors (Table 9.10).

When it comes to research hours, the differences between the two countries are much more salient than the gender differences, consistent with what was observed regarding teaching; Swiss juniors dedicate more time to research than their Italian counterparts. This difference can be explained by the fact that in Italy there is a tacit "rule" for which junior academics should be engaged in didactic duties too and not only in research tasks. This is considered as a part of the socialization to the profession (Table 9.11).

Table 9.8 Percentage of academics whose focus of interest leans towards research or is primarily in research by gender, country, status, and type of institution

Position	Gender	CH	IT
Seniors at universities	Male	78	76
	Female	82	78
Juniors at universities	Male	79	78
	Female	79	71

Question: "Regarding your own preferences, do your interests lie primarily in teaching or in research?"

Table 9.9 Percentage of academics whose focus of interest leans towards research or is primarily in research by gender, country, and discipline

Discipline	Gender	CH	IT
SHS	Male	59	82
	Female	61	72
Bus and Law	Male	70	81
	Female	61	59
Life and Med	Male	74	67
	Female	78	81
Phys and Eng	Male	82	80
	Female	75	76

Table 9.10 Average number of hours per week dedicated to teaching by gender, country, and position

Position	Gender	CH	IT
Seniors at universities	Male	15	17
	Female	19	21
Juniors at universities	Male	8	17
	Female	7	19

Question: "Considering all of your professional work within your current main employment position, how many hours do you spend in a typical week on each of the following activities: preparation of instructional materials and lesson plans, classroom instruction, advising students, reading, and evaluating student work"

Table 9.11 Number of hours per week dedicated to research by gender, country and status

Position	Gender	CH	IT
Seniors at universities	Male	17	18
	Female	19	17
Juniors at universities	Male	25	17
	Female	24	18

Question: "Considering all of your professional work within your current main employment position, how many hours do you spend in a typical week on each of the following activities: research (reading literature, writing, conducting experiments, fieldwork)"

Table 9.12 Percentage of academics who served as members of national/international scientific committees/boards/bodies by gender, country, status, and type of institution

Position	Gender	CH	IT
Seniors at universities	Male	90	60
	Female	87	53
Juniors at universities	Male	35	44
	Female	37	37
Seniors at other HEIs	Male	75	–
	Female	73	–
Juniors at other HEIs	Male	41	–

Question: "Considering all of your professional work within your current main employment position, how many hours do you spend in a typical week on each of the following activities: administration (committees, department meetings, paperwork)"

Table 9.13 Perception of influence at the department level (ordered logistic regression)

	CH	IT
Age	++	+
Female (Male)	–	–
Full-time (Part-time)	++	
Junior Academic (Senior)	–	–
Other Institution (University)	++	
Business and Law (SHS)	–	
Life Sciences and Medicine (SHS)	–	
Physics and Engineering (SHS)	–	

Question: "How influential are you, personally, in helping to shape key academic policies? 1 = Very Influential to 4 = Not At All Influential"

While women appear to be as much engaged in national/international scientific committees in Switzerland as men are, significant differences appear in Italy, where women at both junior and senior levels appear to be less engaged. Women also appear to be less engaged at departmental level in both countries, markedly so in Italy (Tables 9.12 and 9.13).

What Can Be Inferred from These Characterisations?

Italian universities appear to be less gendered regarding access to the academic profession, but the opposite is true for academic activities. Swiss academic women show few differences from men, when it comes to academic activities. In the first case, one could make the hypothesis that women's access to academic careers is a response to higher education massification; women are undertaking more teaching

Table 9.14 Salary progression by experience and gender. This shows the annual salary of researchers by gender and level of experience in each country (2006, all currencies in purchasing power parities)

Country/years of experience by gender	0–4 years	5–7 years	8–10 years	11–15 years	>15 years
	Female	Female	Female	Female	Female
	Male	Male	Male	Male	Male
Italy	12.244	19.777	27.310	34.844	42.377
	12.760	23.488	34.126	44.944	55.672
% Gender salary difference	4.2%	18.8%	25%	29%	31.4%
Switzerland	39.599	55.711	71.823	87.935	104.047
	40.862	61.075	81.288	101.501	121.714
% Gender salary difference	3.2%	9.6%	13.2%	15.4%	17%

http://www.eui.eu/ProgrammesAndFellowships/AcademicCareersObservatory/CareerComparisons/SalaryComparisons.aspx. Own calculations regarding gender salary differences
Source: European Commission (2007), Study on the Remuneration of Researchers in the Public and Private Commercial Sectors

duties. Meanwhile, in Switzerland, women who reach the professoriate have been through such a rigorous process of selection that no difference is to be observed in their activities.

These differences are associated with levels of salary. In both countries, salaries are fixed by law (national law in Italy and cantonal laws Switzerland). When we compare the average salary by years of experience, the gender gap increases over time in both countries; it increases from 3.2 to 17% in Switzerland and from 4.2 to 31.4% in Italy. These results echo differences in status achievement and, in the Swiss case, part-time employment (Table 9.14).

Conclusion: Contextualising Differences

Several levels of contextualisation can help in understanding both the similarities and the differences regarding gendered careers in Switzerland and Italy.

Looking at the similarities (i.e., the relatively low proportion of women academics), one could argue that higher education massification has had a great impact on the opening of academia for women, due to the creation of a large number of positions. In both cases, the level of massification reached is quite low. In 2010, the OECD estimated that enrolment rates of women from 20 to 29 years-old were around 22% in Italy and 24% in Switzerland (OECD 2012).

Considering that women are slightly more represented in the Italian academic profession by comparison with the Swiss one, the structure of academic careers provides some clues to understanding why. In Italy, the main starting position for most academics is a permanent one (e.g., permanent researcher; this position was abolished by the 2010 university reform and replaced by a fixed-term contract position). In Switzerland, there is a long chain of temporary positions that depends on the university (each university has its own academic statuses) and the discipline (faculties can use part or all of the university definition of academic statuses) and leads to a relatively late appointment to the tenured position. The traditional chair system is still partly in place, and the main difference in status appears to be between non-tenured and tenured. The first entails the classification of postdoctoral, researcher, and lecturer positions as teaching and research assistants. The second includes professorship and, in some HEIs, specific positions of lecturer and researcher (e.g., Maître d'enseignement et de recherche). Professorial positions are segmented into several ranks, including tenured or non-tenured positions. Titles and status can vary from one institution to the other. Furthermore, the Habilitation, similar to a second doctorate, is a prerequisite to obtaining a professorial position in the German-speaking part of Switzerland.

These differences in the structure of academic careers are reinforced by differences in the average age of obtaining a PhD. In Italy, this is 31 years old, while in Switzerland this age is the lowest average age for pharmacy and the pure sciences, but it rises to 37 years in human and social sciences (OFS 2010b, p.18). As a result, in Switzerland, access to permanent positions happens at a much later stage compared with Italy, and this can be seen as a barrier for women, due to the conflict between career timing and the biological clock of women.

An analysis of career structure would not be complete without taking recruitment into account.

In Switzerland, we have shown that, at professorial levels, recruitment practices appear to be in the process of standardisation. Multiple factors, with different balances, come into play regarding decisions concerning recruitment at the lower levels. Variety is displayed with common and traditional features. That is, holders continue to control entry into academia (Fumasoli and Goastellec 2015). As Danell and Hjerm emphasized (2012, p.232):

> As long as competition over resources and positions is transparent, competitive women fare as well as men, but when men and women are allowed to compete over resources and networks in a more informal way, women are clearly worse off than men.

The organisation of recruitment thus impinges on the probability of women being appointed. Differences in recruitment also depend on the judgment regimes used (Musselin 2003); women are less disadvantaged by the recruitment processes when standardised evaluation criteria are used as opposed to more subjective criteria linked to personality.

More broadly, the representation of women in academia closely reflects women's place in society. Indeed, a fourth level of contextualisation consists of a societal analysis. Although there is no question of providing a comprehensive understanding of women's rights history in both Swiss and Italian societies, some elements of information might help clarify what is at stake in academic careers.

There are several ways of questioning women's places in society. The most fundamental ones we wish to highlight are women's suffrage and women's rights regarding marriage. The first indicator, the year of adoption of women's suffrage, can be visualised as the expression of the recognition of women's rights in the public sphere (and thus, to some extent, related to their access to education. Remarkably, there was a 26-year gap between the two countries as Italy adopted women's suffrage in 1945, while Switzerland waited until 1971 to see its adoption at a national level, and the last Cantons adopted it in the early 1990s. The second indicator, the citizenship of national women marrying a foreigner –which can be seen as the recognition of a woman's right in the private sphere – presents a different picture. In Switzerland, until 1953, women lost their nationality when marrying a foreigner (Wanner 1998). In Italy, the Law 555 of 1912 stipulating that «women lost their original Italian citizenship if they married a foreign husband whose country's laws gave its citizenship to the wife, as a direct and immediate effect of the marriage. This was only modified in April 1983.

The situation of Italian women was such that, in December 2011, thousands attended public rallies calling for "equality and better representation of women in politics, and in the public eye". They also aimed to protect women's rights, especially the right to work, and the provision of aid for young mothers (Euronews 2011, 11th December).

Finally, differences in the organisation of academic markets are also strongly affected by the degree of internationalisation. In Switzerland, 50 % of academics are foreign born, while this is the case for only 2 % of Italian academics.

The very strong internationalisation of the Swiss academic sectors may be a factor in improving women's access; it potentially counterbalances the historical and societal resistance but also stimulates the increased formalisation of academic career requirements and processes. Thus formalisation and transparency of the processes are among the key factors for improved fairness, be it between genders or between social groups.

References

Altbach, P. G. (Ed.). (1996). *The international academic profession: Portraits of fourteen countries*. Princeton: The Carnegie Foundation for the Advancement of Teaching.

Bianco, M. L. (2002). Effetti della riforma dei concorsi universitari sulle carriere accademiche e dinamiche di genere. *Polis, 16*(2), 417–441.

Bianco, M. L. (2004). Donne all'università. Studentesse e docenti nell'accademia italiana contemporanea. *Annali di Storia delle Università Italiane, 8*, 9–34.

Bourdieu, P. (2001). *The masculine domination*. Stanford: Stanford University Press.

Commission fédérale pour les questions féminines. (1998). Femmes, pouvoir, Histoire. Histoire de l'égalité en Suisse de 1848 à nos jours. http://www.ekf.admin.ch/dokumentation/00444/00517/index.html?lang=fr. Accessed 14 Dec 2012.

Danell, R. & Hjerm, M. (2012). Career prospects for female university researchers: event history analysis of career trajectories at Swedish Universities. *Scientometrics*, 228–235. Published online http://link.springer.com/article/10.1007/s11192-012-0840-4?no-access=true

Euronews. (2011). http://www.euronews.com/2011/12/11/thousands-march-for-women-s-rights-in-italy/

European Commission. (2007). *Study on the remuneration of researchers in the public and private commercial sectors.* Brussels: European Commission.

Facchini, C. (1997). Uomini e donne nell' università italiana. In R. Moscati (Ed.), *Chi governa l'università? Il mondo accademico italiano tra mutamento e tradizione.* Liguori: Napoli.

Fumasoli, T. & Goastellec, G. (2015). Convergence of the Swiss academic markets: E pluribus unum?. In U. Teichler & W. Cumming, Forming, *recruiting and managing the academy*: A varied scene Springer, 145–161.

Goastellec, G. & Crettaz von Rotten, F. (forthcoming, 2016). The societal embeddedness of academic markets: From sex to gender in the Swiss context. In Soares M., Teichler U., Amaral A., Machado-Taylor M., *Approaches to the academic career in Europe: Challenges, issues and developments.* Springer.

Goastellec, G., & Pekari, N. (2014). Gender in the academia between differences and inequalities, findings in Europe. In U. Teichler & E. A. Höhle (Eds.), *The work situation of the academic profession in Europe: Findings of a survey in twelve European Countries.* Dordrecht: Springer, 55–78.

Istat. (2001). *Donne all'università.* Bologna: Il Mulino.

Kogan, M., & Teichler, U. (Eds.). (2007). *Key challenges to the academic profession.* Paris/Kassel: UNESCO Forum on Higher Education Research and Knowledge and INCHER, Kassel.

Musselin, C. (2003). « Academic markets. How they work », Conference paper, Women in European Universities, Training and Research Network. Accessible on-line: http://csn.uni-muenster.de/women-eu/

OECD. (2012). *Education at a glance, highlights.* OECD: OECD publishing. Paris.

OFS. (2010a). *Personnel des hautes écoles universitaires.* Neuchâtel: OFS.

OFS. (2010b). La formation et la situation professionnelle des titulaires d'un doctorat. Résultats issus des données du Système d'information universitaire Suisse et de l'enquête 2007 auprès des personnes nouvellement diplômées. *Education et Science*, 15. Neuchâtel: OFS.

OFS. (2011). *Femmes et hommes dans les hautes écoles suisses. Indicateurs sur les différences entre les sexes.* Neuchâtel: OFS.

Wanner, P. (1998). Les changements de nationalité des étrangers en Suisse. *Revue Européenne des migrations internationales, 14*(3), 185–201.

Part III
Gender Equality?

Chapter 10
Gender Equality in Academic Career Progression: A Matter of Time?

Mary Henkel

Introduction

The twenty-first century has seen the reduction of gender inequalities in the academic profession rise up European, national and institutional policy agendas, as the need to enhance the quality and quantity of higher education and to generate research, technological development and innovation has been perceived as increasingly urgent. Policies have shifted in emphasis from the elimination of direct and indirect discrimination against women to promoting equal opportunities and, to some extent, incorporated the more ambitious aims of gender mainstreaming (United Nations 1997; Rees 2006). Policy analyses of the barriers to equality have become more sophisticated and comprehensive (e.g. European Commission 2012) and programmes have multiplied and diversified. However, it remains the case that the profession is characterised by 'strong vertical gender segregation' (European Commission 2013: 6). There is visible frustration at the slow rate of progress ('It has been estimated that it will take 50 or 80 years before we reach gender equality if we just keep doing the same things, hoping that the pipeline will produce more women scientists' (House of Commons 2013–2014: 5; see also European Commission 2013: 3) and decreasing optimism that it is only a matter of time before there is significant change, particularly in the STEM disciplines and at the top levels of the profession as a whole (European Commission 2013; Barrett and Barrett 2013; Equality Challenge Unit 2014). While in the first two cycles of European higher education, 55 % and 59 % respectively of the students enrolled were female in 2010 (European Commission 2013), women constituted a minority of Ph.D. students, and the figure for Ph.D. graduates stood at 46 %. In other words, the pipeline was already leaking in advance of the lowest academic career level. Further, while an average of

M. Henkel (✉)
Brunel University, Uxbridge, UK
e-mail: henkel864@gmail.com

© Springer International Publishing Switzerland 2017
H. Eggins (ed.), *The Changing Role of Women in Higher Education*,
The Changing Academy – The Changing Academic Profession in International
Comparative Perspective 17, DOI 10.1007/978-3-319-42436-1_10

44% of academics at Grade C were female, the proportions in Grade B and Grade A (professors and senior management in universities) were 37% and 20% respectively (average figures, which mask, for example, the fact that gender equality in higher education is more advanced across the newest EU member countries).

There may be good reasons, therefore, to consider alternatives to thinking about progress on this issue in terms of linear time. Since the turn of the century, there has been a growing interest amongst higher education scholars in what has been happening to time, or more specifically to temporal regimes, in higher education in the face of economic, technological, political and governance change (e.g. Ylijoki and Mäntylä 2003; Neave 2006). Some research has focused on changes in how time is construed and the extent to which they and their implications are gendered (e.g. Menzies and Newson 2008; Rodrigues Araujo 2008; Ylijoki 2013) This chapter will draw on these studies, together with a comparative study of gender equality in German and British higher education, in which the author was involved (Pritchard 2010a, b; Pritchard and Henkel 2011), to consider how analyses of conceptions and experiences of time might contribute to an understanding of the role of gender in the career progression of women academics.[1]

The starting point for this consideration is that time is a fundamental but often implicit dimension of human experience. Adam (1990) suggests that how we theorise time has major implications for how we understand social life and for the richness of our thought about it. She points out that, while the dominance of objective or "clock" time is taken for granted in most societies (2004: 70), it is only one of a number of conceptions of time that inform human understanding of the world. Newtonian concepts of absolute or invariant time contrast but co-exist with Einsteinian concepts in which time is relative to observers and their frame of reference (Adam 1990: 56). Social science, she argues, comprises the whole spectrum of 'times' from the most physical, mechanical and artefactual to the experiential and cultural. In line with other social theorists of high modernity (e.g. Giddens 1991; Beck 1992) she contends that the complexity of conceptions and experiences of time means analysis in terms of dualisms or contradictions is insufficient and misleading. Objective time, for example, is at variance but also co-exists with subjective time, social time and biological time.

There is now an increasing diversity of constructions of time in higher education institutions (Ylijoki and Mäntylä 2003; Ylijoki 2013). A key concern in this chapter is with changes in economic, political, cultural and social relations in which these constructions are embedded and how they affect the careers and experiences of women academics. Changes driven by the growing influence of neo-liberalism, globalisation and new information and communication technologies have resulted in

---

[1] The primary aim of this comparative research project, carried out in 2008 and 2009, was to explore perceptions of gender equality among female academics in British and German universities. The study used quantitative and qualitative methods but this chapter draws on the qualitative data. Semi-structured interviews were conducted with a total of 87 female academics in five universities in each country and four disciplinary areas (biological sciences; economics, finance and management, education and history). For full details of the methodology and findings, see Pritchard (2010a, b).

the loosening and permeation of fixed boundaries and divisions of power, authority, function and labour, and the emergence of new forms of governance and management in higher education, encapsulated in the concept of New Public Management (NPM).

Changing Academic Labour Markets and the Role of Gender in Career Progression

Demands to expand higher education systems in the context of global knowledge economies and increased national and international competition for reputation and resources (public and private) brought pressures for enhanced efficiency and 'entrepreneurial universities'. In differing degrees, academic institutions lost monopoly control of research and educational agendas and of temporal regimes with the introduction of new public evaluation and accountability systems and the growing need to respond to the increasing rate of change in societies' knowledge requirements and, indeed, in knowledge itself.

Academic labour markets became less stable as institutions sought more flexibility in the face of more external demands. Pressures to shrink the primary market (more secure, prestigious and lucrative academic posts) and to raise the barriers to it intensified, while the secondary market (part time, temporary and more narrowly defined appointments} grew substantially (Leisyte and Hosch-Dayican 2014).

Comparative research into gender inequalities in German and British higher education systems in the early years of the twenty-first century is instructive in terms of the impacts of NPM on career structures. Whilst by then NPM was well established in Britain, resistance to it in Germany remained strong.

British higher education provides a particularly clear example of how NPM and the forces underlying it affected academic career structures. Until late in the twentieth century, it remained possible for aspiring academics to achieve an established and often tenured academic post before the age of 30. There was a graduated structure of tenured career grades and little by way of formal eligibility requirements. The adoption of the Ph.D. had been relatively late and, as far as the humanities and social sciences were concerned, only became a normative requirement around the turn of the century. However, by that time, new forms of public management were making themselves felt in the academic labour market. Tenure was effectively abolished under the Education Act 1988. Academic careers in Britain were now marked by a lengthening period of fixed term contracts, each of which might also be short and in a different institution, before the achievement of an established position. The quality of this experience has been unequal, depending on the employing institution and the discipline but it is predominantly a period of insecurity and, for many, of a sense of marginality and isolation (Allen Collinson 2004; Archer 2008) and poor preparation for the primary academic market. Increasingly institutions are dealing with the pressures upon them by employing academic staff on specialised contracts, teaching only or research only. Research achievement is the prime criterion for academic advancement but in the most prestigious institutions the requirement is for maintenance of the research-teaching nexus.

At the same time, institutional expectations of aspiring and early career academics have been significantly raised: publications before and after the award of the doctorate, demonstrable teaching skills and commitment, research funding applications and success, research collaborations, as well as small-scale research management. Institutions seek visible, if not measurable, indicators of continuing excellence in their permanent academic workforce whilst also maintaining a flexibility that is more dependent on short term objectives.

Externally imposed temporal regimes (notably those of external evaluation exercises) are now embedded in academic lives and institutions in Britain and reinforced in the development of internal planning, review and appraisal systems. One consequence is the articulation of compressed temporal norms for academic career progression, not least in the period immediately following the achievement of the first established post. Evidence of long term quality is to be measured by continuity of achievement of short term goals (Cf. Ylijoki and Mäntylä 2003). Space for diversity in modes of knowledge production or in patterns and speeds of intellectual development or productivity is likely to be reduced.

We will go on to argue that women academics were significantly disadvantaged by these developments and their temporal implications. However, this does not mean that their counterparts in Germany were better off by virtue of the fact that NPM had encroached little as yet on traditional academic organisation. If in Britain, there was now a surfeit of formal review and temporal regulation, in Germany problems could arise from a lack of structure or defined temporal norms for career progression, which left women more isolated than their British counterparts and more exposed to personal judgements and assumptions embedded in a strong culture shaped overwhelmingly by men.

In Germany the rank of professor was the main academic career grade and, in contrast to Britain, it was not underpinned by a substructure of tenured posts. In consequence, career progression focused on the achievement of a professorship, the barriers to which were formidable for all but the most highly motivated, with the most substantial social, as well as academic, capital. The eligibility criteria were high and included the completion of a post- doctoral thesis, the *Habilitation*, which involved a prolonged period of further study and financial insecurity (Pritchard 2007).

Although reforms were underway by the late twentieth century, with the introduction of junior professorships and the formal abandonment of the *Habilitation* as a mandatory qualification for a full professorship, *de facto* impact on career progression was slow. For most aspiring academics, the period in which they were financially insecure and without independent status remained a prolonged one (Pritchard 2010a). There was little structure, either organisational or temporal, within which to define and build a career pathway. In what was described in interviews as a 'very person-bound system', in which 'criteria are not transparent' (biomedical scientist), and there was a set of 'feudal structures' (historian), they were dependent for their research programme, for access to research funding and for their reputation upon sometimes one but always a limited number of dominant relationships with (largely male) professors that extended into mid-career.

German academic women reported pressures on them in terms of specific output measures less often than their British counterparts (though publication was clearly critical). They spoke rather of an unbounded and unremitting 'culture of overwork', stress and weight of expectation: 'I work all the time' (full professor, biological scientist). 'German professors … work 24 hours a day' (junior professor of history).

There were common disadvantages in the two systems that were also more gender-specific, which will be more closely examined in the next section, although we will focus primarily on the evidence in Britain of the impacts of new public management.

Maternity and New Public Management: Objective Time, Subjective Time, Biological Time

Women interviewed in both Britain and Germany were clear that child bearing and child care responsibilities were the main reasons why it remained more difficult for women than for men to reach the top in their disciplines (Pritchard 2010a). It is worth noting that in Germany 25 % of all women but 40 % of academic women were now projected to remain childless (Müller 2006). A senior history professor in the British component of our study commented, 'Many of my female colleagues, and not just in [this university], are … deciding that having children is not compatible with this job.'

In Germany the extended and intense preparatory period for the main career grade of professor was (and largely remains) exactly that in which women are biologically fertile. The absence of an obvious 'fertility window' could mean, for example, that individuals could find themselves having to make a final decision about whether or not to have children at a point of extreme pressure, the bringing to completion of the *Habilitation* (still often a *de facto* prerequisite for a 'call' to a chair).

In Britain, careers remain more graduated than in Germany and it is possible to achieve a permanent position earlier. However, the time frame for child- bearing from within a relatively secure career position has narrowed through a combination of more demanding and clearer eligibility criteria and more prolonged years of insecurity. New career structures and increased expectations involve confrontation with the relationships between objective, though not invariant, biological time and subjective time. Extended periods of insecurity at the threshold of academic careers have threatened to close the 'fertility window' provided for women by the achievement of permanent or at least open-ended contracts.

Our interviews give some sense of the interactions between career structures, biological time and subjective time in the early stages in their career to create particular pressures (Pritchard and Henkel 2011). For example:

> If you want to stop and have children, you want to be at a certain level before doing that. And you have to keep quiet about the fact that you would like to have children, in case it impacts on your promotion (early career bio-scientist, Great Britain)

> … although you are not supposed to be judged badly for [taking a break for maternity leave and looking after children], inevitably you would be, and even part-time working is frowned upon… (early career academic in an education department, Great Britain).

The problems posed by the 'maternity gap' (the drop in an individual publication record that goes with pregnancy and maternity) were particularly highlighted in the British data. A historian articulated in some detail what this gap means: not just fewer publications but also conferences not attended, presentations not made, networks lost, weakened or, at best, not developed. The intensity of the individual's engagement with the field may lessen.

It is sometimes argued that the adoption by universities of new public management has brought benefits for women academics. Systematic, external evaluations, based on transparent procedures, rules and criteria, have meant that women have more chance of being judged on their visible achievements. The introduction of 'objective' or 'clock' time frames into performance evaluation makes it possible to take account of and cancel out the disadvantages accompanying pregnancy and maternity, as has happened in the national research evaluation exercises in Britain. However, women have not necessarily availed themselves of the concessions made, feeling the need to compete on equal terms, given the prevailing time economy and an intensely competitive primary academic labour market (Cf. House of Commons 2013–2014: 23ff).

Many participants in our study recognised that overt discrimination had been radically reduced and that they had received strong support from departmental colleagues. Nevertheless, a woman with a young child, discussing an unsuccessful application to senior management for flexible working hours, reflected a feeling shared by several others in the study:

> It's within the light of that…experience that I know there is something out there. It's not said to me [but] it's there still, that being a woman academic puts pressures on departments and universities they'd rather not have (early career historian, Great Britain).

It seems that changes in the academic labour market and their implications for academic career structures have resulted in a compression of time that has exacerbated gender-related problems for women at a critical point in their career. New attitudes to and new policies for the reduction of gender inequalities have not been enough to allay the often intense anxieties felt by many women about how their career aspirations might be damaged by their gender. More powerful are institutional cultures of competitiveness, efficiency, resource and reputation-generating productivity and 'fast time' (Ylijoki 2013).

This study found only one example in Britain of an early career academic, an economist, explicitly adopting a long term perspective on combining motherhood with her career ambitions. She elected to give her children first priority while they were very young. She chose to work in a less demanding university environment than that which she knew to be essential for achieving her ultimate goal, a prestigious Chair. Meanwhile, having accumulated plenty of cultural capital at the beginning of her career, she was laying the foundations for the higher impact publications that she would need for promotions later on by maintaining strong networks, collaborative research relationships and co-authorships. In so doing she could be seen to have expanded the time horizons of her career and so strengthened her control of it (Pritchard and Henkel 2011).

Far more prevalent in the experience of study participants with children was the dominance of what Ylijoki and Mäntylä (2003) call 'scheduled time', externally defined obligations and time frames. This was likely to be more easily managed by those with academic partners. Some academic couples certainly found ways in which both parents could pursue their ambitions. They entailed highly organised forward planning, co-parenting and divisions of time. The personal price would seem to be high for both adults and children, as parents feel compelled to impose temporal regimes of the public world upon that of the family: regular and rigid divisions of time and labour at their most extreme could almost eliminate opportunities for the whole family to be together.

Both these responses to a new ordering of time under NPM suggest that its management lies largely in the hands of individuals and negotiations within private lives. Before considering this more closely we will look at another (perhaps the other) major force for change in organisational lives, which has been seen as both a solution to and an exacerbation of the impacts of temporal change.

Technological Change and the Reorganisation of Time and Space: Cui Bono?

Recent research carried out in Canada, Portugal and Finland (Menzies and Newson 2008; Rodrigues Araujo 2008; Ylijoki 2013) draws attention to the gendered implications of new information and communication technologies in academic lives.

Menzies and Newson found that *prima facie* women were adapting more readily than men to these changes. Significantly more women than men stated that their productivity had improved during the 5 years in which working online had become the norm and that they spent more time on collaborative projects. In some ways it seemed that online connectivity was helping to alleviate women's sense of marginality and minority status in academe. The authors suggest that before these developments, women almost settled for a proxy form of recognition – of their willingness to take on caring roles and administrative responsibilities. Under changed conditions, where the premium on quantifiable productivity had risen even higher, women might be welcoming the option of handling caregiving roles more efficiently through new technologies.

However, online developments were also creating new stresses and on almost every indicator of stress, women were reporting higher levels than men. A common theme in the reporting was that of the increased expectations generated by the compression of time and the new and simpler modes of communication: expectations from students and time pressures arising from the possibility of faster response rates in all contexts. Women not only seemed more affected by these than men but substantially more of them registered an overall increase in their own expectations of themselves.

Women also seemed to feel more ambivalent than men about the connectivity made possible by new technologies. They felt simultaneously 'connected and disconnected.' More specifically, they seemed to feel more deeply the loss of face to face contact with colleagues. Communications were more tightly focused; there was little space for lateral thinking that arises from conversation, from informal (non-scheduled) time with others; this meant less exchange of ideas about the political and cultural context of academic work; and also, it was felt, less penetrating academic critique between colleagues ('there is no one to push or develop me'). Changes in the social relationships generated by the adoption of new technologies had, for women, significant implications for the quality of the knowledge they were producing.

Rodrigues Araujo's research focused more explicitly on the 'profound reconfiguration of working times *and* spaces' brought about by the adoption of information and communication technologies, which allow people to work any time and anywhere. 'University spaces become virtual' but also 'other time-spaces in their social lives' are 'colonized', most importantly the home. She cites the intrusion into the home of work equipment, requiring the reorganisation of domestic space. The critical issue for both men and women is how to 'mark the difference between work time and non-work time'. Rodrigues Araujo argues from broader sociological theory, as well as from her own empirical findings, that the new possibilities for more flexible use of technologies create more anxieties and conflicts for women than for men. Familiar findings from research into the influence of gender on career progression (e.g. Probert 2005) are reflected in this context: that men are more able and willing than women to give priority to their long term career ambitions and the more immediate demands inherent in academic work over domestic responsibilities and parental anxieties. The reorganisation of spaces in the home tends to mean the take-over of bounded or protected work space by men, while women work in open, domestic spaces and often interweave domestic, child care and professional work in the same time-space. In other words, deep-seated cultural norms, values and role definitions reassert themselves, defying contemporary theories positing that the universal processes of change in the era of high modernity provide a new power and autonomy for *individuals* to pursue their own goals. Rodrigues Araujo's conclusions are similar to those of Ulrich Beck: that men are much less constrained than women in the effort to construct their own lives in the current contexts. He suggests that the child is the source of the last remaining 'irrevocable, unexchangeable relationship', and 'as long as women bear children…, feel responsible for them and see them as an essential part of their lives, children remain wanted obstacles in the occupational competition…between men and women' (1992: 111). Probert (2005) points out that this remains the case well beyond the infant years.

Time as Bounded and Unbounded

It appears that the increasingly fierce global and national competition between higher education institutions for resources and reputation, together with the advent of new technologies and new modes of management, has given rise to the imposition of more explicit and structured ordering of time and at the same time the assumption that time for work is unlimited, infinitely elastic. Some manifestations of this emerged in our study (Pritchard and Henkel 2011). For example, as a British professor of biological sciences noted, successful bids for external research funding required commitments to be made within 'clock' timeframes that had no meaning in practice. Applications had to be made in terms of the proportion of the statutory 37.5 h week to be spent on the project. However, funding bodies 'know it is not real' and, indeed, 'if you said that you only work that length of week, people would say, "Are you serious?"' Other female academics from a range of disciplines and institutions suggested that departmental managers, under pressure themselves, while seeming to recognise that they were working to their full capacity, sometimes under inequitable burdens, would still make additional demands on them. A woman recently returned from maternity leave and now mother of two young children was required to take over part of the teaching load of a male colleague on sick leave.

It might be argued that what is described here amounts to requirement of the kind of total commitment that has long represented an ideal in academic life. However, research in Finland based on interviews with academics at various stages in their career (Ylijoki 2013) found that while it remained an ideal for some, it was one perceived as realisable only in the past. Moreover, that past ideal was not externally imposed but chosen by individuals, and in a working context that afforded opportunities for 'timeless time' in academic work: 'internally motivated use of time in which clock time loses its significance.' (Ylijoki and Mäntylä 2003: 62). But time for whom? Tellingly, as Ylijoki (2013) points out, the academic ideal of 'timeless time' was essentially 'a masculine norm', generated within a particular culture (cf. Howie and Tauchert 2002). The equation of work and life in academe was possible with a clear and virtually unquestioned gendered division of labour and responsibility in private and public lives.

The picture of contemporary constructions of academic time that emerges from Ylijoki's research raises old and new questions about academic work and academic values. It contains two, in different ways limited, alternatives: one group of academics in her study saw their time as split between time for 'real work', by which they meant undisturbed immersion in research, and 'wasted time' spent on work which is short term, fragmented into unconnected episodes and compressed into the here and now (251). Many, particularly younger academics, strongly committed to research and wanting to work in a university, nonetheless saw career progression to a Chair entailing too much 'wasted time', too little autonomy and thus unattractive. Two immediately striking issues for academic values are raised here that are more age than gender-related. First, what has happened to teaching as a component of academic work, never mind the academic value of the research-teaching nexus? Second is the judgement of some younger academics that the achievement of a professorial chair is no longer a goal for the academically ambitious. This contrasts with the findings of the Pritchard comparative project, in which women academics in early or mid-career for the most part made a clear distinction between becoming a professor (to be aspired to) and becoming a manager (to be avoided).

Another group, in which women academics with caring responsibilities for young children or elderly relatives were dominant, divided their lives into 'work time' and 'private time'. It was suggested that setting a defined limit to work time 'provides a kind of protective shield against the penetrating power of 'fast time' and 'scheduled time' (Ylijoki: 252). However, there was a sense that the time which could in practice be allocated for work was never enough and that in the current conditions working to the limits of possibility did not necessarily result in meeting internal or external expectations.

In the light of these two sets of perceived temporal regimes, Ylijoki suggests that it is logical to 'question the rationality of adhering to academic ideals in an environment that seems to work against them' and to opt instead for a 'normalisation' of academic work: to see it as 'a job like any other job' (ibid.) to be conducted within set 'clock time' limits.

There were echoes of such sentiments in the study of gender inequality in Britain and Germany. It was most acutely evident in the narratives of the biological scientists, though not confined to them. A representative of this discipline referred to an outstanding postgraduate student in her department, who had declared her intention of getting out of science.

> She feels she cannot stand being 24 hours a day on the job. When she gets home she is still thinking about what she has to do. [We were] trying to explain to her that that is why she should stay in science but she felt she 'wanted to have a life'. (early career biochemist, Great Britain)

As policy makers perceive the need to exploit all the available talent in the STEM subjects, the question of retention has risen up the agenda. A recent report addressing it in the field of chemistry in the UK, found considerable reluctance among women PhDs in the subject to stay in academic work 'because academic careers are too all-consuming, solitary and not attractive to women'; 'short-term contracts did not fit with family life;' they believed that they would have to 'make sacrifices about femininity and motherhood in order to succeed' (Newsome 2013). The House of Commons Select Committee on Women and Science makes a similar point: 'STEM careers are often portrayed as both all consuming and overwhelmingly competitive… with a strong preconception that one cannot participate in science on anything other than a totally immersive basis.' (p. 24)

These views could be seen as primarily a challenge to the scientific disciplines. However, they can also be understood as offering a more fundamental idea: that taking gender equality seriously means not only undertaking the kind of policy approach required by gender mainstreaming but also acknowledging the challenge it presents to long cherished academic ideals, such as total commitment to academic work, forged within cultures and institutions developed by men.

Summary and Conclusions

Despite significant progress in the reduction of gender inequalities in the academic profession, new modes of management, changing structures of academic labour markets and new patterns of career development have created new and unequal pressures for men and women in early careers. Demands on them in terms of output and outcome criteria have increased simultaneously with a compression of time in which to meet them. More explicitly defined temporal norms in career paths are being established that disadvantage women.

Further, day to day 'work time' can, it seems, be almost infinitely expanded by both those managing academic institutions and those who shape the political and economic space in which the institutions operate. Lines between work/public and non-work/private time are constantly being re-drawn. This casts doubt on the possibility of managing them simply by efficient, rational workload allocations and formulae based on clock time. They are often dealt with by repeated adjustments on the part of individual academics, so that the experience of time and work is fragmented and lacking order or regularity.

Men and women, particularly those in academic partnerships, can, and do, provide mutual support within the private space of the family and so mitigate the gendered inequalities. However, the issues are systemic. First and foremost, it can be argued that as yet the consequences of taking gender equality seriously have not been fully acknowledged by policy makers, management or by the academic profession itself. Ambitions for gender equality raise questions about long held academic ideals such as the possibilities and rewards of 'timeless time' in academic life and of the economic, cultural and organisational conditions under which they are achievable and by whom.

There are also broader and deeper cultural issues. Some of the research described here suggests that the fundamental timescapes which men and women construct for their lives are still generally different. Men can more often than women retain more control of their time (and space) than their partners. Work and work time are dominant imperatives in the management of the here and now but also in their conception of what gives meaning to their lives when viewed as a whole or in the long term. For women, the family and the home more often exercise the kind of pull that makes it difficult for them to see work as the primary determinant of their timescape. They tend to move between work and home, so that it has a less clear or permanently defined structure or shape; it is more fluid. Differences in these terms are by no means universal but the patterns and assumptions of cultures with long histories (family and academic) remain powerful.

The other side of this argument is that in a context where the practice of academic work and the organisational and social relationships within which it is carried out are changing, women perhaps are more able to reject change; or because they are worse affected by it, more ready to reject it. The rewards of total commitment are no longer good enough in a range of contemporary academic contexts.

New technologies would seem to offer some solutions to the gendered problems of time; equally, they can exacerbate them and create new ones. Further close grained research on their impacts is needed. The work referred to in this chapter points the way towards identifying differences of response to new temporal orders both within and between genders. Given the expansion and scale of change in knowledge fields, in the processes and participants in the production of knowledge and in modes and media of learning, it is surely necessary to create higher education and research systems that, rather than imposing more rigid and restricted timeframes, accommodate and embrace diversity in academic work patterns, career pathways and time horizons.

References

Adam, B. (1990). *Time and social theory*. Cambridge/Oxford: Polity Press.

Adam, B. (2004). *Time*. Cambridge: Polity Press.

Allen Collinson, J. (2004). Occupational identity on the edge: Social science contract researchers in higher education. *Sociology, 38*(2), 313–329.

Archer, L. (2008). The new neoliberal subjects? Young/er academics' constructions of professional identity. *Journal of Education Policy, 23*(3), 265–285.

Barrett, P., & Barret, L. (2013). *Promoting positive gender outcomes in higher education through active workload management*. Manchester: University of Salford.

Beck, U. (1992). *Risk society: Towards a new modernity*. London: Sage.

Equality Challenge Unit. (2014). *Equality in higher education: Statistical report*, ECU.

European Commission. (2012). In Caprile, M (Ed.), *Meta-analysis of gender and science research: synthesis report*. European Commission.

European Commission. (2013). *She figures 2012: Gender in research and innovation*. Brussels: European Commission.

Galligan, Y. (2014). 'Making sex the dependent variable: Mainstreaming gender equality in higher education', address to 'Equate Scotland' conference, let's talk about sex: Developing and supporting your female STEM students and staff. Edinburgh, Napier University, 14 May.

Giddens, A. (1991). *Modernity and self-identity*. Cambridge: Polity Press.

House of Commons Science and Technology Committee. (2014). *Women in scientific careers*, Sixth Report of Session 2013–14, HC 701.

Howie, G., & Tauchert, A. (2002). Institutional discrimination and the "Cloistered' Academic Ideal". In G. Howie & A. Tauchert (Eds.), *Gender, teaching and research in higher education* (pp. 59–72). Basingstoke: Ashgate.

Leisyte, L., & Hosch-Dayican, B. (2014). Changing academic roles and shifting gender inequalities: A case analysis of the influence of the research-teaching nexus on the academic career prospects of female academics in the Netherlands. *Journal of Workplace Rights, 17*(4–5), 467–490.

Menzies, H., & Newson, J. (2008). Time, stress and intellectual engagement in academic work: Exploring gender difference. *Gender, Work and Organization, 15*(5), 504–522.

Müller. (2006). In M. A. D. Sagaria (Ed.), *Women, universities and change: Gender equality in the European Union and the United States*. New York/Basingstoke: Palgrave Macmillan.

Neave, G. (2006). On time and fragmentation: Sundry observations on research, university and politics from a waveringly historical perspective. In G. Neave, K. Blöckert, & T. Nybom (Eds.), *The European Research University: An historical parenthesis?* New York: Palgrave Macmillan.

Newsome, J. L. (2013). The Chemistry PhD: Impact on women's retention, a report for the UK resource centre for women in SET and the royal society of Chemistry (Quoted in Galligan, Y. (2013)).

Pritchard, R. M. O. (2007). Gender inequality in British and German Universities. *Compare, 37*(5), 651–669.

Pritchard, R. M. O. (2010a). Gender inequality in British and German Universities: A qualitative study. *Compare: A Journal of Comparative and International Education, 40*(4), 513–530.

Pritchard, R. M. O. (2010b). Attitudes to gender equality issues in British and German Academia. *Higher Education Management and Policy, 22*(2), 37–60.

Pritchard, R. M. O., & Henkel, M. (2011). New public management, academic time and gender inequality. In R. Pritchard (Ed.), *Neoliberal developments in higher education: The United Kingdom and Germany*. Oxford: Peter Lang.

Probert, B. (2005). I just couldn't fit it in. *Gender, Work and Organization, 12*(1), 50–72.

Rees, T. (2006). Pushing the gender equality agenda forward in the European Union. In M. A. D. Sagaria (Ed.), *Women, universities and change: Gender equality in the European Union and the United States*. New York/Basingstoke: Palgrave Macmillan.

Rodrigues Araujo, E. (2008). Technology, gender and time: A contribution to the debate. *Gender, Work and Organization, 15*(5), 477.

United Nations. (n.d.). *Report of the economic and social council for 1997*. A/52/3.18 September 1997, Accessed 25 Apr 2015.

Ylijoki, O.-H. (2013). Boundary-work between work and life in the high-speed university. *Studies in Higher Education, 38*(2), 242–255.

Ylijoki, O.-H., & Mäntylä, H. (2003). Conflicting time perspectives in academic work. *Time and Society, 12*(1), 55–78.

Chapter 11
Women and Gender Equality in Higher Education?

Introduction

Over the last 50 years, the pace of change in HE linked to the wider economy has
speeded up such that women now comprise over 50 % of university undergraduate
students across most countries, especially the developed world or 'global north',
although these percentages do not translate into academia and nor do they transform
gender relations (ECU 2011; She Figures 2009; UNESCO 2012). The differences
are stark, as I shall show: the gender gap has reversed for undergraduate students but
for women as academics it remains resistant to change as male power dominates.
The question of gender equality in universities, and the contribution of feminist or
women's studies is a highly contentious topic. The claim that gender equality has
been achieved only refers to the question of the balance of male and female students, whether of undergraduate or graduate degrees and courses (HEPI 2009). It is
not at all about women as academics, teachers or researchers, and yet feminist
knowledge, pedagogies and wisdom have developed apace as feminists have entered
global academe. *She Figures*, an European Union publication, illustrates how limited women's penetration into the senior ranks of university research and administration has been, whilst the annual reports of the UK's Equality Challenge Unit
(ECU) do not acknowledge the rampant inequalities between students and
academics.

Drawing on *Feminism, Gender and Universities: Politics, Passion and Pedagogies*
(2014), I present a global picture to contextualise the collective biography and life
history of international feminists entering HE over the last 50 years. I argue that the
feminist project to transform women's lives in the direction of gender and social

M.E. David (✉)
University College London (UCL) Institute of Education and Visiting Professor, Centre for
Higher Education and Equity Research, University of Sussex, Brighton, UK
e-mail: miriam.david@ucl.ac.uk

© Springer International Publishing Switzerland 2017
H. Eggins (ed.), *The Changing Role of Women in Higher Education*,
The Changing Academy – The Changing Academic Profession in International
Comparative Perspective 17, DOI 10.1007/978-3-319-42436-1_11

equality became not only a political but also an educational and pedagogical one. Feminism has transformed women's lives and the processes of knowledge-making but it has yet to have a wider impact upon gender and sexual relations, given the parallel changing socio-economic contexts towards managerial and business approaches to university. I interviewed over 100 international academic feminists and activists, across three generations, and whilst their particular biographies and experiences were different, all felt that feminism had transformed their personal and professional lives. HE was critical to this with comments like:

- *Feminism has been my life project*
- *It changed my life*
- *My entire life has been shaped by feminism*
- *As a scholar I write from a feminist perspective*
- *I began to self-identify as a feminist when I was in graduate school…*

The first generation (born around the second world war), those who are now known as second-wave feminists, to distinguish them from first-wave feminists who fought for women's suffrage, tended to become feminists through their political and personal circumstances, *after being students* at university, when 'second-wave feminism broke on the shores of academe'. The second generation illustrate the ripple effects of feminism moving into academe, mainly becoming feminists through their studies as teachers or researchers, whilst the third generation are illustrative of the 'crest of the wave' of academic feminism: when feminist and gender studies become part of the curriculum of undergraduate studies. Whilst all feel passionate about feminist knowledge and feminist pedagogies, none are sanguine about the future, feeling that issues about gender and social equality have been captured by neo-liberal discourses and where they have lost their radical and transformative edge.

Global Commitments to Gender Equality in HE

UNESCO's *World Atlas of Gender Equality in Education*, published in 2012, is the clearest example of this international commitment to global gender equality across and including all levels of education. This atlas provides a vast amount of statistical information about where women and men are as *students* across the globe, relating the information to international criteria. It is quite clear from the publication of a global atlas that education is a vital ingredient of economies today and that the goal of universal education for all is fast becoming a reality. The title of illustrates quite how normal the issue gender equality has become. So has the goal of gender equality been accomplished, or are there still issues about the relations between men and women in higher or tertiary education and beyond? Or, on the other hand, has the notion of gender equality been captured by the ruling classes or governing elites and been changed to a modest one of access and inclusion, rather than a wider notion of transformation of power relations?

Even the UNESCO Atlas argues that whilst there has been enormous growth in student numbers, including a 500 % increase across the globe, over the last 40 years, women do not benefit as well as men from their involvement in HE. This is their headline: *Women now account for a majority of students in most countries* [and this is part of] *an increase of around 500 % in enrolments over less than 40 years (1970–2009)*. They add that 'the capacity of the world's education systems more than doubled – from 647 million students in 1970 to 1397 million in 2009…[and] from 33 to 164 million in higher education' (UNESCO 2012, p. 9). They go on that *'female enrolment at the tertiary level has grown almost twice as fast as that of men over the last four decades* (my emphasis) for reasons that include social mobility, enhanced income potential, international pressure to narrow the gender gap…[but] access to higher education by women has not always translated into enhanced career opportunities, including the opportunity to use their doctorates in the field of research' (2012, p. 75). So whilst *'the female edge is up in tertiary enrolment through the master's level [it] disappears when it comes to PhDs and careers in research'* (my emphasis) (2012, p. 107).

They also say that 'Even though higher education leads to individual returns in the form of higher income, women often need to have more education than men to get some jobs…Women continue to confront discrimination in jobs, disparities in power, voice and political representation and laws that are prejudicial on the basis of their gender. As a result well-educated women often end up in jobs where they do not use their full potential and skills' (2012, p. 84). Clearly, there is much that remains to be done to transform the relations between men and women both in HE and beyond. Men still wield more powerful positions within and beyond HE.

How much of these changes are to do with feminism or to do with other socio-economic and cultural changes? As feminists we argued for political changes on the basis of our emerging views of the ways that our personal lives were not unique. We argued that the relations between men and women, in the family, and in the wider public and social world, were political, in the sense of being about power, and inequalities of power in the minutiae of everyday relations. The slogan 'the personal is political' was coined to express these sentiments almost 50 years ago. It is being re-invoked today and used to think about the nuances of the power relations within the new forms of HE in a changed and now knowledge economy. The question of the future of feminist knowledge and pedagogies as well as gender equality in neo-liberal forms of HE remains contested. How are we to create a feminist friendly future?

Contested Evidence About Gender and Equality in HE

Lord David Willetts, when Minister for Universities and Science in the UK Coalition government, produced a pamphlet entitled *Robbins Revisited: Bigger and Better Higher Education* (2013) for the fiftieth anniversary of the report. He claimed that 'in 2011–12 … 54 per cent of full time students at UK HEIs were female' (2013, p. 26), arguing that this comes from 'a shift in the gender balance in higher education'. He added that 'the situation we face in today's society is one that might have seemed unlikely in 1960s Britain, with more women entering university than there are men even submitting a UCAS form. This is a remarkable achievement for women, who were outnumbered in universities by men as recently as the 1990s. *It is also the culmination of a longstanding educational trend, with boys and men finding it harder to overcome obstacles in the way of learning. It is a real challenge for different policy-makers* (my emphasis) (2013, p. 27–8)'. Willetts laments this shift in the gender balance in HE.

In his book *The Pinch* (2010) he argued for policies to rectify the balance towards men, as he feared that 'feminism had trumped egalitarianism' and university-educated women were to blame for taking working class men's jobs. The book was published in April 2011 in paperback with a new justifying afterword which restates the book's purpose: to deal with *injustice between generations* rather than social or ethnic groups, while gender relations are taken for granted. He wants to ensure that working class men are encouraged into HE, at the expense of middle class women, albeit that the overall numbers of students applying for HE are declining, given the imposition of tuition fees. Heralded as a brilliant scholar or 'two-brains' (*The Guardian* 15.07.2014, p. 4) it seems to me that these arguments are not at all brilliant and that he is the reciprocal of this, namely a 'half-wit'.

Similarly *She Figures* from the European Union in 2009 show that *the proportion of female students (55 %) and graduates (59 %) exceeds that of male students*. Another example has been expressed in the USA, by *The Chronicle of Higher Education*, the magazine for academe, in a special issue on 'Diversity in Academe: The Gender Issue' (November 2, 2012). As the editor notes: …It's well known, for example, that *female undergraduates outnumber their male counterparts* (my emphasis)…the undergraduate gender gap is especially striking among black students…women are advancing in the professoriate as well…(Carolyn Mooney, senior editor, special sections, B3, 2012).

There are several sources of evidence providing the detail that confirm the overall picture of moves towards gender equality amongst *students* in the UK. Willetts does not seem at all abashed by providing comments to right 'the gender balance'. And he is supported in this by several independent organizations, for example, the Higher Education Policy Institute (HEPI), under the directorship of Barham Bekhradnia, produced a study in 2009 entitled *Male and female participation and progression in higher education*, which purported to show that since women were now in the ascendance as full-time undergraduate students there was no longer any problem with questions of gender equity, let alone equality in HE.

As regards universities, the organization of university leaders or vice-chancellors, now the Universities UK (UUK), set up a unit to gather together gender statistics, initially named as its Equalities Unit, in the early twenty-first century. It has been transformed over the last decade in line with neo-liberal tendencies. Although continuing to be financed by public funds, across the four nations of the UK, the unit is no longer under the umbrella of the UUK, but has become an independent and autonomous organization, renamed the Equalities Challenge Unit (ECU). In its current guise it provides detailed evidence about *Equality in Higher Education* in annual reports that gather together statistics across various social groups including *gender*, ethnicity, disability, and age, and bringing them together in what are referred to as 'multiple identities'. Its mission statement declares: 'ECU works to further and support equality and diversity for staff and students in HE and seeks to ensure that staff and students are not unfairly excluded, marginalised or disadvantaged because of age, disability, gender identity, marital or civil partnership status, pregnancy or maternity status, race, religion or belief, sex, sexual orientation, or through any combination of these characteristics or other unfair treatment.'

In announcing the ECU's *Equality in higher education: statistical report 2011* (December 2011) on the website it was argued that: 'This report presents an equality-focused analysis of information on staff and students during the 2009/10 academic year, plus a year-on-year comparison showing the progress of equality across the sector over the last 5 years. For the first time the report looks at the inter-play of multiple identities (for example female black staff, male disabled students). Covering England, Wales, Scotland and Northern Ireland, the report provides a use-ful benchmark for institutions to compare their local statistics. New legal require-ments across England, Scotland and Wales mean that HE institutions need to set equality objectives or outcomes. The figures in this report, alongside information gathered at a local level, will provide an evidence base that will inform these objectives.'

This was ECU's most detailed report so far, and was split into two parts. *Part 2 students* (2011) does not start with headline figures about gender equality or parity but provides detail on other equalities such as disabilities, with the comment that 'the statistic on the cover shows the difference between students declaring a dis-ability in different subjects. 14.4 % of students studying creative arts and design declared a disability, compared with 4.5 % of students on business and administra-tion studies courses ...' (2011, cover). The overwhelming impression is that *gender equality has become so normalized that it hardly bears comment.* The authors argue that: 'in the academic year 2009/10, women made up 56.6 % of the student popula-tion. Female students were in the majority across all four countries (England, Wales, Scotland and Northern Ireland)'. Of the almost 2.5 million students in the UK, 1.4 million are women, and the rest – just over a million – are male. However, this fact is qualified, as was the case with UNESCO atlas, although a similar gloss is not put on the figures, with the statement that 'Women were in the majority across all degree levels and modes with the exception of full-time postgraduates where 50.4 % were male... The proportion of female students was highest amongst other undergradu-ates (64.7 %)...'

Willetts also elaborates on these figures with the comment that: 'In the 1960s only 25 % of full-time students at UK institutions were female... The number of women studying has grown by a larger proportion than the number of men across every subject. Women are still under-represented in sciences (maths and physics) and the applied sciences (computing, engineering, technology and architecture), but the margin has narrowed from the 1960s when only three per cent of students studying "applied science" were women. Arguably the most dramatic increase is in medicine: in the 1960s only 22 in every 100 medical students were women, but by 2011–2012 this had risen to 59 in every 100 (2013, p. 27)'.

Rampant Gender Inequalities in HE: The UK Academic Labour Market

It is fascinating that the two reports on *Equality in HE* by the ECU in the UK can be written and published together without any overarching comment about the *dissonance between the two* in terms of gender equity. It is abundantly clear that despite the huge increases in educational opportunities up to postgraduate research where women have been sufficiently able to attain as much if not more than men, that they remain subordinate across all sectors of academic employment. The picture painted by the ECU for students is one of gender having become a *minor* issue in relation to student attainment and progression, across a range of subjects and disciplines. The ECU's report *Equality in higher education part 1: staff* (December 2011) paints an entirely different picture: it is one of *rampant gender inequalities*. The headline figures are prefigured on the cover with the caption: 16.3 % median gender pay gap and 20.3 % mean gender pay gap. 'The statistic on the front cover shows the median and mean pay gaps between male and female staff working in higher education across the UK (Fig. 1.28)'. The headline figures also paint a similar story of gender inequalities with the following highlighted:

- Overall in 2009/2010, 53.8 % of all staff were women.
- Female staff made up 46.8 % of full-time staff and 67.1 % of part- time staff.
- *A higher proportion of staff in professorial roles were male (80.9 %) than female (19.1 %).*
- *The mean salary of female staff was £31,116 compared with £39,021 for male staff, an overall mean pay gap of 20.3 %.*
- **76.1 % of UK national staff in professorial roles and 67.4 % of non-UK national staff in professorial roles were white males** (my emphases)

All the policy discussion is focused upon *students*, and especially the dilemma of there being more female than male undergraduates. There is no concern at all about the fact that women are still subordinate within the staffing of HE. As we look across the echelons of HE women become more and more rare, most especially for Black and Minority Ethnic groups. The *white male* remains legitimately in power in HE.

HE and Women 50 Years Ago

It is clearly the case that HE is far more prominent in public life and employment than 50 years ago globally and nationally. The Robbins report was commissioned in 1961 by a British Conservative government. There was anxiety at the time about how to sustain and develop economic growth in the post-war era, and education was gradually seen as a key strategic component, given other international developments. The government therefore appointed an eminent economist to chair the proceedings, namely Lord Lionel Robbins, who was a professor at the London School of Economics. He was commissioned to report on the state and future of HE and its contribution to economic growth. The commitment to economic growth was one of a series of measures embarked upon by the then Conservatives, given that Robbins' report was published less than 20 years after the ending of the Second World War.

The policy to expand HE was not initiated through the Robbins report, but rather the Government wanted Lord Robbins and his committee to legitimate and enhance a policy already set in train. By the beginning of the 1960s, the government, through its autonomous University Grants Committee (UGC) had already sanctioned the expansion of HE and the creation of new universities on green field sites. It was a time of commitment to social and economic change, to human and civic rights, in the shadows of the war. Governments were committed to trying to bring about social change and peaceful solutions. There was what has since been described as a bipartisan social consensus on the role of the state in social and economic policies, and especially around the uses of education and the expansion of educational opportunities. But at that time there was no system for education beyond the compulsory stage, which in the UK had only just been raised to the age of 16. Institutions had grown up in response to different and specific economic needs such as teaching and technologies. Hence there were separate and often locally funded and supported colleges of technology and teacher training.

The Robbins report on *Higher Education* was published in Autumn 1963.[1] Its main recommendations were to create a system whereby HE could expand. To that end, the committee recommended that 'university places should be available for all…qualified by ability and attainment'. This quickly became known as *the Robbins principle*. To ensure that the recommendations were enacted the committee also recommended a commitment of public funds to expand and create a *system* of HE. The report also concluded that such institutions should have four main 'objectives essential to any properly balanced system: instruction in skills; the promotion of the general powers of the mind so as to produce not mere specialists but rather cultivated men and women; to maintain research in balance with teaching, since teaching should not be separated from the advancement of learning and the search for truth; and to transmit a common culture and common standards of citizenship.'

---

[1] Committee on Higher Education (23 September 1963), *Higher education: report of the Committee appointed by the Prime Minister under the Chairmanship of Lord Robbins 1961–1963*, Cmnd. 2154, London: HMSO.

At the time, HE reached a very small segment of the population, and university education was an even smaller proportion and the official figures and statistics in the UK did not routinely produce them in terms of sex or gender. There were 216,000 undergraduate (and postgraduate) students overall then (*Robbins Report*, Cmnd 2154, 1963, p. 15). Given that university was not crucially important for professional employment, such as the law, many men did not go. And some of the women who went on to gain qualifications in what were then seen as key female occupations – teachers, nurses and social workers – did not have to go to university but to specialist schools and colleges. Willetts makes the point that of the 216,000 students in 1962–1963, only 118,000 went to universities, and the other 98,000 went to other institutions, such as colleges of technology, teacher training colleges (2013, p. 22–24). He adds 'in the 1960s only 25 percent of full time students at UK institutions were female' (Willetts 2013, p. 26).

The period was also about the rise of the social sciences within universities, linked as it was to social reforms and social welfare. Indeed, Willetts' newly constructed tables for his commentary on Robbins show these developments and changes quite dramatically. In his Table 3.2 entitled *Full-time university students by sex and faculty, 1961–1962 and 2011–1912* he shows that in 1961–1962 there were only five groups of faculties or subjects, namely humanities, social studies, science, applied science and medical subjects. The balances for all students were that a third were in humanities, a quarter in science, and almost 20 % in applied science, with just over one in ten in social studies and almost a sixth in medical subjects. So in 1961–1962 across all faculties there were 75 % men and 25 % women. Women's proportion was the highest in humanities where there were 42 % women and this represented over half of all women students (53 %).

By 2011–2012, these faculty groupings had increased to include other subjects and, far more importantly for my story the balances between both the faculties and men and women had completely reversed! In 2011–2012 social studies accounted for almost a third of all students, and humanities had dropped to one in ten, whilst science and applied science had also reversed in balance too so that a quarter of all students are now in applied sciences and only 12 % in science, with now only 4 % being in medical subjects! It is clear, then, that there has been a major growth in the social sciences and accompanying this phenomenal growth has been the rise of women as students. Women now represent 54 % of such students and men only 46 %, with women being the majority (almost two-thirds in humanities and other subjects (65 %), and well over half in medicine (59 %) and social studies (57 %). It seems clear where the rise in interest in social change has been developed, and how feminism might have taken hold.

In considering ways to finance all of this expansion, the Robbins committee also considered the nature of the culture and society of the time. It noted the balance between male and female students and noted how few women students were attending university at the time: there were far more than twice as many men as women as students at the beginning of the 1960s. Only 2.5 % of 17–30 year old women went to university, whereas almost 6 % of men went. It also, however, noted that parents were then expected to support their daughters on marriage. The Robbins committee, therefore, argued against the implementation of student loans, especially as to the potential impact that they would have on parental decision-making about their daughters. They were opposed to student loans because: 'In particular, where women are concerned, the effect might well be either that British parents would be strengthened in their age-long disinclination to consider their daughters to be as deserving of higher education as their sons, or that the eligibility for marriage of the more educated would be diminished by the addition to their charms of what would be in effect *a negative dowry* (my emphasis) (Robbins report 1963, Cmnd 2154, paragraph 646).

They also added that: 'On balance we do not recommend immediate recourse to a system of financing students by loans. At a time when many parents are only just beginning to acquire the habit of contemplating higher education for such of their children, *especially girls*, as are capable of benefiting by it, we think it probable that it would have *undesirable disincentive effects*. But if, as time goes on, the habit is more firmly established, the arguments of justice in distribution and of the advantage of increasing individual responsibility may come to weigh more heavily and lead to some experiment in this direction (my emphasis) (ibid, Chap. 14).

The government of the time accepted all the recommendations of the Robbins committee and set about expanding the university system, including encouraging the provision of more places for women, although this might, as Willetts mentions, have proved difficult: 'The Robbins report appeared 50 years ago, in October 1963. It was a remarkable year: ... staggered by the assassination of JFK in November. Aldous Huxley died but the title of his most famous book, *Brave New World*, was an apt description of the age. It was a big political year too. On 1 October 1963, Harold Wilson promised the 'white heat' of a new technological revolution at the Labour Party Conference. A few days later, during the Conservative Party Conference, Harold Macmillan resigned as Prime Minister, citing some health problems. From the vantage point of 2013, the case for a technology focused industrial strategy still resonates – but there is no parallel crisis in leadership, despite the constraints of coalition...the new Conservative ... Prime Minister... Alec Douglas-Home ...took charge. Less than a week later, on 23 October, his new Government formally received the Robbins report, entitled *Higher Education*. A day later, the new administration accepted Lord Robbins's conclusions in full. This was widely expected... (2013, p. 8)

Willetts adds that: 'Because existing universities were not keen to deliver all the extra places [needed as seen by the UGC], there was an unprecedented opportunity to bring some embryonic ideas to life. New universities were established ... [its] *origins owe more to an academic debate about modern forms of higher education than to the numbers game* (2013 p. 12) (my emphasis). He also comments, more pertinently for this discussion, about the issues pertaining to women as students. A key point that he makes that: 'The report makes two key assumptions about this growth which proved hard to reconcile in practice. First, it assumed a substantial proportion of these extra places would be in science and technology...Secondly, as women were particularly under-represented at university and their forecasts for growth rested on forecasts of better school attainments, this would mean a particularly dramatic surge in the number of female students from 68 in 1962 to 253 k in 1980). Together these assumptions required a massive shift of girls towards science and technology. This may have been right and desirable but it required a shift in cultural attitudes and patterns of school teaching which could not be delivered in the time available. Robbins correctly forecast a big increase in female students but many more of them went into arts and humanities, which is where overcrowding and resource pressures proved most intense… (Willetts 2013 p. 25–7).

The gloss that Willetts puts upon the issue of student loans seems to be very different from my interpretation: '…to pay for all of this Robbins toyed with the idea of loans repayable as a percentage of future earnings. He decided not to go down this route as he was afraid that positive attitudes to higher education were not sufficiently widespread, especially among young women. Looking back he increasingly came to regret his caution… (Willetts 2013, p. 70).

Indeed, he shares the views about women's role in the family that were current at the time of Robbins and which were clearly articulated in the report. For many of us, women and feminists especially, these views are now very old-fashioned and do not accord with the ways we now live our lives. Willetts, however, seems to want a return to what he might think of as halcyon days. But he does mention the changing balances between subjects and faculties in universities, which may have implications for graduate and professional employment. His concerns are about what are now called STEM subjects, namely science, technology, engineering and maths or medicine. And in his case, the focus is firmly on medicine and the fact that nowadays even here there is a predominance of women as students, and therefore presumably of doctors.

1963, Robbins and Me

The Robbins report illustrates the changing times dramatically. Fifty years ago most women were not expected to pursue a career throughout their adult lives: marriage and motherhood remained a more important official focus. The Robbins report's reflections on the funding of HE and the way students should be helped through illustrates neatly what a different world it was then. Whilst I did not know the Robbins arguments at the time, their arguments confirm the expectations that many women myself included were brought up with then. And it was the year that I went to university. How things have changed for us all as a society, and in terms of the balances between employment and education in an expanding knowledge economy.

Having mapped out the landscape of HE 50 years ago, and the changing values and views about students and women's role and place, it is clear that the changes have indeed been enormous. In the UK alone we now have more than two million students in HE in the UK, making for a massive increase over the last 50 years. And since the publication of the Robbins report there have been dramatic changes in male and female participation such that females are in the ascendance. Whilst, quite clearly the colleges, schools and universities to which students go vary now in ways they did not at that time. Whilst all of this is welcome news, the question of how it happened and in what ways still needs to be addressed. We still do not know very much from this landscape about who the teachers and academics are in these various different kinds of university and HE. And perhaps more importantly, we still do not know what the future holds, and this is increasingly a time of austerity.

Students were not commonly on the public agenda for discussion and as women students we were even more rare. We were a tiny minority of a small minority of young people becoming of age in the 1960s. But students became increasingly vocal as the decade wore on, and this led to the emergence of a strong and campaigning women's liberation movement (WLM), of which I quickly became a part. None of the terms now used about the relations between men and women in HE and beyond were then in either common currency or in the official lexicon. These are all part of the changing discourse of HE and its political situation – terms like gender equality, feminism and the women's movement. And even less so notions of sexual harassment or abuse, patriarchy and misogyny (David 2016).

Origins of Second-Wave Feminism 50 Years Ago

The anniversary celebrations for the Robbins report took place alongside several other events in 2013: for example, in the UK as well as the USA about the publication of the American feminist Betty Friedan's book *The Feminine Mystique*. This book arguably launched the feminist movement in the USA initially and later in Europe and beyond. The book was based upon Friedan's study of suburban housewives, the majority of whom lived in middle class areas and had been college students, prior to becoming wives and mothers. They all identified what Friedan called 'the problem that has no name', namely women's dissatisfaction with their lives as merely wives and mothers, hidden from public and professional lives for which they had studied. This was a major cry for social change and the book quickly became a best-seller and launched the National Organisation of Women (NOW) in the USA. Indeed, several of the women that I interviewed mentioned this as most formative in their becoming feminists. For example, Professor Helen Taylor, the feminist literary critic, and Professor Sandra Acker, the feminist sociologist of education both mentioned reading the book as students in the USA and remarking without prompting how influential it was in their journey of thinking about new ways of being a woman and Professor Bronwyn Davies, an Australian feminist sociologist, was also captivated by the book and it transformed her life.

Friedan, along with other feminist writers such as Eva Figes 1970, Shulamith Firestone (1970), Germaine Greer (1970), Juliet Mitchell (1966, 1973), Adrienne Rich (1977) and Sheila Rowbotham (1972, 1973a, b) were all passionate about changing women's lives: in the family as daughters, sisters, wives and mothers, as sexual beings, and in education, paid and unpaid work or employment. How could women's lives be transformed and made more equal with men's lives in both public and private? How could patriarchy and sexual oppression be overcome? These books led to the enormous development of feminist knowledge and scholarship in global academe, slowly at first but eventually quickening its pace as the twentieth century wore on.

From my study, what is particularly significant is how the feminists I interviewed across the 3 generations were not, as Willetts (2011) argued, all middle class but from a variety of family backgrounds. The vast majority of the women – whether middle class or working class – were 'first-in-the-family' (a UK concept) or first generation (an American concept) to go to university or college. Of the middle class women, many were the '*first-girls-in-the-family*', demonstrated the early impact of some form of gender equity, whilst across my three generations of women increasingly the women were both from working class and first in the family to go to university. Importantly too the vast majority of the women are 'full' professors in the American sense, and having doctorates, with only tiny numbers of the oldest generation not having them, given the changing requirements of a changing form of HE. This illustrates how expansions of HE, set in train in the UK by the Robbins report, have had an effect on gender equity as a form of social mobility, despite the fact that Conservatives, as represented by Willetts (2011) might abhor such developments.

What Is the Complex Jungle of HE Today and Where Is SHE Internationally?

It is clear from the UNESCO atlas that gender equality is nowhere near being achieved in academe today anywhere in the world but it also signals how gender equality in education is on the global public agenda in ways in which it was not at the beginning of the twenty-first century, and certainly not as an international issue during the twentieth century. The production of this 'evidence' is an important indicator of public policy debates about gender equality, including both the economic and social interests of the global powers. As the Director-General of UNESCO, Irina Bokova, argues in her foreword: 'This …responds to this need on one of the most important questions for human rights and sustainable development today. *Girls and women remain deprived of full and equal opportunities for education* (my emphasis). There has been progress towards parity at the primary level, but this tapers off at the secondary level in developing regions. The global economic crisis is deepening inequalities, made worse by cuts in education budgets and stagnating development support.'

Gender equality in education has been accepted as a global human right, but how is this interpreted? UNESCO's commitment to gender equality in education has a long history but is it linked to political and feminist campaigning during the twentieth century? It is partly but not only and it has now become embroiled in neo-liberal policies and politics too. The discourses used about these dramatically increasing numbers are overly optimistic with notions of women being either 'favoured' or 'beneficiaries'. The Atlas argues that *Women are the biggest beneficiaries of rising tertiary enrolments* (2012, p. 77). Using a rather odd phrase '*globalization has led to more attention to gender egalitarianism*' the authors conclude that this is not because of government action – there has rarely been any government policies on affirmative action – but because of social and economic reasons. 'Over-representation of women in HE is not necessarily the result of affirmative action in their favour, for such legislation is rare. Rather, empirical research highlights several reasons for the growing participation of women in post-secondary education, beginning with the fact that higher levels of schooling are now required to attain social mobility and escape poverty... (2012, p. 84).

They also conclude that whilst there has been an enormous increase in educational participation within and through HE, this has not been matched by greater participation in the labour market. This is then one of the key paradoxes of gender equality in education: is it an indication of continuing forms of sexism, misogyny or patriarchal relations in the wider society? This is what UNESCO says: 'Despite the narrowing of the gender gap in tertiary enrolment, significant differences are observed in the fields in which men and women choose to earn degrees ...The proportion of female graduates is much higher in the social sciences, business and law, where women are the majority of graduates in all but one region and in all of the sub-fields of social and behavioural science, journalism and information, business and administration, and law... (2012, p. 80–82). The fact remains that men predominate in jobs after the Ph.D. and especially in relation to research posts. The arts and social sciences overall are dominated by women, and also in education '*education is the most popular with women* (my emphasis) (2012, p. 82).

The conclusion is that: It is often the case where a better level of education doesn't necessarily translate into better employment opportunities. Even though women outperform men in education, they still face significant shortfalls and discrimination in the labour market and end up in jobs where they don't use any of their skills. However, *even though education is not the only input into women's empowerment it is nonetheless a central one.*' (2012, p. 107).

It is quite clear that there has been a sea-change in the role of HE in international economies, and that HE is now critical to economic growth throughout the world, known as 'academic capitalism'. And students are clearly very important to this, including women as students. But what differences does this really make to women's positioning relative to men in the public world of employment and politics, whether in HE or not? Does the fact that there are more women than men students across the globe make any to the relations between men and women in subsequent employment, whether academic or not, and in politics or the public? At a statistical level, as we have already seen from the UNESCO Atlas women have a harder time than men in academic employment, despite getting better grades.

Gender Equality Now Part of the Neo-liberal Project?

The term *gender equality in education* is everywhere accepted or acknowledged in political arenas but it has lost its meaning and radical edge. It has been hijacked by government and neutralized. European policies are frequently strongly in favour of gender equality not on social grounds but for economic competition and business innovation, such as a recent gender summit about research in Europe with Mr Robert-Jan Smits, EC Director General for Research and Innovation arguing that: 'The promotion of *gender equality is part of the European Commission's strategic approach* in the field of research and innovation. It contributes to *the enhancement of European competitiveness* (my emphasis) and the full realisation of European innovation potential' (2011, p. iv).

The European Commission (EC) has produced specific statistics on gender equality in 'science', where science is the umbrella term for research across all subjects and disciplines in universities. Their nicely named *She Figures – Statistics and Indicators on Gender Equality in Science* (EUR 23,856 EN) have provided evidence and indicators on gender equality in universities every 3 years during the twenty-first century. It is argued that: 'The *She Figures* data collection is undertaken every 3 years as a joint venture of the Scientific Culture and Gender Issues Unit of the Directorate-General for Research of the European Commission (EC) and the group of Statistical Correspondents of the Helsinki Group'.

She Figures 2009 published by the EC paints an interesting picture: in the preface to the report Janez Potočnik, a Slovenian politician who serves as European Commissioner for Science and Research, states that 'while there are equivalent numbers of women and men working in the field of Humanities, only 27 % of researchers in Engineering and Technology are female. And what about researchers' career progression? *Women account for 59 % of graduates, whereas men account for 82 % of full professors. Do you find that hard to believe? Check out chapter 3*' (my emphasis).

He then presents the case for more action by policy-makers: 'She Figures 2009 tells us that the proportion of female researchers is actually growing faster than that of men …The figures are encouraging but the gender imbalance is not self-correcting. She Figures is recommended reading for all policy-makers, researchers, teachers, students, and for parents *who share a vision of a democratic, competitive and technologically advanced Europe*' (my emphasis).

The report argues for serious action to make gender equality across all science and research more of a reality: 'Women's academic career (sic) remains markedly characterised by strong vertical segregation: the proportion of female students (55 %) and graduates (59 %) exceeds that of male students, but men outnumber women among PhD students and graduates AND academic staff. The proportion of *women among full professors is highest in the humanities and the social sciences.* The situation thus appears more favourable for the youngest generations of female academics but *the gender gap is still persistent* (my emphasis).'

Feminist Research on Global HE: Changing the [Patriarchal] Rules of the Game?

The landscape of HE not only in the UK but across Europe and other nations of the 'global north' remains uneven in terms of gender equality, especially for women working as professionals and in HE. There is not only statistical evidence but increasingly feminists are developing critical studies of forms of management and leadership in HE to show how enduring patriarchal patterns are. Is there any evidence to show whether there are any changing gendered patterns of leadership within HE? Barbara Bagilhole and Kate White (2011, 2013), for example, conducted research studies on this theme. In *Gender, Power and Management: A Cross-Cultural Analysis of Higher Education* they put together a most exciting and innovative study of women as feminists in global HE. Using feminist perspectives and methods and drawing upon the collaborative network they analyzed gender and power in senior management in universities. What they were specifically interested in were the dynamics of women and men working together in HE management teams and how these dynamics operated cross-culturally. Taking an explicitly 'feminist standpoint theory' approach (Harding 1987) and locating themselves clearly in the study, they are able to tease out women's experiences in the different universities they studied. Kate White provides an excellent contextual analysis of legislative frameworks for equal opportunities, including employment and issues around the overarching gender pay gaps, including the impact and influence of specific frameworks on the careers of women within comparative countries. Whilst it is extremely exciting that the Women in HE management (WHEM) network have collaborated to produce this nuanced and carefully executed study, it is also disheartening to find that the picture remains quite bleak for women in senior management. This is largely because there have been contradictory trends both in HE and in the developing economies of which they have become a more critical and central part. So women are now far more in evidence in HE and in senior management but the effects of neo-liberalism and managerialism have been to confine women to relatively limited roles, and not the most senior leadership positions.

Similarly, using *She figures*, Louise Morley (2013) argues trenchantly about how what is now called 'new managerialism' and the so-called 'leaderist turn' in HE, are subverting and reinforcing the 'rules of the game' in patriarchal ways. She provides 'an international review of feminist knowledge on how gender and power interact with leadership in HE… to unmask the 'rules of the game' that lurk beneath the surface rationality of academic meritocracy'. She argues that: 'curiously, in a culture of measurement and audit in HE, women's representation in different roles and grades is not always perceived as sufficiently important to measure, monitor or map comparatively. The Centre for Higher Education and Equity Research (CHEER) at the University of Sussex had to construct its own tables. The data that do exist suggest that women disappear in the higher grades i.e. when power, resources, rewards and influence increase… The highest shares of female rectors (vice- chancellors) were recorded in Sweden, Iceland, Norway, Finland, and Israel. In contrast, in

Denmark, Cyprus, Lithuania, Luxembourg and Hungary, no single university was headed by a woman when She Figures reported in 2009… This under-representation reflects not only continued inequalities between men and women, but missed opportunities for women to influence and contribute to the universities of the future'.

Conclusions

Morley (2012) concludes that 'we need new rules for a very different game'. It is abundantly clear that gender equality is a highly politicized and contested notion in HE today, given the changes towards neo-liberalism and its impacts upon women's participation in global [and academic] labour markets. Whilst there has been huge transformation in women's participation as *students*, especially undergraduates, in HE across the globe, this is *not* matched by significant change in women's participation in academic labour markets as this brief trip through the various statistics for Europe, the UK and the USA amply illustrate. The expansion of universities has gone hand-in-hand with new systems of ranking and changes to academic capitalism (Slaughter and Rhoades 2004). The discourses have changed but the key relations intensified through business and marketing strategies. This intensification is particularly the case in terms of the culture of student and academic life, whereby sexualisation has become increasingly marked. So whilst it is true that there are far more students nowadays and the majority are women this does not mean that there is more than formal equality in terms of 'the numbers game'. This is controversial as the 'numbers game' is a mask for continuing power plays whereby the 'rules of the game' remain misogynistic. To develop a more feminist-friendly future we need to transform the rules of the game. Given the growth of a 'laddish culture' in HE (Jackson 2014; Phipps and Young 2014) and the increase in campus sexual assaults in the US which has been made public by President Obama in creating a task force to deal with it (January 22, 2014) the task of transforming HE to make women more equal as both students and academics remains a distant prospect.

References

Bagilhole, B., & White, K. (Eds.). (2011). *Gender, power and management: A cross-cultural analysis of higher education.* London: Palgrave Macmillan.

Bagilhole, B., & White, K. (Eds.). (2013). *Gender and generation in academia.* Basingstoke: Palgrave Macmillan.

Bekhradnia, B. (2009). *Male and female participation and progression in higher education.* Oxford: Higher Education Policy Unit http://www.hepi.ac.uk/466-1850

David, M. E. (2014). *Feminism, gender and universities: Politics, passion and pedagogies.* London: Ashgate.

David, M. E. (2016). *Reclaiming feminism: Challenging everyday misogyny.* Bristol: Policy Press.

Equality Challenge Unit. (2011). *Equality in higher education: Statistical report 2011 part 1 staff* and *part 2 students*. Dec.

Figes, E. (1970). *Patriarchal attitudes: Women in society*. London: Stein and Day.

Firestone, S. (1970). *The dialectic of sex: The case for feminist revolution*. New York: Morrow.

Friedan, B. (1963). *The feminine mystique*. Harmondsworth: Penguin.

Greer, G. (1970). *The female eunuch*. London: Picador.

Harding, S. (1987). *Feminism and methodology*. Bloomington: Indiana University Press.

Jackson, C. (2014). Laddism and the culture of higher education. Seminar presentation at CHEER, University of Sussex. 27th Jan.

Mitchell, J. (1966). Women: The longest revolution. *New Left Review*. Republished In J. Mitchell ed., 1984. *Women: The longest revolution: Essays on feminism, literature and psychoanalysis*. London: Virago Press.

Mitchell, J. (1973). *Women's estate*. Harmondsworth: Penguin.

Morley, L. (2012). Cycles of domination of top roles by men must be broken. *Times Higher Education, 6*, 29.

Morley, L. (2013). The rules of the game: Women and the leaderist turn in higher education. *Gender and Education, 25*(1), 116–131.

Phipps, A., & Young, I. (2014). *Neoliberalisation and 'lad cultures' in higher education*. Sociology. ISSN 0038–0385.

Report of the Committee on Higher Education. (1963). *Higher education. The Robbins report. Cmnd 2154*. London: Her Majesty's Stationery Office (HMSO).

Rich, A. (1977). *Of woman born: Motherhood as experience and institution*. New York: W.W. Norton.

Rowbotham, S. (1972). *Women, resistance and revolution*. Harmondsworth: Penguin.

Rowbotham, S. (1973a). *Hidden from history*. London: Pluto Press.

Rowbotham, S. (1973b). *Women's consciousness: Man's world*. Harmondsworth: Penguin.

She Figures. (2009). *Statistics and indicators on gender equality in science*. Brussells: European Commission Directorate-General for Research http://ec.europa.eu/research/research-eu

Slaughter, S., & Rhoades, G. (2004). *Academic capitalism and the new economy markets, state and higher education*. Baltimore/London: The John Hopkins University Press.

The Chronicle of Higher Education. (2012). *Diversity in Academe The Gender Issue* section B November 2, USA.

UNESCO. (2012). *World atlas on gender equality in education*. http://www.unesco.org/new/typo-3temp/pics/d7af2fe604.jpg

Willetts, D. (2011). *The pinch: How the baby boomers took their children's future – and why they should give it back* (2nd ed.). London: Atlantic Books.

Willetts, D. (2013). *Robbins revisited: Bigger and better higher education*. London: Social Market Foundation.

Chapter 12
Women Academic Researchers: Still Interlopers in the UK Academy?

Carole Leathwood

Women Academic Researchers: Still Interlopers in the UK Academy?

Interloper, 1. Person who pushes himself into the affairs of others, or into a position to which he has no right; an intruder. (Wyld n.d.)

Interloper, A person who becomes involved in a place or situation where they are not wanted or are considered not to belong. [Oxforddictionaries.com]

How many of us have not, at times, felt like interlopers in the academy? Whether we are the only woman on a committee full of men, or the only black academic in a sea of white conference delegates? Perhaps we are new to this field, or to a senior role in it? Or maybe we are painfully aware, yet again, of being identified as that dangerous interloper, the feminist killjoy (Ahmed 2010), and/or the only voice raising issues of inequality? Puwar's (2004, p. 8) account of the 'space invaders' of a public sphere historically (and often still) marked as white male territory, is particularly evocative:

> While all can, in theory, enter, it is certain types of bodies that are tacitly designated as being the 'natural' occupants of specific positions. Some bodies are deemed as having the right to belong, while others are marked out as trespassers, who are, in accordance with how both spaces and bodies are imagined (politically, historically, conceptually), circumscribed as being 'out of place'.

But, as Puwar goes on to articulate, our presence changes the space that we enter and, in the context of the academy, offers a potential challenge to dominant constructions of intellectual subjectivity.

C. Leathwood (✉)
London Metropolitan University, London, UK
e-mail: c.leathwood@londonmet.ac.uk

© Springer International Publishing Switzerland 2017
H. Eggins (ed.), *The Changing Role of Women in Higher Education*,
The Changing Academy – The Changing Academic Profession in International
Comparative Perspective 17, DOI 10.1007/978-3-319-42436-1_12

227

Historically, women were certainly seen as interlopers in the field of higher education, with men's resistance to women students entering university, and being awarded degrees, well documented (Dyhouse 1995). As Davies (2006, p. 500) noted, in academia in the first half of the twentieth century, 'women were transgressive just by virtue of being there. Their very presence transgressed the boundaries of "correct practice"'. And as the twentieth century came to an end and the twenty-first century began, the dramatic increase in the number of women entering the academy as undergraduate students brought its own response, with this often seen, not as a cause for celebration, but as a threat – i.e. that women are taking (over) men's (rightful) place in the academy (Leathwood and Read 2009). But given that women students now outnumber their male counterparts in the UK and in many parts of the world, how can women academic researchers still be seen as interlopers?

In this chapter I consider this question with a particular focus on the gendered effects and affects of contemporary trends in higher education research policy and the academic subjectivities produced and performed through research policy discourses and practices. I am interested in the work policy does, in the production of 'research' and researcher subjectivities, that keeps women researchers out, or down, indeed as interlopers, in a policy arena constructed as neutral, rational and meritocratic.

The context is one in which there is a heightened focus on research 'excellence' and the utility of research outcomes globally, with universities and nations competing to assert their 'world-class' status. Research has become an increasingly high stakes activity, critical to institutional positioning in national and international league tables and a key signifier of material and symbolic capitals for universities, departments and individual academics. Technologies of research audit are well-established in the UK, with the Research Assessment Exercise (RAE), first conducted in 1986, and reframed as the Research Excellence Framework (REF) in 2014, periodically assessing the quality of research outputs of individual academics, departments and universities. In REF 2014, 30 % of the research submitted from 154 UK universities was judged as 'world-leading' or '4*' and 46 % as 'internationally excellent' (3*) (HEFCE 2015b). The assessments for the REF are conducted on a discipline specific basis by national panels of research experts and users in those disciplines. The research funding that individual universities receive in direct grant from the government is based on these assessments (and the number of researchers entered), with 4* research now receiving four times the funding of 3*. Research judged to be 2* ('recognised internationally') or 1* ('recognised nationally') receives no funding allocation. Academics are, therefore, often under considerable pressure to produce research outputs of the required quality, usually meaning four highly rated journal articles, to conduct research that can be shown to have made a demonstrable impact outside academia, and to bring in significant amounts of research grant funding (see Leathwood and Read 2012). Such research assessment activities, legitimised through the process of academic peer review, are constructed as meritocratic and fair, with the subsequent rewards – material and symbolic – deemed to be just recompense for what is seen as unquestionably excellent research.

Yet women academics continue to be marginalised in this research economy, excluded from the most senior research positions, less likely to receive research grants, and less likely to be deemed research 'excellent'. It is to these persisting inequalities, with specific reference to the UK, that I now turn.

Research as a Gendered Field

Although women are now attaining doctorates (ISCED 6) at levels nearing parity with men, women are far less likely to be employed as researchers, with women constituting 46 % of all doctoral graduates in the UK, but only 38 % of researchers in 2012 (European Commission 2015). In England in 2013–2014 (HEFCE 2015a), over half (54 %) of all staff employed in higher education were women, but women constituted only 44.5 % of academic staff, just 23 % of professors[1] and merely 19 % of Vice Chancellors/Principals. Both disabled and Black and minority ethnic (BME) staff are also far less likely to hold senior academic posts. In 2012–2013, just 5.3 % of all UK professors were BME men, and only 1.3 % were BME women (ECU 2014).

Women and minority ethnic staff are more highly represented in professional and support roles than in academic posts. Women constitute the majority of professional and support staff (62.6 %), (2012–2013), and make up 52.9 % of managers, directors and senior officials on professional and support contracts. UK BME staff constitute very similar proportions of academic and professional/support roles overall (7.8 %, 7.9 %),[2] but they are slightly more likely to make it to manager/senior level on professional support contracts (constituting 5 % of such posts) than on academic contracts (just 2.6 %) (ECU 2014).

There are also differences in type of academic contract, with more women than men on 'teaching-only' contracts (51.7 % women) and fewer on the traditional academic 'teaching and research' contracts (39.8 %). A higher proportion of men academics are on permanent/open-ended contracts than women (57.5 % compared to 42.5 %) and men are far more likely to be in full-time posts. The higher education gender pay gap remains at 19 % overall (12.6 % amongst academic staff and 14.8 % amongst senior academic staff) and there is evidence of both an ethnicity and a disability pay gap (ibid.).

Gendered disciplinary differences persist, as in many other countries, with disproportionately low numbers of women academics across most of the natural sciences, technology, engineering and maths. This is reflected at professorial level, with, for example, just 6 % of maths professors being women in 2010–2011, despite women constituting 44 % of maths undergraduates (McWhinnie and Fox 2013).

---

[1] A 'professor' in the UK is a senior academic.

[2] Though note there are distinct differences between BME groups. For example, Chinese staff are more likely to be in academic than in professional/support roles, whereas the reverse is the case for black staff.

There are also stark differences between institutions in what is a highly stratified higher education system in the UK, with proportionately fewer women professors in the high status 'research leading' 'Russell Group'[3] of universities where, on average, 20.8% of professors were women in 2013–2014, compared to 25.9% on average across the 'Million+' group of more teaching-focused institutions. In one Russell Group university, the University of Cambridge, only 15.4% of professors were women in 2013–2014, in contrast with 33.3% women in three different Million+ universities. These gendered disciplinary and institutional differences matter, with the majority of research funding going to the STEM (sciences, technology, engineering and mathematics) subjects and concentrated in the elite universities. What becomes clear is that academic, and particularly senior academic research posts, continue to be dominated by white men.

A range of explanations have been offered for these persistent gender inequalities, including the discredited 'pipeline theory', the difficulties of combining academic work with caring and domestic responsibilities, gender differences in rates of application for senior posts, and unconscious or explicit bias and discrimination (see, e.g. Leathwood and Read 2009; Brink and Benschop 2012; Mervis 2012; Morley 2014; Aiston 2015; Nielsen 2015). Less attention has been paid to the service and caring work that women and minority ethnic staff do in the academy and to the inequalities in the time that men and women academics are able to devote to research (see e.g. Brooks 1997; Lynch 2010; Misra et al. 2011; Bhopal and Jackson 2013). What is most interesting for this chapter, however, is the now extensive body of feminist research showing how constructions of excellence, and of the 'excellent' researcher are gendered. For example, Wenneras and Wold (1997, p. 341), in the now classic study of grant applications for post-doctoral fellowships to the Swedish Medical Research Council, concluded that 'peer reviewers cannot judge scientific merit independent of gender' and either over-estimated men's achievements and/or underestimated those of women. Their analysis indicated that 'a female applicant had to be 2.5 times more productive than the average male applicant to receive the same competence score as he' (ibid. p. 342). More recent research (Sandström et al. 2010), also conducted in Sweden, has shown how funding for research deemed to be of strategic 'excellence' favoured men researchers over women by a ratio of almost 9:1 over the preceding decade. Markers of 'excellence' such as citation indexes, journal editing, membership of research panels, the prioritisation of research over teaching all tend to favour men, so it is men who are more likely to be deemed to be 'excellent' (Brink and Benschop 2011; Coate and Howson 2014; Morley 2014).

Hence, as Brink and Benschop (2011) argue, it is important to challenge the pervasive idea that the academy operates as an objective, neutral meritocracy where 'excellence' is an objective characteristic that can be objectively measured. Of course, this 'pervasive idea' has long been central to the academy and academics tend to be highly invested in it (Rees 2011) – after all, to become academics we have

---

[3] The Russell Group is a 'mission group' of 24 'research-leading' universities in the UK – i.e. those universities that tend to have the highest levels of prestige.

'proved ourselves' to some extent through an education system legitimised through meritocratic ideals. But the discourse of meritocracy, along with powerful gendered cultural signifiers of excellence and the 'natural order', produce what Skeggs refers to as a 'form of mis-recognition – not a hiding of the operations of the powerful, but a hiding of the systems of inscription and classification (which work in the interests of the powerful)' (Skeggs 2004, p. 4). In this way, 'excellent' research and 'excellent' researchers are continually produced through research policy and the technologies of research audit, with the 'excellent' prefix, to paraphrase Bourdieu (2001, p. 33), not merely a mark of 'academic distinction', but 'a warrant of natural intelligence, of giftedness'. And when it is men who are more likely to be judged 'excellent', women researchers are inevitably 'other' to the masculine norm.

I now want to turn to the gendered effects and affects of research policy, and to explore in more detail the ways in which policy texts construct research and researcher subjectivities that contribute to the ongoing re/production of a gender binary.

Gendering Research Policy

The ways in which research policy impacts on academics and academic work has been the subject of a range of research (e.g. Lucas 2006; Gill 2010), including my own research, conducted in collaboration with Barbara Read (Leathwood and Read 2012, 2013) which specifically explored academics' accounts of the impact of dominant trends in research policy on their research. The focus on research 'excellence' and utility, along with the prioritisation of knowledge production to serve the needs of the economy (Slaughter and Leslie 1997), works to exclude research and researchers that are not seen to fit the priorities of pre-determined programmes or constructions of 'excellence'. The move, in the UK and elsewhere, towards funding larger grants as part of specific programmes, with fewer small grants available, privileges well established renowned (and usually senior) academics in research-intensive universities leading large, and often international, teams of researchers (i.e. those who are more likely to be men), and works to further exclude or marginalise newer researchers and/or those prioritising qualitative, feminist work etc. The 'grants culture' (Baez and Boyles 2009) that has become increasingly pervasive across the higher education sector has led to concerns about what research is funded and hence what knowledge is produced (Leathwood and Read 2012), whilst the intensive pressure on individual academics in the UK to bring in grant income (Morley 2003), has been implicated, not only in high levels of academic stress (Kinman and Wray 2013) but also in at least one academic committing suicide (Parr 2014). And although research audit has been established in the UK since the mid-1980s, increasing emphasis on global competition, ranking tables and the striving for 'world-class' excellence in a context in which individual performance is under heightened levels of surveillance appears to have intensified the pressure on academics – a pressure that tends to be felt more acutely by women (Harley 2001; Morley 2003; Leathwood and Read 2012).

In a recent article (Leathwood 2013), I not only discuss the ways in which intellectual subjectivity has historically been constructed as masculine (and white) but go on to show how the contemporary visual iconography in the field of higher education continues to reify the intellectual as a white male subject. Here I want to take this further to examine how research policy texts work to establish boundaries and exclusions, and to mark research spaces, activities and subjectivities as 'naturally' privileged and masculine – an arena in which white senior men are, in Puwar's (2004) terms, 'the somatic norm'.

Research policy does so, I suggest, through the discursive elision between 'research' and 'science', the reification of the natural sciences and technologies over and above other disciplines, a neoliberal framing of research as innovation, and a privileged and imperialist assertion of research 'excellence'.

An example of the slippage between 'research' and 'science' can be seen in the following text from the UK Government department responsible for universities and research – the Department of Business, Innovation and Skills (BIS):

> BIS is committed to developing a world class UK research base responsive to its users and the economy, with sustainable and financially strong universities and public laboratories and a strong supply of scientists, engineers and technologists. (BIS 2012, p. 4)

The 'Research and Development' policy section of the BIS website contains numerous links to specific policies, news items and reports, almost entirely devoted to business innovation and/or the natural sciences, technology and engineering. Although Government policy uses the phrase 'science and research' on occasion (for example in the title of a document: 'The Allocation of Science and Research Funding 2015-16'), this predominantly morphs into 'science' alone. In a context in which the dominant cultural signification of 'science' tends to be the natural sciences, and the image most frequently invoked in the public imagination is of men in white coats in laboratories, the arts, humanities and social sciences disappear into insignificance in most government policy texts. Despite, therefore, a statement in another government policy text, 'Our Plan for Growth: Science and Innovation' (BIS 2014), that the word 'science' is used to encompass all the sciences, including the social sciences, arts and humanities, the almost total absence of any other reference to these disciplines in a 71-page document in which the natural sciences and technologies feature heavily highlights the values and exclusions that are set in place and the boundaries that are, in effect, established around 'science'. It is the natural sciences, technology and engineering that are seen to provide the basis for innovation and economic growth, and this is where the bulk of public investment in research, or 'science' goes, with the ontologies and epistemologies dominant in these disciplines being the taken-for granted norm. 'Objectivity', neutrality and a search for evidence of 'what works' as well as the resurgence of a demand for randomised control trials as the gold standard of research for policy are all apparent in the current policy context in the UK. Despite, therefore, policy assertions and initiatives to improve 'diversity' in science and research (noted in the concluding comments of this chapter), policy works to re-produce the field of research as a highly gendered arena. Given that men dominate the natural sciences, technology and engineering in particular, 'science', or 'research' is reaffirmed as a masculine arena, further signified through the references to '*strong* universities' and 'a *strong* supply of scientists'.

The following text, taken from the Forward of 'Our Plan for Growth', and signed by the Chancellor of the Exchequer, the Secretary of State for Business, Innovation and Skills and the Minister of State for Universities, Science and Cities, reaffirms the emphasis on the natural sciences, innovation and the utility of research to meet the demands of the economy, despite an opening statement on its intrinsic value:

> Scientific endeavour is inherently worthwhile. It expands the frontier of human understanding. Whether exploring the first moments of the universe, or the deep structure of matter, or the power of genetic code, Britain will continue to take the lead in pursuit of the fundamental scientific challenges of our time.
>
> Science and innovation are also at the heart of our long term economic plan. The UK's science base is extraordinary – our cutting edge research base is world leading, our universities are world-class, we develop and attract the world's brightest minds and we are second in the world when ranked by Nobel prizes. Science is one of our clear comparative advantages in the global race. (ibid. p. 3)

It is notable that the 'fundamental scientific challenges of our time' do not include, for example, tackling violence against women, global poverty or ever-increasing social inequalities. The continual reassertion of 'world-classness' (Amsler and Bolsmann 2012), of how 'our cutting edge research base is world leading' signifies national power and prestige in the context of the global higher education market (Hazelkorn 2008). As Amsler and Bolsmann (2012, p. 284) note, rankings of universities 'may be understood not as neutral methods for understanding the quality or value of education, but as political-ideological technologies of valuation and hierarchisation that operate according to a principle logic of inclusion and exclusion'. Drawing on a Bourdeusian framework, they argue that the practice of ranking universities:

> ..constitutes a powerful new sociodicy that produces 'the belief that the dominant are endowed with the properties of nature that legitimate them to rule' (Wacquant 1993, 28); this in turn serves to legitimise the divisions between universities that are produced. (ibid. p. 288)

In Britain, the '*world class*' or 'world leading' epithet tends to be adopted by, and to signify, the elite research-intensive institutions (e.g. the universities of Oxford and Cambridge). It draws upon not only the contemporary positioning of these universities in national and global league tables, but also on their historically constructed identities of long-standing tradition, class and privilege – the 'dreaming-spires' of Oxbridge. This is a history, and a present, that is gendered, classed and racialised, with 'world-classness' coming to signify not only the elite universities themselves but also the bodies that populate them (see Taylor and Allen 2011). The association of world-classness and research excellence with Oxbridge and a few other elite universities is maintained through dominant research policy discourse and practices – including the increasing concentration of research funding in these institutions.

In the research economy of contemporary higher education, 'world-classness' is what matters, and it is *the mind*, in particular 'the world's brightest minds' that is/ are extolled. The academy has long been marked as the definitive site of objectivity, rationality and the mind. Bodies, or at least those bodies that are marked as different from the normative white male and middle-class body, are symbolically (and have been, or are, materially) excluded in this discursive arena – it is 'the mind' and ratio-nality, coded as masculine in contrast to the feminine association with nature and bodies, that is recognised and valorised. The values of objectivity and rationality, further reified through the traditional epistemologies of the natural sciences, are positioned against their binary opposites of subjectivity and emotion – a gendered, classed and racialised binary that has a long history. But it is to emotion, and the emotional work of policy texts, that I now want to turn.

Despite the construction of the academy as a realm of pure rationality, of the unfettered and objective search for truth, in which emotion has no place (see, e.g. Hayes 2005), both the field of higher education (Clegg and David 2006; Leathwood and Hey 2009; Hey 2011) and policy (Ahmed 2003, 2004a, b, c; Hey and Leathwood 2009) are replete with emotion. As Valerie Hey and I have argued (Leathwood and Hey 2009, p. 438), it is necessary 'to work with an imagination that is attuned to, rather than turned from, emotion' if we are to begin to make sense of the inequalities and power relations of the academy. So I want to explore the emotional work of research policy and to examine the gendered effects and affects this policy gener-ates. I am drawing here on a conceptualisation of emotions as social rather than individual (Boler 1999; Hey and Leathwood 2009) and on what emotions do rather than seeing them as things we possess:

> Rather than seeing emotions as psychological dispositions, we need to consider how they work, in concrete and particular ways, to mediate the relationship between the psychic and the social, and between the individual and the collective. (Ahmed 2004a, p. 119)

In particular, I am utilising Ahmed's work on the 'emotionality of texts', on how texts name or perform emotions, or 'how words for feeling, and objects of feeling, circulate and generate effects' (Ahmed 2004c, p. 14). Ahmed does not discuss emo-tion as being 'in' texts:

> We need to avoid assuming that emotions are 'in' the materials we assemble (which would transform emotion into a property), but think more about what the materials are 'doing', how they work through emotions to generate effects. (ibid. p. 19)

She discusses the effects 'of the very naming of emotions', but also explains that words for emotions do not have to be in a text for it to be read in terms of that emo-tion. Some of the texts that Ahmed uses are awash with affect and appear to have been produced with the explicit and direct intention to signify and produce emo-tional (and other) responses. This is the case with the opening extract in 'The Cultural Politics of Emotion', from a British National Front[4] poster, about how

---

[4] A far-right fringe political party in the UK.

'swarms of illegal immigrants and bogus asylum seekers invade Britain … seeking the easy comforts and free benefits of Soft Touch Britain. All funded by YOU – The British Taxpayer!' (ibid. p 1). The politics of race and immigration have long been fraught and contentious in Britain, and this text seeks to exploit that further. In contrast, my focus in this chapter is on an area of policy that rarely incites, or excites, the wider public. Instead, the fields of science and research are more likely to signify objectivity, rationality and neutrality, i.e. the absence, rather than the presence, of emotion.

Nevertheless, words for emotions are sometimes used, as in a recent speech by the Minister for Universities and Science, where he argued that 'we couldn't have a Chancellor more committed to research' – one who has 'a personal passion' for science (Johnson 2015). Words for emotion, 'passion' and 'commitment', emphasised with the word 'personal', are clearly designed to reassure the audience about future spending on science and research. Whilst such words may generate, or be designed to generate, warm feelings and reassurance, a sense that 'we are with you, on the same side', they can also be read as prime examples of utilitarian new managerialism speak, inspired by management texts such as Peters and Waterman's 'In search of Excellence' (1982) which called for a move away from a purely rational model of management and leadership to one which encompassed emotion. But as King (2005, p. 3) noted, 'In business, emotions are useful only if in the service of achieving a "rational", business- oriented goal. Managers can have a passion for success for excellence, or to win as long as it helps the business grow and secure returns to investors.' Here 'passion' and 'commitment' are safe acceptable statements of emotions, as opposed to 'being emotional' which, as Ahmed (2004a, b, c, p. 4) notes, 'comes to be seen as a characteristic of some bodies and not others' – and certainly not of privileged senior white men who are Government ministers. In this way, the emotionality of the text, just as the use of 'passion' in management speak, does nothing to challenge the gendered binary that associates men with rationality, and hence with 'science' (and 'research'), and women with its opposite.

I want to briefly turn now to another text from the research policy arena that illustrates how policy texts can work to establish boundaries and to exclude. It is a document produced by the Russell Group of 'world-leading universities' entitled 'Jewels in the crown: the importance and characteristics of the UK's world-class universities'(Russell Group 2012). It argues for the (ongoing and further) concentration of research funding in these elite universities. The text seeks to present these universities as the height of excellence, but also locates its case for the concentration of research funding in terms of perceived threats:

> In the UK we are fortunate enough to have some of the world's very best universities. […]
> Many countries of a comparable size and world influence would dearly love to possess even
> a tiny handful of our leading universities. Worryingly for us, right now many of them are
> doing everything they can to emulate what we already have. (ibid. p. 1)

So we are the best, top, 'jewels in the crown' and other countries can only look on enviously. The intention, presumably, is to generate feel good affects (aren't *we* wonderful?) whilst also constructing the other as a threat, as deliberately trying to 'emulate' and by implication, steal, what we have. The nationalistic and imperialist discursive undertones cannot be ignored, helping to establish what Puwar (2004 p. 45) refers to as 'a psychic/social/physical territorial boundary'. This discursive emotional framing also serve to align us, the collective 'very best', against the other, and so focus all attention externally and away from the inequalities and divisions within the nation. The text continues:

> The amount of money they are spending is astounding. Of course America and China invest substantial sums in research and higher education. But other countries are also **deliberately** and **consciously** concentrating public funding in order to build up a small number of research intensive universities. Already more that £1.2 billion has been invested in South Korea and there are plans to invest £2 billion in Germany. And we **fear** their approach will pay dividends. If our world-class universities don't get the support they need, there is a real **danger** that overseas universities will not only equal us but will overtake us. (Russell Group 2012, p. 1, my emphasis)

Ahmed's (2004a, b, c, p. 25) insight that emotions 'work to align some subjects with others and against other others' can be seen here. The danger located in the other reaffirms our collectivity through a sense of fear, more so as the other are deemed to be 'deliberately and consciously' attempting to threaten us. Although these others are other nations, and other nations' universities, the imagined/feared presence/invasion can be read 'as an invasion of bodily territory as well as the territory of the nation' and one framed by histories of racism (ibid. p 31). The 'we' here, however, is the Russell Group of 'world-class' universities, characterised, in their own words, by their 'high concentration or critical mass of talent', of 'outstanding staff and students' and 'leading researchers', establishing clear boundaries around who can be part of this club. The visual iconography in the document is almost entirely of the natural sciences, medicine, engineering and technology, and the one image used to convey the 'employability' of Russell Group university students is of a handshake between two suited white masculine hands, further signifying the space as a privileged, white and masculine one.

This fear of the other is not unique to the Russell Group, with several of the Government research policy documents discussed here referencing the 'challenges' presented by developments in other countries, albeit in rather more constrained language. What is evident in all of these, however, is the affective economy of the market, of risk, threat, fear and danger, and of winning or losing in the global race for supremacy.

This affective economy is one in which the pleasures of winning, for example being awarded a research grant or getting an article through the peer review process, can be off-set by the fears and despondency of failure, and of the 'terrors of performativity'(Ball 2003) generated by the surveillance technologies of research audit (Gill 2010). The shame of 'letting the side down' by not producing enough, or good enough (i.e. internationally excellent or world-leading) research outputs for the REF emerged strongly from the study I conducted with Barbara Read (Leathwood and Read 2012, 2013). This study, which consisted of email interviews with 71 academic researchers in Britain in 2011–2012, highlighted the often intense pressures experienced by academics, and in particular reported by academic women in this hyper-performative research economy. Most of the participants expressed a great deal of concern about the impacts of these policy trends and technologies on the research that is conducted and the kinds of knowledge that can be produced in such a climate, as well as on the future for early-career researchers. But here I want to focus on the affects of research policy discourses and technologies, and in particular on the imperative to produce research outputs deemed to be 'internationally excellent' or, preferably, 'world-leading'. One lecturer's comments conveys the sense of not being 'good enough' as she explains:

> I have had a number of articles published since the previous RAE and I was quietly proud of this! Now I am fully aware that it is not really good enough – they are not in the right journals or on the right topics. I almost feel like everything I've done so far counts for nothing and I have to start from scratch (Paula, lecturer).

Her account draws attention to the place of affect in the academy, not only in the construction and performance of academic subjectivities, but in the cultures, practices and structures of inequality in higher education (Hey and Leathwood 2009). Failure to attain the hallowed status of 'REFability' is located with the individual academic, producing in many cases 'personal anguish and public shaming' (Leathwood and Hey 2009, p. 437). Paula identifies her background as working class and her words evoke the 'hidden injuries' of class (Sennett and Cobb 1977), and gender, with the sense of never being good enough and feeling she has to work doubly hard to avoid derision (Reay 2000; Hey 2001). However, many middle class women in the study reported not dissimilar feelings and pressures, as did a few men, though it was the gendered subjectivities that ran through participants' accounts that stood out. The sense of not being good enough was exacerbated through the public aspects of the audit process, with one woman senior lecturer reporting:

> Our research review process (unlike appraisal) is not confidential – so everyone knows how everyone else is doing, and who may be "letting the side down". Some departments are now very difficult places to work for some colleagues. (Lucy, senior lecturer)

Again, the sense of 'letting the side down' was expressed mostly, though not entirely, by women, and reflects Bartky's (1990) account of how shame is produced within systems of oppression. In her discussion of some women students' reluctance to hand in work because of a feeling that they, or it, was not good enough, argued that 'this shame is manifest in a pervasive sense of personal inadequacy that . . . is profoundly disempowering' and reveals 'the "generalized condition of dishonour" which is women's lot in a sexist society' (ibid, p. 85, citing Bulhan 1985). She went on to explain that 'the shame of some of these women was not a discreet occurrence, but a perpetual attunement, the pervasive aftertaste of life'. The overwhelming sense that women in particular still have to prove them/ourselves in an academy where we are still, in many ways, interlopers, came through strongly in our study.

The imperative of the pursuit of excellence and world-classness, indeed of becoming world-leading, that runs through these research policy texts generates and incites the affects of a win or lose, local and global game – affects which circulate between and amongst nations, institutions and individual academics forming and re-forming binaries of the successful and the failing, of elite universities and the rest, of excellent research/ers and the mediocre[5] – binaries that are sustained and solidified through research audit technologies and global league tables. Such binaries can be seen in the words of another research participant in our study, a woman professor at a research-intensive university, showing how such hierarchies and divisions operate within (elite) universities, as well as between institutions differently positioned in this prestige economy. She explained:

> You know what it is like – you feel a complete failure without money in my place –but its soooo hard to get! Pressure is there and the rewards are great if you get it – so we get racehorses and carthorses – if you don't get money, you get to do more marking/teaching etc. (Kathleen, professor)

Here, more marking or teaching are the punishments for research grant failure. This then becomes a vicious circle as, overloaded with teaching and marking, it becomes harder to devote the time to research and to accruing the prestige indicators so essential to attaining the heights of research/er 'excellence' (Coate and Howson 2014). This highlights the material conditions of research production that are implicated in what masquerades as a meritocratic activity, where those deemed 'excellent' or 'world-class' are seen to have achieved this status through their natural talents and abilities (Bourdieu 2001). In this binary construction, research is associated with abstract thinking, cerebral activity and pure rationality, and teaching as an embodied presence and care for students – although as Reay (2000, p. 15) notes, research itself tends to be similarly gendered, with the 'legwork' of fieldwork often conducted by women research assistants: 'the presumption being, I suppose, that the head work goes on elsewhere'. The 'racehorses'/'carthorses' metaphor points to the production and embodiment of researcher subjectivities and the ways in which these can become fixed – it isn't easy for carthorses to turn themselves into the racing variety.

The words of another woman participant, a professor, further highlights the ways in which gendered academic subjectivities are continually constituted through these disciplinary technologies:

> Only the workaholics or downright ruthless seem to preserve their time or steal time from themselves to stay in the game or redistribute the 'other' work to less powerful colleagues. (Margaret, professor)

Being a 'workaholic' appears to be a necessary characteristic/identity for women to survive in the academy at all, as the accounts of a number of our participants indicated, evoking Acker and Armenti's (2004) Canadian research highlighting the fatigue and stress reported by academic woman, with the main survival strategy being to work harder and sleep less. Similarly in our study, it was predominantly

---

[5] The term 'mediocrity' has been used by a Russell Group spokesperson and a Government Minister to describe research not seen to meet the heights of research 'excellence' – see Corbyn, Z. (2009). V-c: focus research cash or 'mediocrity' awaits. *Times Higher Education.* http://www.timeshigher-education.co.uk/story.asp?storycode=408770, THE. 22 October. Cable, V. (2010). 'The role of science, research and innovation in creating growth' Speech by the Secretary of State, 8 September. London, Department of Business, Innovation and Skills.

women who conveyed this extreme sense of endless hours of work (and often desperation), with work on research often only possible at the weekends and through the night. In addition, being 'ruthless' stands at odds with traditional constructions of femininity and is hardly consonant with being 'good girls' (Evans 2005) in the academy. In contrast, ruthlessness is often portrayed as a desirable aspect of masculinity, particularly in managerial and neo-liberal discourse, with men who are ruthless in pursuit of their goals more likely to be admired than derided, providing another example of how the 'excellent' researcher tends to be coded as masculine.

Conclusion

In this chapter I have highlighted some of the ways in which the discourses and practices of research policy reaffirm the research arena in the UK as a 'naturally' masculine one. It is senior white men, and in particular, senior white men in elite institutions, who continue to be constituted as the 'somatic norm' (Puwar 2004) of research/er excellence through research policy technologies.

There are, however, some aspects of policy in this field that could be seen to challenge my overall conclusions and demonstrate that policy makers are addressing 'diversity' issues. One example is policy designed to enhance women's carers in the STEM academic fields, operationalised through the Athena Swan[6] awards allocated to universities that demonstrate a commitment to gender equality, with evidence of some positive outcomes (Munir et al. 2013). A second example is of the 'Equality and Diversity Policy' that was developed for REF2014,[7] which introduced a range of measures in an attempt to ensure 'fairness' in the selection of staff entered. In the previous Research Assessment Exercise (RAE) in 2008, women, black and minority ethnic academics, and disabled staff were all less likely to be entered than their white able-bodied male peers (HEFCE 2009). Despite the new 'fairness' measures, however, this has been replicated for REF 2014, with women far less likely to be entered (and hence deemed 'research active') than men (51 % compared to 67 %), and black, Asian and disabled academics also less likely to be entered (HEFCE 2015c). It seems likely that practice in universities in relation to the new equality and diversity policy may have been more about 'doing the document than doing the diversity' (Ahmed 2007, p. 590). As Morley (2014) has argued, if the higher education sector is serious about tackling inequalities, then a step in the right direction would be to include 'equality' as a performance indicator in audit activities, with gender equity recognised in international league tables. But, as she also acknowledges, equality is seen as a threat to 'excellence' (Morley 2009).

---

[6] http://www.ecu.ac.uk/equality-charters/athena-swan/join-athena-swan/ This scheme has now been extended to other disciplines.
[7] http://www.ref.ac.uk/equality/

So it seems highly likely that women and other 'others' will continue to be positioned as interlopers in the academy for the foreseeable future. But as another dictionary definition of 'interloper' is 'To interfere; meddle' (Collins 1985), I suggest that a bit more feminist interfering and meddling is precisely what is called for to destabilise and disrupt the prestige economy of the academy.

References

Acker, S., & Armenti, C. (2004). Sleepless in Academia. *Gender and Education, 16*(1), 3–24.

Ahmed, S. (2003). The politics of fear in the making of worlds. *International Journal of Qualitative Studies in Education (QSE), 16*(3), 377–398.

Ahmed, S. (2004a). Affective economics. *Social Text, 22*(2), 117–139.

Ahmed, S. (2004b). Collective feelings: Or, the impressions left by others. *Theory, Culture and Society, 21*(2), 25–42.

Ahmed, S. (2004c). *The cultural politics of emotion.* Edinburgh: Edinburgh University Press.

Ahmed, S. (2007). 'You end up doing the document rather than doing the doing': Diversity, race equality and the politics of documentation. *Ethnic and Racial Studies, 30*(4), 590–609.

Ahmed, S. (2010). Feminist killjoys (and otherlful subjects). *The Scholar and Feminist Online, 8*(3), 1–8. http://sfonline.barnard.edu/polyphonic/print_ahmed.htm

Aiston, S. J. (2015). Women academics and research productivity: An international comparison. *Gender and Education, 27*(3), 205–220.

Amsler, S., & Bolsmann, C. (2012). University ranking as social exclusion. *British Journal of Sociology of Education, 33*(2), 283–301.

Baez, B., & Boyles, D. (2009). *The politics of inquiry: Education research and 'the Culture of Science'.* Albany: State University of New York Press.

Ball, S. J. (2003). The teacher's soul and the terrors of performativity. *Journal of Education Policy, 18*(2), 215–228.

Bartky, S. L. (1990). *Femininity and domination: Studies in the phenomenology of oppression.* New York: Routledge.

Bhopal, K., & Jackson, J. (2013). *The experiences of black and minority ethnic academics: Multiple identities and career progression.* http://blackbritishacademics.co.uk/wp-content/uploads/2013/04/Research-Report-The-Experiences-of-Black-and-Minority-Ethnic-Academics-Dr-Bhopal.pdf

BIS. (2012). *BIS and the overseas territories.* London: Department of Business, Innovation and Skills.

BIS. (2014). *Our plan for growth: Science and innovation.* London: Department of Business, Innovation and Skills.

Boler, M. (1999). *Feeling power: Emotions and education.* London/New York: Routledge.

Bourdieu, P. (2001). *Firing back: Against the tyranny of the market 2.* New York: The New Press.

Brink, M. V. D., & Benschop, Y. (2011). Gender practices in the construction of academic excellence: Sheep with five legs. *Organization, 19*(4), 507–524.

Brink, M. V. D., & Benschop, Y. (2012). Slaying the seven-headed dragon: The quest for gender change in Academia. *Gender, Work and Organisation, 19*(1), 71–92.

Brooks, A. (1997). *Academic women.* Buckingham: Open University Press.

Cable, V. (2010). *'The role of science, research and innovation in creating growth' Speech by the Secretary of State, 8 September.* London: Department of Business, Innovation and Skills.

Clegg, S., & David, M. (2006). Passion, pedagogies and the project of the personal in higher education. *21st Century Sociology, 1*(2), 149–165.

Coate, K., & Howson, C. K. (2014). Indicators of esteem: Gender and prestige in academic work. *British Journal of Sociology of Education, 37*(4), 567–585.

Corbyn, Z. (2009). V-c: Focus research cash or 'mediocrity' awaits. *Times Higher Education*, THE. 22 October. http://www.timeshighereducation.co.uk/story.asp?storycode=408770

Davies, B. (2006). Women and transgression in the halls of academe. *Studies in Higher Education, 31*(4), 497–509.

Dyhouse, C. (1995). *No distinction of sex? Women in British universities 1870–1939*. London: UCL Press.

ECU. (2014). *Equality in higher education: Statistical report 2014*. London: Equality Challenge Unit.

European Commission (2015). *SHE figures 2015: Gender in research and innovation – statistics and indicators*. European Commission. http://ec.europa.eu/research/swafs/pdf/pub_gender_equality/she_figures_2015-leaflet-web.pdf

Evans, M. (2005). *Killing thinking: The death of the universities*. London: Continuum.

Gill, R. (2010). The hidden injuries of the neoliberal university. In R. Ryan-Flood & R. Gill (Eds.), *Secrecy and silence in the research process* (pp. 228–244). London: Routledge.

Harley, S. (2001). Research selectivity and female academics in UK universities: From gentleman's club and barrack yard to smart macho? *Gender & Education, 15*(4), 377–392.

Hayes, D. (2005). The touchy-feely brigade: Coming your way soon. *The Times Higher Education Supplement*. 4 November: http://www.thes.co.uk/search/story.aspx. Accessed 22 Nov 2007.

Hazelkorn, E. (2008). *The rising popularity of university rankings: Lessons and implications* (Presentation given at Centre for the Study of Higher Education (CSHE) seminar). Melbourne: University of Melbourne.

HEFCE. (2009). *Selection of staff for inclusion in RAE2008: Issues paper 2009/34*. Bristol: HEFCE.

HEFCE. (2015a). *Equality and diversity tables: Staff data*. Higher Education Funding Council for England. http://www.hefce.ac.uk/data/Year/2015/eddata/Title,104183,en.html

HEFCE. (2015b). *Higher education in England 2015: Key facts*. HEFCE. http://www.hefce.ac.uk/media/HEFCE,2014/Content/Analysis/HE,in,England/HE_in_England_2015.pdf

HEFCE. (2015c). *Selection of staff for inclusion in the REF 2014*. Higher Education Funding Council for England. http://www.hefce.ac.uk/pubs/year/2015/201517/

Hey, V. (2001). The construction of academic time: Sub/contracting academic labour in research. *Journal of Educational Policy, 16*(1), 67–84.

Hey, V. (2011). Affective asymmetries: Academics, austerity and the mis/recognition of emotion. *Contemporary Social Science, 6*, 207–222.

Hey, V., & Leathwood, C. (2009). Passionate attachments: Higher education, policy, knowledge, emotion and social justice. *Higher Education Policy, 22*, 101–118.

Johnson, J. (2015). *Research, innovate, grow: The role of science in our long-term economic plan*. 2 July, Queen Elizabeth II Conference Centre, London, https://www.gov.uk/government/speeches/research-innovate-grow-the-role-of-science-in-our-long-term-economic-plan

King, D. (2005). In pursuit of passion: a frame analysis of the popular managment literature. *TASA Conference*. University of Tasmania.

Kinman, G., & Wray, S. (2013). *Higher stress: A survey of stress and well-being among staff in higher education*. London: Universities and Colleges Union.

Leathwood, C. (2013). Re/presenting intellectual subjectivity: Gender and visual imagery in the field of higher education. *Gender & Education, 25*(2), 133–154.

Leathwood, C., & Hey, V. (2009). Gender/ed discourses and emotional sub-texts: Theorising emotion in UK higher education. *Teaching in Higher Education, 14*(4), 429–440.

Leathwood, C., & Read, B. (2009). *Gender and the changing face of higher education: A feminised future?* Buckingham: SRHE and Open University Press.

Leathwood, C., & Read, B. (2012). *Final report: Assessing the impact of developments in research policy for research on higher education: An exploratory study*. London: Society for Research into Higher Education. http://www.srhe.ac.uk/downloads/Leathwood_Read_Final_Report_16_July_2012.pdf

Leathwood, C., & Read, B. (2013). Research policy and academic performativity: Compliance, contestation and complicity. *Studies in Higher Education, 38*(8), 1162–1174.

Lucas, L. (2006). *The research game in academic life*. Buckingham: Open University Press.

Lynch, K. (2010). Carelessness: A hidden doxa of higher education. *Arts and Humanities in Higher Education, 9*(1), 54–67.

McWhinnie, S., & Fox, C. (2013). *Advancing women in mathematics: Good practice in UK university departments*. London: The London Mathematical Society.

Mervis, J. (2012). U.S. study shows unconscious gender bias in Academic Science. *Science, 337*(6102), 1592–1592.

Misra, J., Lundquist, J. H., Holmes, E., & Agiomavritis, S. (2011). The ivory ceiling of service work. *Academe, 97*(1), 22–26.

Morley, L. (2003). *Quality and power in higher education*. Maidenhead: SRHE and Open University Press.

Morley, L. (2009). *Gender equity in higher education: Celebrations and challenges*. University of Sussex. https://www.sussex.ac.uk/webteam/gateway/file.php?name=gender-equity-in-higher-education-presentation---helsinki-and-tampere.pdf&site=43

Morley, L. (2014). Lost leaders: Women in the global academy. *Higher Education Research and Development, 33*(1), 114–128.

Munir, F., Mason, C., McDermott, H., Morris, J., Bagihole, B., & Nevill, M. (2013). *Advancing women's carrers in science, technology, engineering mathematics and medicine: Evaluating the effectiveness and impact of the Athena SWAN Charter*. Equality Challenge Unit. http://www.ecu.ac.uk/publications/evaluating-athena-swan/

Nielsen, M. W. (2015). Gender inequality and research performance: Moving beyond individual-meritocratic explanations of academic advancement. *Studies in Higher Education*, 1–17.

Parr, C. (2014). Imperial college professor Stefan Grimm 'was given grant income target'. *Times Higher* (December 3): https://www.timeshighereducation.co.uk/news/imperial-college-professor-stefan-grimm-was-given-grant-income-target/2017369.article

Peters, T., & Waterman, R. (1982). *In search of excellence*. New York: Harper and Row.

Puwar, N. (2004). *Space invaders: Race, gender and bodies out of place*. Oxford: Berg.

Reay, D. (2000). "Dim Dross": Marginalised women both inside and outside the academy. *Women's Studies International Forum, 23*(1), 13–21.

Rees, T. (2011). The gendered construction of scientific excellence. *Interdisciplinary Science Reviews, 36*(2), 133–145.

Russell Group. (2012). *Jewels in the crown: The importance and characteristics of the UK's world-class universities*. London: The Russell Group.

Sandström, U., Wold, A., Jordansson, B., Ohlsson, B., & Smedberg, Å. (2010). *Hans Excellens: om miljardsatsningarna på starka forskningsmiljöer ('His Excellency…')*. Stockholm, http://www.hsv.se/download/18.328ff76512e968468bc80003456/DJ-satsningar-starka-forskningsmiljoer.pdf

Sennett, R., & Cobb, J. (1977). *The hidden injuries of class*. Cambridge: Cambridge University Press.

Skeggs, B. (2004). *Class, self, culture*. London: Routledge.

Slaughter, S., & Leslie, L. (1997). *Academic capitalism: Politics, policies and the entrepreneurial university*. Baltimore: John Hopkins University Press.

Taylor, Y., & Allen, K. (2011). *Sinking or swimming? Academic strokes, anxious provokes*. BSA Sociology and the Cuts blog. http://sociologyandthecuts.wordpress.com/2011/11/22/sinking-or-swimming-academic-strokes-anxious-provokes-by-yvette-taylor-and-kimberly-allen/

Wenneras, C., & Wold, A. (1997). Nepotism and sexism in peer-review. *Nature, 387*, 341–343.

Wyld, H. C. (Ed.) (n.d.). *The universal dictionary of the English language*. London: The Amalgamated Press, circa 1932.

Chapter 13
Women Teaching Languages in Higher Education: Voices from the European Union

Elisabeth Lillie

Introduction

The twentieth century saw the gradual enfranchisement and empowerment of women across the continent of Europe as they gained the right to vote, became able to avail of better educational opportunities and increasingly entered a wider range of employment.

From an early stage the European Union (EU) and its predecessors have played a major role in supporting women in their search for equity in employment, social justice and an education commensurate with their abilities and adapted to the demands of the modern workplace. The economic imperative of developing fully the talents of citizens in all member states was certainly a key motivation. Yet the volume and scope of the work undertaken go beyond the purely economic.

A crucial element was the establishment of a legal framework for enforcement. Largely launched in the 1970s, a range of directives, applicable in the member states, created a legal basis for equality of pay and treatment in employment and these have been subject to ongoing scrutiny, additions and amendment. From this period too, judgements on infringements of European Treaties or laws from the European Court of Justice (now Court of Justice of the European Union) have also been a major and ongoing factor in the implementation of equality measures.

The 1980s saw the development of Action Programmes, each covering a span of years, to address in a more purposeful way the problems faced by women and promote and implement good practice, an approach which continues to be used to map out activities, strategies and forward looking plans. Also effective in fostering change

E. Lillie (✉)
Faculty of Arts, Ulster University, Coleraine, UK
e-mail: em.lillie@ulster.ac.uk

© Springer International Publishing Switzerland 2017   243
H. Eggins (ed.), *The Changing Role of Women in Higher Education*,
The Changing Academy – The Changing Academic Profession in International
Comparative Perspective 17, DOI 10.1007/978-3-319-42436-1_13

through the dissemination of information and communication with stakeholders in member states has been the setting up of specialist advisory groupings and networks.

Regular evaluations of achievement have been undertaken by Europe and although they have shown progress, they also reveal the need for continued action and a more sustained approach in order to attain fuller gender equality. It was to address such concerns that, principally from the 1990s, gender mainstreaming, the 'principle of integrating the equal opportunities dimension in all policies and activities' at both Community and Member State levels was evolved and adopted as a more holistic approach to equality for both men and women (Council Decision of 22 December 1995 on a medium-term Community action programme on equal opportunities for men and women, 1996–2000: 95/593/EC, Article 2) (on the evolution of European strategies see, for instance, Burri and Prechal 2014; Earles 2014; Hantrais 2007; Rees 2005, 2007; Costello and Davies 2006; Booth and Bennett 2002).

The policy of mainstreaming and the use of actions to counter specific inequalities have been maintained. In addition the policy of equality for both men and women has been strengthened and broadened by inclusion in Treaty revisions. Thus, for instance, the Treaty of Amsterdam of 1999 stated the promotion of 'equality between men and women' (Articles 2 and 3) as an aim of the Community in its areas of competence (Treaty of Amsterdam, p. 23; Burri and Prechal 2014; Masselot 2007). Yet, in the twenty-first century, despite much that is positive, women at work as well as writers on gender issues are all too conscious of the fact that significant inequalities remain. In relation to Higher Education, a European Union paper, the *Background document. Strategy for Equality between women and men 2010–2015* points to the fact that while there are now more women university graduates than men 'they are *under-represented among researchers and university staff*' (*Background document. Strategy for Equality between women and men 2010–2015* 2010, p.14, emphasis in the original). One commentator speaking of women within science has also noted: 'the extraordinary persistence with which gender remains a powerful organizing principle of the Academy' (Rees 2010, p. 61).

Ongoing evidence on the position of women in research as well as in certain other related areas is provided in the *She Figures: Gender in Research and Innovation* which have been published every 3 years since 2003, the latest full publication to date at the time of writing relating to 2012 (*She Figures 2012. Gender and Innovation* 2013), although a short leaflet indicating certain advance results from the 2015 study appeared in July 2015 (*She Figures 2015*). These statistics show that, while there have been improvements in the position of women, problems and inequalities remain. Indeed, as the first Action Plan 1982–1985 already pointed out: 'equal opportunities for men and women will only be attained by sustained action over a long period' (European Commission, COM(81) 758, 1981, p. 5, para 5) and the Union is currently preparing the next stage of action on gender equality (Bettio and Sansonetti 2015).

The Study: Women Teaching Languages in Higher Education

The paucity of women in more scientific and technological domains has led to a European focus and a range of analyses, as in the report of the European Technology Assessment Network working group on women in science published in 2000 (ETAN *Science Policies in the European Union* 2000) with ongoing evaluation of this issue being included in the *She Figures*. However, little attention has been paid to fields such as languages that have traditionally been more attractive to women and where there is normally a strong female presence. Yet, these areas may offer instructive insights into the position, problems and successes of women in a context where the numbers of female staff are higher and where the ethos should potentially be more friendly towards them.

The study described here is based on a small survey undertaken in selected member states, targeted for different reasons. Scandinavian countries of Northern Europe are reputed for their longstanding concern with the position and rights of women and, in line with this, both Denmark and Finland were chosen. France was picked as a country where female suffrage was only granted in 1944 but which also has a policy of offering considerable support to women in the labour market as well as favouring childbearing to counter population losses in various wars (Crompton and Le Feuvre 2000). A former Communist country – Poland – was selected given the very different attitudes to the employment of women which prevailed in the Communist era and also its relatively recent accession to the European Union in 2004. The United Kingdom (UK) from which the author comes was taken as a representative of an English speaking country with its own particular traditions and needs (the chapter was written prior to the June 2016 referendum in the UK on membership of the European Union). The Republic of Ireland, a small country, traditionally considered conservative with a strong religious influence (although less so now than in the past), offers a sample from the English-speaking world with slightly different traditions from the United Kingdom. It may also in its religious outlook be considered to be to some extent comparable to post-Communist Poland.

The actual study was conducted by email survey with the possibility of requesting further clarification from respondents. Within each country a contact of the author was asked to circulate the questionnaire to colleagues teaching languages whether within their department, institution or country. In all, 41 completed questionnaires were received, 8 from Scandinavian countries – 6 from Denmark and 2 from Finland; 11 from France; 2 from Poland; 8 from Ireland and 12 from the United Kingdom.

Within the different jurisdictions, the sample confirmed the spread of nationalities from which language teachers come with a considerable number not being natives of the country in which they now work. Staff active in the Republic of Ireland have, however, been counted as nationals if they come from anywhere in Ireland or the United Kingdom since the two areas share a common language and also have very similar education systems with considerable movement between them for the purposes of employment and study. In effect, some 48.78 % of the sample (n.20) came originally from the state in which they now teach whereas 51.22 % (n.21) came from another country and of this latter group one third or 33.33 % (n.7) were from areas outside Europe. The employment of foreign nationals was particularly marked in the United Kingdom where 10 of the 12 respondents fell into this category, a situation which may, at least in part, be attributed to the decline in language study in the country following the 2002 governmental decision to make languages optional in the first school leaving examination from 2004 (on the reduction in language learning in the UK see, for instance, Elliott 2013; Chen and Breivik 2013; Worton 2009). While the majority of those originally from a different country had worked solely as teachers or had held stop-gap jobs prior to teaching, a small number had been engaged in other types of careers before taking up posts in higher education.

Among the respondents to the questionnaire, there was a spread of responsibility and age range. Where age is concerned, the breakdown was as follows: 2.44 % (n.1) in the range 25–30; 14.64 % (n.6) aged between 30 and 39; 19.51 % (n.8) between 40 and 49; 46.34 % (n.19) between 50 and 59; while 17.07 % were over 60 (n.7). It is, of course, difficult to compare levels of post between countries but if, on the one hand, those with professorships and/or a significant level of responsibility within the subject or institution and, on the other, staff finding themselves at lecturer/senior lecturer/reader are considered, in this sample there were almost twice as many in the latter grades, a factor which may to some extent have influenced their views. A small number of those in this category were part-time in their posts or had impermanent contracts.

Family and Personal Life

The extent to which family life and commitments may impinge on the careers of women, is an ongoing issue of discussion (as in Shaw and Cassells 2007 who point to the 'continuing work/domestic role conflict of female academics', p. 510). Overall the majority of participants in this study indicated that they were married, engaged or partnered, namely 78.1 % (n.32); 7.3 % (n.3) were widows (widowed or divorced and remarried is counted as married or partnered); 7.3 % (n.3) were divorced while a further 7.3 % (n.3) said they were single.

Views on the effect of marriage or similar relationships on professional life were, perhaps inevitably, mixed, with over half of those concerned stating that marriage or a partnership had proved helpful to them. Certain of these women spoke in very positive tones about the support and encouragement which they had received from their spouses. Some of them had (or had had, now deceased) academic husbands who understood the situation, being in the same profession and with whom they had been able to share domestic responsibilities. Other participants were slightly more nuanced in their views, linking the impact that marriage might have to the individuals involved, as in: 'whether the relation is positive or negative depends largely on the relations between the couple' or (from a different country): 'it depends on the kind of marriage you are in'. This was borne out by observations from a small number who were able to make comparisons between different partners as in: 'with my first husband, it was an impediment. With my second husband it is stabilising and supportive'. Some, while clearly positive about their own situation, did point out that marriage might nonetheless require 'compromise' and certain 'sacrifices'. Other people and their needs had to be taken into account, although this was not necessarily a negative factor since, despite the 'stress' that home commitments might impose on a 'schedule', such 'obligations', nonetheless, could also serve to keep one 'grounded'. On occasion marriage might entail moving to live abroad and this was noted by a small number of those concerned to have impacted, at least to some extent, on how their career developed. Even within the same country, if the two partners were employed, there could well be geographical issues arising from the need to find a compromise agreeable to both 'if one region does not offer ... equal career opportunities for the couple' (see also Farwell 2013; Shaw and Cassell 2007 on this topic).

Motherhood and Academe

The effect of marriage and the need to consider others may refer not just to a spouse but also to children, particularly those of school age or under. Different commentators highlight the effect children may or may not have on professional activity and progression (for instance, Pritchard 2010; Damiano-Teixeira 2006; Deem 2003; Munford and Rumball 2000) and the *She Figures 2012* speak of there being 'not just a "glass ceiling" but also a "maternal wall" hindering the career of female researchers' (*She Figures 2012*, 2013, p. 7).

A majority of those replying to the survey had children, namely 68.29 % (n.28) while 31.71 % (n.13) did not. 21.43 % of the group of 28 with children had one child (n.6), while the largest families had four (7.14 %; n.2). The most common number of children was two at 53.57 % (n.15), with five respondents having three children (17.86 %). Given the age range of respondents, unsurprisingly, the majority of those with children had adult offspring of 18 or over (i.e. 60.7 %; n.17) while the remaining 39.3 % (no.11) had children under 18 (included in this category are two mothers with one of their children under 18). However, even if they were not currently caring for young children, respondents were able to reflect on what their experience had been and give their reaction to support and attitudes within the institution and country in which they work.

A number of these respondents thought that their offspring had no impact on career (21.42 %; n.6 out of the 28 with children), a view found elsewhere (O'Connor 2012). While a further four participants also said that children were not detrimental, three of these mentioned the importance of back-up from their spouse and the fourth stated that, even if it was not damaging, it was difficult, at least for a time, 'to work at the same pace' after having them. The helpfulness of family support networks was raised by some – an advantage not always available to language lecturers living outside their original country: 'no grandparents to stand in for mum or dad if need be' (on 'a social informal network (mainly family-based)', see Zimmer and Siemieńska, p. 13).

In fact, the needs and care of the young were described as a key element in the approach to work and career development: 'children (their wellbeing being more important than one's own) definitely influence your career prospects because your choices are informed by their existence'. This is particularly the case with children at an early stage of their lives, something which was encapsulated in: 'naturally small children may slow down career development'. There is subsequently a need to 'juggle' and 'prioritise' and also to accept increased constraints, with, for instance, the issue of geographical mobility becoming even more of an obstacle than within a childless couple. For professionally active mothers the loser was sometimes said to be research, even if only for a number of years: 'the major challenge for me now is to find the time to carry out meaningful research while teaching and raising children' (France). Another had to: 'wait until they grew up to do some research' (UK).

Attitudes to employment and participation in the workplace may be conditioned by a variety of factors both economic and personal. Sometimes the woman academic may be the main or, indeed, the only bread winner in the family, leading to a rather different reaction as in: 'my career enables my family's education ..., interests, and household stability' and 'my children increase my dedication to my working life'. Others, despite the problems that could arise, had chosen employment in third level teaching as it offered a certain flexibility and was thus better suited to the demands of child-rearing. One respondent currently employed in the UK indicated that her original job as an interpreter and its work at 'odd hours' had proved incompatible with the care of her two young children. For a participant from France: 'being a teacher is a wonderful compromise. You DO work but you are available for your kids when they need you' (capitals in original), while another from the same country had switched to academic life on having children because she wanted 'an intellectual and international job' as well as one that would give her greater freedom in organization (underlining in her response).

Time Out to Raise Young Children

Some respondents had decided to work part-time or to take leave for a period while the children were small in order to devote themselves more fully to them. As one put it, rather defensively perhaps: 'raising children and having a career break meant for me that working in employment is not my ... biggest goal in life. To be there for your children is more important, although this might sound very old fashioned'. She also added 'looking after children full time took only 10 years out of my life, I will still work about 30 years'. Those who decided on the traditional route of a period of leave and full-time concentration on parental responsibilities were not unhappy with their choice: indeed their satisfaction may even have surprised them as in the case of the last quoted participant: 'I never thought that I would enjoy being at home and raising my children'. Others too stressed the importance of children and how positive they always are. In the view of one: 'my children have been given to me as gifts and … I need to treat them as such. For this reason I made an active choice, equally with my husband, to take care of my children until they entered their school years'. For her motherhood had in no sense been detrimental and 'only ever added to the richness of a full life, including work'.

Divided Loyalties

A number of those concerned indicated a clear conflict between the two sets of demands imposed by family, on the one hand, and work on the other. A respondent whose husband had played a key role was of the view that in order to 'live up to' her 'professional obligations' she had perhaps spent less time with her children than she would have wished. Another, from a different country, spoke of her ongoing sense of guilt, a sentiment often associated with working mothers (as in, for example, Majcher 2007, Seeking the guilty – academics between career and family in Poland and Germany). She described herself as having 'total support' from a husband able to offer considerable help, but still said that 'throughout my career, I have felt guilty, guilty for not being with the children when working and guilty for not working when I was with the children'. A woman of a different nationality expressed her sense of conflicting allegiances by saying that she was '"torn" between children and work' (her double inverted commas). A further respondent had reacted to the problems posed in another way, namely by having only one child as she considered that it would not have been possible to bring up more than one properly and deal with the demands of her job.

Similar situations and responses in the United States were described by Damiano-Teixeira in her study of women academics. She suggests that the women she surveyed tended to prioritise either their family or their professional lives, with fewer or no children in the latter case (Damiano-Teixeira 2006). In this regard, it would seem that the dilemmas for women in language departments and the solutions they adopt resemble those found in other academic areas.

Support for Working Mothers

The type of support offered by different countries to mothers in employment was found to influence the ease with which they could pursue their careers. Where France is concerned, it was notable that two respondents originally from elsewhere spoke of the excellent facilities available in the country, with 'easy to find day care (both private and nursery school from age 2)', or as the other put it 'superb pre- and after-school childcare', even if this did not necessarily solve all the difficulties.

The United Kingdom was rather less favourably viewed. A French national pointed to the more supportive situation in her native land where 'the whole child-care system is geared towards encouraging women/young mothers to go back to full time employment as soon as possible'. In similar vein, a lecturer from the UK noted that 'good but affordable childcare' was 'generally poor' in England.

In Ireland too a number of negative comments were made about the context and facilities. Childcare was said to be 'patchy in both quality and availability. And phenomenally expensive' (cf. also O'Connor 2012). Another bemoaned the fact that there was 'no support from the state (for example, through tax-free-allowances for child-care) nor from the employer for people with small or teenage children'.

The end of communist rule in Poland led to considerable changes in this area. Under the Communists, women had been encouraged to take up employment, something which was seen as representing 'progressiveness and gains of the system'. If only as compensation for the very low income levels during this period, better and more extensive services were available to women which were 'cheaper (if not free of charge)'. These included 'creches, kindergartens,..summer camps for youth and children and also family holidays in state-owned holiday centres etc.etc. [*sic*]'. Given this scenario, that era offered more to working mothers, a fact recognised by the respondent in question (on the transition from communism to a post-communist state and attitudes to women, see, for instance, Plomien 2006). Despite the changes in support for women in employment, as one participant put it, Poles now: 'are free. Free to choose, free to move…'. In addition, the ever-present threat of arbitrary arrest has been lifted: 'I shall not fear that my husband or son (or I myself) will be interned or imprisoned' (as had happened to a family member in 1948). For this participant, the reduction in certain types of support was clearly a small price to pay for liberty and government under the democratic rule of law. Furthermore, with the passage of time in the EU, there are signs, as suggested by the other respondent, that European measures may be influencing governmental attitudes: 'every year politicians promise to improve and increase the number of kindergartens and the system of child care, so that having a child would not be a barrier for working women' who wish 'to continue their professional careers'.

Parenting Skills and Teaching

Different aspects of a person's life can interact and impact on one another as people mature and develop through experience. One of the questions was thus aimed at seeing if staff with children felt that they had gained any skills or techniques from motherhood that were found helpful in their university teaching and careers. While some participants did not see any connection at all, a number pointed particularly to attributes that arose not only from working with and organising the younger generation but also frequently from the management of multiple commitments in a time-span that was, as ever, too short. Thus organisation, time-management, efficiency and multitasking were mentioned (qualities which also arise in other studies as in

Pritchard 2010 who speaks of the acquisition of efficient organisation or Priola 2004 who discusses multitasking as an attribute of female managers as does Deem 2003). It was also suggested that children 'keep you young' and that you gain 'another perspective' both of which were considered beneficial. Other qualities were more directly connected to work in the classroom or sometimes with colleagues, as in 'all kinds of management and negotiation skills'. Teaching and parenting are, as one said, two different roles which should not be confused; however, she pointed to factors that contribute to a teacher's effectiveness such as 'listening, explaining, encouraging, making the rules clear and sticking to them'. A further respondent indicated that the ability to act as 'a facilitator' and offer 'support' were important attributes. Seeing how one's own children learnt and raising bilingual children were also seen by some as not irrelevant to language lecturers, while the experience of children as students could also serve to enlighten practice and increase understanding of student needs.

Motherhood: A Worthwhile Challenge

The answers to questions relating to different aspects of motherhood reveal a variety of individual responses to family life and employment, influenced by personal situation, temperament, world view and, at least to some extent, the national context. It emerges clearly, however, that while there were different reactions to its challenges, in general those concerned were positive about child-rearing. It was also seen as an experience that could make a positive contribution to professional practice. The 'maternal wall' was undoubtedly problematic at times but it was not necessarily viewed as an unwelcome impediment.

Unattached or Childless

While it might seem that single and childless women should be freer and have less stress and career problems than their married or partnered counterparts with children, some research suggests that this may not be the case with single women being expected to be more available and take on extra work (as in Ramsay and Letherby 2006 who found that some of the single or childless women felt that they fell foul of '"greedy institutions"', p. 35, and their 'unreasonable expectations of non-mothers', p. 34 or Cummins 2005 who argues that single, childless academics are often expected to undertake additional caring type duties as well as helping out when other academic staff have problems). Although support for this view was limited among participants, a French respondent reported frequent comments by women with children about the greater freedom of single women, the implication being that they could well assume extra responsibilities. Another, working in Denmark, who had not felt disadvantaged as an unattached woman, had noticed that colleagues with families sometimes used their family as a 'legitimate reason' for declining to accept additional work. Unlike those with partners, she went on to say, 'in a sense, single people have to justify being stressed'. A further participant had noted that single women seemed to accept a great many tasks but was not sure whether this was due to their having more time or because 'the additional work was forced upon them' (France). Two (married) respondents (both from the same country: Poland), indicated that it was expected that single people, whether women or men, would undertake more work and additional duties. As one put it: 'their superiors often believe that there is nothing wrong' in giving them 'extra hours or duties and they should not refuse because they are freer than their colleagues who have families/are married/have children to look after'. It was, however, suggested by a further respondent (based in Ireland) that this sort of treatment was generally meted out to women whatever their marital or family situation and 'of course women concur in this, feeling all too often that they must prove they are as capable as their male colleagues'.

Institutional Policies

Institutional equal opportunity policies should create a positive ethos for women in the exercise of their profession. Although a majority of respondents (68.3 %, n.28) stated that policies existed in their place of work a number did not know if this was the case (19.5 % n.8) while some showed a certain hesitancy about the topic with replies such as 'I'm not sure' or 'I suppose it does' (12.2 % n.5) . Apart from France, all those who either did not know or were hesitant were, in fact, working in a country to which they were not native, and while a strong emphasis is placed on such policies in Europe, sometimes they came from other continents.

   To have policies is obviously an important starting point but it is not enough for them to exist on paper: they have to be translated into reality. Of course, some staff had never had to have recourse to them while others indicated that they were indeed effective, with one adding that in her university 'they are also implemented'. In another university, there was said to be 'an equal opportunities committee/network at the university and they organise events [and] sometimes courses for female academics'. The necessity of having such policies in place should one have occasion to seek some form of redress was acknowledged even if 'such challenges are lengthy processes and may be difficult to prove'. However, certain doubts were expressed with regard to the tangible benefits conferred by policies and institutional measures: 'In reality, I am not sure they count for much', while in an establishment in another country they were characterised as 'a politically correct move of the university authorities' without any real teeth and in yet a further country as being effective 'up to a point, provided they are not just lip service' and in a fourth country, they were 'theoretically [effective], yes'. In a fifth country, they were described as being 'not at all' effective while a participant from a sixth country stated even more graphically that despite the policies: 'in the end every institution ends up doing what they like'. Scepticism regarding such policies, at least on the part of some, is not confined to any one national setting but was found in all the countries included in the survey.

Attitudes and Treatment in the Workplace

Specific evidence of positive attitudes and equal treatment was found in all countries included in the survey, although it was notable that the highest levels of satisfaction came from France (90.9 % (n.10) with only one (i.e. 9.1 %) being unsure about the position). Across the survey, there were indications that the existence of a larger number of women in a unit could have a bearing on outcomes, as with one who supported the view that there was equal treatment in her department: 'being the majority, I'd say yes' while another said: 'yes – we are almost all women in language teaching'. Or again: 'I was very well welcomed. The majority of teachers are women, the head of school is a woman'. A woman leader had particular praise for her university which made efforts to ensure a gender balance on committees: '… especially when I was in a leadership position, I was often chosen for different councils, committees, etc. because I was a women – i.e. there was a wish, or even a requirement, that the committee in question should be gender balanced'. While such an approach is sometimes viewed as tokenism (see, for example, Kettle 1996), this woman clearly thought of it as a positive factor and saw it as indicative of the institution's good intentions in introducing a practice recognised as being effective in reducing 'gender bias' and 'symbolically' changing 'institutional cultures' (European Commission 2012, *Structural change in research institutions*, p. 31).

Other respondents, however, pointed to a discrepancy between their area and the wider university with comments such as: 'the engendered attitudes … do lurk in the wings, but not so much at departmental level'. Sometimes, the position was linked to the nature of the subjects concerned, with there being less equitable treatment in more technical areas such as: 'universities of technology, also science'. Another from a different country stressed the importance of 'the head of department' and also the level of activity of 'the elected members' of relevant bodies.

The difficulties evoked by those who had caveats or were overall less positive and indeed, on occasion, very negative, about approach and treatment were not dissimilar to observations and research findings in the field of gender studies. For instance, in one institution even though the treatment of women was judged favourably, it was noted that: 'the men, even with the best intentions do tend to form groups among themselves' and women 'have to assert themselves specially to get into the inner sanctums' (on networks, see, O'Connor 2012; Zimmer and Siemieńska 2007; Shaw and Cassells 2007; Heward 1996, Bagilhole 1993; Hicks 1993). In addition to networks not easily accessible to women, the tendency for men to command more respect and attention was raised by another respondent: 'there are still a lot of engendered attitudes – men tend to get listened to more especially by other men, their opinions valued more etc'. One put this issue even more strongly saying:

'as a woman, I have found it difficult: follow the experts who seem to be mostly men'. Another raised the problem of women having to do more than men so that for her things were: 'hard, you have to work double to have half of the recognition'. A further participant experienced a need to 'do everything with a smile', to accept authority and not speak up or be awkward. In addition, she spoke of having her ideas 'stolen' by her male director (cf. Kettle 1996) 'even if he was happy to ridicule you when you first suggested them'.

Overall, the position was perhaps best summed up in the view of the respondent who suggested that that while, legally, there might be equality of treatment, laws and the reality of interpersonal approach are not necessarily the same thing and: 'a lot of non-equal-treatment attitudes survive, actually, to an amazing degree'.

Promotion

Participants expressed different views about whether in reality the same opportunities for advancement existed for women as for men. In one country, Poland, there was unqualified agreement that there was no difference but in others the reaction was often rather more mixed. One participant from Finland indicated that: 'I have always felt that women can go as far as they desire to go'. For the other, despite equal opportunities within her university: 'the number of women in full professorships .... is smaller than that of men'. One UK lecturer observed that: 'men progress more rapidly than women' while a further respondent, again in the UK, said that 'most important department positions are still headed by men'. Beyond the department, senior management was sometimes perceived as a largely male preserve so that, while there might in the main be equal opportunities for progression, this was not necessarily the case at that level in which: 'there seems to be a higher representation of men' (Ireland) or again: 'while there is a nice gender balance at the lower levels of the career ladder, there are still more men as full professors, deans, rector/vice-rector' (Denmark). In fact, it would seem that the less prestigious the category of post, the more likely it is that women will be found in it with, from Ireland: 'as in most institutions, the % of women is higher in the lower grades. And even higher in part-time/temporary positions' (cf. also *She Figures 2012*). A further respondent linked the problems experienced by women to the fact that men were 'better able to argue their "case" and be heard as regards working conditions and promotion'. She felt that in order to be listened to, she had 'to pursue my goal in a more aggressive manner' but this did not 'suit' her 'character' so 'I am at risk of just abandoning the pursuit'. This may touch on the problem of the initial education and conditioning of women to play certain roles (see, for instance, Hicks 1993) so that 'women may choose not to adopt a competitive masculinised model of working' (Fletcher, pp. 272–273).

There is, of course, an element of personal choice and inclination which may be influenced more by individual aspiration than by inhibiting factors as seen in the following: 'lots of my female colleagues have no interest whatsoever in becoming managers' even if they aspired to be senior lecturers, a goal they were thought likely to achieve. A further participant attributed her current level of achievement to her 'own personal desire to have a wide variety of life experiences and not focus on only developing a university career'. Thus any 'limitations' she had encountered 'have been self-imposed'. Another respondent who was positive about her own career, characterising it as 'good', explained that this was 'because I never wanted more than I have reached'. Nonetheless, she did think that 'many situations are easier for men than women' and further expanded this by indicating that in this comment she was pointing to matters such as 'leadership'. This reply in particular offers an interesting perspective into the dichotomy between what certain individuals seek and are happy with, on the one hand, and, on the other, their ability to view the general situation and perceive that for others with different aims and ambitions, there may indeed be problems.

Together with a preponderance of women in an area, a clear method for according promotion was seen as helpful (in this connection, cf. also *Structural change in research institutions*, 2012). One respondent from France outlined the country's system in a sector with high numbers of females: 'in the French public university system, promotion is partly granted by the Conseil National des Universités [the National Council of Universities which has to certify that people are properly qualified for the post in question] and partly automatic. Women also represent a majority in higher education, and in juries [i.e. selection panels]. As a consequence, it would be difficult to apply unequal treatment' (see also Le Feuvre and Latour 2007; Pigeyre 2006). However, she did wonder what happened in secret ballots for elected positions where: 'you can never know whether male voters actually support a female candidate and vice versa'. Despite a high positive rating among French participants, a small number of doubts were expressed as to whether or not actual practice matched the legal position as in: 'on paper, yes. In reality?' French satisfaction in this regard may also owe something to the fact that tenured academic staff are civil servants with clearly defined conditions of service (Lefeuvre and Latour 2007). A different explanation came from a further respondent employed in France: 'it is definitely true that there were few women Full Professors in my field 15–20 years ago and that that has changed (but it is also true that this may be due to the fact that fewer and fewer men are to be found as students in my field…)'. Again the suggestion is that as areas become more feminised there are increased possibilities for women to advance.

Despite the largely positive nature of the replies from the country, there is evidence to suggest that beyond arts and languages with their higher proportions of women, current trends, at least at the upper levels of management, are not necessarily favourable. A recent (2013) report to the Senate (the upper house of the French legislature) on the results of university reforms noted that the small number of women who were university presidents has been in decline. For the most part, those who move into such posts come from the ranks of the professoriate of which women constitute 20 %, as against 41.5 % at the level below (maître de conférences: roughly, senior lecturer level) (Gillot and Dupont 2013).

Career Patterns: Similarity or Difference?

Linked to the issue of promotion is the rate at which women progress, perhaps reaching certain responsibilities later than their male colleagues (cf. *Structural change in research institutions* 2012; Barrett and Barrett 2011; Ledwith and Manfredi 2000). While there were differing opinions about this, a number of participants considered that the trajectory followed by women was indeed not altogether the same as that of their male counterparts (31.71 %; n.13), something which was attributed to the impact of children in terms recalling observations on the effect of motherhood. For one, women's progression was only comparable to that of men: 'for the women that don't have children' while for another: 'I would say many only begin to develop their careers when their children have grown up'. The dilemmas involved were well illustrated in a response outlining not only the persistence of cultural pressures but also the responsibility felt by women and the choices that this may lead them to make, choices for which they often fully accept the consequences: 'The traditional pattern of "women take care of the home" is still very vivid. Reconciling a career and a family is therefore still rather difficult for women: there is a period of time in a married woman's life with children where family necessarily comes first if a woman cannot rely on substantial help at home'. As ' my family has always been my utter priority' she continued, 'on two occasions, I refused to take extra responsibilities because I knew it would be detrimental to my family. However I can lay the blame on no-one but myself and have no regrets'.

Salary Levels

In the past women were frequently paid less than men for work of equivalent value, a practice which has been combatted by European and national legislation, yet despite this 'Member States still have a gender pay gap' (*Structural change in research institutions* 2012, p. 23). Research undertaken recently in the United States also suggests that when academic men and women are assessed on essentially the same curriculum vitae, the men are judged worthy of higher salaries (Anon. *Guardian* 2013; on salary levels see also McCrudden 2006; Deem 2003). Even in situations of apparent equality with basic rates of pay, additional bonuses and differential ways of grading achievements may lead to some inequity in salary. In Denmark, for instance: 'the official salary scales are the same, but you can negotiate performance pay as an individual. What happens there, I do not know. But it may be that women are less good at doing this negotiation. I don't know'. In Ireland, although respondents were in the main confident that women were equally remunerated in their teaching posts, one did not know what the position was. Another hoped that equality of remuneration obtained, 'although I have in the past heard of examples where this was most definitely not the case'. She also felt that women: 'are less likely to challenge or doubt inequality', an observation which like that from the Danish participant may be interpreted as raising the issue of education and conditioning.

Lack of certainty was also exhibited in the United Kingdom where national salary scales exist at the various levels of post but where there can also be some recourse to performance related pay and bonuses. A third of the respondents indicated that salary scales were equitable (n.4) while two just thought that they were. A third of respondents stated they did not know (n.4) while two were of the view that they were not.

Employment conditions for university lecturers in Finland have undergone certain changes and it was not yet clear at the time of response what this might entail in the longer term: ' … the legal status of Finnish universities was changed a few years ago – we are no longer state employees, but have a contract with the university directly. This means that there is also a new salary system: basic salary + performance bonus (which is reviewed every 2 years), whereas previously there was a fixed salary + increments based on years of service. All posts and government positions have clear requirements in terms of degrees and experience, as well as criteria for appraisal. What all these changes will mean in terms of gender differences in salaries and positions is not known yet'.

In the case of both Poland and France, however, there was little dissension or lack of clarity. In Poland, 'the salaries are exactly the same for both groups'. In France, where, as seen above, tenured university staff are also civil servants, the existence of transparent national pay scales meant that there was a general feeling that work of equal value attracted the same reward: 'Yes: there is a salary scale for Civil servants, regardless of gender'. While additional powers to award bonuses have recently been granted, national pay scales remain in place guaranteeing, at the very least, a basis of equity (Ministère de l'Éducation nationale 2011).

Women as Managers and Leaders

The approach adopted by women if they are in a position of leadership has been the subject of discussion (as in: Priola 2004; Deem 2003). The participants in this study held a range of views about whether or not women in posts of responsibility managed and led in ways different from men and on this issue there was no clear country link. Almost half of the respondents thought that there was no difference (41.5 %, n.17): 'their responsibilities and the ways they manage do not differ' (Poland) or 'not in my work environment. Women are totally accepted in positions of responsibility and have nothing to prove' (France). There was, however, evidence that women assuming a leadership role may experience at least some sense of resistance. A woman, also from France, who had held a head of department post suggested that: 'accepting … female authority is still difficult for a lot of male colleagues'. This may be why another respondent (from the UK) thought that women needed: 'to do something to prove themselves to earn the respect from the beginning'.

One participant had observed 'a certain amount of hardening' in the behaviour of women who assumed a position of authority, which she believed happened so that 'these females ... can be perceived as leaders within the (male dominated) ... hierarchy' (Ireland). Another considered that while there was no difference in the ways in which women managed, this was simply because: 'most women that are leading in management are doing so because they behave like men' as otherwise they would not have been promoted (Ireland) (on the topic of 'honorary men' and women aligning themselves with 'the masculine values of competition' see Fletcher 2007, p. 272; p. 276).

Other participants did, however, think that women approached the process of management differently from their male counterparts. For some it was not so much that women found that they needed to adopt a distinctive style but rather this was something that might be more spontaneous or innate, as in: 'they do not have to, they simply do it in a different way' (Poland). One who offered a similar observation was less sure as to why it happened: 'they do certainly do things differently, but whether they "find they have to" or they just do so, I am unsure' (Ireland). One, working in France, thought that a problem, at least in her generation, might be the fact that there were not: 'many women as role models (since most women didn't work when I was a child) '. The paucity of female role models was an issue raised in Bagilhole's article of 1993 at a time when women were less prevalent among university staff but it has also been discussed more recently in Fletcher 2007.

Various suggestions were offered as to what the difference in style or approach on the part of women might involve. One described it as 'using more subtle means' (Poland) while for a further participant women were 'more protecting more like a mother'. Rather than leading, they often 'manage'. In contrast to this, she said that men tended to be more direct, to say what they meant and to want immediate answers to questions whereas women were 'more indirect' and 'hide everything and it comes out as frustrations' (Denmark). Traditional female qualities were also evoked in an answer highlighting greater understanding on the part of women: 'I do believe we take into account, much more than men, other men or -mostly- women's personal situations (for example, secretaries or colleagues who have children, who are divorced, etc.) and that we are therefore more flexible and caring' (France). These participants thus tended towards a view of management by women based on so-called feminine and masculine characteristics, with women showing what Fletcher terms 'a more feminised model of collegial working practices' (Fletcher 2007, p. 272).

Some eschewed an explanation solely based on gender, linking the approach adopted in management to temperament as in: 'I think individuals have different styles' (Ireland). Another indicated that: 'in my experience, women leaders are either very tough (trying to play the male game) or tend to work according to more feminine values such as e.g. a high level of empathy. In other words, like men, women are also a diverse group. There are also men with a high level of, say, empathy' (Denmark). Similar views came from a further participant working in Denmark: 'I think leadership style can have a lot to do with personality and ethos rather than gender. I have experienced caring male leaders and ruthless, hard as nails female leaders'. She had also known women to: 'put other women down because they are clearly seen as competition' (a behavioural practice discussed, for instance, by Cummins 2005). There are, in effect, a variety of approaches and managers can have a positive or negative effect on the people with whom they interact which is perhaps why one respondent (from Finland) suggested that it was essential: 'to develop a good rapport with the employees in order to be a good manager'.

Part-Time Work and Casualisation

For women wishing to return to teaching or for those seeking employment compatible with childcare, one solution may be to work in a part-time mode, a route women may choose as the lesser '"of two evils" – part-time work vs no work at all'. Yet this was a solution which could create very real difficulties and uncertainties: 'being hourly paid …in HE puts women (and men) in a very precarious situation'. What this meant was clearly exemplified in another response: 'I never know whether I will be called from one term to the next' or if 'my hours may be reduced or not increased'. The problems created by part-time and impermanent contracts were raised in this survey by respondents to some extent from Ireland but mainly from the United Kingdom. This may simply reflect the profile of participants or it may also be an indication of trends towards casualisation being more pronounced, particularly in the United Kingdom, with a lower degree of protection for those who choose this route. A lecturer originally from the Netherlands certainly considered the part-time situation in the UK to be less favourable than in her home country. One French woman working in the UK would have liked a 'real "part time" Lecturer' job. This respondent went on to say that she felt that such posts would only ever be put on a proper footing when 'men want to make that choice for themselves' which would mean that this route would become an experience that was 'real' and 'positive' for those opting for it. In fact, a UK national placed the whole issue firmly onto the equality agenda when she commented that while equal opportunities existed in the country, they were not applied to part-timers.

Overuse of part-time and impermanent contracts has been considered an exploitative mechanism and the ongoing casualization in academia in the United Kingdom has been highlighted by recent studies (see for, instance, Else 2015; McCrudden 2006). It has been argued that women in general are being more adversely affected by the austerity measures that have been introduced in the UK following the global financial crisis (Gayle 2015). Recent figures from the Equality Challenge Unit (an organisation with charitable status based in the United Kingdom whose main aim is to promote equality and diversity in institutions of higher education) show that in Modern Languages 64.2 % of the workforce are female and 35.8 % male. Their statistics also reveal that in the academic workforce as a whole 'women comprised the majority of … part-time academic staff (54.7 %)' (Equality Challenge Unit 2014, p. 215). As more cuts are planned in the country, with the already high feminisation of Modern Languages, the situation may well get worse with, potentially at least, an increase in casualisation and the type of badly paid and sometimes rather erratic part-time work to which women language teachers often have to have recourse.

Discrimination, Harassment and Sexual Innuendo?

Encouragingly, a sizeable body of participants (70.7 %; n.29), including women at different stages of their career and at varying levels of seniority, indicated clearly that they had never suffered discrimination. Replies to this effect came from a range of countries, including comments, such as: 'I've never had to think of myself or my career and experience from the point of view of gender' (Finland) or 'I have never felt that being a woman was a disadvantage and I have never experienced any discrimination with regard to gender' (Poland) or, again: 'being a woman has been neither advantageous or disadvantageous to me in my career' (Ireland).

Nonetheless, there was evidence that discrimination could happen and had happened, The examples of differential treatment varied in their impact and seriousness. Sometimes, they could be more or less laughed off as was the case with the woman who had in her younger days been mistaken for a secretary and asked to serve coffee. Other types of discrimination had had more serious repercussions, in that, at least for a time, they impacted directly on progression in employment. One, a UK national teaching in the UK, cited instances at an earlier stage of her life, in two different institutions where she had formerly worked with an impermanent contract (one in the school sector and the other in higher education), when she felt that pregnancy had been detrimental to her prospects. Instances, where promotion was at stake, were cited by two professors, both in an age range over 50 (and based in different countries). In one of these not only was there a question of gender discrimination, there was also an element of prejudice towards someone originally from another jurisdiction. She described how her request for support for advancement had been brushed aside by a male professor unsympathetic to the careers of women, coupled with a disparaging remark relating to her country of origin. She was not the only participant to draw attention to unfavourable treatment on the grounds of nationality. One said that when she was younger, her 'foreign' (UK) qualifications were seen as 'not as good' but then went on to wonder if it was not in fact 'a combination of factors - young, female and foreign'. Another, in a different country (Ireland) considered her problems were not related to her gender but rather to the tendency for there to be 'a glass ceiling when it comes to "outsiders" in jobs of high responsibility'.

Harassment may take various forms but serious inter-sexual harassment did not prove to have been an issue, although some, from all countries in the survey except Finland and Poland, had been the recipients of inappropriate suggestions and sexist allusions (but they were not in a majority: 26.9 %, n.11). For the most part, the feisty attitudes of those concerned revealed that they had been more than able to deal with the situation, as in: 'once as a young research fellow, a senior professor made a very sexist remark when he came to my office. My own reply ensured that he never did it again!' Another typical comment in the same vein indicated: 'any remarks that I have received that I consider sexist, I handle myself with a quick verbal volley'.

As was seen to be the case for discrimination, sexist comment was sometimes linked to the country of origin. One woman from Latin America reported having been the recipient of a rather suggestive joke about a dance from the continent but as incidents like this were said by her to be 'commonplace' in her homeland, she described herself as being: '"trained" to survive' in this type of situation and felt that her overall experience in the UK had been 'good'. Another, who was decidedly more concerned by such behaviour, indicated that she had had to deal with: 'not only sexist remarks but remarks about my country of origin'. She found that there had been a less than helpful response from the relevant university body: 'the advice to get thicker skin has been mentioned a number of times'.

The answers given in this survey would seem to suggest that, although it could surface, overtly sexist behaviour was not a widespread issue. In addition, the most blatant examples of gender discrimination were experienced by older respondents and, in particular, those who aspired to be rise to the higher levels of the lecturing hierarchy and become professors. However, it would seem that, despite the tendency of modern foreign language departments to attract native speakers to their staff, it may in some cases (but by no means all) be disadvantageous to be both female and working outside one's native land.

Academe: Better In Than Out?

It has already been noted that some women chose to enter academic life as it offered them employment that was more compatible with raising children. In fact a striking result of the survey was the consistency with which participants from a number of countries considered that even if life in academe was not without difficulty, conditions in it were generally better than elsewhere. This was so even in Scandinavia with two respondents from Denmark indicating that while the situation in teaching and the public sector was positive, in the private sector there were problems which were 'often discussed in news from the unions'. In Finland too, a similar theme emerged when it was suggested that there were ways around the letter of the law, particularly in certain fields of work: 'the problem of always having equal salaries, for example, has not been solved in business and technology in particular; it is always easy to create new job titles to manipulate legislation and policies'. In addition, it was noted that there were less women in 'top company positions'. In Poland, a comparison was made between education and other sectors of the economy 'beyond HE' where the issue of equal rights 'was not perceived as something very important'. In France too, a distinction was drawn between education and other domains. Although both sexes received the same salaries 'in teaching' where 'the salary scales' were 'very controlled', the same was not the case in the private sector. Also in France, while higher education was judged to fit well with personal responsibilities as 'the organisation of hours is very flexible', apart from teaching and the public sector, there was some doubt about the reality of gender equality. It was also clear that in certain types of employment in the country, long established routines could prove problematic for women with there still being much to do 'in terms of … sticking to reasonable and family-compatible office hours (managers like to come in at 9.00 a.m and linger around – including meetings – until 8.00 p.m)'.

The work patterns in academic life were not, however, found to be equally acceptable in institutions in all countries as seen in a comment by an Irish respondent who spoke of the '24/7 culture of academia', which is 'geared toward single or at the very least childless people, and men with stay-at-home wives', together with 'an assumption that you will prioritise your work life over your personal life'. A (single) woman based in another country (Denmark) commented on the high number of hours undertaken by her which would 'impact negatively on a marriage. I would not be able to work the hours I do if I had a partner'.

Surprisingly, perhaps because the majority of respondents from the United Kingdom worked part-time, the long hours culture in the country did not emerge as a concern in the survey, although it was possibly alluded to by one who had previously been employed part-time and indicated that the transition to full-time was not 'easy to manage'. The issue has, however, been the subject of ongoing comment in reports and the educational press. One writer on the topic, for instance, has pointed to its disadvantages for women with family responsibilities (Fletcher 2007). A recent study undertaken on behalf of the University and College Union found high working hours in the higher education sector. Over three-quarters of full-time staff did more than 40 h per week with over a quarter from higher education going beyond the 48 h maximum laid down in the EU working time directive (Kinman and Wray 2013).

Conclusion: A Multi-faceted Scenario

The women surveyed in this study had had diverse experiences in employment in the course of their careers, both positive and negative with some having experienced fewer difficulties than others. Languages is an increasingly feminised area and, in some cases at least, this made for a more favourable ethos. Even if there were problems in the academy, teaching in higher education was for most a desirable career. Yet the picture was mixed with many traditional stereotypes and prejudices still remaining.

The reconciliation of family and working life was often found to be problematic, as participants struggled to achieve an acceptable compromise between the two. Different strategies were adopted by those involved, depending on circumstances, personal outlook and priorities. Care of young children led some mothers to pause their careers while others reduced their commitment in the workplace or refused additional and potentially beneficial responsibilities. Yet, many respondents accepted the situation and professed themselves to be happy with any sacrifices they had had to make, epitomised in the observation: 'I am convinced that if I had no children, my work opportunities would be better, but I would not not have them'. In coming to this type of judgment, it would seem that they viewed their lives and the different elements in them in the round with the positive nature of motherhood often compensating for deficiencies or lack of progress in the workplace.

While for some the provision of good and affordable childcare as well as other national measures to support families certainly alleviated the problems, a measured work-life balance remains a goal yet to be achieved in language departments as elsewhere. The issue has been highlighted repeatedly by the European Union as, for instance, in a study from 2012 which points to the fact that the success of women in education and their advances in employment have all too often not been matched by facilities 'such as child-care services or the emergence of suitable flexible work schedules for working parents' that would enable the reconciliation of 'career aspirations and private life' (*Structural change in research institutions* 2012, p. 24). Yet, for the Union a balance between these two areas is 'a key element in achieving gender equality' (*She Figures 2012* 2013, p. 7).

Despite the increasing numbers of women in languages, improvements in equality and enhanced opportunities for advancement, the persistence of aspects of male privilege and better career prospects for men were still observed, particularly (but not only) in the wider university and society as a whole. The existence of a transparent, nationally agreed system for promotion and salary in certain countries could certainly act as an antidote to unequal treatment. Yet with changes to contracts as in Finland or the extension of disadvantageous working practices such as casualisation and part-time employment in the United Kingdom, there are also considerable threats to women throughout higher education. Even if departments of languages often offer women a more positive and congenial working environment, they exist within a broader context and are subject to a range of outside influences. The progress achieved by women is real but if it is not to be eroded, vigilance, support and pressure at all levels, institutional, national and European, continue to be required.

References

Anon. (2013, January 15). Sexist science. Or how 'John' was offered more money and respect than 'Jennifer' despite having the same qualifications. *Guardian*, p. 12.

Bagilhole, B. (1993). Survivors in a male preserve: A study of British women academics' experiences and perceptions of discrimination in a UK University. *Higher Education, 26*(4), 431–447.

Barrett, L., & Barrett, P. (2011). Women and academic workloads: Career slow lane or Cul-de-Sac? *Higher Education, 61*, 141–155. doi:10.1007/s10734-019-9329-3.

Bettio, F., & Sansonetti, S. (Eds.). (2015). *Visions for gender equality*. European Commission. Luxembourg: Publications Office of the European Union. doi:10.2838/00811; http://ec.europa.eu/justice/gender-equality/files/documents/vision_report_en.pdf. Accessed 27 July 2015.

Booth, C., & Bennett, C. (2002). Gender mainstreaming in the European Union. Towards a new conception and practice of equal opportunities? *European Journal of Women's Studies, 9*(4), 430–446. doi: 10.1177/1350506820090040401.

Burri, S., & Prechal, S., updated Burri. (2014). *EU gender equality law. Update 2013*. European Union. http://ec.europa.eu/justice/gender-equality/files/your_rights/eu_gender_equality_law_update2013_en.pdf. Accessed 24 May 2014.

Chen, S., & Breivik, A. (2013). *Lost for words. The need for languages in UK diplomacy and security*. London: The British Academy. http://www.britac.ac.uk/policy/Lost_For_Words.cfm. Accessed 07 June 2014.

Commission of the European Communities (1981). A new community action programme on the promotion of equal opportunities for women 1982–85 (Commission Communication to the Council, presented on 14 December 1981). COM(81) 758, 9 December 1981. *Bulletin of the European Communities*, Supplement 1/82. http://aei.pitt.edu/3954/1/3954.pdf. Accessed 25 July 2014.

Costello, C., & Davies, G. (2006). The case law of the court of justice in the field of sex equality since 2000. *Common Market Law Review, 43*, 1567–1616.

Council of the European Union (1995). Council decision of 22 December 1995 on a medium-term community action programme on equal opportunities for men and women (1996 to 2000). 95/593/EC. *Official Journal of the European Communities*. L35/337, 30.12.95. http://eur-lex.europa.eu/legal-content/EN/TXT/PDF/?uri=CELEX:31995D0593&from=EN. Accessed 01 Aug 2014.

Crompton, R., & Le Feuvre, N. (2000). Gender, family and employment in comparative perspective: The realities and representations of equal opportunities in France and Britain. *Journal of European Social Policy, 10*(4), 334–348.

Cummins, H. (2005). Mommy tracking single women in academia when they are not mommies. *Women's Studies International Forum, 28*, 222–231.

Damiano-Teixeira, K. M. (2006). Managing conflicting roles: A qualitative study with female faculty members. *Journal of Family and Economic Issues, 27*(2), 310–334. doi:10.1007/s10834-006-9012-0.

Deem, R. (2003). Gender, organizational cultures and the practice of manager-academics in UK Universities. *Gender Work & Organization, 10*(2), 239–259. doi:10.1111/1468-0432.t01-1-00013.

Earles, K. (2014). Gender equality identity in Europe: The role of the EU. In D. MacDonald & M.-M. DeCoste (Eds.), *Europe in its own eyes, Europe in the eyes of the other* (pp. 103–124). Waterloo: Wilfrid Laurier University Press.

Elliott, E-A. (2013). *The case for language learning. Language teaching is facing a state-independent divide*. http://www.theguardian.com/education/2013/oct/04/state-independent-language-learning-divide. Accessed 07 June 2014.

Else, H. (2015, June 04). Zero points: The persistence of temporary measures. *THE, Times Higher Education*, p. 38.

Equality Challenge Unit (2014). *Equality in higher education: Statistical report 2014, Part 1: Staff*, http://www.ecu.ac.uk/wp-content/uploads/2014/11/2014-08-ECU_HE-stats-report_staff_v19.pdf. Accessed 01 June 2015.

ETAN. (2000). *Science policies in the European Union. Promoting excellence through mainstreaming gender equality. A report from the ETAN Expert Working Group on Women and Science*. Brussels: European Commission. ftp://ftp.cordis.europa.eu/pub/improving/docs/g_wo_etan_en_200101.pdf . Accessed 24 May 2014.

EUR-Lex. Access to European law. Fundamental rights and non-discrimination. http://eur-lex.europa.eu/legal-content/EN/TXT/HTML/?uri=URISERV:a10000&from=EN. Accessed 10 June 2015.

Europa. The treaty of Amsterdam, a comprehensive guide, fundamental rights and non-discrimination. http://europa.eu/legislation_summaries/institutional_affairs/treaties/amsterdam_treaty/a10000_en.htm. Accessed 19 Sept 2014.

European Commission. (2010). *Background document accompanying the communication from the Commission to the European Parliament, the Council, the European Economic and Social Committee and the Committee of the Regions. Strategy for equality between women and men*

2010–2015. COM(2010) 491; SEC(2010) 1079. Commission Staff Working Document. http://www.europarl.europa.eu/registre/docs_autres_institutions/commission_europeenne/sec/2010/1080/COM_SEC(2010)1080_EN.pdf. Accessed 20 Sept 2014.

European Commission. (2012). *Structural change in research institutions: Enhancing excellence, gender equality and efficiency in research and innovation, Report of the Expert Group on Structural Change*. Luxembourg: Publications Office of the European Union. http://ec.europa.eu/research/science-society/document_library/pdf_06/structural-changes-final-report_en.pdf. Accessed 20 June 2015.

European Commission. (2013). *She figures: 2012 – Gender in research and innovation. statistics and indicators*. Luxembourg: Publications Office of the European Union. http://ec.europa.eu/research/science-society/document_library/pdf_06/she-figures-2012_en.pdf. Accessed 06 May 2015.

European Commission. (2015). *She Figures: 2015. Gender in research and innovation. statistics and indicators*. Luxembourg: European Union. http://ec.europa.eu/research/swafs/pdf/pub_gender_equality/she_figures_2015-leaflet-web.pdf#view=fit&pagemode=nonefit&pagemode=none. Accessed 21 July 2015.

Farwell, R. (2013 August 22). My own experience has made me conscious of the choices women must make and keen to help others progress. *Times Higher Education*, pp. 34–35.

Fletcher, C. (2007). Passing the buck: Gender and management of research in UK higher education. *Equal Opportunities International, 26*(4), 269–286.

Gayle, D. (2015, May 28). Women disproportionately affected by austerity, charities warn. *Guardian*. http://www.theguardian.com/society/2015/may/28/women-austerity-charities-cuts-gender-inequality. Accessed 01 June 2014.

Gillot, D., & Dupont, A. (2013). *L'Autonomie des universités depuis la loi LRU: le big-bang à l'heure du bilan*, Sénat, un site au service des citoyens. http://www.senat.fr/rap/r12-446/r12-446_mono.html#toc19. Accessed 06 June 2015.

Hantrais, L. (2007). *Social policy in the European Union* (3rd ed.). Basingstoke: Palgrave Macmillan.

Heward, C. (1996). Women and careers in higher education: What is the problem? In L. Morley & V. Walsh (Eds.), *Breaking boundaries: Women in higher education*. London: Taylor and Francis.

Hicks, E. K. (1993). Policy strategies for the career development of women at European Universities. *Higher Education in Europe, 18*(4), 3–16.

Kettle, J. (1996). Good practices, bad attitudes: An examination of the factors influencing women's academic careers. In L. Morley & V. Walsh (Eds.), *Breaking boundaries: Women in higher education* (pp. 51–65). London: Taylor and Francis.

Kinman, G., & Wray, S. (2013). *Higher stress. A study of stress and well-being among staff in higher education*. UCU (University and College Union). http://www.ucu.org.uk/media/pdf/4/5/HE_stress_report_July_2013.pdf. Accessed 02 June 2015.

Le Feuvre, N., & Latour, E. (2007). Understanding women's academic careers in France. In R. Siemieńska & A. Zimmer (Eds.), *Gendered career trajectories in academia in cross-national perspective* (pp. 43–74). Warsaw: Wydawnictwo Naukowe Scholar.

Ledwith, S., & Manfredi, S. (2000). Balancing gender in higher education. *The European Journal of Women's Studies, 7*(1), 7–33.

Majcher, A. (2007). Seeking the guilty – academics between career and family in Poland and Germany. In R. Siemieńska & A. Zimmer (Eds.), *Gendered career trajectories in academia in cross-national perspective* (pp. 298–325). Warsaw: Wydawnictwo Naukowe Scholar.

Masselot, A. (2007). The state of gender equality law in the European Union. *European Law Journal, 13*(2), 152–168.

McCrudden, C. (2006). United Kingdom. Progress, problems and opportunities. In R. Blanpain & A. Numhauser-Henning (Eds.), *Women in academia and equality law: Aiming high – falling short?* (pp. 199–216). The Hague: Kluwer Law International.

Ministère de l'Éducation nationale, de l'enseignement supérieur et de la recherche: Enseignement supérieur et recherche. (2011). Les bénéfices de l'autonomie des universités. http://www.enseignementsup-recherche.gouv.fr/pid24651-cid54338/autonomie-les-benefices-pour-les--universites.html. Accessed 06 June 2015.

Munford, R., & Rumball, S. (2000). Women in university power structures. In M.-L. Kearney (Ed.), *Women, power and the academy. From rhetoric to reality* (pp. 92–98). New York: Berghahn.

O'Connor, P. (2012). Irish universities: Male-dominated? Limits and possibilities for change? *Equality, Diversity and Inclusion: An International Journal, 31*(1), 83–96.

Pigeyre, F. (2006). Gender and the careers of French University instructors and researchers. In *Women and scientific careers: Unleashing the potential* (pp. 139–146). Paris: OECD.

Plomien, A. (2006). Women and the labor market in Poland: From socialism to capitalism. In H.-P. Blossfeld & H. Hofmeister (Eds.), *Globalization, uncertainty and women's careers. An international comparison* (pp. 405–432). Cheltenham: Edgar Elgar.

Priola, V. (2004). Gender and feminine identities – women as managers in a UK academic institution. *Women in Management Review, 19*(8), 421–430. doi:10.1108/09649420415754149.

Pritchard, R. (2010). Gender inequalities among staff in British and German universities: A qualitative study. *Compare, 40*(4), 515–532. doi:10.1080/03057925.2010.490375.

Ramsay, K., & Letherby, G. (2006). The experience of academic non-mothers in the gendered university. *Gender, Work and Organization, 13*(1), 25–44.

Rees, T. (2005). Reflections on the uneven development of gender mainstreaming in Europe. *International Feminist Journal of Politics, 7*(4), 555–574. doi:10.1080/14616740500284532.

Rees, T. (2007). Pushing the gender equality agenda forward in the European Union. In M. A. D. Sagaria (Ed.), *Women, universities and change. Gender equality in the European Union and the United States* (pp. 7–21). Basingstoke/New York: Palgrave Macmillan.

Rees, T. (2010). Creativity needs diversity. In R. Gruhlich (Ed.), *Cultures of creativity: The challenge of scientific innovation in transnational perspective. Proceedings of the third forum on the internationalization of sciences and the humanities* (pp. 60–63). Bon-Bad Godesberg: Alexander von Humboldt Foundation. http://www.humboldt-foundation.de/pls/web/docs/F7981/iab-broschuere-2009.pdf. Accessed 2 June 2014.

Shaw, S., & Cassell, C. (2007). 'That's not how I see it': Female and male perspectives on the academic role. *Women in Management Review, 22*(6), 497–515. doi:10.1108/09469420710778727.

Worton, M. (2009). *Review of modern foreign languages provision in higher education in England.* London: HEFCE. http://webarchive.nationalarchives.gov.uk/20100202100434/http://hefce.ac.uk/pubs/year/2009/200941/. Accessed 07 June 2014.

Zimmer, A., & Siemieńska, R. (2007). Introduction: Career paths and aspirations – results of the research network "Women in Universities". In A. Zimmer & R. Siemieńska (Eds.), *Gendered career trajectories in academia in cross-national perspective* (pp. 9–39). Warsaw: Wydawnictwo, Naukowe Scholar.

Chapter 14
Early Career Women in Academia: An Exploration of Networking Perceptions

Terhi Nokkala, Bojana Ćulum, and Tatiana Fumasoli

Instrumental or Evolutionary? Understanding Networking of Female Academics

The old saying 'It is not what you know, but also who you know' has a host of implications when it comes to career development strategy and one's career outcomes. This phrase refers to the connecting of (like-minded) people, meaning creating relationships and networks that are a valuable asset as they can provide the individual with support as well as intangible and tangible benefits, like access to information and social resources (Nahapiet and Ghoshal 1998). Although building relationships and networking is not a novelty for academia, some authors argue it is the internationalization of higher education and the growing need for international activities and strategic alliances between universities that has made professional linkages and networking with other scholars worldwide essential for academics (Ismail and Rasdi 2007). Mavin and Bryans (2002), for their part, suggest that the networking process in academia has redrawn the departmental and geographical boundaries. This affects how the arena for networking is conceived: on the one hand we relate academia to the organized settings of the higher education institution where academics are located; on the other hand we understand academia broadly as a

T. Nokkala (✉)
University of Jyväskylä, Jyväskylä, Finland
e-mail: terhi.nokkala@jyu.fi

B. Ćulum
University of Rijeka, Rijeka, Croatia
e-mail: bculum@ffri.hr

T. Fumasoli
University of Oslo, Oslo, Norway
e-mail: tatiana.fumasoli@iped.uio.no

© Springer International Publishing Switzerland 2017
H. Eggins (ed.), *The Changing Role of Women in Higher Education*,
The Changing Academy – The Changing Academic Profession in International
Comparative Perspective 17, DOI 10.1007/978-3-319-42436-1_14

transnational scientific community which researchers relate to and which is mainly defined by disciplinary fields.

Much of the literature on networking and specifically gender differences in networking practices is based on studies on career advancement and success, conducted in non-academic settings, such as companies, banks, social services etc. Although such studies contributed significantly to our knowledge of the nature of networking, differences between academic and non-academic setting have to be acknowledged as well. Besides providing support for career development (Mavin and Bryans 2002; Forret and Dougherty 2004), support for attaining power within an organisation (Brass 1992), and psychological support (Kram and Isabella 1985; Ibarra 1992; Mirvis and Hall 1996), as many of the studies done in non-academic settings suggest, networking in academia seems to entail a dimension that is closer to core academic activities, particularly of research.

Fetzer (2003) views networking in academia as a mechanism to build a sense of community among scholars within a specified disciplinary field. Maack and Passet (1993) argue that in academia, networking is about keeping up with the literature, doing innovative work, and presenting research work at conferences and in publications with other academics of the same interests. Nabi (1999, 2003) suggests networking is about self-promotion, as it increases the visibility of the academics by signaling their quality, ability and potential to the academic community.

Some authors argue that one's personal and professional reputation in academia is heavily dependent upon integration into formal and informal networks in the research community (Bagilhole 1993, 2000; O'Leary and Mitchell 1990). Atkinson and Delamont (1990) further argue that success in the academic community is not achieved by publishing more, or even by doing better research, but through personal contacts, friendships and cooperative work with key players in the disciplinary field. As academics often identify themselves with the chosen discipline rather than the university where they are employed, it is of no surprise they also identify themselves with important (national and international) disciplinary networks (Ismail and Rasdi 2007; Välimaa et al. 2014) and key players in the chosen field (Atkison and Delamont 1990). Just like the ability to successfully publish high quality research, the social competence in creating networks that benefit not only the individual therein embedded, but also the research group or institution in which he or she works, contributes to the labour market attractiveness of a scholar. Thus, some authors see networking as one's most valuable career management strategy, having in mind that individuals are responsible for their own employment and career development (Altman and Post 1996; Arthur and Rousseau 1996; Hakim 1994; Sullivan 1999). The two main concepts arising from these premises are networks and networking. We define networks as more or less durable linkages between academics; such networks allow the flow of a particular resource, which is social capital. We assume thus that the degree of social capital possessed by an academic affects one's opportunities to advance in the career trajectory (Bourdieu and Wacquant 1992, 113–114; Burt 2000). Quinlan (1999), for example, suggests that connections with powerful people such as highly respected scholars, members of grant committees, editors of journals or one's department head or dean, make for an influential network in the academic arena. Similarly, we define networking as an activity of acquiring those networks.

Previous research shows the importance of networking and networks for academic work and career paths. Bagilhole and Goode (2001) argue that networking is a skill necessary to develop in order to create professional relationships acting as a 'capital' in making academic career progress. Networking enables the individuals engaged in it to gain access to new information and collaborations, contributes to career planning and strategy, provides them with better professional support and encouragement, and ultimately impacts on their upward career mobility (Ismail and Rasdi 2007). It is increasingly acknowledged that not only having a mentoring relationship (so common for academia), but especially a network of developmental relationships may be essential to achieving career success (e.g. Baugh and Scandura 1999; De Janasz and Sullivan 2004; Higgins 2000, 2001; Higgins and Thomas 2001). Seen as the process of building and nurturing of personal and professional relationships to create a system of information, contact, and support, networking is crucial not only for career progress but personal success as well (Whiting and De Janasz 2004). Peluchette (1993) and Greenhaus and Callanan (1994) have pointed out three mechanisms found in networking: (I) increased support and advice, both emotional and practical; (II) enhanced sense of competence through skill development; and (III) greater access to power and control over one's career prospects through self-promotion of abilities and aspirations.

Although recognized as a 'highly time and energy consuming' activity (Šadl 2009), networking seems to evolve into one of the crucial determinants of one's academic career, as academics usually find themselves embedded in both formal and informal networks. Beside mentor-related relationships, broader networks of supporters have also been identified as influential to career success (Ibarra 1993) as both mentors and interpersonal networks may have instrumental value (i.e. enhancing job performance and career advancement) and expressive value (i.e. providing psychosocial support), as argued by Tichy (1981). Aisenberg and Harrington (1988) emphasize the need for both formal and informal networking in academia, showing that, in contrast, isolation is costly in terms of 'intellectual and informational exchange'. However, the networks that are relevant for one's career may be located at different levels: along the same corridor, in the same institution, nationally or globally. Still, some authors recognize the successful development of relationships and networks as one of the key challenges faced by early career academic staff (Bazeley et al. 1996), especially junior female academics (Quinlan 1999). This is further supported by Rothstein and Davey's study (1995) as their data reveals that networks are seen as more important to younger, less established female academics who are more in need of support at this particular stage of their academic careers.

While we acknowledge that networks are functional to academic career advancement, we also aim to define them in the broadest possible manner. Networks may be the outcome of external pressures – e.g. conducting collaborative research in order to get funding, or the output of a deliberate strategy – e.g.to foster one's own career. We argue that networks can also be the unintended consequence of socialization –

e.g. attending a doctoral school, satisfying group or personal needs or expressing individual traits. Thus we characterize as networks *any linkages academics hold or have held with colleagues*; in other words, networks are linkages that do not have to be focused primarily on academic tasks, but that can also be framed by more personal relationships: friendship, partnership, or acquaintance. Networks may be born out of conscious activity to "network" but also as an unintended consequence of meeting people in work or social contexts. Šadl's study (2009) suggests that academics create networks both to gain political power and advantage in organizational politics (e.g. 'old boy networks', Kaufman 1978) and to satisfy practical needs, such as socializing with sympathetic colleagues.

In this paper we want to further explore women's networking perceptions by focusing on a specific group: early career women in social sciences. Our motivation for this exploratory study arises on the one hand from a research interest focusing on the changing academic profession, in particular the challenges academics face with increasing competitive working conditions, internationalization agendas, big-consortia research. On the other hand, our personal interests and experiences as early career women position us in the midst of precarious career situations resulting from short term funding, discrepancy between scarce academic positions and abundant new graduates, the toughening competition for upward career mobility and the importance of networks for our personal career paths. These experiences and the perception that they are widely encountered by early career scholars in Europe and sparked our interest in studying how the early career women carry out and think of networking.

We ask three empirical research questions. Firstly, we ask how early career women define the early career stage in academia. We consider this relevant in understanding the self-perceptions of female academics who, on the one hand, may share a group identity of being early career women, on the other hand present heterogeneous characteristics in terms of institutional affiliation, national context, specific position and age. Secondly, we ask what definitions, meanings and interpretations they give for networks and networking. Thirdly, we inquire how they construct the networking process and their ability to establish and/or join networks, as early career researchers and as women. Given the exploratory nature of our research, this paper starts by discussing different analytical perspectives, and then presents in detail the empirical setting. We then offer our analysis according to our three research questions, we discuss our empirical findings from a conceptual perspective and conclude by presenting a potential future research agenda.

Gender Studies, Social Capital, Academic Profession

This paper addresses the perceptions early career women in academia hold about networking for career purposes. Despite a plethora of studies that scrutinize differences in male and female networks in the workplace (Brass 1985; Moore 1990; Ibarra 1993, 1997; McGuire 2002), the perceptions of networking held by women in academia, as well as the patterns of their networking, remain less understood. Previous research offers two possible approaches to understanding the difference in the ways in which women network in academia for the purposes of advancing their career.

According to the first approach, women and men foster qualitatively different patterns of interaction within their work settings. Kaufman's study (1978) reveals that women have larger, more integrated and more homogeneous networks than their male colleagues and surround themselves with same-sex colleagues more than males would. Furthermore, her study reveals that women tend more to associate with those of similar or lower rank, as well as with those whose research interests are (very) different from their own. Similar patterns were detected in other studies as well. Rothstein and Davey's study (1995) also reveals that female faculty had significantly more females in their networks than did male faculty, suggesting homophilous networking by both men and women. Furthermore, their study indicates that female faculty realize the importance of social support more than men, and make a greater effort than men to extend their networks to obtain higher levels of support. Šadl's study (2009) reveals that men and women use different strategies to attract attention and visibility and to enhance their chances and opportunities. Men are more willing to use confrontation and public relations strategies to put themselves forward, whereas women seem to be more worried about their legitimacy and the appropriateness of their actions. The male respondents' in Šadl's study (2009) showed political manoeuvring and the practical and purposive nature of their information-seeking practices stand in contrast to the female respondents' 'no-planning' approach to social networking. Similarly, Ledwith and Manfredi's study (2000) showed little signs of gain-seeking networking amongst junior or senior women in academia. Other studies suggest women tend to have network compositions with more diverse participants and connections to several other networks, and tend to be linked to fewer influential connections in their networks (Brass 1985; Moore 1990; Ibarra 1993, 1997; McGuire 2002).

Female academics are often excluded from academic networks, especially in their early career phase, which puts them at a disadvantage (Kaufman 1978; O'Leary and Mitchell 1990; Toren 1991, 2001; Vazquez-Cupeiro and Elston 2006). Exclusion results in them experiencing greater isolation, a higher level of stress, a lower level of self-efficacy and self-confidence (Vasil 1996). Women are often excluded from the most resourceful networks despite their career location (Miller et al. 1981; Ibarra 1992), and there are gender differences in the rewards of social capital (Ibarra 1997; Burt 1998). Men appear more able than women to leverage credentials such as hierarchical rank, existing network contacts, or educational degrees, in addition to managing a higher number of relations. Even female academics in executive positions are frequently excluded from the networks through which male academics hold more powerful positions in decision-making (Šadl 2009). Brass (1985) argues that women's networks may be valued less, as women are perceived to be less competent.

The second approach to studying women's networking addresses this imbalance through social capital theory and argues that women – along with young men – are

perceived as "outsiders" in the workplace (Burt 1998, 2000; Aisenberg and
Harrington 1988; Atkinson and Delamont 1990). Thus, Burt argues, women do not
have the legitimacy or capacity to network successfully, nor are they recognized as
able and/or entitled to build and maintain fruitful connections in order to advance in
their careers. This outsider position requires women to act differently in order to
increase their social capital through networking. Instead of creating their own network women are better off if they "borrow" the network from a "sponsor", who is
high(er) in the hierarchy, such as a mentor or a supervisor. Women in Burt's sample
profit the most from close relations to superiors, and from being in dense networks
with direct ties to close colleagues. Burt attributes this to the need for women to
attain "borrowed social capital" in the eyes of their superiors, who make decisions
about their upward mobility (1998, p. 6). They can thus achieve quicker career
advancement than if they stay on their own or attempt to build networks exclusively
from their position (Burt 1998). Also Šadl (2009, p. 1251) in her study of 22 mid-
career male and female academics, identified senior (usually male) academics as
holding the most powerful positions and acting as 'sponsors' for female colleagues
in networks. She also suggests that the combination of age and gender hierarchies
deprives younger women in academia, while in the case of their male colleagues
their disadvantageous position in the age hierarchy is offset by their privileged position with regard to the gender hierarchy. Atkinson and Delamont (1990) conclude
that the position for women as 'outsider' scientists is therefore complex and less
under their own control than is publicly portrayed.

However, Leathwood and Read's study (2009: 176) suggest many female academics continue to 'construct a "space of their own" within academia that provides
many pleasures, comforts and rewards'. Other studies suggest women actively seek
out satisfying career supportive relationships, often within the group of peers, but
mostly among other women as the women's network plays a significant role in providing them with the instrumental, emotional, psychological, and social support that
is vital for survival in the male-dominated workplaces (Quinlan 1999; Ismail and
Rasdi 2007). Ibarra (1992) suggests that women's homophilous ties – those with
other women – may be chosen to serve primarily expressive functions, while ties
with men may be for more instrumental purposes.

Empirical Setting: Exploring Networking of Early Career Women in Social Sciences

Our starting point is an explorative study rooted in social constructivist methodology (Broido and Manning 2002). This approach makes sense of the experience and
perceptions of early career women in academia by interpreting the meanings they
make of their own thoughts on and engagement with networking in different arenas
and with various agendas in mind (Denzin and Lincoln 1994). It highlights the
salient phenomena in our own academic contexts and draws attention to women's

self-understanding of their position and opportunities. The qualitative group interviews used to collect the empirical data allow us to gain a holistic understanding of the context in which early career women operate, while capturing data on participant perceptions "from the inside" (Miles and Huberman 1994, p. 6). The analysis aims to understand "the complex world of lived experience from the point of view of those who live it" (Schwandt 1994, p. 118). Therefore, despite our personal preconceptions regarding networks, we aimed not to predefine the concept of networks or networking, or assume the perceptions of the interviewees. In a similar vein we present our case as a valuable starting point to develop new research – new concepts, hypotheses, methods and cases – on how female academics interact with their colleagues in academia.

In keeping with our personal interest, we decided to limit our study to our own disciplinary field and context, higher education research. In collecting the data through group interviews of early career women, we made use of two international conferences, as they provided access to potential participants in our field. These were the 34th Annual Forum of the EAIR – the European Higher Education Society), organised in Stavanger, Norway, 5–8 September 2012 and the 25th Annual Conference of The Consortium of Higher Education Researchers (CHER), in Belgrade, Serbia, 10–12 September 2012. The selection of these conferences formed a setting for a purposeful selection of the desired target group: an international set of early career women in a particular academic context and the European arena for higher education research.

Both interview events were planned and organised in close collaboration with the conference organizers. Relevant information about the study and how to participate in the interviews was announced on the conferences' websites and through mailing lists, and interview groups were included in the official programme as additional academic activities. We also contacted selected participants of the two conferences and sent them a personal invitation. The Call for Participation included relevant information about the background of the study, and introduced us and our research. Participation in interview groups relied on the voluntary engagement of interested parties. The guidelines concerning the definition of early career women were loose, and we welcomed everyone who perceived themselves as part of that group.

The first conference yielded a group interview with three and the second one with nine early career women (see Appendix 1).[1] There was also some interest amongst established female academics and early career male researchers to participate, which indicates the timeliness and genderless-ness of this exercise.

The group interview sessions lasted for 1 h 40 min and 2 h respectively. Our main goal as facilitators was to encourage all members to participate, while trying to prevent the discussion from being dominated by few. Before the group interviews, participants were invited to sign a letter of consent and fill a background questionnaire containing information about the participant's highest degree, current position,

[1] Additionally, the interview session at EAIR was briefly visited by another person, who did not however, fill the participant information questionnaire or sign the letter of consent. Thus the few remarks made by her are not taken into account in the analysis.

institutional affiliation, age, nationality, and membership in formal academic networks and associations. The interview sessions were semi-structured (see Appendix 2), and the discussions were audio-taped, and later transcribed, amounting to more than 26,000 words. In the following text, the quotes have been lightly edited for grammatical clarity. The participants were later offered an opportunity to comment on a draft version of this chapter.

We have analysed the transcripts individually and collectively at several stages, as we have discussed our impressions, and detected emerging issues and recognizable patterns. Furthermore, we have considered several strands of literature that we thought resonated with our empirical data. During the process many possible interpretations were debated and then discarded. All in all, the process has allowed us to get to know our data in meaningful depth, to develop a common frame for discussion, and finally to come up with a shared fine-grained analysis.

In order to triangulate our analysis further, we have also applied a different method to verify the robustness of our findings. Thus, once we achieved an advanced draft of this chapter, we coded the group interviews with NVivo software by testing our concepts and dimensions, while at the same time challenging ourselves with new interpretations (see Appendix 3). This exercise has proven helpful in systematizing further our previous findings and in examining them with different lenses. Concomitantly it has confirmed our major findings, hence strengthening our analysis and interpretation.

Perceptions of Early Career Women on Networking in Academia

Early Career as Stage and Agency

The group interview participation was based largely on a self-selection framed by a loose set of guidelines and thus the participants held varying positions in academia, from PhD student positions to associate professorships. Yet they had all elected to participate, thus presumably identifying themselves as early career scholars, or at the very least wanting to express their opinions regarding early career scholars. This discrepancy between self-identification as an early career scholar and relatively speaking advanced position may have several explanations. It may indicate the simultaneous fuzziness and sharp definition of boundaries between the different ranks in academia: PhD positions and several post-doctoral stages are all considered early career; yet at the same time they are removed from the full professorial position, which stands at the top of the academic hierarchy (Clark 1983, 112–113; Neave and Rhoades 1987; Fumasoli et al. 2015). Early career was perceived to mark the stage of entering the academic society; or as a testing period where both the individual and 'the academia', especially department or the individual supervisor, are testing the person's suitability for an academic career. Early career stage was variably considered to start when an individual entered into an employment contract with the university with a purpose of completing a PhD, or alternatively, start after the completion of a PhD degree.

I would say that in (country) perhaps that (the early career stage) would be when you enter as a PhD student, then you start in a way your career, because you are an employee and you get money and you are supposed to do your own project, and after you are finished you can work as a researcher or apply for another job within the academic community. (A7)

The concepts of "early career" and "young" or "junior" person were also perceived to differ from the rest of the society, reflecting a sense of academia as a specific institution or field (Fumasoli et al. 2015). The early career stage was considered to be longer in academia than in other professional sectors, and to be populated by older people than elsewhere. Similarly, someone who has already held a more "senior position" outside academia may well hold a "junior position" in academia.

The perceptions related to the early career thus reflect the twofold nature of academic careers. On the one hand, the perceptions represent a linear understanding of the career, with early career as a stage or phase in (academic) life, with a beginning, duration and an end, as well as specific capacities and responsibilities that are embedded in the hierarchical structure of academia. In the case of second careers, early career does not necessarily denote young:

For me this is kind of my second career because I have put 10 years into an administrative position so this is kind of a new career [...] but I agree with (name) it's like, during your PhD it is like you are percolating around all of this different ideas trying to figure out who you are and what you want to do. (A3)

On the other hand, the early career is characterised by a particular type of agency, focusing on a search for legitimation, and coping with limitations of capacity to act:

I think about being legitimated and maybe an early career person, or woman, is still someone that is looking for, or in need of, legitimation. (A11)

Even if you are young it doesn't necessarily mean that you would be considered unequal or less important. It's maybe more up to you to find your own reassurance, to know that you are able to do this and that you are able to find something and then to speak about your findings with some authority. (A10)

The perception of a researcher's agency as changing over time and being dependent on the career stage implies that those who have acquired responsibilities for other people are no longer early career researchers. The broadening scope and capacity to act in relation to one's job and tasks, and a sense of responsibility going beyond matters related to oneself to those over other people are part and parcel of the transition from early to midcareer position.

Understanding, Joining, and Maintaining Networks

We address networks and networking through four questions, namely what definitions early career women give to networks; what they perceive to be the ways of acquiring or joining networks, what they perceive to be the reasons affecting their ability to form or join networks and, finally, what motivations they give for networking and whether they consider networking as an intentional or unintentional process.

At the beginning of the paper, our empirical characterization of a network was that of *"any linkages academics hold or have held with colleagues "*. When analysing the data, a much more fine-grained picture of describing networks and networking emerges, as indicated by the following quotes. Firstly, we can identify a functional idea of a network, based on shared work and tasks, rather than on individual or institutional attributes or values. It emphasizes outcomes, tangible or intangible, as ways to pin down the existence of a network.

> *Collaboration with other research teams or other researchers, researchers from other countries or even in the same country but other institutions but above all collaboration and exchange of ideas, of work, of doing something together, papers or participating in the same research projects, networking, yes. (A1)*

> *Ok, so for me the question is who do I collaborate with and I collaborate with people from my department, people in (country) who work as researchers on the issue of higher education, people who work in the civil society in those issues and people who work in states institution like ministry on these issues and then internationally I collaborate with researchers who work on these issues… (A9)*

The second definition of network arising from the interviews is that of a peer group sharing interests and values. This similarly reflects a functional idea of a network, although the function is more tacit than in the first case. Instead of coproduction of something tangible, such as a shared article, the function in this second case is social, based on the social aspects of interaction between people.

> *I have maybe very wide and superficial ideas of network. For me it is just to get to know other people […] to speak a little bit just to get to know people and then one day maybe we will strongly collaborate on a project or maybe not … it is for me is something very social, so first step of networking for me is something just a social-ish, not really work-ish. (A4)*

The third definition of networks relates to knowing people, who are in a position to provide help or information, or, more profoundly, support an early career researcher to develop their own research or move ahead in academia. The participants constructed two types of examples of such networks: hierarchical ones with an imbalance of power within the network members, and non-hierarchical ones without a power imbalance and larger reciprocity among participants. The extract below demonstrates the perception of network as essential element in establishing oneself in academia, and how one's own position mediates access to networks as well as enables one to do one's own job.

I first understood how important networking is when I started a large project and we started looking for people to bring into the project. My senior colleagues who were in the middle of very important networks, were very able to bring people into the group [...]It was very easy to gain information about those people because you can always write your colleague, who is in the network and ask their opinion about a person. And when I approached somebody, they would ask "Who are you? [...]Why are you writing to me?" After a couple of years I found that the situation is slowly changing and that people respond in a very different way now. It seems that this may be because I am part of a network now. (A11)

The participants had divergent views regarding the locations of such networks at local or institutional scale, national scale and international scale, reflecting the multilevel character of higher education (c.f. Marginson and Rhoades 2002). They are also mediated by the national and institutional contexts, and the career stages of the participants themselves. The following excerpt illustrates the perception that in contexts where academic mobility is limited, institutional networks and mentors become important.

In my country, there is little mobility between universities. It means that if you start your career in one university, you will end your career at the same place with 80% probability. So, for us networking in the university normally is much more important than between universities. It is really hard to gain external ties because people just stay at one place. [...] the main tie of young people within a university is, I would say, only the PhD advisor or the faculty or department chair. (A11)

If you are just stuck in your institution as you explained, I guess that would mean your relevant network is with the other people within the institution. But if you have the opportunity to have also international activities that of course then means that you are going to meet relevant authorities in the field internationally. (A10)

While discussing networking and networks, the interview participants also construed different ways of accessing or joining networks. We can identify three primary ways, which we are calling *work-based*, *attribute-based*, and *mediated network access*. Firstly, in *work-based network access*, a clear collaborative task and/or prolonged collaborative work facilitate the emergence of or inclusion to a network. This may be participation in mutual research projects, professional and scholarly associations, and contacts outside academia related for example to one's research topic or earlier career.

There is one network that is particularly important to me. It is related to a group of people who have come together to deal with different issues like sustainable development and economics and different people come together to see whether there can be a new platform for change in [country]... (A9)

The interview participants construed the joining and creating of networks as taking place through meeting and bonding with other people in a similar career stage so that the career stage was the determining factor in joining a network. We may call this mode of *attribute-based network access* and it is based on common traits of the participants, such as being female PhD students of a roughly similar age.

If I look behind the first year of my PhD, I did a lot of networking with my colleagues, other PhD students.[...] My first step was just to go to seminars and workshops. [...] After two years of my PhD I think I knew more or less all the PhD students in my faculty. (A4)

I've networked with my PhD fellows… informally and of course they were friends but also… sometimes you also kind of need to know somebody to help out, to advice you or whatever, just for socialization. It's networking as well. (A6)

Burt's (1998, 2000) argument about early career women needing to canvas for support of their supervisors in order to gain access to networks also finds support amongst our participants, who noted that they acquire networks through supervisors and other senior colleagues acting as mediators or gatekeepers to pre-existing networks. As one participant pointed out, before one becomes known, being part of networks is based on other people around oneself being already known in the scientific community. We shall call this *mediated network access*:

So you always need to reveal some information, which is familiar to other people to build a trust relationship. […] So for example how can I invite you to write paper if I know nothing about you? But if I know that you are working with some important people who produce good work, I would be happy to invite you. (A11)

The ability to join networks was considered a social skill, at which some people were naturally more adept, or which they had learned. Also personal characteristics and career stage were seen to impact on the ability to join or build networks. Alternatively, the ability to join or acquire networks was seen to depend on the reputation and prestige of the institution and one's supervisor, and by the support the early career women were able to get from their institution. This is important as it relates to the organizational structures, where networking takes place, which empower or constrain academics' behaviour according to reputation and legitimacy (March and Olsen 1989, 1995). This seems to point to the perceived necessity of being legitimized by formal attributes, like institutional affiliation or supervisor's reputation. The relevant networks may be located at one or several layers at the same time, which reflects the understanding of academia as a field which is twofold: constructed around organized settings and professional and disciplinary communities (Clark 1983). Networking opportunities are thus shaped by several arenas, which overlap each other and/or are embedded into one another, as well as operate at different levels (Gornitzka 2009). The process through which these networks can be joined thus also varies.

If you have a very well established supervisor or a very well established institution then you are much better off […]. And if you are not in a network, if nobody knows you, you have huge problems.[…] So if you want to be part of this cutting edge research you simply must be in a very good and very well established and very well-known and very famous network . If you are not there, you are out […] If you are in a good university with good people, then you somehow automatically become a part of it. It is much easier for you. (A10)

The perception of our respondents provides a complex picture of networking, which was simultaneously construed as an activity that was intellectually and personally stimulating and related to developing new ideas for one's research and thinking; as a natural part of the job, of working and growing as a researcher; and as a way of acquiring useful contacts to help early career researchers progress on their careers and acquire future positions. Networking was thus construed both as driven by intellectual curiosity and the desire to do one's job well, or portrayed as a purposeful activity arising from strategic considerations for some explicit gain. A logic of instrumentality and a logic of appropriateness (March and Olsen 2006) appear to co-exist in the words of some of our respondents, who recognize blending their academic interests with career goals.

> Networking is about getting to know useful contacts. It can be from just exchanges of ideas to introducing yourself to potential employer...so yeah it's a strategy and I think I don't know to what extent I can separate how I embody that through my socialization, professional socialization process. (A9)

On the one hand, networking arising from intellectual curiosity-driven and socially-driven motivation, networking with one's peers and colleagues with whom one shares similar values and interest, or networking in a context, was presented with a positive connotation.

> But sometimes it is also a way to stay there for the others and to help each other, because one of the networks that I belong to, we are developing some research projects, [topic], and we have never been able to get financial support for the project until now and we keep going with that. We are from 8 different countries and we are actually supporting each other and trying to see: "Well we have an opportunity here let's see" – and it's more, it's not hierarchical...it is different I think. (A8)

On the other hand, many participants expressed some ambiguity towards networking as a purposeful activity. It was recognised as an important process in academic contexts, yet rejected as something too "planned", evoking feelings of awkwardness and being uncomfortable, as well as going against one's nature.

> My association with networking is a piece of advice I was given early on in my career that it is very important to network and I remember thinking at the time that it seemed so planned. [...] I think networking actually involves more planned, more directed approach, and it is about identifying people from whom you can benefit in some way. And I often find myself feeling almost awkward at conferences about meeting useful contacts. (A9)

For the sake of analytically distinguishing these two different construals of networking, we may call them 'organic' and 'strategic' networking. Organic networking refers to an incremental activity, in which networks arise either through social means or through research groups or collaborations. Organic networking also includes an idea of egalitarian, peer-based reciprocity. Strategic networking refers to networking as a purposeful activity done in order to advance one's career, or deliberate attempts to network with people in more powerful positions, especially outside the context of a shared research project.

Whilst the value connotations of these two understandings were by no means unanimous, strategic networking was often given a negative connotation, even presenting a caricature of a networker, implying a rude and self- important person, somebody one does not want to identify with.

> I am not comfortable with that idea of getting to know someone only for specific purposes, [to have] lunch with someone at a conference or sit near someone just because I want something. I don't like that kind of meaning for networking. (A1)

> I don't think I would become a strong networker ... you know this type of person who takes the initiative, go to interrupt people while they are chatting with others just to say hello. (A4)

However, the portrayal of strategic networking was not wholly negative, and its importance was perceived to increase over one's career. Participants also pointed out that funding schemes and the general competitiveness of academia nowadays requires strategic collaborative partners, and that external funding requires increasing networking in order to submit applications based on collaborative research. This represents a way to construe a positive notion of strategic networking. The necessity of establishing networks of researchers in order to apply for funds and conduct research appears to nuance the perceived negative features of strategic networking. Perhaps funding acquisition provides a sense of common enterprise towards a shared goal, thus liberating strategic networking from its individualistic traits, such as personal career progression, and adding a sense of collective endeavour benefitting a group of colleagues. However, the distinction between organic and strategic networking processes was not always easily identifiable.

Perceptions of Networking and Gender

While the participants approached networking as a purposeful activity with an ambiguous attitude, they also indicated having encountered a whole host of cultural expectations as to how women should behave, which seemed to discourage networking. For example, women are perceived to rely on their looks to get ahead, they should be seen but not heard, they should not make a big deal of themselves, they should have appropriate topics for discussion, or be interested in particular research methods. Some participants also expressed feeling uncomfortable being 'visible' in a way implied by the activity of networking.

> For me [networking] is about making yourself visible. I don't often feel comfortable making myself visible in front of men, seniors, academics, researchers etc. So I think that's something I bear in mind. And I also find as a woman I think about how I dress[…] whether I'll be taken seriously depending on how I look and how I talk. So I am definitely aware of the male gaze more. With women I feel much more comfortable. (A9)

However, despite the fact that participants explicitly voiced a perception of gender bias in academia, where they even expected to be treated differently from men, some participants also wanted to challenge what was perceived to be the role assigned for women, namely one based on looks or certain kind of behaviour.

> I know it's there and I've seen research on how young female scholars are not taken seriously but I just choose to ignore it, just literally. I mean, I know the evidence is there but I ignore it because I will not let this sort of thing influence the type of research I can make. I know if I want to get anywhere I have to produce quality work. (A5)

Some of the participants told of having encountered bullying or gendered jokes in the work place and presented different responses to that. They portrayed a discrepancy between the official discourse and the reality of (in) equality encountered by some of the women. One of the interviewees presumed that women play along with the gendered jokes in order to gain access to the "boys' club", while two others pointed out conscious resistance to the expected stereotypes of female behaviour, and refusal of the participants to acknowledge in their behaviour that these existed.

Although this study does not reveal anything about the real differences in the networking of men and women, the participants themselves perceived there to be a difference (Ibarra 1997; Burt 1998). Men were thought to have a more strategic or perhaps more competitive approach to networking than women, and some participants pointed out that they had received encouragement from male peers or mentors or colleagues to "better stick up for themselves".

I have a feeling that yes [men network more strategically], but it's just a hunch. […] When I scan through people that I know, I would say that in men's group the majority do that, in the women's group only some. (A10)

I've got the same advice from numerous I would say male bosses. […] They think that (networking) is very important. You need to go out there, you know, shake hands with people and introduce yourself. And to me, I am just like … I mean I do it because I am more curious, not because I want to get something. […] So I think maybe it works, maybe there is this gender thing. I don't know, but for me it doesn't feel comfortable. (A7)

Discussion

The different understandings of networks and networking presented by our participants can be summarised in the following tables: functional networks and work-based networking are linked, as are peer group networks and access to them based on shared attributes; or strategic networking motivation and purposeful networking process. The participants often saw two sides of the networking coin: i.e. although some individuals indicated that they were not comfortable with strategic networking, they at the same time thought it important or necessary in academic careers (Tables 14.1 and 14.2).

While this empirical observation is easy to understand, and aligns well with the previous research on women's networking in academia (Kaufmann 1978; Brass 1985; Burt 1998; Higgins 2000), it is more challenging to discuss its implications for our conceptual understanding of networking and networks as pertaining to the social capital and its use in leveraging positions in academia. As our case illustrates, early career women adopt different opinions regarding networking in the field of academia. We find examples where strategic networking with more established

Table 14.1 Networks and network access

Definition of networks	Functional networks	Peer group networks	Information sharing networks (hierarchical/non-hierarchical)
Access to networks	Work-based	Attribute-based	Mediated by institutions or seniors

Table 14.2 Networking motivations and process

Motivations for networking	Curiosity-driven or socially-driven	Strategic
Networking process	Organic	Purposeful

people in the academic field is preferred, but also examples of preferred networking with other early-career peers based on social relations and mutual interests. However, as some participants pointed out, their ability to network is partially dependent on the leverage their supervisors, mentors and senior colleagues, as well as the standing of the institutions they are affiliated with can offer, in order to be able to access a targeted network, and thus position themselves in the field.

The participants seemed to have a nuanced awareness of the stratification of the field and the operation of the two types of power in academia, namely academic power related to the control over resource distribution and scientific power, linked to scientific knowledge production and its related reputation (c.f. Bourdieu 1988; Delanty 2005). On the one hand they perceived as important connections those with academics who possess academic power and therefore are able to offer a potential contact for job opportunities. On the other hand they deem as important those link-ages to academics with scientific power, considered valuable contacts in terms of advice for research activities while also offering reputation gains through their own status. Academic and scientific power also play out differently at different points of the process, and the nature of the power dynamics are very different in a context of a local competitive horizon of one's own institution (Hoffmann et al. 2011), than when operating on a global competitive horizon, where the relevant networks may be less immediate and localised. The gendered nature of networking in academia is evident in the way our participants reported having encountered gendered treatment, stereo-typing or jokes as women; and in their perception that women's networking differs from men's. Previous research argues that (younger) women are outsiders in aca-demia with less legitimacy, and thus less capacity to network on their own, and that they are better off if they are able to use mentors and supervisors to mediate their access to networks in the field (Burt 1998). Our participants demonstrated a desire to consciously challenge and step over the gender divide, for example by actively chal-lenging the stereotypes of appropriate behaviour for women; or by seeking to strate-gically network even if they were uncomfortable with it or by emphasising networking as a social, curiosity driven activity amongst peers rather than an activity aiming at personal gains through connecting with more senior colleagues.

In the comment stage for this study, a question was raised about how the early career women in our sample seemed to be determined to network, even when they did not necessarily feel very comfortable with it. Our commentator pointed out that perhaps our sample comprised ambitious 'high flyers', who were determined to 'get on'. The importance of networking was, indeed, not challenged in the interviews, which tells about the widely held, deeply seated belief in the importance of network-ing for an academic career, but also to the nature of academic work itself. Instead of abandoning efforts to network when it clashed with their personal inclination, our participants reframed what counted as networking, what were the motivations for doing it and whom to network with. The concepts of compliance and differentiation (Deephouse 1999) are useful here. On the one hand, we may view networking with actors holding higher positions or prestige as an example of compliance with the established rules of the field and the perceived traditional goal of reaching higher positions. On the other hand networking with lower-prestige peers is a way of dif-ferentiating or distancing oneself from the mainstream rules and creating a new set of rules for playing the 'game'. The multiple voices from the group interviews demonstrate that early career women construe networking strategies along the lines of both compliance and differentiation (Deephouse 1999), often at the same time. While networking along the lines of compliance strategy is recognised as important, the early career women also demonstrate a desire to redefine the rules of the field by using differentiation strategy in their networking, thus challenging Burt's findings (1998) and his notion that only mediated networking is available for women, while they do not hold enough credibility for more autonomous types of networking. Following our reasoning on compliance and differentiation, we can assume that early career women act as strategic as well as organic networkers. These two different roles carry different types of agency as the individuals engage through the strategic or organic networker roles to find space for themselves in the academic field.

Strategic networkers accept the dominant rules of the field and strive to follow them by engaging in networking with established seniors in the field and thus seek to legitimate their position. Organic networkers contest those rules and try to establish an alternative set of rules in order to legitimise themselves and establish agency for themselves. In Bourdieu's words, early career women are aware of the struggle for stakes in the academic field and perceive themselves as carriers of alternative stakes. Along this continuum, it is relevant to scrutinize the different roles combining both strategic networker and organic networker characteristics. This will allow us to characterise more in-depth the dynamics between agents – individuals and groups – and the field as well as the perceptions of early career women on their mutual relationships. Early career women are aware of and do consider strategies of compliance and differentiation with respect to networking. In this sense they reflect the shifting balance between structure – rules, norms, values – and agency – the capacity of individuals and groups to originate change in the field and its social institutions. Further research is needed to determine to what extent socialisation into the rules of the field influences the networking strategies selected by the early career women. We may hypothesise that longer stay and a higher position in academia contributes to a more traditional understanding of the rationales, uses and implications of networking.

Conclusion

This paper has sought to sharpen our understanding of the topical phenomenon of networking in academia, as perceived by those who are presented with multiple disadvantages in networking both on the account of their gender as well as of their junior position in academia. This may have implications for the attractiveness of and retention on the academic career especially on the crucial early career stage. Previous research shows that networking on the early career stage is linked to higher research productivity of early career researchers and enhances the post-doctoral experience (Scaffidi and Berman 2011), thus contributing to attractiveness and retention. Also, junior academics might become discouraged about their career prospects when they face rejections for publications (Hermanowicz 2012). Against this backdrop, participating in networks – particularly with peers – can help over-coming such difficult phases in one's career, and can prevent selecting out from submitting papers or dropping out altogether from academia. Similarly, the role of mentors as contributing to academics' decision to pursue an academic career (Lindholm 2004), or to foster the scholarly agency of early career researchers (Griffin et al. 2015) is significant. Finally, the impact that socialization experiences, such as the access to networks, have on the self-perceptions of female academics and their perception of their career opportunities cannot be overlooked (c.f. Astin 1984), if we are interested on the retention of early career female scholars.

In terms of understanding the networking perceptions of early career female scholars, this study has certain obvious limitations and gaps, that could be remedied in future research. Empirically, the most conspicuous omission is that the notions of family and children are missing on practical grounds from the group interviews, even given that networking in relation to gender was one of the topics discussed, and that as previous research consistently points out, female academics with chil-dren are at a disadvantage in terms of their career progression (Levinson et al. 1989; Carr et al. 1998; Thanacoody et al. 2006). The most likely reason for there being hardly any mention of family in the data is that we as researchers did not include it in the agenda when designing the study. Another gap arises from the European focus of the study, as all but two of the participants were of European origin, and all but one were working in European higher education institutions. All but one of the par-ticipants were of Caucasian ethnicity and mainly worked in what can be classified as research universities. In the next stage, therefore, it is important to include wider institutional and disciplinary perspectives, as well as the broader cultural and ethnic diversity of early career women to enable us to reflect upon the salience of the find-ings of the study. An international comparative setting would offer a potential for the critical discussion of networking perceptions of early career female scholars, highlighting the potential differences in a global context, whilst a comparison with early career male scholars, or alternatively with more established female academics, would offer valuable comparisons to contrast with the identified perceptions of early career female academics.

Finally, the organized settings of academic careers have not been used explicitly in our analysis. Recent research has shown that what Neave and Rhoades (1987) describe as department structure (with lower status distance between juniors and seniors) and chair structure (with higher status distance between the chair holder and his/her assistants) affect academic career prospects differently (Fumasoli 2015; Fumasoli et al. 2015). Hence a future venue for research would be to investigate how department and chair models influence the networking of early career women.

Conceptually, examining the different roles combining both strategic networker and organic networker characteristics would allow us to characterise more in-depth the dynamics between individuals, groups, and the field as well as the perceptions of early career women on their mutual relationships. Early career women are aware of and do consider strategies of compliance and differentiation with regard to net-working and its uses. In this sense they reflect the shifting balance between struc-ture – rules, norms, values – and agency – the capacity of individuals and groups to originate change in the field and its social institutions. Further research is needed to determine to what extent socialisation into the rules of the field influences the networking strategies selected by early career women.

Appendices

Appendix 1 Respondents' Characteristics[a]

	Position	Country	Age	Memberships	Year of PhD
A1	Post-doc researcher	Portugal	37	ECHER, APS, EAIR	2009
A2	Post-doc researcher	Portugal	33	CHER	2011
A3	PhD student	Finland	39	ECHER, EMA	–
A4	PhD student	Switzerland	30	EGOS	–
A5	PhD student	Norway	30	ECHER	–
A6	PhD student	Norway	37	Euredocs	–
A7	Post-doc researcher	Norway	41	CHER, 4S, NEON	2006
A8	Assistant professor	Portugal	41	CHER, ESA	2006
A9	Assistant professor	Croatia	34	HSD	n.a.
A10	PhD student	Slovenia	30	ECHER, CHER, EAIR	–
A11	Associate professor	Russia	38	n.a.	2003
A12	Associate professor	South Africa	47	HELTASA, BERA, EAIR	2002

[a]The name of the institution and the nationality of the participants have been deleted for considerations of anonymity.

Appendix 2

Early career women in academia (ECW): perceptions of networking
Interview template and tentative research questions
General RQ: What does our case tell us about early career women's networking in academic community?

RQ1: What is the self-perception of ECW like?

☐   What does early career mean to you?
☐   When is the early career stage finished?

RQ2: What definitions do ECW give for networking?

☐   What does networking mean for you?

RQ3: For what reasons do ECW network?

☐   Within the context of how you understand the networks, think about your own networking, and reasons for making any…why did/do you network?
☐   What did/do you want to achieve?
☐   What motivated/motivates you?

RQ4: With whom <u>do ECW mostly network?</u>

☐   Who do you network with?
☐   Whom do you find out to be most/least successful for networking and why?

RQ5: <u>To what extent is networking an active or passive process – are ECW borrow-ing or constructing their own networks?</u>

☐   Please describe how you go about networking.
☐   Are you getting included in the existing networks, or creating your own ones? Whose networks are those existing ones? Do you find one of them more/less successful and why do you think so?

RQ6: <u>How do ECW perceive the effects of their gender and/or of the people they networking with on the networking processes?</u>

☐   Is it harder or easier for you to network because you are women, and why do you think so?
☐   Is it/was it easier/harder for you to network yourself or to tap into existing network?
☐   Do you think gender have any effect on the process of your networking?
☐   Have you ever been excluded from some network on the basis of gender?
☐   Is there is anything you would like to add?

Appendix 3: NVivo Coding

1. Networking rationale
   Functional
   Information sharing
   Learning and socializing
   Normative
   Opportunistic
   Social
2. Networking access
   Collaborative
   Mediated
   Social
3. Networking approach
   Institutional
   Personal
4. Networking motivation
   Organic
   Strategic
     Identity-based
   Impediments to networking
5. Networking type
   Formal
   Informal

References

Aisenberg, N., & Harrington, M. (1988). *Women of academe: Outsiders in the scared grove.* Amherst: University of Massachusetts Press.

Altman, B. W., & Post, J. E. (1996). Beyond the 'social contract': An analysis of the executive view at twenty-five large companies. In D. T. Hall, & Associates (Eds.), *The career is dead – long live the career: A relational approach to careers* (pp. 46–71). San Francisco: Jossey-Bass.

Arthur, M. B., & Rousseau, D. M. (1996). The boundaryless career as a new employment principle. In M. B. Arthur & D. M. Rousseau (Eds.), *The boundaryless career* (pp. 3–20). New York: Oxford University Press.

Astin, H. S. (1984). The meaning of work in women's lives: A sociopsychological model of career choice and work behavior. *The Counseling Psychologist, 12*(4), 117–126.

Atkinson, P., & Delamont, S. (1990). Professions and powerlessness: Female marginality in the learned occupations. *Sociological Review, 38*(1), 90–110.

Bagilhole, B. (1993). Survivors in a male preserve: A Study of British Women Academics' experiences and perceptions of discrimination in a UK University. *Higher Education, 26,* 431–447.

Bagilhole, B. (2000). Against the odds? Reflections on women's research opportunities. In G. Howie (Ed.), *Feminist pedagogy.* London: Ashgate.

Bagilhole, B., & Goode, J. (2001). The contradiction of the myth of individual merit, and the reality of a patriarchal support system in academic careers: A feminist investigation. *The European Journal of Women's Studies, 8*(2), 161–180.

Baugh, S. G., & Scandura, T. A. (1999). The effects of multiple mentors on protege attitudes toward the work setting. *Journal of Social Behavior & Personality, 14*(4), 503–521.

Bazeley, P., Kemp, L., Stevens, K., Asmar, C., Grbich, C., Marh, H., & Bhathal, R. (1996). *Wailing in the wings: A study of early career academic researchers in Australia* (National Board of Employment, Education and Training Commissioned Report No. 50). Canberra: Australian Government Publishing Service.

Bourdieu, P. (1988). *Homo academicus.* Cambridge: Polity Press.

Bourdieu, P., & Wacquant, L. (1992). *Towards a reflexive sociology.* Oxford: Polity.

Brass, D. J. (1985). Men's and women's networks: A study of interaction patterns and influence in an organization. *Academy of Management Journal, 28,* 327–343.

Brass, D. J. (1992). Power in organizations: A social network perspective. *Research in Politics and Society, 4,* 295–323.

Broido, E. M., & Manning, K. (2002). Philosophical foundations and current theoretical perspectives in qualitative research. *Journal of College Student Development, 43*(4), 434.

Burt, R. S. (1998). The gender of social capital. *Rationality and Society, 10*(1), 5–46.

Burt, R. S. (2000). The network structure of social capital. *Research in Organizational Behaviour, 22,* 345–423.

Carr, P. L., Ash, A. S., Friedman, R. H., Scaramucci, A., Barnett, R. C., Szalacha, E., Palepu, A., & Moskowitz, M. A. (1998). Relation of family responsibilities and gender to the productivity and career satisfaction of medical faculty. *Annals of Internal Medicine, 129*(7), 532–538.

Clark, B. R. (1983). *The higher education system.* Berkeley: University of California Press.

De Janasz, S. C., & Sullivan, S. E. (2004). Multiple mentoring in academe: Developing the professorial network. *Journal of Vocational Behavior, 64,* 263–283.

Deephouse, D. L. (1999). To be different, or to be the same? It's a question (and theory) of strategic balance. *Strategic Management Journal, 20,* 147–166.

Delanty, G. (2005). The sociology of the university and higher education: The consequences of globalization. In C. Calhoun, C. Rojek, & B. Turner (Eds.), *The SAGE handbook of sociology.* London: Sage.

Denzin, N. K., & Lincoln, Y. S. (Eds.). (1994). *Handbook of qualitative research.* Thousand Oaks: Sage Publications.

Fetzer, J. (2003). Becoming an integral part of your field (or networking for more success). *Building a Professional Career, 376*(7), 943–944.

Forret, M. L., & Dougherty, T. W. (2004). Networking behaviours and career outcomes: Differences for men and women? *Journal of Organizational Behaviour, 25*(3), 419–438.

Fumasoli, T. (2015). Strategic management of personnel policies: A comparative analysis of Flagship universities in Norway, Finland, Switzerland and Austria. In F. Ribeiro, Y. Politis, & B. Culum (Eds.), *New voices in higher education research and scholarship*. Advances in Higher Education & Professional Development. IGI Global.

Fumasoli, T., Goastellec, G., & Kehm, B. (Eds.). (2015). *Academic work and careers in Europe – trends, challenges, perspectives*. Dordrecht: Springer.

Gornitzka, Å. (2009). Networking administration in areas of national sensitivity: The commission and European higher education. In A. Amaral, G. Neave, C. Musselin, & P. Maassen (Eds.), *European integration and the governance of higher education and research* (Higher Education Dynamics, Vol. 26, pp. 109–131). Dordrecht: Springer.

Greenhaus, J., & Callanan, G. A. (1994). *Career management* (2nd ed.). New York: Dryden Press.

Griffin, K., Eury, J., Gaffney, M., York, T., Bennett, J., Cunningham, E., & Griffin, A. (2015). *Digging deeper: Exploring the relationship between mentoring, developmental interactions, and student agency*. New Directions for Higher Education, 171.

Hakim, C. (1994). *We are all self-employed*. San Francisco: Berrett-Koehler.

Hermanowicz, J. C. (2012). The sociology of academic careers: Problems and prospects. In J. C. Smart & M. B. Paulsen (Eds.), *Higher education: Handbook of theory and research* (pp. 207–248). Dordrecht: Springer.

Higgins, M. C. (2000). The more, the merrier? Multiple developmental relationships and work satisfaction. *Journal of Management Development, 19*, 277–296.

Higgins, M. C. (2001). Reconceptualizing mentoring at work: A developmental network perspective. *Academy of Management Review, 26*(2), 254–288.

Higgins, M. C., & Thomas, D. A. (2001). Constellations and careers: Toward understanding the effects of multiple developmental relationships. *Journal of Organizational Behavior, 22*, 223–247.

Hoffman, D., Raunio, M., & Korhonen, M. (2011). Finnish Universities: Car dealerships, churches or cultural institutions? In P. Teixeira & D. Dill (Eds.), *Public vices, private virtues? Assessing the effects of marketization in higher education* (pp. 273–296). Rotterdam: Sense Publications.

Ibarra, H. (1992). Homophily and differential returns: Sex differences in network structure and access in an advertising firm. *Administrative Science Quarterly, 37*, 422–447.

Ibarra, H. (1993). Personal networks of women and minorities in management: A conceptual framework. *Academy of Management Review, 18*, 56–87.

Ibarra, H. (1997). Paving an alternative route: Gender differences in managerial networks. *Social Psychology Quarterly, 60*, 91–102.

Ismail, M., & Rasdi, R. M. (2007). Impact of networking on career development: Experience of high-flying women academics in Malaysia. *Human Resource Development International, 10*(2), 153–168.

Kaufman, D. R. (1978). Associational ties in academe: Some male and female differences. *Sex Roles, 4*(1), 9–21.

Kram, K. E., & Isabella, L. A. (1985). Mentoring alternatives: The role of peer relationships in career development. *Academy of Management Journal, 28*(1), 110–132.

Leathwood, C., & Read, B. (2009). *Gender and the changing face of the higher education. A feminized future?* New York: SRHE/Open University Press.

Ledwith, S., & Manfredi, S. (2000). Balancing gender in higher education: A study of experience of senior women in a 'New' UK University. *The European Journal of Women's Studies, 7*, 7–33.

Levinson, W., Tolle, S. W., & Lewis, C. (1989). Women in academic medicine, combining career and family. *The New England Journal of Medicine, 321*(22), 1511–1517.

Lindholm, J. (2004). Pathways to the professoriate: The role of self, others, and environment in shaping academic career aspirations. *The Journal of Higher Education, 75*(6), 603–635.

Maack, M. N., & Passet, J. E. (1993). Unwritten rules: Mentoring women faculty. *Library and Information Science Research, 15*, 117–141.

March, J., & Olsen, J. (1989). *Rediscovering institutions: The organizational basis of politics.* New York: The Free Press.

March, J., & Olsen, J. (1995). *Democratic governance.* New York: The Free Press.

March, J., & Olsen, J. (2006). The logic of appropriateness. In M. Moran, M. Rein, & R. E. Goodin (Eds.), *The Oxford handbook of public policy.* Oxford: Oxford University Press.

Marginson, S., & Rhoades, G. (2002). Beyond national states, markets, and systems of higher education: A glonacal agency heuristic. *Higher Education, 43*(3), 281–309.

Mavin, S., & Bryans, P. (2002). Academic women in the UK: Mainstreaming our experiences and networking for action. *Gender and Education, 14*(3), 235–250.

McGuire, G. (2002). Gender, race, and the shadow structure: A study of informal networks and inequality in a work organization. *Gender & Society, 16*, 303–322.

Miles, M. B., & Huberman, A. M. (1994). *Qualitative data analysis: An expanded sourcebook* (2nd ed.). Thousand Oaks: Sage Publications.

Miller, J., Lincoln, J., & Olson, J. (1981). Rationality and equity in professional networks: Gender and race as factors in the stratification of interorganizational systems. *American Journal of Sociology, 87*, 308–335.

Mirvis, P. H., & Hall, D. T. (1996). New organizational forms and the new career. In D. T. Hall & Associates (Eds.), *The career is dead—long live the career: A relational approach to careers* (pp. 72–101). San Francisco: Jossey-Bass.

Moore, G. (1990). Structural determinants of men's and women's personal networks. *American Sociological Review, 55*, 726–735.

Nabi, G. R. (1999). An investigation into the differential profile of predictors of objective and subjective career success. *Career Development International, 4*(4), 212–224.

Nabi, G. R. (2003). Situational characteristics and subjective career success: The mediating role of career enhancing strategies. *International Journal of Manpower, 24*(6), 653–672.

Nahapiet, J., & Ghoshal, S. (1998). Social capital, intellectual capital, and the organizational advantage. *Academy of Management Review, 23*(2), 242–266.

Neave, G., & Rhoades, G. (1987). The academic estate in Western Europe. In B. C. Clark (Ed.), *The academic profession. National, disciplinary, and institutional settings* (pp. 211–270). Berkeley: University of California Press.

O'Leary, V. E., & Mitchell, J. M. (1990). Women connecting with women: Networks and mentors in the United States. In S. S. Lie & V. E. O'Leary (Eds.), *Storming the tower: Women in the academic world.* London: Kogan Page.

Peluchette, J. (1993). Subjective career success: The influence of individual difference, family and organizational variables. *Journal of Vocational Behavior, 43*, 198–208.

Quinlan, K. M. (1999). Enhancing mentoring and networking of junior academic women: What, why and how? *Journal of Higher Education Policy and Management, 21*(1), 31–42.

Rothstein, M. G., & Davey, L. M. (1995). Gender differences in network relationships in Academia. *Women in Management Review, 10*(6), 20–25.

Šadl, Z. (2009). We women are no good at it: Networking in academia. *Sociologický časopis/Czech Sociological Review, 45*(6), 1239–1263.

Scaffidi, A. K., & Berman, J. E. (2011). A positive postdoctoral experience is related to quality supervision and career mentoring, collaborations, networking and a nurturing research environment. *Higher Education, 62*(6), 685–698.

Schwandt, T. A. (1994). Constructivist, interpretivist approaches to human inquiry. In N. K. Denzin & Y. S. Lincoln (Eds.), *Handbook of qualitative research* (pp. 118–137). Thousand Oaks: Sage Publications.

Sullivan, S. E. (1999). The changing nature of careers: A review and research agenda. *Journal of Management, 25*, 457–484.

Thanacoody, P. R., Bartram, T., Barker, M., & Jacobs, K. (2006). Career progression among female academics: A comparative study of Australia and Mauritius. *Women in Management Review, 21*(7), 536–553.

Tichy, N. M. (1981). Networks in organizations. In P. C. Nystrom & W. H. Starbuck (Eds.), *Handbook of organization design* (Vol. 2). New York: Oxford University Press.

Toren, N. (2001). Women in academe: The Israeli case. *International Journal of Sociology and Social Policy, 21*(1/2), 50–56.

Toren, N. (1991). Women at the top: Female full professors in higher education in Israel. In G. P. Kelly & S. Slaughter (Eds.), *Women's higher education in comparative perspective* (pp. 165–184). Dordrecht: Kluwer Academic Publishers.

Vasil, L. (1996). Social process skills and career achievement among male and female academics. *Journal of Higher Education, 67*(1), 103–114.

Vazquez-Cupeiro, S., & Elston, M. A. (2006). Gender and academic career trajectories in Spain: From gendered passion to consecration in a sistema endogamico? *Employee Relations, 28*(6), 588–603.

Välimaa, J., Stenvall, J., Kuoppala, K., Lyytinen, A., Nokkala, T., Pekkola, E., & Siekkinen, T. (2014). *Enter, exit and being in academic careers.* Unpublished manuscript.

Whiting, V. R., & De Janasz, S. C. (2004). Mentoring in the 21st century: Using the Internet to build skills and networks. *Journal of Management Education, 28*(3), 275–293.

Chapter 15
Beyond the Academic Glass Ceiling: Notes on the Situation of Women Professors in Brazil

Marília Moschkovich

Since the second half of the twentieth century the participation of women in higher levels of education has been increasing, after centuries of systematic exclusion. In many countries women are now both graduate as well as undergraduate students, and also researchers and professors. In 1962 in France, for example, 64 % of women aged 25 or more had higher education diplomas, a proportion that was dramatically increased in the following decades, reaching 79 % in 1990 (Maruani 2006). In Brazil, women have been the majority of PhD earners annually since 2004 (Galvão 2010).

Recent studies have pointed out, however, that although women's access to different roles in universities is fundamental to achieve gender equality, it is definitely not enough. A well-known metaphor that describes the difficulty of women achieving higher positions in society or in a career is the idea of a *glass ceiling*. Thus, if a "*glass ceiling*" can be found in a certain career, it means that although women are present there, they seem to be held back by invisible barriers, and not be able to reach for positions with higher status, power or salary (those three are often associated with each other).

However, broader studies on various types of careers to which women have access show two kinds of gender inequality that are also present in the academic workplace. The first one is often called "*horizontal concentration*": an expression which refers to the concentration of women in certain areas or careers when compared to others. In simpler words, *horizontal concentration* takes place when women have access to specific fields of study or careers but not to others. This would be similar to – still in the "glass" metaphor – *glass walls* that allow women to move "freely" at their own field, or between fields, but only within certain limits.

M. Moschkovich (✉)
State University of Campinas, Campinas, Brazil
e-mail: mari.moscou@gmail.com

© Springer International Publishing Switzerland 2017
H. Eggins (ed.), *The Changing Role of Women in Higher Education*,
The Changing Academy – The Changing Academic Profession in International
Comparative Perspective 17, DOI 10.1007/978-3-319-42436-1_15

At the same time, careers and fields of study to which women have either low or high access are reported to have shown what Maruani (2006) called "*vertical concentration*". This is also known as being a "*pipeline*" of inequality or disadvantage: women have trouble getting to the higher levels inside a specific career. This is the "*glass ceiling*" mentioned above.

When it comes to the academic career, the glass (either in the shape of walls or ceilings) seems to be quite thin, transparent and clean. Spotless, it gives us the realistic impression that there are no barriers on our way. In countries such as the USA (DiPrete and Buchmann 2013), Brazil (Carvalho 2003) or France (Baudelot and Establet 1992), throughout the whole school system, from preschool to graduate schools, women are the majority of students and/or have better grades. Logic tells us, then, that they should also do well in their academic career. Unfortunately, this is not their current situation in many universities around the world (Acker et al. 2012; Bagilhole 1993; Bordi and Vélez Bautista 2007; Fox 2001; Moschkovich and Almeida 2015; Musselin 2008).

In this chapter, the case of Brazil is considered, in the hope of investigating which mechanisms operate in keeping such invisible walls and ceilings going – and if they are maintained, given certain specificities of the Brazilian academic career. The particular case of Brazilian public research universities may bring a new perspective on the subject of gendered vertical and horizontal concentration in the academic career for different reasons. First, because professors at such institutions are public employees, and they are granted permanence in their posts, regardless of their circumstances. This also means that their salary and conditions of employment do not need to be negotiated within the individual institution. Men and women have identical conditions of employment. Secondly, being a professor in a research university is a well-paid job (Barbosa Filho et al. 2009; Schwartzman 2012), making it possible for both male and female professors to hire domestic employees and other services in order to spare more time for work if needed. Such characteristics suggest that gender inequality in the academic career ladder in Brazil could be significantly less than in other countries (at least potentially).

As will be seen further in this chapter, both the situation of different institutions in the Brazilian higher education system and the actual practices which go on within universities show us that gender definitely has an impact on how male and female professors develop their careers – although in an unexpected way. This chapter gives a broader view of the Brazilian higher education system, the variety of types of institutions and work conditions associated with each of them, as well as the presence and distribution of women in such jobs and careers. It then investigates the case of one of the top research universities in the country, to examine how its male and female professors are distributed in different areas and disciplines. The chances of arriving at the top position of the academic career are considered, as to whether there is any difference among men and women in each of these areas and disciplines, and if there is any relationship between women's access to a certain area or discipline and their actual chances of arriving at the top position. The results show, in the end, that glass ceilings and walls are not as present as they might seem, but, at the same time, that the lack of a glass ceiling does not mean that there are no hindrances.

To understand the particular position of being a professor in a public state university in Brazil it is important to keep in mind that the category "professor" as a whole is very diverse in this country. This diversity is especially strong when comparing the different institutions where they work and the working conditions they experience there. Higher education institutions differ from each other in terms of their organizational structure and in terms of their administrative model. As to the organization, legislation defines three main kinds of institutions: universities, university-like centers ("*centros universitários*") and non-university institutions. Universities should be multidisciplinary, and must work on teaching/learning as well as research and community service ("*extensão*"). University-like Centers can also be multidisciplinary, but focus primarily on teaching/learning. Both of them have the autonomy to create their own courses. Non-University Institutions, on the other hand, can be mono-disciplinary, are dedicated to teaching/learning only and do not have the autonomy to create courses. In terms of administrative model, they can be public or private. Public institutions can be federal, state or city-level managed; this is dependent on which State structure is responsible, administratively and financially, for them. Private institutions can be philanthropic or non- philanthropic. These are the main distinctions made by the Ministry of Education (MEC) among higher education institutions in Brazil.[1]

Differences in working conditions and contracts are also found between each of these kinds of institutions, and sometimes within them. They vary between more and less stable contracts, higher and lower salaries and more and less time dedicated to either teaching or research. At one end of the spectrum there are those who have PhDs, who work exclusively in teaching and research, have employment stability and higher salaries. At the other end, there are those who have just finished a BA and work as substitute professors, are paid lower salaries based on hours of work and are hired on temporary contracts. In between these two extremes there is a great variety of trajectories and work conditions among Brazilian professors. Women are not equally distributed among them.

When considering the whole of Brazilian higher education institutions, women constitute 44,8 % of professors, with 44,3 % of them in the public universities – the type of institution with the highest prestige, where research can be done, and generally with better work conditions such as stable contracts, higher salaries, etc. This proportion drops when one analyzes only the southeast of Brazil (the wealthiest region, with the highest concentration of prestigious universities), and even more when considering only the state of São Paulo (where the top research universities are concentrated). These data, shown below in Graph 15.1, indicate that women appear to be slightly horizontally concentrated in institutions with worse work conditions and salaries, and less scientific and academic prestige. Graph 15.2 reinforces

---

[1] For a broader discussion on the differences among institutions and work conditions for higher education professors in Brazil, see Balbachevsky (2007), Balbachevsky and Quinteiro (2003), Schwartzman (2012) and Stromquist et al. (2007).

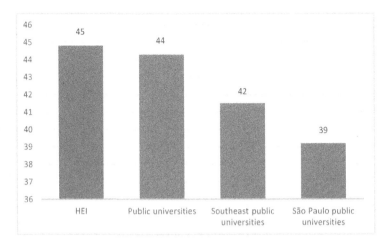

Graph 15.1 Proportion of women among professors in higher education institutions (HEI) in general and specifically in public universities – Brazil, Southeast Brazil and São Paulo State (2010) (Source: Sinopses estatísticas do Censo Nacional de Educação Superior (INEP 2010))

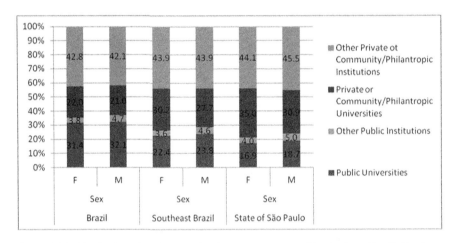

Graph 15.2 Distribution of professors of each sex among types of institution – Brazil, Southeast Brazil, State of São Paulo (2010) (Source: Sinopses estatísticas do Censo Nacional de Educação Superior (INEP 2010))

that perception by showing how women and men are differently distributed among types of institutions – and how women concentrate, a little more than their male counterparts, in private higher education institutions.

It is noteworthy that the State University of Campinas (Unicamp).[2] is located in the southeast region of Brazil, in the state of São Paulo, because it is one of the most

---

[2] The case study of the State University of Campinas presented here derives from the work done by Moschkovich (2013) and by Moschkovich and Almeida (2015).

important research universities in Brazil. According to its institutional website, it alone is responsible for 10 % of all of graduate courses in the country, and its professors are authors of at least 15 % of all research done nationally (Unicamp 2015). However, it is also less accessible to female professors, in general, than other central research universities and had a lower than the average proportion of women professors (only 36,7%) found in the state in 2011. Why is it so?

One could wonder whether that would be an effect of its history and, specially, of the role it was meant to play in the Brazilian higher education system when it was created. Since its foundation in the 1960s, Unicamp has been designed to play a central role in the development of the State of São Paulo and of the whole country. That meant boosting technological research and putting more effort into applied scientific areas at that time (Castilho and Soares 2008). As women have historically been excluded from such disciplines and research areas, it would indeed be expected for them to be less present as Unicamp professors. However, an overview of the number of professors allocated to each research area in that university nowadays, shown in Table 15.1 below, removes this impression.

As shown above, in 2011 professors working in biomedical sciences and human sciences and arts – research areas that have been reported as being more open to women than engineering or pure sciences – represented 53,72 % of the total. Of course such areas are not exclusively feminine, but nor are pure sciences and engineering exclusively masculine. That is enough to exclude a supposedly heavier concentration of applied science disciplines as the cause of the low access of women professors to Unicamp. Judging only by the faculty data that were available at the time of this research, however, it is impossible to determine the causes of such a low access to women as professors at Unicamp. What the faculty data show us, though, is equally valuable and interesting: they reveal how gender differences and inequalities are expressed in the positions achieved by female professors in a permanent career, governed by impersonal rules (rules which are actually disputed by them and formulated by the faculty as a whole).

Unicamp professors are, as previously explained, public employees. They are hired by the State (more specifically by the state of São Paulo's government) to teach in undergraduate as well as in graduate courses, and also to do research. More than 90 % of its professors are exclusively dedicated to teaching and research (Unicamp 2012, 2015). They enter the career by a public process of selection called

Table 15.1 Professors allocated in biomedical sciences, human sciences and arts, engineering sciences and exact sciences – number (n) and proportion in total (%) – Unicamp, 2011

Research area	Number of professors (n)	Proportion in total (%)
Biomedical Sciences	556	31.11
Human Sciences & Arts	404	22.61
Engineering Sciences	529	29.60
Exact Sciences	298	16.68
Unicamp total	1787	100.00

Source: Unicamp, Human Resources Secretariat 2011

"*concurso*", in which they apply to teach a specific course in a bachelor's program. However, research is considered an essential duty of its professors, something to be demanded from them and something that plays a central role in career promotion criteria (Unicamp 2008).

In 2011, the year whose data we have analyzed, the institutionalized career of professor was organized in three levels at Unicamp: MS3 (entrance level), MS5 (middle level) and MS6 (top level). The promotion from MS3 to MS5 depends on an evaluation made by peers in the specific school or college (called "*faculdades*" or "*institutos*") in which the applicant works. The promotion to MS6 involves a new "*concurso*", which means a post is open not only to internal applicants (those who are already professors at MS5 level at Unicamp), but publicly to anyone who meets the requirements.

At least two other characteristics of this career pattern make Unicamp an interesting case for researching gender inequality in the academic career. First, tenure is granted shortly after professors are approved in their entrance "*concursos*". Second, there is no such thing as an obligatory progression rhythm for all. Progression depends uniquely on the professor. There are hardly any material losses or sanctions of any kind if a professor decides to postpone progression/promotion or not do it at all, apart from accumulated salary loss for not having been promoted as they could have. These two characteristics combine to produce more flexibility in the career, which benefits those who have other responsibilities beyond their work at universities. Thus, if female professors in these universities aren't forced to follow a fixed pattern of career progression, they can, at least supposedly, dedicate themselves to their children who might need more attention when young, and invest in their careers in other periods of their lives.

Besides that, in public research universities it is the professors themselves who make decisions including career promotion and progression, as mentioned. At different levels, not only do they evaluate their peers' promotion, but they also make the rules that guide these evaluations and decisions. One can suppose, therefore, that rules are negotiated and that there is space to accommodate different groups of professors' interests. One can also imagine that this decision-making structure makes the processes more explicit and less personal, assuring universality in the principles that guide promotions. This can benefit groups of people who arrived only recently in this professional environment, such as female professors, when the ones in positions that concentrate decision-making power (a director of a certain college or school, for example) are representatives of their peers and must account for their decisions.

Such characteristics of the career of professor at Unicamp give grounds to the following hypotheses: (i) due to the career stability and its progression's flexible timing, women would arrive as frequently as men to MS6, the top position of the ladder; (ii) work environments where women are the majority or are well represented would be more sympathetic to their needs, thus making it even easier for them to progress in their career. To examine those hypotheses, we first looked at the presence of women professors in different disciplines and fields of study at Unicamp. Then, we moved to an analysis of their chances of achieving the top position in each discipline or field of study, comparing it to their male counterparts'. The results were surprising.

To make the calculations necessary for this investigation, information was collected from Unicamp's following sources: (i) their administrative website and their Human Resources department; (ii) their internal system of professors' research registry and (iii) from the Lattes online platform (a national academic curriculum database maintained by the scientific research council of the Ministry of Science and Technology).

The formal bureaucratic division of professors in campuses, colleges, schools, programs and departments, however, didn't always seem to translate in terms of their professional or disciplinary identities. They were, then, grouped according to other criteria, called here by the name of "units". The basic unit used to group and classify professors was their correspondent college or school. In cases where the college or school offers more than one undergraduate program with totally separated curricula (meaning professors do not teach in more than one program), professors were grouped according to the department that engenders the undergraduate program in which they teach. Each of these groups of professors were called units – the complete list of units and the schools, colleges or departments they engender is available in Chart 15.1, in the annexes of the chapter. Table 15.2, below, shows the whole of Unicamp professors in 2011 as grouped in such 'units'. The standard deviation was also included in the end, to show how diverse units can be.

Besides that, a new generational category had to be developed to help us capture the real situation of male and female professors regarding their chances of achieving the top position of the career. It was considered, first, that the term "professors" includes people from various generations, and that they are not all equally competing for the top positions (a recently hired professor wouldn't have yet had the chance of trying the *concurso* for MS6, for example). At the same time, the mere year of appointment was not necessarily a good measure of their actual possibilities of achieving the MS6 level, since someone can be hired directly to the middle level of the career, or even directly to the top level (once the top level *concursos* are open to public). To check if there was really any kind of glass ceiling or vertical concentration among Unicamp professors, then, the category of *"professional generation"* was used.

To define the *professional generation* the key reference was the year when the most recent MS6 professor obtained his or her PhD. Every professor who obtained his/her PhD that same year or before, regardless of the position they now held in their career, was considered belonging to that particular "professional generation" – it was assumed, therefore, that once a professor who earned his or her PhD in a certain year had achieved the top level of the career, all those who had earned their PhDs that same year or before could hypothetically have done the same. Each unit has a different rhythm of progression and different promotion cultures among professors, and thus it was important to find references from within units and not those that were arbitrarily set. A general overview of the cohort included in the *professional generation* of each unit is shown in Table 15.3, below. The reference years for each unit are shown in Table 15.7, in the annexes of this chapter.

Table 15.2 Professors by sex in each unit; number (n) and proportion (%) – Unicamp, 2011

| | Professors | | | | | |
| | Number (N) | | | Proportion (%) | | |
	F	M	Total	F	M	Total
Acting and Drama	7	8	15	46.7	53.3	100
Agricultural Engineering	6	32	38	15.8	84.2	100
Applied Mathematics	9	27	36	25	75	100
Applied Sciences	21	28	49	42.9	57.1	100
Architecture	13	10	23	56.5	43.5	100
Biology	54	61	116	47	53	100
Body Arts and Dance	11	1	12	91.7	8.3	100
Chemical Engineering	21	27	48	43.8	56.3	100
Chemistry	24	51	75	32	68	100
Civil Engineering	10	40	50	20	80	100
Computing	10	37	47	21.3	78.7	100
Economics	14	59	73	19.2	80.8	100
Education	54	36	90	60	40	100
Electrical Engineering	4	82	86	4.7	95.3	100
Food Engineering	23	26	49	46.9	53.1	100
Geosciences	14	33	47	29.8	70.2	100
History	7	12	19	36.8	63.2	100
Letters and languages	13	1	14	92.9	7.1	100
Linguistics	19	12	31	61.3	38.7	100
Literary Theory and Literature	5	12	17	29.4	70.6	100
Mathematics	6	30	36	16.7	83.3	100
Mechanical Engineering	7	72	79	8.9	91.1	100
Media and Communications	1	16	17	5.9	94.1	100
Medicine	118	178	296	51.9	48.1	100
Music	6	25	31	19.4	80.6	100
Nursing	26	3	29	89.7	10.3	100
Odontology	29	50	79	35.4	64.6	100
Pharmacology	3	5	8	37.5	62.5	100
Philosophy	3	12	15	20	80	100
Physical Education	8	21	29	27.6	72.4	100
Physics	7	78	85	8.2	91.8	100
Social Sciences	20	28	48	41.7	58.3	100
Statistics	6	13	19	31.6	68.4	100
Technology	21	39	60	35	65	100
Visual Arts	10	12	22	45.5	54.5	100
Unicamp	**610**	**1177**	**1787**	**36.7**	**63.3**	**100**
Standard deviation	21.06	32.65	49.75			

Source: Unicamp, Human Resources Secretariat 2011

Table 15.3 Professors included in the reference cohort (professional generation) of each unit, by sex – Unicamp, 2011

Unit	Professors included in the reference cohort (professional generation)					
	Number (N)			Proportion in the total of the unit (%)		
	F	M	Total	F	M	Total
Agricultural Engineering	4	26	30	66.7	81.3	78.9
Chemical Engineering	15	21	36	71.4	77.8	75.0
Physics	5	57	62	71.4	73.1	72.9
Applied Mathematics	8	17	25	88.9	63.0	69.4
Chemistry	17	35	52	70.8	68.6	69.3
Electrical Engineering	1	58	59	25.0	70.7	68.6
Medicine	81	120	201	68.6	67.4	67.9
Mechanical Engineering	5	48	53	71.4	66.7	67.1
Mathematics	5	19	24	83.3	63.3	66.7
Biology	37	39	76	68.5	63.9	65.5
Letters and Languages	9	0	9	69.2	0.0	64.3
Odontology	15	32	47	51.7	64.0	59.5
History	3	8	11	42.9	66.7	57.9
Food Engineering	13	15	28	56.5	57.7	57.1
Computing	6	19	25	60.0	51.4	53.2
Statistics	2	8	10	33.3	61.5	52.6
Pharmacology	1	3	4	33.3	60.0	50.0
Geosciences	4	17	21	28.6	51.5	44.7
Economics	3	27	30	21.4	45.8	41.1
Civil Engineering	3	17	20	30.0	42.5	40.0
Social Sciences	7	10	17	35.0	35.7	35.4
Literary Theory and Literature	2	4	6	40.0	33.3	35.3
Linguistics	5	3	8	26.3	25.0	25.8
Media and Communications	0	4	4	0.0	25.0	23.5
Education	11	9	20	20.4	25.0	22.2
Philosophy	1	2	3	33.3	16.7	20.0
Physical Education	1	4	5	12.5	19.0	17.2
Architecture	3	0	3	23.1	0.0	13.0
Acting and Drama	0	0	0	0.0	0.0	0.0
Body Arts and Dance	0	0	0	0.0	0.0	0.0
Visual Arts	0	0	0	0.0	0.0	0.0
Applied Sciences	0	0	0	0.0	0.0	0.0
Nursing	0	0	0	0.0	0.0	0.0
Music	0	0	0	0.0	0.0	0.0
Technology	0	0	0	0.0	0.0	0.0
Unicamp	**185**	**499**	**684**	**30.3**	**42.4**	**38.3**

Source: Calculations by the author using data from Unicamp's Human Resources Secretariat, 2011

Based on the professional generation as described above, new calculations were made in order to establish in each unit the chances of achieving the top position (MS6) for women, as well as for men and the general chances for professors regardless of sex. Those were then compared to explore in which cases women or men had advantages and disadvantages in climbing the career ladder or, in other words, in which cases there seemed to be a glass ceiling. We also examined whether the supposed glass ceilings would be found more or less frequently when dealing with units where women are the majority of professors or with units that have more women professors than the university average.

The calculations of chances were done according to the following, considering each unit and the whole of Unicamp. Units were excluded from calculations when it was not possible to define a professional generation due to the lack of MS6 professors teaching in them. Table 15.4 below shows the number of professors in the professional generation and the number of MS6 professors in each unit.

$$CF = Ft / Fg$$
$$CM = Mt / Mg$$
$$CT = Tt / Tg$$

Where C = Chances; F = Female professors; M = Male professors; T = Total of professors; t = Total of MS6 professors within the professional generation; g = Total of professors within the professional generation.

In regard to horizontal concentration, Unicamp seems to be no different from other universities around the world. The few women who are professors there do not have equal access to all disciplines and fields of study, being concentrated in some of them and but virtually absent from others. There are some other peculiar characteristics, however, regarding their presence in different fields. Table 15.5, below, shows the proportion of women in each unit, from the highest to the lowest.

Considering the fact that 36,7 % of professors at Unicamp are women it is possible to say that there are 16 units more accessible to female professors than the average. They are all classified as human sciences and arts or as biomedical sciences units, areas where women are indeed more prevalent, as shown before in Table 15.2. Such division into areas, however, does not seem to help in understanding how female professors are distributed in the university: many human sciences and arts and many biomedical sciences units also show very low proportions of women among their professors – such as in the cases of Media Studies, Music, Philosophy, Economics, Physical Education, Literature and Odontology. These data show that there isn't an automatic association between more scientific areas and the absence of women, nor that women have more access to human sciences and arts or to biomedical sciences as a whole. On the contrary, they seem to be very specifically located in a few areas, disciplines or fields of study, that can't be translated by a simplified impression of opposing "humanities" and "hard sciences".

Table 15.4 Professors included in the professional generation and total of MS6 professors among them in each unit, by sex – Unicamp, 2011

Unidades	Professors included in the reference cohort			MS6 professors in the reference cohort		
	Number (N)			Number (N)		
	F	M	Total	F	M	Total
Agricultural Engineering	4	26	30	2	11	13
Applied Mathematics	8	17	25	1	5	6
Architecture	3	0	3	2	0	2
Biology	37	39	76	14	23	37
Chemical Engineering	15	21	36	9	7	16
Chemistry	17	35	52	7	19	26
Civil Engineering	3	17	20	1	9	10
Computing	6	19	25	2	6	8
Economics	3	27	30	0	6	6
Education	11	9	20	5	5	10
Electrical Engineering	1	58	59	0	37	37
Food Engineering	13	15	28	5	8	13
Geosciences	4	17	21	2	8	10
History	3	8	11	3	5	8
Letters and Languages	9	0	9	5	0	5
Linguistics	5	3	8	3	2	5
Literary Theory and Literature	2	4	6	1	3	4
Mathematics	5	19	24	2	7	9
Mechanical Engineering	5	48	53	3	15	18
Media and Communications	0	4	4	0	2	2
Medicine	81	120	201	15	36	51
Odontology	15	32	47	8	23	31
Pharmacology	1	3	4	1	1	2
Philosophy	1	2	3	1	2	3
Physical Education	1	4	5	1	2	3
Physics	5	57	62	0	23	23
Social Sciences	7	10	17	6	9	15
Statistics	2	8	10	1	1	2
Unicamp	**185**	**499**	**684**	**100**	**275**	**375**

Calculations by the author using data from Unicamp's Human Resources Secretariat, 2011

These data also show that units where women are the majority are more open to male professors than are those units where men are the majority to females. In only seven units the proportion of female professors is 50 % or higher. Among these, male professors are less than 30 % in only three of them (Languages, Dance, Infirmary). On the other hand, there are 15 units where women are 30 % of professors or less, out of the 28 where men are the majority. That shows that units where men are more present are significantly less open to women than the other way round.

Table 15.5 Proportion of male and female professors in the total of each unit, organized by highest to lower proportion of women in faculty – Unicamp, 2011

Units	Proportion of female and male professors (%)		
	F	M	Total
Letters and Languages	92.9	7.1	100
Body Arts and Dance	91.7	8.3	100
Nursing	89.7	10.3	100
Linguistics	61.3	38.7	100
Education	60	40	100
Architecture	56.5	43.5	100
Medicine	51.9	48.1	100
Biology	47	53	100
Food Engineering	46.9	53.1	100
Acting and Drama	46.7	53.3	100
Visual arts	45.5	54.5	100
Chemical Engineering	43.8	56.3	100
Applied Sciences	42.9	57.1	100
Social Sciences	41.7	58.3	100
Pharmacology	37.5	62.5	100
History	36.8	63.2	100
Unicamp	**36.7**	**63.3**	**100**
Odontology	35.4	64.6	100
Technology	35	65	100
Chemistry	32	68	100
Statistics	31.6	68.4	100
Geosciences	29.8	70.2	100
Literary Theory and Literature	29.4	70.6	100
Physical Education	27.6	72.4	100
Applied Mathematics	25	75	100
Computing	21.3	78.7	100
Civil Engineering	20	80	100
Philosophy	20	80	100
Music	19.4	80.6	100
Economics	19.2	80.8	100
Mathematics	16.7	83.3	100
Agricultural Engineering	15.8	84.2	100
Mechanical Engineering	8.9	91.1	100
Physics	8.2	91.8	100
Media and Communications	5.9	94.1	100
Electrical Engineering	4.7	95.3	100

Calculations by the author using data from Unicamp's Human Resources Secretariat, 2011

There are many possible explanations as to why discipline and field of study choices are gendered in our society. It is not appropriate to explore them in detail here, but it could very well be that this is because they seem to be more related to general social phenomena than to the specific case of Unicamp – an academic career is usually a choice made after one opts for a profession or discipline at undergraduate level during early adulthood. This is why the main focus on this chapter is the vertical concentration and the chances of women who do enter Unicamp as professors to achieve the top position of their career.

As mentioned earlier, the career structure of Unicamp professors and its requirements to get a promotion are all governed by bureaucratic rules that do not admit differentiation by sex. The same is also true for the determination of their salaries and the general norm they must follow. At Unicamp the recruitment, promotion and salaries are the same for all disciplines, fields of knowledge and units, which allowed this comparative study to be undertaken most effectively.

Progression in one's career is associated directly with increasing income and power. Being an MS6 professor means an increase of salary and also access to some positions of power in the university system, such as dean (one must be a MS6 professor in order to be appointed as a dean). This is why the calculation of chances of achieving the top level of the institutional career ladder is meaningful to provide evidence about gender inequality at Unicamp. Such calculations, as previously described, resulted in a quite unexpected new perspective on the matter. These results are shown in Table 15.6.

The data above show very similar chances of achieving the top position for professors of both sexes when considering the whole of Unicamp (a ratio of 1.0 between female and male professors' chances). This could give a false impression of equality if differences among units hadn't been considered. One of the first things that attracted our attention regarding these data is the fact that in four units no woman at all achieved the top position in the referred professional generation. The same only happened in two units for men.

Considering only the units where both men and women have achieved the top, for a more solid comparison (thus considering only the units where the calculation of the ratio of female over male chances was possible), we found that in 10 of them women were at a disadvantage and in other 10 the same happened to men. At the same time, women's advantage seems to be, in most cases, lighter than men's.

Surprisingly, from the 10 units where women of the particular professional generation had an advantage over men in achieving the top of the career, only one belonged to the area of human sciences and arts, and one to the area of biomedical sciences – precisely those which were previously found to be more open to female professors. In contrast, the data showed also that women had an advantage in some of those units where they were not so well represented as professors. Therefore, there wasn't a direct correspondence between feminization of a unit and women's chances of succeeding to the top level of the career ladder there.

The data presented here show that there is no systematic glass ceiling that can be considered as such in the career of professors at Unicamp. Since our data are quite

Table 15.6 Chances of achieving the top position: number of professors in the reference cohort who achieved the MS6 position, by sex, in each unit – Unicamp, 2011

Unit	Chances F	Chances M	Chances F/M	General chances
Statistics	50.0	12.5	4.0	20.0
Pharmacology	100.0	33.3	3.0	50.0
Physical Education	100.0	50.0	2.0	60.0
Mechanical Engineering	60.0	31.3	1.9	34.0
Chemical Engineering	60.0	33.3	1.8	44.4
History	100.0	62.5	1.6	72.7
Agricultural Engineering	50.0	42.3	1.2	43.3
Geosciences	50.0	47.1	1.1	47.6
Mathematics	40.0	36.8	1.1	37.5
Computing	33.3	31.6	1.1	32.0
Philosophy	100.0	100.0	1.0	100.0
Social Sciences	85.7	90.0	1.0	88.2
Unicamp	**54,1**	**55,1**	**1,0**	**54,8**
Linguistics	60.0	66.7	0.9	62.5
Education	45.5	55.6	0.8	50.0
Chemistry	41.2	54.3	0.8	50.0
Odontology	53.3	71.9	0.7	66.0
Literary Theory and Literature	50.0	75.0	0.7	66.7
Food Engineering	38.5	53.3	0.7	46.4
Biology	37.8	59.0	0.6	48.7
Civil Engineering	33.3	52.9	0.6	50.0
Medicine	18.5	30.0	0.6	25.4
Applied Mathematics	12.5	29.4	0.4	24.0
Architecture	66.7	0.0	–	66.7
Letters and Languages	55.6	0.0	–	55.6
Economics	0.0	22.2	–	20.0
Electrical Engineering	0.0	63.8	–	62.7
Physics	0.0	40.4	–	37.1
Media and Communications	0.0	50.0	–	50.0

Source: Calculations by the author using data from Unicamp's Human Resources Secretariat, 2011

limited, it is important to note theses limits before rushing to conclusions as to whether this is or isn't a gender unequal professional area.

The limitation of the data presented is related to the complexity of the Brazilian academic career. In the first place, because of the variety of kinds of institutions and work conditions as described in the first section of this chapter, working for certain universities offers, by definition, a more prestigious position than working for others, in terms of salary, stability and social recognition. Women are, indeed, concentrated as professors in some kinds of institutions to which they have more access. This provides the first evidence of an unequal profession beyond the ladder within the institutions themselves.

When hired by prestigious universities to work as professors, they also do not have the same access as men to all fields of study and disciplines, as shown by our data regarding Unicamp's case. Even considering the existence of disciplines and fields of study where women are the majority of professors, they definitely do not appear as well-represented as in those where men are the majority. That means that men have more access than women to all fields of study and disciplines, even in those where they aren't many. This is the second evidence exposed here of gender inequality in the academic career that is often neglected by the idea of a "glass ceiling" in the career ladder.

As to the career ladder itself, however, inequality was not as prevalent as it is sometimes thought to be. This chapter intended to show how it can vary between disciplines and fields of study, and how this variation is not directly related to either the presence or absence of women professors in each of them. This inconsistency might be a direct effect of their work conditions which are quite particular in the case of Unicamp and other Brazilian public universities, as previously discussed. Further qualitative research is needed in order to examine that.

At the same time, it is important to emphasize that even within an institution there are other measures of prestige that should be considered in any future and more profound analyses of the Brazilian academic career. Based on the work of Bourdieu (1984), Hey (2008), for instance, described different kinds of capital associated with academic prestige in Brazil. They are not only related to being in or out of the top level of the institutionalized career ladder within an important university, but also to occupying power positions in administration or even in the State, for example. More studies are needed in order to investigate the situation of women when considering all such multiple forms of prestige in the Brazilian academic space.

No less important seems to be the detailed process that led women to the top position of the career in different universities. As pointed out by previous work (Moschkovich 2013; Moschkovich and Almeida 2015), the trajectories of male and female professors at Unicamp are strongly marked by their genders, even when they are bureaucratically classified as being in the same top position in the same discipline or field of study. Their experiences during the course of their progression to their way there definitely matter to better understand what gender means in the Brazilian academic career, and how it shaped professional experiences and possibilities.

In the end, it is noteworthy that when it comes to detecting and analyzing the glass ceilings or glass walls, neither organizational structures, work conditions or historical gender patterns can be isolated as the final cause (and, therefore, source of solution) of gender inequality in the academic career.

Annexes

Chart 15.1 List of units built for this work, related to field and REI/departaments. Unicamp, 2011

Field (Unicamp)	REI	Unit (in this study)	Departments
Biomedical Sciences	School of Medicine	Medicine	Anatomical Pathology
			Anesthesiology
			Surgery
			Clinic
			Genetics
			Neurology
			Ophthalmic/Otolaryngology
			Clinical Pathology
			Pediatrics
			Medical Psychology and Psychiatry
			Radiology
			Social Healthcare
			Gynecology
		Infirmary	Infirmary
		Pharmaceutical Sciences	Pharmacology
Biomedical Sciences	Physical Education School	Physical Education	Sports Sciences
			Motor Education
			Adapted Physical Activities
			Leisure Studies
Biomedical Sciences	Odontology College of Piracicaba	Odontology	Physiological Sciences
			Oral Diagnosis
			Morphology
			Restoration
			Children Odontology
			Social Odontology
			Prosthesis and Periodontics
Biomedical Sciences	Institute of Biology	Biology	Animal Biology
			Structural and Functional Biology
			Plant Biology
			Biochemistry
			Genetics, Evolution and Bio Agents
			Histology and Embryology
Engineering Sciences	College of Applied Sciences	Applied Sciences	There are no departments

(continued)

Chart 15.1 (continued)

Field (Unicamp)	REI	Unit (in this study)	Departments
Engineering Sciences	Food and Engineering School	Food Engineering	Departamento de Alimentos e Nutrição
			Departamento de Ciência de Alimentos
			Departamento de Food Engineering
			Departamento de Technology de Alimentos
Engineering Sciences	Agrarian Engineering School	Agrarian Engineering	Não há divisão por departamentos
Engineering Sciences	Civil Engineering, and Architecture School	Architecture	Architecture and Buildings
		Civil Engineering	Structures
			Geotechnical and Transportation
			Water Resources
			Sanitary and Environment
Engineering Sciences	Electrical and Computational Engineering School	Electrical Engineering	Communications
			Electronics and Microelectronics
			Biomedical Engineering
			Computational Engineering and Industrial Automation
			Systems Engineering
			Machine Components and Intelligent Systems
			Microwaves and Optics
			Semiconductors, tools and photonics
			Systems of Electrical Engineering
			Energy Systems and Control
			Telematics
Engineering Sciences	Mechanical Engineering School	Mechanical Engineering	Energy
			Fabrication Engineering
			Material Engineering
			Oil Engineering
			Thermic and Fluids Engineering
			Computational Mechanics
			Mechanical Project
Engineering Sciences	Chemical Engineering School	Chemical Engineering	Biotechnological Processes
			Chemical Processes
			Polymer Technologies
			Thermic fluid dynamics
			Chemical Systems Engineering
Engineering Sciences	College of Technology	Technology	There are no departments
Engineering Sciences	Institute of Computer Sciences	Computer Sciences	Systems of Computers
			Information Systems
			Computer Sciences Theory

(continued)

Chart 15.1 (continued)

Field (Unicamp)	REI	Unit (in this study)	Departments
Exact Sciences	Physics Institute "Gleb Wataghin"	Physics	Quantic Electronics
			Applied Physics
			Condensed Matter Physics
			Cosmic Rays and Chronology
Exact Sciences	Geosciences Institute	Geosciences	Applied Geosciences in Education
			Geography
			Geology and Natural Resources
			Science and Technology Policies
Exact Sciences	Institute of Mathematics, Statistics e Scientific Computing	Statistics	Statistics
		Mathematics	Mathematics
		Applied Mathematics	Applied Mathematics
Exact Sciences	Chemistry Institute	Chemistry	Physics-Chemistry
			Analytical Chemistry
			Inorganic Chemistry
			Organic Chemistry
Human Sciences & Arts	College of Education (FE)	Education	Social Sciences in Education
			Education, Knowledge, Language and Art
			Teaching and Cultural Practices
			Education History and Philosophy
			Educational Politics and Management Systems
			Educational Psychology
Human Sciences & Arts	Arts Institute	Theatre	Theatre
		Dance	Body Arts and Dance
		Arts	Arts
		Music	Music
		Midialogy & Communications	Multimedia
			Cinema
Human Sciences & Arts	Institute of Economic Sciences	Economic Sciences	Economic Politics and History
			Economic Theory
Human Sciences & Arts	Institute of Language Studies	Linguistics	Linguistics
		Languages	Applied Linguistics and Languages
		Literature	Literature
Human Sciences & Arts	Institute of Philosophy and Human Sciences	Social Sciences	Anthropology
			Political Science
			Demography
			Sociology
		Philosophy	Philosophy
		History	History

Table 15.7 Year of oldest and most recent PhD titles among MS6 professors and time gap, in years, between them, by unit – Unicamp, 2011

Units	Year of most recent PhD	Year of oldest PhD	Gap
Biology	1994	1969	25
Medicine	1999	1974	25
Chemistry	1995	1970	25
Mathematics	1998	1974	24
Food Engineering	1994	1971	23
Agricultural Engineering	1997	1974	23
Physics	1994	1971	23
Chemical Engineering	1996	1974	22
Odontology	1997	1975	22
Social Sciences	1992	1974	18
Education	1991	1975	16
History	1992	1976	16
Applied Mathematics	1994	1978	16
Mechanical Engineering	1994	1978	16
Electrical Engineering	1994	1978	16
Geosciences	1996	1980	16
Civil Engineering	1995	1980	15
Letters and Languages	1995	1980	15
Literature and Literary Theory	1992	1980	12
Computing	1997	1985	12
Economics	1996	1984	12
Architecture	1990	1980	10
Media and Communications	1992	1982	10
Pharmacology	1991	1983	8
Linguistics	1985	1979	6
Statistics	1997	1993	4
Physical Education	1992	1989	3
Philosophy	1983	1982	1

Source: Calculations by the author using data from Unicamp's Human Resources Secretariat, 2011

References

Acker, S., Webber, M., & Smyth, E. (2012). Tenure troubles and equity matters in Canadian academe. *British Journal of Sociology of Education, 33*(5), 743–761. doi:10.1080/01425692.2012.674784.

Bagilhole, B. (1993). Survivors in a male preserve: A study of British women academics' experiences and perceptions of discrimination in a UK university. *Higher Education, 26*(4), 431–447. doi:10.1007/BF01383737.

Balbachevsky, E. (2007). Carreira e contexto institucional no sistema de ensino superior brasileiro. *Sociologias* (17). doi:10.1590/S1517-45222007000100007.

Balbachevsky, E., & Quinteiro, Maria da Conceição. (2003). The changing academic workplace in Brazil. In P. G. Altbach (Ed.), *The decline of the guru. The academic profession in the third world* (pp. 75–106). New York: Palgrave Macmillan.

Barbosa Filho, Fernando de Holanda, Pessôa, Samuel de Abreu, & Afonso, L. E. (2009). Um estudo sobre os diferenciais de remuneração entre os professores das redes pública e privada de ensino. *Estudios Economics 39*(3). doi:10.1590/S0101-41612009000300006.

Baudelot, C., & Establet, R. (1992). *Allez, les filles!.* Paris: Seuil (L'Epreuve des faits).

Bordi, I. V., & Vélez Bautista, G. (2007). Género y éxito científico en la Universidad Autónoma del Estado de México. *Revista Estudos Feministas, 15*(3), 581–608. doi:10.1590/S0104-026X2007000300005.

Bourdieu, P. (1984). *Homo academicus.* Paris: Editions de Minuit.

Castilho, F., & de Soares, A. G. T. (2008). *O conceito de universidade no projeto da UNICAMP.* Campinas: Editora UNICAMP.

Carvalho, Marília Pinto de. (2003). Sucesso e fracasso escolar. Uma questão de gênero. *Red Educação e Pesquisa, 29*(1), 185–193. doi:10.1590/S1517-97022003000100013.

DiPrete, T. A., & Buchmann, C. (2013). *The rise of women. The growing gender gap in education and what it means for American schools. New York.* New York: Russell Sage Foundation.

Fox, M. F. (2001). Women, science, and academia: Graduate education and careers. *Gender & Society, 15*(5), 654–666. doi:10.1177/0891243101015005002.

Galvão, A. C. F. (2010). *Doutores 2010: Estudos da demografia da base técnico-científica brasileira.* Brasília: CGEE.

Hey, A. P. (2008). *Esboço de uma sociologia do campo acadêmico: A educação superior no Brasil.* São Carlos: EduFScar.

INEP – Instituto Nacional de Pesquisas Educacionais Anísio Teixeira. (2010). Sinopses estatísticas do Censo Nacional de Educação Superior. Brasília. Available online at http://portal.inep.gov.br/superior-censosuperior-sinopse. Checked on 01/01/13.

Maruani, M. (2006). *Travail et emploi des femmes* (3rd ed.). Paris: Découverte.

Moschkovich, M., & Almeida, A. M. F. (2015). Desigualdades de Gênero na Carreira Acadêmica no Brasil. *Dados, 58*(3), 749–789. doi:10.1590/00115258201558.

Moschkovich, M. B. F. G. (2013). Teto de vidro ou paredes de fogo?: Um estudo sobre gênero na carreira acadêmica e o caso da UNICAMP. Masters dissertation. Unicamp, Campinas and SP and Brasil. Faculdade de Educação. Available online at http://www.bibliotecadigital.unicamp.br/document/?code=000905752&opt=4. Checked on 6/20/2015.

Musselin, C. (2008). *Les universitaires.* Paris: la Découverte.

Schwartzman, S. (2012). Brazil: The widening gap. In P. G. Altbach et al. (Eds.), *Paying the professoriate. A global comparison of compensation and contracts* (pp. 72–82). New York: Routledge.

Stromquist, N. P., Gil-Antón, M., Colatrella, C., Mabokela, R. O., Smolentseva, A., & Balbachevsky, E. (2007). The contemporary professoriate. Towards a diversified or segmented profession? *Higher Education Quarterly, 61*(2), 114–135. doi:10.1111/j.1468-2273.2007.00342.x.

Unicamp. (2012). Anuários de Pesquisa da Unicamp. Available online at http://www.prp.rei.unicamp.br/site/portal/index.php?option=com_content&view=article&id=111&Itemid=96. Checked on 1/5/2013.

Unicamp – Universidade Estadual de Campinas. (2015). Official website – Unicamp. Available online at www.unicamp.br. Checked on 6/20/2015.

Unicamp. (2008). Perfil docente nas unidades de ensino e pesquisa. On-line, available at http://www.sg.unicamp.br/download/documentos-e-legislacoes/485c78066dc1c2a4d4ec2d40e36d700f. Last access in 22 Jan 2013.

Lightning Source UK Ltd.
Milton Keynes UK
UKOW05n1324201016

285764UK00001B/65/P

9 783319 424347